THE

MINES OF THE WEST:

A REPORT

TO THE

SECRETARY OF THE TREASURY,

BY

ROSSITER W. RAYMOND, Ph. D.,

COMMISSIONER OF MINING STATISTICS.

NEW-YORK:

J. B. FORD AND COMPANY.

39 PARK ROW.

1869.

CONTENTS.

LETTER OF INSTRUCTIONS.

TREASURY DEPARTMENT, *April* 1, 1868.

SIR: An appropriation having been made by Congress to enable the Secretary of the Treasury to collect reliable statistics of the mineral resources of the United States, a special appointment was conferred upon Mr. J. Ross Browne, under which he performed this service in the States and Territories west of the Rocky mountains.

To Mr. James W. Taylor the duty of collecting similar statistics east of the Rocky mountains was assigned.

The position held by Mr. Browne having become vacant, and it being in the opinion of the department important that the work should be continued, you have this day been appointed a special commissioner for the collection of statistics in the western division above specified. A copy of the instructions under which Mr. Browne performed his duties is herewith enclosed.

Inasmuch as his preliminary report, printed by Congress in 1867, and his subsequent report for 1868, now in the hands of the public printer, cover the material points embraced in the instructions, it will be unnecessary for you to enter into similar investigations in detail, except in cases where omissions may have occurred, or where the information obtained may appear to be erroneous or imperfect.

The most important subjects for inquiry at present seem to be—

First. As to the different processes of treating the ores, their chemical combinations, and the system demonstrated by practical experience to be the most successful.

Second. The relative merits of the various inventions, machines, and mechanical contrivances now in use or projected for the reduction of the precious metals, and for all other purposes connected with the business of mining and metallurgy.

Third. The special needs of the great mining interest, how it can be encouraged and rendered most productive, how far individual enterprise should be left untrammelled by legislative action, and to what extent and in what instances government might properly lend its aid to facilitate the development of the mines and thus arrest the present annual decrease in the production of bullion.

Fourth. What has been the experience of other countries, resulting from the establishment of national institutions for the education of miners, and how far would the systems prevailing in Europe be applicable to our people or appropriate under our government?

General suggestions of this kind cannot of course always be implicitly carried out, but it is expected that your scientific and practical experience will enable you to furnish valuable information on the subjects indicated.

It will be necessary, in the performance of the duties assigned to you, that you should visit in person the principal States and Territories embraced within your division.

You will be pleased to submit your report to this department on or before the first day of October next.

I am, very respectfully,

HUGH McCULLOCH,
Secretary of the Treasury.

R. W. RAYMOND, Esq.,
New York City.

LETTER

FROM

ROSSITER W. RAYMOND,

COMMISSIONER FOR THE COLLECTION OF MINING STATISTICS,

TO

THE SECRETARY OF THE TREASURY.

WASHINGTON, D. C., *January* 18, 1869.

SIR: The report which I have the honor to transmit herewith is mainly my own work. At the time when I received my appointment as Commissioner of Mining Statistics, there was but a small remnant of previous appropriations left in the treasury which could be applied to the work with which I was charged. Preferring to go into the field as soon as possible, and prepare myself by personal observation for my task, I decided, with your approval, not to wait for the necessary appropriation, but to use the money already applicable, to enable me to see as much as possible of the districts within my department. I am happy to say that by the almost universal courtesy of railway, steamboat, stage, and express companies, my expenses of travel were much reduced, and I was able, with the small sum at my disposal, to complete during the summer a journey of some 13,000 miles. In this connection it is my duty especially to acknowledge the interest manifested in my mission, and the facilities put at my disposal by the Pacific Mail Steamship Company, the North American Steamship Company, the California Steam Navigation Company, the Union Pacific Railroad Company, the Central Pacific Railroad Company, and Wells, Fargo & Co.

The lack of means put it beyond my power to engage competent assistants, or even to employ a clerk for tabulating and calculating statistics. Obliged to do the whole work myself, I am nevertheless indebted to numerous gentlemen of the States and Territories I visited for their hearty sympathy and assistance, and feel bound to mention particularly the members of the California Academy of Sciences, Mr. Sherman Day, Mr. Titus Cronise, Mr. William Ashburner, and Mr. Henry Janin, of San Francisco; Messrs. Watt, Crossman, Lee, Merchant, and others, superintendents at Grass Valley; Messrs. Brumagim, connected with the Mariposa company; Mr. A. P. K. Safford, United States surveyor general, Mr. Louis Janin, and Mr. Cæsar Luckhardt, of Virginia City; Messrs. Boalt, Stetfeldt, and Riotte, of Austin; Messrs. Eaton, Keyes, De Lacy, and others, of Montana. Many of these gentlemen put themselves to trouble and expense to further my objects; some of them furnished me with valuable information, which will be found credited to them in the proper place.

Under these circumstances, the report now presented is necessarily partial. I have not attempted to make it comprehensive, at the cost of accuracy. It contains my own observations and such others as I have collected from perfectly trustworthy sources. Many papers promised to me, which I would be glad to have included in it, have not yet arrived; and as the writers are under no obligation but that which their own courtesy imposed, I cannot well hurry or blame them. The report is in two parts, the first containing such observations of the present condition of our mining industry as I could collect, and the second discussing at considerable length the subjects involved in the relation of the government to that industry.

The subject of methods and processes of mining and reduction I have entirely postponed, proposing to treat it in my next report with more care and thoroughness than would have been possible in the brief period, and with the limited means, at my disposal last year. I hope to be able to present such a description and discussion of the different methods and apparatus used or proposed in this country as will be of practical value, not only as a means of determining the progress of the country in these respects, but also as a convenient summary for the benefit of the mining communities, and the great number of our citizens directly or indirectly interested in mining and metallurgy.

As my object has been to make a plain and simple statement, I have avoided, as far as possible, the use of technical or obscure terms, using only, I believe, such as can be found in the ordinary English dictionaries, or readily explain themselves from the context. There are also introduced a few sketches of underground workings, selecting such mines as were capable of being represented by simple profiles. These profiles are taken *on the plane of the vein*, (local irregularities being disregarded,) and show the quantity of ground already excavated, and the quantity remaining, either unopened or so far opened as to come under the head of "reserves," which includes the portions of a vein where "stoping," or extracting ore, may at once be commenced, the preparatory shafting and drifting (or opening of galleries) being complete. The Eureka mine, of Amador county, California, and the Social and Steptoe mine, of Egan cañon, Nevada, are examples, in which the amount of reserves, or ground opened in advance, is very large. Many of the Grass Valley mines are characterized by the same peculiarity, as the sketches show; and in this case, the prudence of the management is worthy of high praise, since the Grass Valley veins are narrow and hard, and the maintenance of large reserves is a matter of difficulty and expense. I ought to add that many mines of celebrity and interest are not represented by sketches, not because I desired to omit them, but because (as is the case with the Comstock mines) they could not be shown in simple profile, or because the expense of making the necessary measurements and drawings (in cases where none were accessible to me) was greater than I felt justified in assuming, or finally, because the character of the underground workings was so irregular and unskilful as to confer no credit upon the owners, and convey no instruction to the public.

The bullion product of the present year is more difficult to be estimated than that of almost any preceding one. The bullion tax having been abolished, the best source of knowledge on the subject is taken away. Wells, Fargo, & Co.'s express returns, which have hitherto been an important aid in estimating the movement, and thus the product, of bullion on the Pacific coast, have lost their comprehensive character by the establishment of a rival express company (the Union Pacific,) the amount of the business of which is said to be considerable, but has not been, to my knowledge, thus far authoritatively reported. From the best authorities, and such official returns as I can collect, I estimate the product of the whole country as follows:

California	$22,000,000
Nevada	14,000,000
Montana	15,000,000
Idaho	7,000,000
Washington and Oregon	4,000,000
Arizona	500,000
New Mexico	250,000
Colorado and Wyoming	3,250,000
All other sources	1,000,000
	67,000,000

This is a decrease of $8,000,000* from the product of 1867, which showed a falling off of some $8,000,000 as compared with that of the year before. Montana, Idaho and Colorado manifest a satisfactory improvement; but there is a decrease of $5,000,000 from California, and $6,000,000 from Nevada, the latter being due to the exhaustion of many of the Comstock ore-bodies.

It is an instructive fact that the greater part of the product from deep mining is furnished by the same mines this year as last year and the year before, indicating that a more general adoption of systematic and economical methods would result in greater stability of production. The yield from placer mining must be expected to decrease, and its place must be supplied by the cement and quartz mines. The causes of the decrease in our production of bullion may be enumerated as follows:

1. The exhaustion of many surface deposits.
2. The reaction following upon a period of excited speculation, and the collapse of numerous dishonest schemes.
3. The increasing and novel difficulties attendant upon the management of deep mines and the reduction of refractory ores.
4. The lack of communications, capital and knowledge, such as are required for the creation of enterprises based on the extraction and reduction of ores of low grade in large quantity—the only stable form of mining.
5. The vexatious and ruinous litigation which waits upon mining on the public domain, and which is most troublesome and expensive where mining is, in other respects, most profitable—thus operating to destroy those enterprises which have overcome other difficulties.

All these may be summed up in one sentence. Mining has been found in too many instances to be unprofitable; and the individuals who have lost money have retired from the business. It certainly is not the duty of the government to give bounties to bolster up mining industry, if that industry is by the nature of the case an unprofitable one. Yet it cannot be denied that the decrease of the product of gold and silver in this country is a matter which particularly concerns the government at this time; and it may well be inquired, whether the causes of it are remediable. I believe that time will remove many of them, and that the action of the government, based upon a just appreciation of its relations to the mining industry, will do away with the rest. Concerning the extent of our "mineral resources," the half has never been told; but those resources are but one factor, which must be joined with labor and

* Part of this apparent decrease may be accounted for by the item of $5,000,000 in Mr. Browne's estimate from "unknown sources," which I have reduced to $1,000,000.

intelligence to make the product wealth. When the industry of mining in these rich fields is based upon a foundation of universal law, and shaped by the hand of educated skill, we may expect it to become a stately and enduring edifice, not a mere tent, pitched to-day and folded to-morrow. This industry has been the pioneer in our far western territory. It has founded States, attracted population, enlarged the boundaries of civilization; and it has done this great work in a lawless and careless way, without much regard to the future. All other parts of society springing from it, are gradually becoming systematized and consolidated, but the primitive industry remains in its primitive condition. Establishing everything else, it has not established itself. I believe that with the extension of the government surveys over the public domain, and the reduction of its vast area to order and law, the consolidation and definite adjustment of the mining interests will become imperatively necessary; and inasmuch as mining outruns all other activities in our new territories, and needs more than any other the aid of judicious legislation, I believe it should receive immediate attention. I may venture to hope that the views and suggestions contained in the following pages, based as they are upon much personal observation, experience and study, will not be without value to the government and the country.

Very respectfully, your obedient servant,

ROSSITER W. RAYMOND.

Hon. HUGH MCCULLOCH,
Secretary of the Treasury.

PART I.

OBSERVATIONS

ON

THE PRESENT CONDITION AND PROSPECTS OF THE MINING INDUSTRY.

SECTION I.

NOTES ON CALIFORNIA.

CHAPTER I.

NEW ALMADEN QUICKSILVER MINES.

The traveller visiting these mines leaves San Francisco by rail for San José, a pleasant city at the southern end of the bay. At several intervening stations and along the road may be observed the good effects of irrigation, in beautiful gardens and orchards. At one place, a magnificent stream of water is supplied by an artesian well. The numerous windmills used for the elevation and distribution of water are a most picturesque feature in the landscapes of California, and might be introduced with advantage in many older States, perhaps for other purposes than those of irrigation. The boring of artesian wells is doubtless destined to be widely practiced, since there are few countries where they are rendered at once so necessary by climatic conditions, and so successful by topographical features. The valleys along the mountain ranges and their foot-hills do not receive, in surface streams, an adequate proportion of the water which so vast a mountain area must collect, partly because the excessive evaporation dries up the streams, and partly because they sink into the sandy soil. But the water thus apparently lost in the earth can be recovered by artesian borings, in which it frequently rises in vast volume and force. Wells judiciously located in such a region could hardly fail to be perennial fountains. In fact, the disappearance of water by sinking, which seems at first sight a great disadvantage to the country, is probably the means of preserving for man that necessary moisture without which the land would remain a desert, as it appeared, in many places, to the eyes of its discoverers. If the rivers ran in tight channels, doubtless this dry and ever-shifting air would carry away the last drop of their moisture, and deposit it in the sea, or on remote mountain summits out of reach.

The mines of New Almaden are about 13 miles from San José, in the Coast range. The drive thither, through the valley, and winding up among the hills, is beautiful in the extreme. There is a good deal of timber along the road—that is, a good deal for California. The valley looks like some large park. Magnificent oaks overshadow the smooth wide road; great gardens and wheat fields, such as never Atlantic States dreamed of, border it on either hand. The distant mountains, seeming near at hand through the clear air, are constant companions of the journey. New Almaden itself is, perhaps, the prettiest spot for residence in all California.

The mines and furnaces have been frequently described. At the time of my visit the ore from the deepest and newest *labores* was among the best that I saw; and the prospects for future production were as good as ever. There is quicksilver, irregularly distributed, at so many points in the Coast range, that the business of mining and reducing the ores would be open to ruinous competition, but for the peculiar commercial status of the question. As, from time to time, quicksilver mines are offered for sale in New York, and many persons imagine that this branch of mining involves large, prompt, and sure profits, it will be worth while, perhaps, to exhibit the commercial aspect of the question for the benefit of the public.

The quicksilver trade of the world is substantially an armed truce between Spain and California. The mine of Old Almaden, in Spain, supplies the market of London and a large part of Europe, and ships its product as far west as the city of Mexico. Until recently, it also controlled the great Chinese market, but Mr. Butterworth, shipping 10,000 flasks to Hong Kong, and selling at far below the cost, forced the re-shipment to Spain of all the Spanish quicksilver; and the market has since been in his hands. The same tactics on the part of Spain keep him from the London market; and the two great producers are thus forced to divide the world between them. But the New Almaden company is not the only producer of quicksilver in California, and is obliged for self-preservation to accede to a combination with the New Idria and the Redington; and it is this combination which now controls the production of quicksilver, and will probably, for a long time to come, prevent the successful establishment of any rival enterprise.

It must be borne in mind that the consumption of this metal is limited. A certain amount for manufactures, a certain amount for metallurgical purposes, and the diminishing quantity required for calomel, with what the Chinese manufacture into vermilion, comprise the principal demands. Now, the quantity used in metallurgy, which is the most considerable, is hardly affected by the price of mercury. If it were $1 a pound instead of 60 cents, there would be no less consumed; if it were 25 cents, the demand would scarcely increase. In fact, the cost of quicksilver lost in amalgamation is (to wasteful men, like our mill-men) very trifling. In Mexico, where the *patio* process is employed, perhaps a pound and a half of quicksilver is lost for every pound of silver extracted; but in Washoe the loss is (I am told) not more than a third as much. The Pacific States and Territories require altogether about 1,200 flasks, or 91,800 pounds per month; Mexico and South America, 1,000 flasks each; China, 1,000. The total annual demand does not exceed 50,000 flasks, the production of which is divided among different companies as follows: New Almaden, 24,000; New Idria, 10,000; and Redington, 10,000. These three companies have agreed to confine themselves to the above limited amounts (the works at New Almaden, for instance, are only run to half their capacity to furnish the allotted 24,000 flasks) and to buy up the quicksilver made by all other companies. There are a number of smaller mines, like those of Guadalupe, which I visited, about eight miles from New Almaden, and which produce perhaps 150 flasks monthly. All these mines are forced to sell to the before-mentioned combination, which pays them 40 cents a pound, and sells to the public at 60. This margin of profit may seem excessive, but it must be remembered that the returns from sales are extremely slow. The metal is sent to distant agents, and must be sold at retail before the money is received by the producer. It takes perhaps two years to work off the whole of one annual crop. With money at two per cent. a month, this delay is serious. The present combination, which includes the Barrons, (who were in a certain degree forced to go into it, to save their profits on a large amount of quicksilver, which they had scattered through the western hemisphere at the expiration of their well-known contract with New Almaden,) is able to command foreign capital at comparatively low rates; and hence can afford to wait for the slow remuneration of the trade.

The following is the number of flasks of quicksilver ($76\frac{1}{2}$ pounds each) produced at the New Almaden mines, California, during the year 1868:

	Flasks.		Flasks.
January	3,000	August	2,000
February	3,001	September	1,600
March	2,501	October	1,600
April	2,000	November	2,262
May	2,000	December	1,660
June	2,000		
July	2,000	Total	25,624

Or 1,960,236 pounds. For these returns I am indebted to the courtesy of William Bond, Esq., president of the company.

CHAPTER II.

THE MOTHER LODE OF CALIFORNIA.

It is not easy to describe that formation known in this State as the Mother Lode, and extending, it is said, from Mariposa through three counties, into the neighborhood of Placerville. I traversed it through nearly its whole length, and studied with some care its general characteristics; but I confess myself puzzled to answer the very first question which arises concerning it, namely, is it a lode at all? In spite of the statements so often and so positively made, there is not the evidence of a continuous outcrop for 60 miles to support that supposition. Frequently the vein cannot be found on the surface; frequently it is "split up" (according to theory) into several branches. Nor have careful surveys established the identity of the individual outcrops exposed. In fact all that can be held as proven is, that there is a certain belt of the slates, within which occur, parallel with the stratification, the outcrops of veins or layers of auriferous quartz, which bear, on the whole, a certain resemblance to each other in general features. Yet even this resemblance is not invariable. Different mines on the Mother Lode have different kinds of rock, different quality of quartz, different associated minerals. The Pine Tree and Josephine, adjacent mines, and known to run together, carry distinctly different ores. It is only fair to say, however, that the Mother Lode itself is held by some to be a double vein, the two halves being of different ages, (as is always the case in a double fissure vein,) and showing, throughout the course, a steady antithesis of character.

This question I will not argue. At many points, the double nature of the deposit cannot be recognized. At other points, especially in Tuolumne county, there is a talcose companion vein east of the main quartz deposit, and at the celebrated Amador mine, by Sutter creek, there is a so-called boulder vein in the east. It is very difficult to identify these various formations so as to prove (what it is quite as difficult to disprove) that the Mother Lode is indeed a great master vein, occupying the central fissure in a system. It is even almost impossible to decide whether the different veins which are included under the one name are really fissure veins. Ashburner hints that they are veins of segregation, intercalations among the slates; Blake thinks them true fissures, though always or nearly always conformable to the layers of slate. I incline to the latter view, but I cannot bring forward absolute proof of the pre-existing fissures. Without any doubt, there are evidences enough of the movement of one wall on the other, of dislocations of vein matter, producing "slickensides," which sometimes run directly across the vein.

The quartz is sometimes (as in the Amador mine) knit to the hanging wall by ribs or cross-flaws of quartz, at right angles to the vein sheet; and these can be traced into the vein mass. It is hard to explain this without the hypothesis of a fissure gradually filled. "Horses" are not uncommon—another significant fact. The quartz itself has lost the comby structure so often seen in fissure veins, and appears dense, laminated, and streaked parallel with the walls. Some of it actually has a cleavage like felspar; and one intelligent man whom I have met believes most positively that the so-called quartz of the Mother Lode *is* felspar. He is mistaken. Felspar sometimes appears in these mines; but it is yellow, not white; and the gangue is genuine quartz, but quartz which has undergone so severe and long-continued a pressure as to lose the traces of its original structure, and receive new peculiarities from circumstances. In the Eureka at Grass Valley I saw (and no doubt the same might be observed on the Mother Lode) portions of the vein where the comby structure could still be traced, though with difficulty, in the solid mass of quartz.

All these, and other signs, are interpreted by me to mean "fissure vein." If I am right, then the Mother Lode presents to us either a huge continuous fissure, or a succession of similar ones, remarkably regular in strike and dip, and remarkably free from cross-courses or branches.

This regularity results, no doubt, from the conformability of the fissure or fissures to the slate-strata. But what force could open those strata in such a way, to such an extent, and with so little disturbance of the walls, or creation of faults and cross-courses? In reply to this question I can only offer a suggestion. Future observation may throw the needed light upon the subject.

Let it be borne in mind that the auriferous slates which here flank the Sierra Nevada do not dip westward, as one would naturally expect them, tilted by the upheaval of that range, to do; but on the contrary, dip towards the east, at various angles, though in general very steeply. This strange phenomenon, analogous to some Alpine occurrences which long perplexed the geologists of Europe, finds its probable explanation in the observations made by Professor Whitney, the State geologist, in the ridge between the north and middle forks of the American river. "This ridge," I quote from Cronise's Natural Wealth of California, "is cut by deep cañons or gorges, in one instance 2,000 feet in depth, with sides sloping at as high an angle as 45 degrees. The auriferous slates beneath are sometimes eroded to a depth of 1,500 feet, and peculiar facilities are thus afforded for the study of their structure. It was in this vicinity that Professor Whitney observed the very interesting fact, illustrative of the probable fan-like structure of the strata flanking the central portion of the Sierra. These usually show an easterly dip, towards the chain; in these deep vertical sections, it was noticed that the upper 1,000 or 1,200 feet had the normal dip to the east, but below this there was a gradual curve, and at the bottom the dip was to the west, as if the upper portion of the strata had been forced back by immense pressure from above." If the slates, first lifted on the east by the rising Sierra, were afterwards slowly overborne by its weight, we have precisely the cause requisite for longitudinal fissures on a grand scale. Further speculation would lead us too far.

An account of one or two of the principal mines, visited during my examination of the Mother Lode, taken together with the details given in the report of my predecessor (1868, pp. 14–19,) will throw some light on the nature and commercial importance of this extensive deposit.

The Mariposa mines, Mariposa county, the property of the Mariposa company, are now being worked under a new arrangement by the company itself. The financial adjustment which has been effected does not come within the province of this report; nor shall I repeat the general description of the property, with which the public has been made familiar, but content myself with adding, by way of illustration to what is said in Mr. Browne's last report, (pages 21–30,) two profile sketches of the Josephine and Pine Tree mines, showing their present condition and amount of reserves.

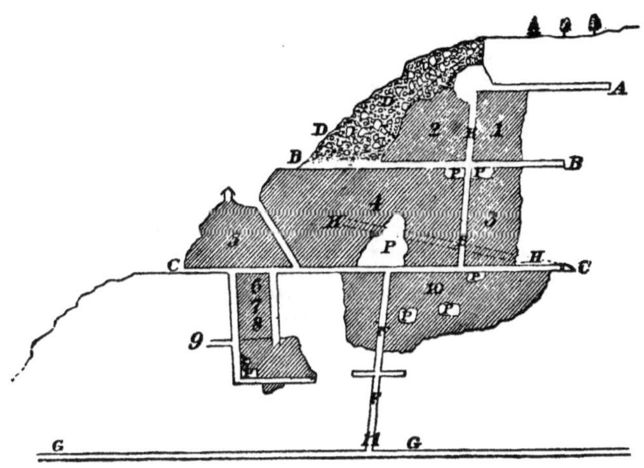

Josephine Mine.—Profile—Scale, 200 feet to the inch.

Course of vein, northwest and southeast; dip, northeast. A, Ketton drift; B B, Josephine drift; C C, Black drift; D D, caved ground; E E, Swiss shaft; F F, main shaft; G G, English drift; P P, pillars of quartz, left to support the vein; H H, Pine Tree drift, connecting the Josephine and Pine Tree mines.

	Yield per ton.
1. Stoped out, vein 20 feet thick	$22 00
2. Stoped out, vein 18 feet thick	22 00 to $42 50
3. Stoped out, vein 20 feet thick	22 00
4. Stoped out, vein 18 feet thick ... average..	22 00
5. Stoped out, vein 4½ feet thick	13 50
6. Stoped out, vein 4 feet thick	.....
7. Stoped out, vein 5 feet thick	.....
8. Stoped out, vein 11 feet thick	25 00 to 50 00
9. Ground standing, vein 8 feet thick	.....
10. Stoped out, vein 16 feet thick	20 00
11. Black talc slate, very rich.	

The quantity of low-grade ore still in the reserves is immense, and the amount of mining ground not yet open, beyond calculation. The problem here, as everywhere, is the reduction of the second-class ore. By the Ryerson process, the company expects to do this successfully. The working results obtained by that process are given below.

The Josephine and Pine Tree are the two mines on which the immediate development of the Mariposa estate, and the recovery of the company's fortunes, depend. The Princeton is in a bad condition, and would cost too much to reopen and extend; the Mariposa is for the present exhausted; the Ophir and Green Gulch offer no known productive ground. It is evident that on the great extent and excellent position of the Josephine and Pine Tree the first operations must be based. The following is a profile of the Pine Tree:

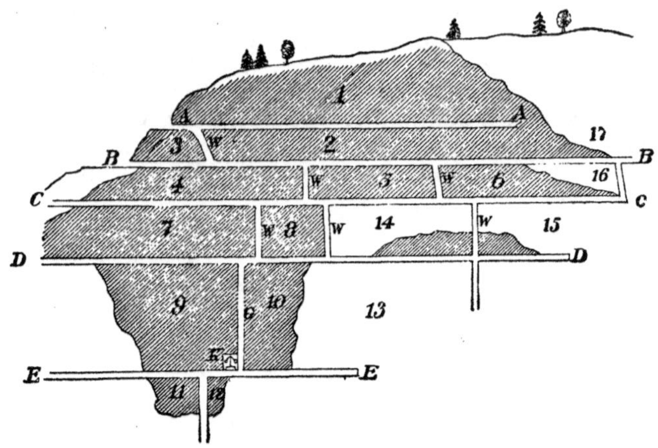

Pine Tree Mine.—Profile—Scale, 200 feet to the inch.

Course nearly northwest and southeast; dip, northeast. A A, Frémont drift; B B, upper or railroad tunnel; C C, Garden drift; D D, Wet drift; E E, lower tunnel, the mouth of which is 720 feet west of the west shaft; G, west shaft; K, engine underground; W W, winzes, or interior shafts.

	Yield per ton.
1. Stoped out and carved in, vein 14 feet thick	$26 00
2. Stoped out, vein 14 feet thick	26 00
3. Stoped out, partly caved in, vein 14 feet thick	26 00
4. Stoped out, vein 14 feet thick	24 00
5. Stoped out, vein 30 feet thick	9 00
6. Stoped out	......
7. Stoped out	8 00 to $12 00
8. Stoped out	......
9. Stoped out	9 50
10. Stoped out	9 50
11. Stoped out	......
12. Stoped out	14 00

Yield of 12, by Ryerson process, produces $25 to $45 per ton.

13, 14, 15, reserves, estimated by Captain Ketton to contain 20,000 tons of workable ore.

16, 17, reserves, of little value; vein small. The ore, however, at the extremity of drift A, yielded $60 per ton.

All the above yields, except in a single instance, refer to the ordinary process of stamping and amalgamation, as practiced in the two mills on the Merced, known as the Benton mills, and celebrated in California for their cheap crushing and great loss of gold. The Ryerson process of amalgamation, which has been tried for more than a year on the estate, is more expensive, but more thorough than that formerly in use; and for the ore of the Josephine and Pine Tree mines appears to have given very encouraging results. At the little Bear Valley mill, 1,500 tons of Josephine rock have been reduced, yielding $36,944 83, or $24 66 per ton. When it is remembered that the Josephine was abandoned because it would not pay $8 per ton at the Benton mills, the gain by the new process is apparent. The ore is first coarsely crushed with stamps, then reduced to powder in revolving drums, containing chilled iron balls, about as large as musket balls, and then introduced into a cylinder, in which it is exposed to mercury and steam. The Josephine rock worked by this process at Bear Valley is the same in appearance as that which formerly yielded $6 to $8 per ton at the Benton mills. Mr. Hicks, in charge of the Bear Valley mill, thinks the Pine Tree ore still better. Since my visit, the Bear Valley mill has been destroyed by fire, and the company has finished once more the dam across the Merced, and will soon be producing large amounts of bullion, the Benton mills having been adapted to the Ryerson process.

THE ONEIDA MINE OF AMADOR COUNTY.

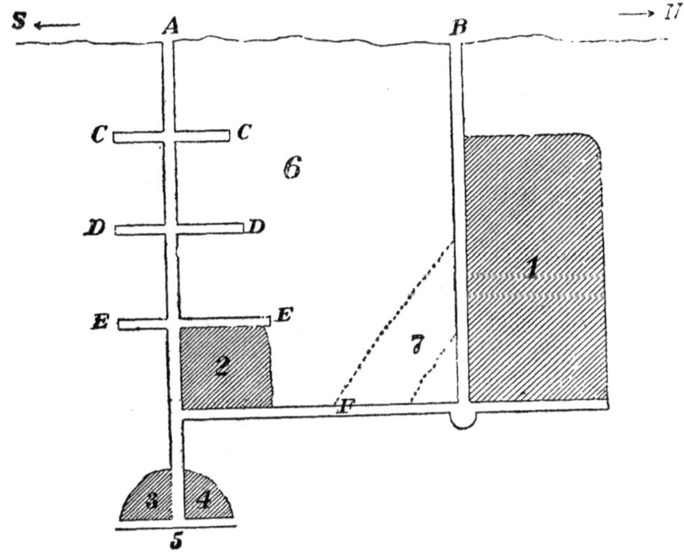

Profile—Scale, 200 feet to the inch.

Course nearly north and south; dip 65° to 80° east. A A, south shaft, 500 feet deep; B B, middle shaft, 400 feet deep; C C, D D, E E, F—100, 200, 300, and 400 foot levels; 1, stoped out, good vein, over 10 feet thick; 2, ditto; 3, 4, present stopes, vein 20 feet thick; 5, bottom workings of mine, vein 20 feet thick; 6, ground standing, not supposed to be rich; 7, hardly any vein.

The average width of the vein is about 14 feet. Seven hundred feet north of B is the north shaft, 150 feet deep, on a vein of 12 feet. Water is lifted from this mine in buckets, like those formerly used in the Hayward. The heavy gouge along the footwall renders extraction of rock easy, as in the Hayward also, *q. v.* Mr. Morgan, the superintendent, states the cost of mining at $3 25, and milling at $1 25, per ton. Giant powder has been tried, but not adopted. The circumstances neither require nor favor it. The mine is heavily timbered, and in good condition. The yield of rock in 1867 was $22 per ton; this year the vein is broader and not so rich, yielding, on the average, only $16 per ton. The shipments of bullion from this mine were, in March $21,500; in April, $10,500; in May, $18,300, and in the first shipments of June, $10,100—the variations being due to the times of cleaning up, once in three weeks, and the average monthly shipment being $15,000. The Oneida mill contains 60 stamps—40 at 450 pounds, and 20 at 650 pounds. The latter give the best satisfaction. Amalgamation with copper in battery and a narrow strip outside, then blankets, then concentrators, (four Hungerford and four Hendy,) pan and setler. In mine and mill together 105 men, all told, are employed. Mr. Morgan thinks he could save 20 men by opening another shaft.

THE EUREKA MINE OF AMADOR COUNTY.

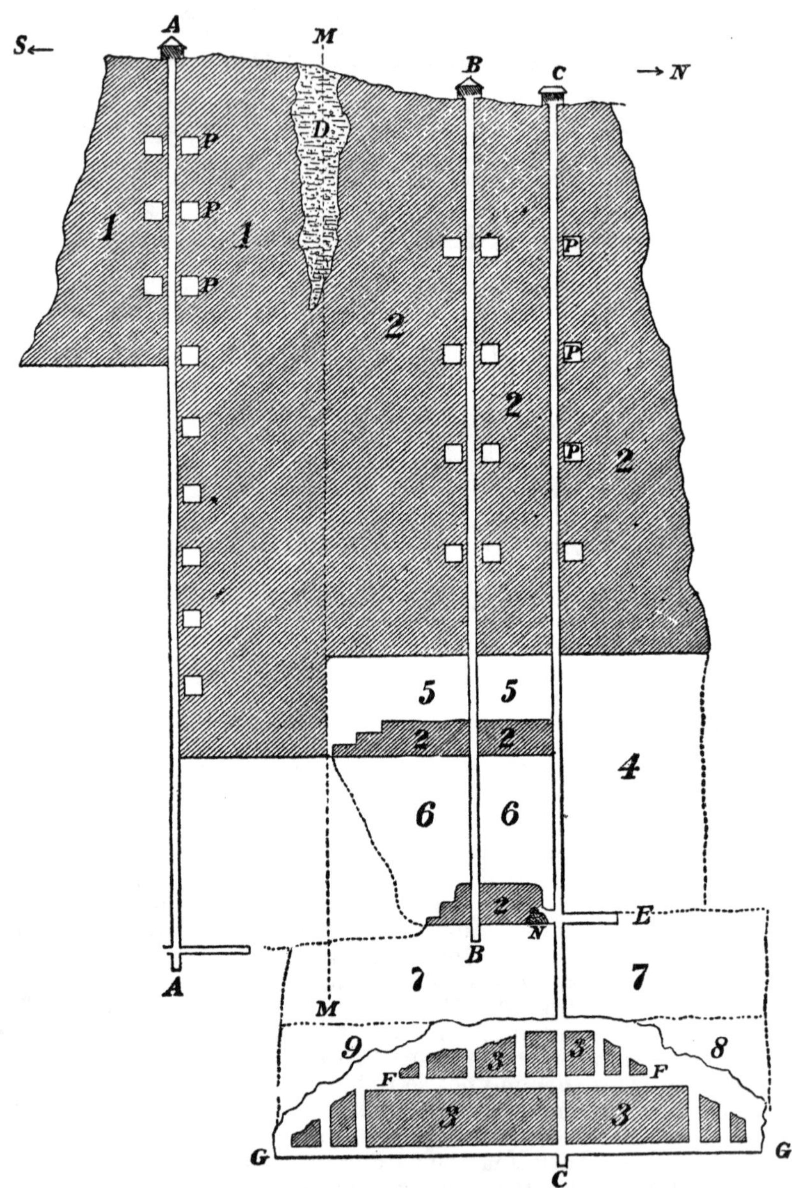

Profile—Scale, 200 feet to the inch.

A A, the Badger shaft; B B, the middle shaft; C C, the north shaft; D, caved ground on the old Badger line; E, F, G, levels; M M, the Badger line, formerly separating the two mines; N, a dam holding the water of B B from C C; 1 1, old Badger stopes; 2 2, ground worked out in the Eureka; 3 3, present stopes; 4, 5, 6, 7, 8, 9, reserves, the splendid extent of which is evident when we consider the width of the vein, which is in the lowest levels over 15 feet; P P, pillars of ground left standing as supports.

This profile is the same as that given in the report of Mr. Bowie, of San Francisco, except that it is not a vertical section, but a map on the vein, showing the amount of ground open and the extent of reserves.

The far-famed Amador, *alias* Eureka, *alias* Hayward's mines, is situated at Sutter creek, in Amador county, on the "Mother Lode." Sutter creek is about 18 miles from Latrobe, a station on the Sacramento railroad—which was intended to run from Sacramento to Placerville, but stopped ingloriously at Shingle Springs, and now that the Central railroad has adopted the river route via Dutch Flat, over the mountain, may perhaps never get any further. The difference which railroad and river transportation make in some of the incidental expenses of mining operations is illustrated by the fact that freight from San Francisco to Latrobe costs but $5 50 per ton, while the cost from Latrobe to Sutter creek is $12 per ton.

The claim now owned by the Amador company is 1,850 feet in length upon the course of the ledge, north 22° west. The average dip is 71° east, and the width varies from 3 feet to more than 20, being 15 feet in the lower stopes at the present time.

Mr. Browne's report, based upon such data as were attainable in June, 1867, represents the main or Eureka shaft to be 1,230 feet in depth. Accurate surveys made since that time establish the exact depth as 1,109 feet on the incline, or 1,054 feet vertically. The lowest level is 1,084 feet on the vein, the remaining 25 feet being used as a sump. This was especially required by the system of drainage employed. Up to the present time there have been no pumps in the mine, the water being hoisted in large buckets. Most of the water was from the surface. Old exhausted stopes in the upper part of a mine are often very troublesome in collecting water and conducting it into the deeper workings, from which it must be hoisted or pumped at considerable expense. The system of bailing instead of pumping is practicable where the water is not too abundant; and this was the plan adopted and obstinately adhered to by Mr. Hayward, as long as he owned and managed Eureka. The system has certain advantages. The plant is inexpensive and easily kept in repair. There is no trouble in sinking deeper, such as the readjustment of pumps, or perhaps replacing them with others of larger calibre. The same hoisting gear may raise water part of the time and ore the rest. On the other hand a pump works steadily, without interfering with other operations in the shaft, without constant manual labor in emptying buckets, &c., and is adequate (if selected with proper forethought) to all the sudden or climatic variations in the quantity of water entering the mine. The Eureka mine at its present depth needs two shafts constantly available for hoisting rock. Mr. Hayward's positiveness as to the superiority of buckets, enforced by his great pecuniary success in managing the mine, went far to convince many minds that, for this mine at least, pumps were not necessary. But Mr. Inch, a very experienced mining captain, now superintendent for the company, no sooner took charge than he determined to change the system of drainage. He will run a drain-tunnel near the surface to catch the water on the vein and keep it out of the lower levels; and the drainage in depth will be effected by means of pumps, to be placed in the south or Badger shaft, (now being deepened for the purpose,) while the Eureka and middle shafts will be devoted to hoisting rock. This is true economy.

It is possible that the popular reports that the profits of this mine amount to $50,000 monthly, were at one time true. But it is difficult to arrive at a just estimate of such a point, without considering the condition in which the mine and mills are kept. About the first of March last

Hayward & Company sold the property to the Amador company for about $750,000. (The Amador company which was formed in October, 1867, seems to have been merely Haywood & Co. under a new name.) The production of the mine for several months preceding and following this transfer is as follows:

October.	Production	$38,371 00
	Expenses	14,123 04
	Profit	24,247 96
November.	Production	$37,060 97
	Expenses	13,505 43
	Profit	23,555 54
December.	Production	$35,000 89
	Expenses	11,073 12
	Profit	23,927 77
January.	Production	$43,021 03
	Expenses	11,255 01
	Profit	31,766 02

Total profit of four months, $103,497 29, of which $88,000 was declared in dividends during that period. There were 3,700 shares, the par value of which was $400. The dividends were $6 per share monthly, or 18 per cent. annually on the capital stock, yet the mine was sold at $200 per share. This is a fact which eastern capitalists would do well to ponder. In the San Francisco market, where the value of mines is best understood, the stock of an active, successful mine is not intrinsically worth par, unless it is paying from 30 to 40 per cent. annually. In other words, a mine earning profit at the rate of $300,000 per annum is worth in cash, under the most favorable circumstances, only $750,000.

I say "under the most favorable circumstances," for it is not often that a mine is sold while it is in good paying condition, with ample promise for the future. When mine-owners look forward to selling they are apt to neglect the necessary preparatory work for the future, to make old timbers, old ropes, and old machinery last a little longer, and in every way to get as much immediate profit, and postpone as much inevitable expense, as possible. This was sadly true of the Mariposa mines. And, to a certain extent, it may be said of the Hayward. The new company has spent a good deal of money in repairs, and will have to spend more in necessary improvements. But the mine itself was well opened. Messrs. Ashburner and Janin, two of the most careful and impartial engineers on the Pacific slope, examining the property for the purchasers, measured the quartz in the stopes, calculated its value from the actual returns of large amounts worked in the mills, and computed the total reserves in sight at 108,027 tons, with a gross value of $1,778,366. The cost of mining and milling does not exceed $6 per ton, leaving an apparent profit of $1,130,204. A reduction of 25 per cent. for contingencies, over-estimate, &c., leaves $847,653 as the final net value of the reserves. At the present rate of about 2,000 tons a month, it would take some five years to exhaust the ore actually in sight and ready for extraction.

The statement of this mine, from the books of the company, is as follows:

Statement of the Eureka or Amador mine, at Sutter creek, Amador county, California, formerly known as Hayward's mine.

Date.	Number of tons mined.	Gross yield.	Per ton.
1867.			
October	1,650	$38,837 44	$23 53
November	1,568	37,395 56	23 85
December	1,773	35,103 06	19 80
Total	4,991	111,336 06	
Average per month		$37,112 03	$22 31
1868.			
January	1,885	$43,077 05	$22 85
February	2,106	47,245 46	22 43
March	2,259	52,787 25	23 37
April	1,885	42,023 43	22 29
May	2,203	43,769 82	19 87
June	2,156	45,474 32	21 09
July	2,229	47,198 69	21 17
August	2,243	45,094 33	20 10
September	1,823	42,420 54	23 27
October	(Not given.)	46,518 97	
Total yield for 10 months		$455,609 86	
Total yield for 13 months		566,945 92	
Monthly average, 1868		45,609 86	
Monthly average whole period		43,611 22	
Average yield per ton, 1868			$21 77
Average yield per ton, 1867 and 1868			21 88

Dividends for 1868, $7 per share monthly	$259,000
Investments in property and improvements, equivalent to about $1 per share monthly	40,000
Expenses of running mine and mill have varied from $14,000 to $22,000 monthly, averaging about $18,000, or, for 1868, about	180,000
Total disbursements therefore about	479,000

THE KEYSTONE MINE OF AMADOR COUNTY.

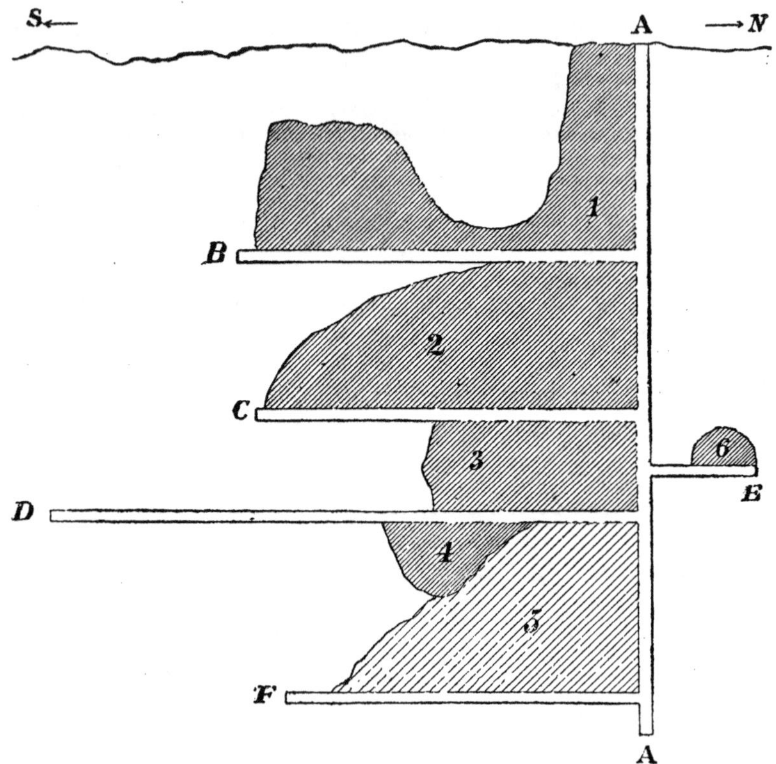

Profile of north shaft and workings—Scale, 100 feet to the inch.

Course of vein, north-northwest and south-southeast; dip 43° east. A A, north shaft of Keystone, 380 feet deep; B, 110 feet level; C, 190 feet level; D, 250 feet level; E, 220 feet level, north; F, 360 feet level; at D the vein is pinched; 1, 2, old ground stoped out; 3, old stope, in which the vein was 20 feet wide; 4 ditto, vein 15 feet; 5, the vein here is spliced, and the bottom seam only worked out; 6, stope in four-foot vein.

The south Keystone shaft, 640 feet south of these workings, and the Geneva workings, on a vein west, said to be the true mother lode of Amador, are both unconnected with the north shaft, and at present (June, 1868) full of water, having been drowned out by the severe rains of the winter of 1867 and '68, and not yet reopened. The company owns 2,800 feet on the Keystone vein, and 800 on the Geneva. The quartz, like that of the Eureka and Oneida, is hard but not tough—a "kindly mill-rock." The gold is apparently contained, for the most part, in sulphurets. There are steam hoisting works at the south Keystone, and a whim on the Geneva. The Keystone mill has 24 stamps (550 pounds) and no rock-breaker; blankets, sluices, and Hepburn pans are employed in amalgamation; Hendy concentrators and shaking tables in the concentration of tailings. The sulphurets (about 2 per cent.) assay $300 to the ton, and have been treated by chlorination. A new process was being tested during my visit, with what result I have not learned. The company pays $60 and $40 gold, with board, monthly to the first and second class miners; $50, with board, to mill-hands.

Statement of the Keystone mine, Amador county, California, for the year ending July 31, 1868.

Receipts:

Bullion	$154, 354 87
Premium on sales of bullion	1, 167 42
Cash on hand August 10, 1867	844 83
Amount of superintendent's account, August 10, 1867	7, 555 47
Total receipts	163, 922 59

The above quantity of bullion was derived from about 12,000 tons of quartz; average yield, $12 86 per ton.

Disbursements:

Real estate—house and lot		$100 00
Assay account—assays of bullion and ores		250 59
Tax account—government tax on bullion	$515 52	
tax on property at mine	549 18	
		1, 064 70
Insurance at mine		556 25
Freight account—on bullion received	546 90	
on coin forwarded to the mine	132 74	
on materials, provisions, &c	982 81	
		1, 662 45
Stationery at mine and in San Francisco		46 55
Interest paid		66 82
Team account—feed and livery		392 05
Boarding-house account—provisions, &c	7, 939 17	
cook and help	1, 227 00	
		9, 166 17
Machinery account—pump, &c		501 25
Expense account, at mine and in San Francisco		296 71
Salary of superintendent	3, 600 00	
Salary of secretary	600 00	
Salary of clerk at mine	465 00	
		4, 665 00
Bills payable August 10, 1867		1, 696 33
Mine account—timbers	4, 428 32	
wood	1, 393 97	
stones and materials	6, 123 22	
sundries	282 91	
		12, 228 42
Mill account—wood	11, 568 91	
castings	3, 002 66	
stores and materials	1, 523 58	
working sulphurets	1, 563 11	
		17, 658 26
Labor account—mine	29, 638 48	
mill	7, 124 47	
		36, 762 95
Water ditch account		1, 644 13
Dividends paid stockholders		75, 000 00
Total disbursements		163, 758 63

CHAPTER III.

THE QUARTZ AND PLACER MINES OF NEVADA COUNTY, CALIFORNIA.

THE EUREKA MINE, GRASS VALLEY.

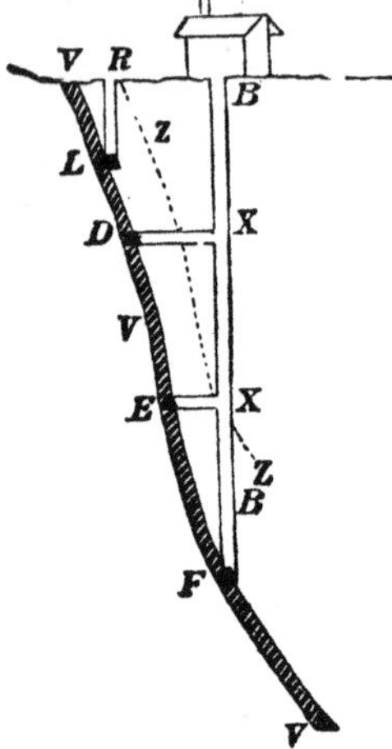

Cross Section—Scale, 200 feet to the inch.

The mines of Grass Valley and Nevada City were described at considerable length in Mr. J. Ross Browne's last report. I only add sketches and explanations as to a few of the principal mines, from which their condition and prospects may be inferred. The management of the mines and mills of this county may be studied by the engineer with profit. There are no fitter illustrations of workmanlike mining, timbering, hoisting, crushing, and amalgamating, than some of these companies present.

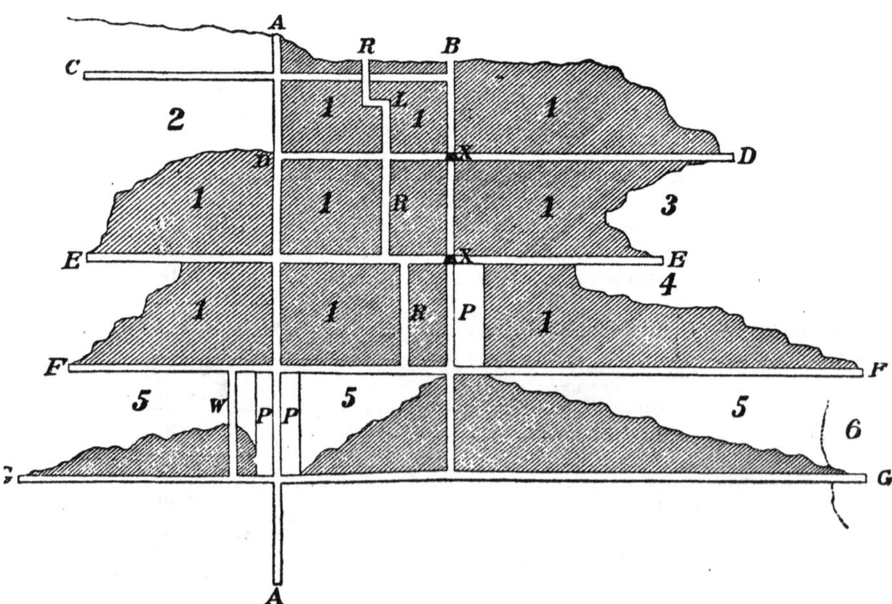

Profile—Scale, 200 feet to the inch.

Course east and west, dip about 78° south. Thickness of vein, 2.16 feet; average, 5 feet. A A, incline; B B, a shaft, vertical (and so not properly in the incline profile) as far down as the 300 foot level F; C, drain tunnel; D, E, F, G, 100, 200, 300, and 400 foot levels; X X, cross-cuts from vertical shaft to vein; L, 60 foot level; R, roadway into mine; W, winze; P P, pillars of ground left standing, to support the vein-walls around the shaft; V V, vein: Z Z, stringer accompanying the vein, at a distance of, say, 30 feet; 1 1, old stopes; 2, old ground, not valued for much; 3, 4, vein small and poor; 5, reserves; 6, vein 2½ feet thick, along hanging wall, and horse on foot-wall. Good ore.

The total reserves in the Eureka amount to 15,000 or 20,000 tons, one year's work in advance.

The Eureka mine, the foremost in California, is described in Mr. Browne's report, page 130. At the time of my visit in July, there were 122 men at work in the mine, and 21 in the mill, besides 19 surface hands, and five in the sulphuret works. Average wages were, at the sulphuret works, $2 75 daily; at the mine, $2 75 above ground, $3 under ground; foremen under ground $5, shift captains $4. The production was 376 tons weekly, yielding $40,000 to $60,000 per month. The mill has 30 stamps, 10 at 700 pounds, dropping 68 per minute, and 20 at 850 pounds, dropping 60 per minute. The light stamps crushed without a rock-breaker 16 tons daily, and the heavy stamps 40 tons; the relation between them is, therefore, as 1.6 to 2 in favor of the heavy stamps. A large Varney rock-breaker increases the capacity of the mill 40 tons in six days. Screens, No. 5 Russia-punched, equivalent to 40 brass wire. The pulp flows over blankets, and the tailings of these pass through "Eureka amalgamators;" the blanket washings are passed through Atwood amalgamators first and Eureka afterward, the whole finally passing over broad copper-plate sluices into a system of tubs and settlers, whence it is finally drawn into large improved Stevens buddles, 18 or 20 feet in diameter. The more quickly the sulphurets are concentrated the better, since they lose in specific gravity by oxidation. The last concentration from the buddles is put in a tossing tub, after which it is ready for chlorination. The sulphurets in the Eureka amount to about 1 per cent. of the quartz. In this mine the richer the rock in sulphurets, the richer the sulphurets in gold. The Eureka sulphurets formerly yielded $420 per ton, then $400, then as low as $115, and now $200. Some of this is free gold that escapes the amalgamating apparatus. Mr. William Watt, the very able and successful superintendent, and Mr. Deetken, the chemist in charge of the chlorination works, say that when the Eureka amalgamator was introduced, the yield of the sulphurets in the tailings fell off at once $100 per ton, so much more free gold being saved in the first process.

The chlorination works of the Eureka mine are under the charge of Mr. G. Deetken, who was the first to introduce the process successfully in California. In accordance with my resolution to abstain in the present report from all discussion of processes, I postpone the description of chlorination until a future occasion.

Statement of the Eureka mine, Grass Valley, California, for the year ending September 30, 1868.

The amount of quartz worked during the year was 15,944 tons. The apparent cost of mining and milling was $12 54 per ton; but as there was an excess last year of 610 tons of quartz on the surface and 500 tons in the mine, the actual cost of working is reduced to $12 44. The apparent yield for the year is $30 36 per ton; but as $14,000 belonging to last year's account was carried over to this year, the actual yield has been $31 24 per ton.

Receipts:

15,944 tons of quartz at $28 36	$452,103 76
142¾ tons of sulphurets, at $154 32	22,030 10
Other receipts	9,752 33
	483,886 19

(The total given in the statement furnished me by authority of the company was $484,076 23, but the individual items were the same as above. There was a mistake somewhere of $190 04.)

Disbursements:

Dividends	$270,000 00
Extraordinary expenses	24,924 74
Mining and milling expenses	209,479 87
Cash on hand	22,604 93
	527,009 54

Statement of the Eureka mine for the three years ending September 30, 1868

Receipts:

Bullion	$1,578,701 41
Other receipts	13,221 05
	1,591,922 46

Disbursements:

Paid for original and additional ground, settling title, &c.	$240,650 75
Dividends	670,000 00
Extraordinary expenses, construction, &c.	96,604 18
Mining and milling expenses	562,062 60
Cash on hand	22,604 93
	1,591,922 46

THE NORTH STAR MINE.

(One and three-quarter miles from Grass Valley.)

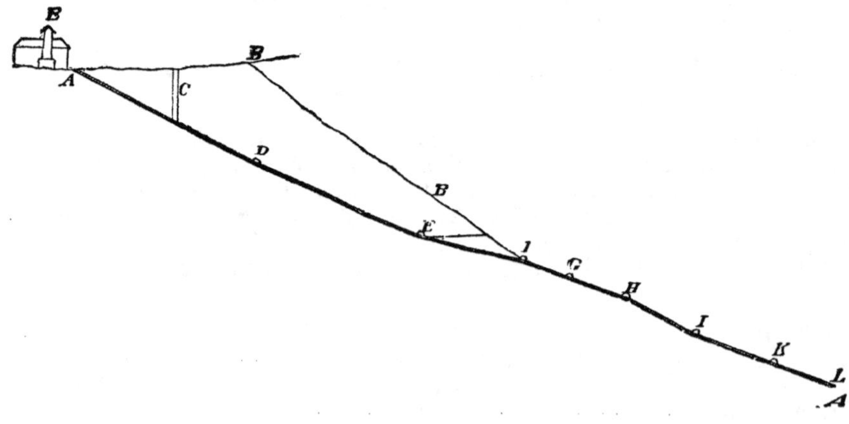

Cross-section—Scale, 200 feet to the inch.
[For explanation of lettering see note under profile.]

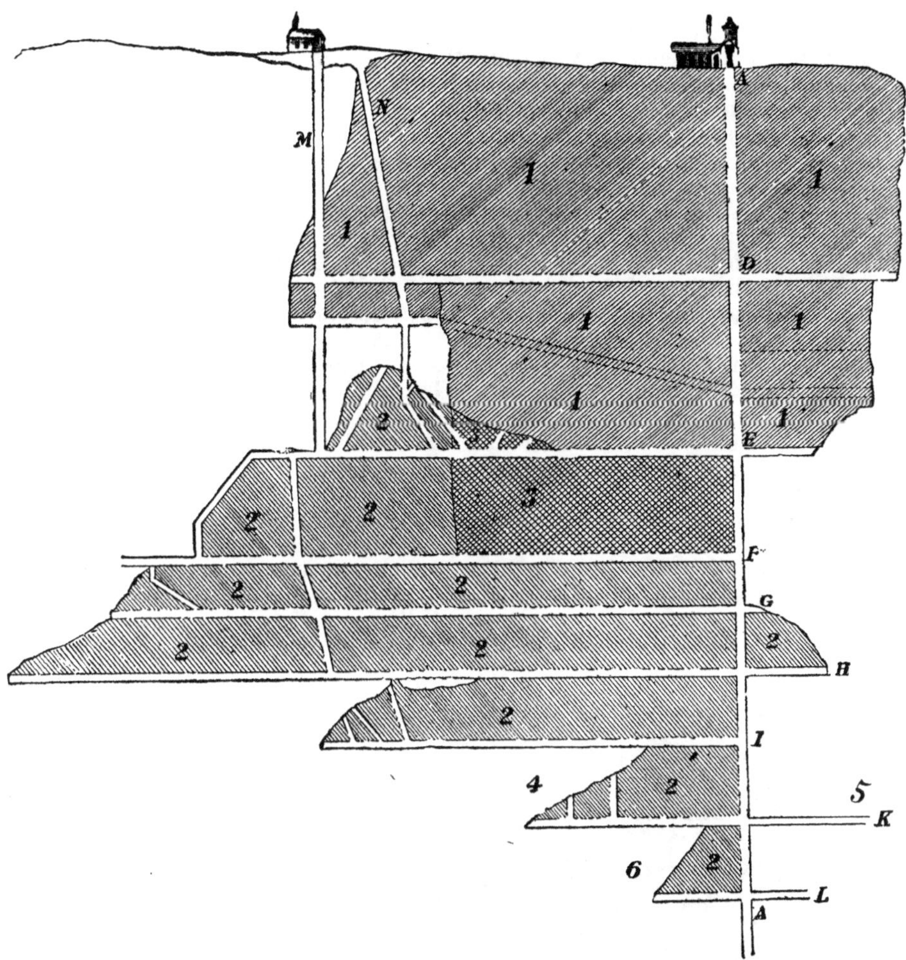

Profile—Scale 200 feet to the inch.

Course, east and west; dip, on the average, 21° 50′ north, in the lowest level only 12°. A A, main incline; B B, upper lode; C, pumping shaft, to raise water into mill; D, drain tunnel; E, first level; F, second level; G, third level; H, fourth level; I, fifth level; K, sixth level; L, seventh level, something over 300 feet vertical depth, and 892½ feet on the incline: M, shaft; N, Larimer incline; 1, 2, 3, stoped out; 4, 5, 6, reserves.

The ground shaded from right to left has been worked out on the upper vein; from left to right on the lower vein; and that shaded in both directions is worked out on both veins. The rock at either end of the sixth and seventh levels, and at the bottom of the shaft, is very rich, and the reserves of the mine are extensive and valuable. The gross proceeds of bullion from this mine in the sixteen months between July 6, 1867, and November 11, 1868, were $320,390 66. Further particulars are not in my possession. I judge that 50 per cent. of the above sum must have been net profit. Discoveries of great importance are said to have been made in the mine since my visit to it in July last. The value of the ore was then about $34 per ton, and total cost of mining, milling, superintendence, and interest account, about $12 per ton. The vein varies from 10 inches to four feet in width, averaging about 14 to 18 inches. Contracts for mining only are let underground at $1 50 to $2 50 per ton of quartz raised, which seems very reasonable for a narrow vein. The arrangement of pumps to be hereafter employed is a 16-inch plunger from the fifth level up, and lift below, for sinking. This apparatus will have a capacity of 1,000 gallons per minute. The maximum of water last winter (a very wet season) was 668 gallons per minute. There were 208 men employed in the mine and mill.

The North Star mill now contains 24 stamps, (950 pounds,) with a crushing capacity of 45 tons daily. The power is supplied by a 40-horse power engine, built in this county, where excellent mining machinery is made. A similar engine in the same building does the mine-pumping. The pulp from the batteries is run over blankets, which are washed every 10 minutes. The washings are slowly fed into a close Atwood amalgamator, and run afterwards over riffles with quicksilver. All tailings are concentrated in Hendy machines. The rock contains five to eight per cent. of sulphurets, of which about four-fifths are saved; buddles will be introduced to save the remainder. The sulphurets are sold or worked at custom chlorination works in the neighborhood. They yield $80 to $200 per ton, (being from $4 to $18 per ton of quartz.) The clean-up of the mill, July 8, after 12 days' run with 16 stamps, was $22,000, exclusive of sulphurets. This is extraordinary, as it shows an average of $61 per ton, or thereabouts. The high result is due to the occurrence in the lower levels of quartz thickly filled with free gold.

EMPIRE MINE, OPHIR HILL, GRASS VALLEY.

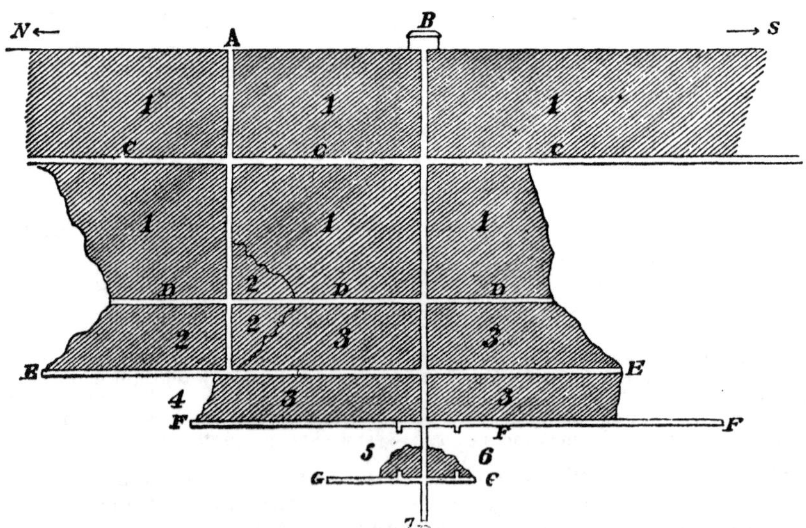

Profile—Scale, 300 feet to the inch.

Course, north and south, or more exactly north-northwest and south-southeast; dip, 21° to 40° west; average 31° west; A A, old incline shaft 500 feet deep; B B, working incline, 740 feet deep, (these depths are not vertical, but, like all profiles given, measured on the incline of the vein, the only true way to obtain a knowledge of the quantity of ground open;) C C, drain tunnel; D D, 400 foot level; E E, 500 foot level; F F, 580 foot level; G G, 680 foot level; 1 1, ground worked out; 2 2, ditto, poor ore; 3 3, ditto, rich ore; 4, new ground, vein poor; 5, new ground, vein two feet, very good; 6, new ground, vein 15 inches, very good. At the south end of level D, the ledge failed; at the south end of F, on the contrary, there is a good vein of 18 inches.

The claim of the company covers 2,100 feet, viz: 1,500 feet of the Ophir Hill, of which 1,200 are shown above, and 600 feet of the Rush and Lawton, adjoining the mine on the south. This latter ground has been opened to the depth of 300 feet and found very rich. The ledge in the Empire mine varies in width from nothing up to five feet. The wall rock is "greenstone," (altered slates?) and the casings and horses between the stringers of quartz on either wall are a rock of lighter color. A year and a half were spent in shafting and other dead work, to get the mine into its present shape, which, as the sketch shows, is highly workmanlike and symmetrical, giving assurance of reserves adequate to the capacity of the mill. The pumps in the mine comprise a lift for sinking the shaft; a 10-inch plunger for raising the mine water to the drain tunnel, and an eight-inch plunger, sitting 100 feet below the tunnel, raises to the surface the water needed in the mill. The company's 30-stamp mill is considered the most magnificent in the State, though other mills, employing different apparatus, claim equally good results. The weight of stamps is 800 pounds, drop 58 to 65 per minute; screens No. 40 brass wire; daily capacity, with a Blake crusher, 40 tons; amalgamation in battery: copper plates, Hendy concentrators and pans. About four tons of sulphurets in 24 hours are caught in the mill. Below the tail-race two men working on shares catch about six tons (they say) per month—probably more; which they sell at $23. Still further down, another man catches two tons per month. The ore averaged $30 38 last year, and the monthly expenses were about $12,000 per 1,000 tons reduced.

Statement of the Empire Mining Company of Grass Valley, California, for fourteen months, ending October 15, 1868.

Proceeds of reduction of 8,735 tons of ore	$253, 632 15
Cost of milling and mining, including dead work and explorations	159, 328 22
Net proceeds of 8,735 tons of ore	94, 302 93
Average gross yield per ton	29 04
Average cost of mining and milling	18 24

(*Note by the secretary of the company.*—The two last reductions were from a low grade of ore, now exhausted, and produced from 1,950 tons but $34,911 27, or $18 18 per ton; while the remaining 6,815 tons realized $218,720 88, or at the rate of $32 09 per ton, which is considered the average value of the reserve.)

BANNER MINE, NEVADA CITY.

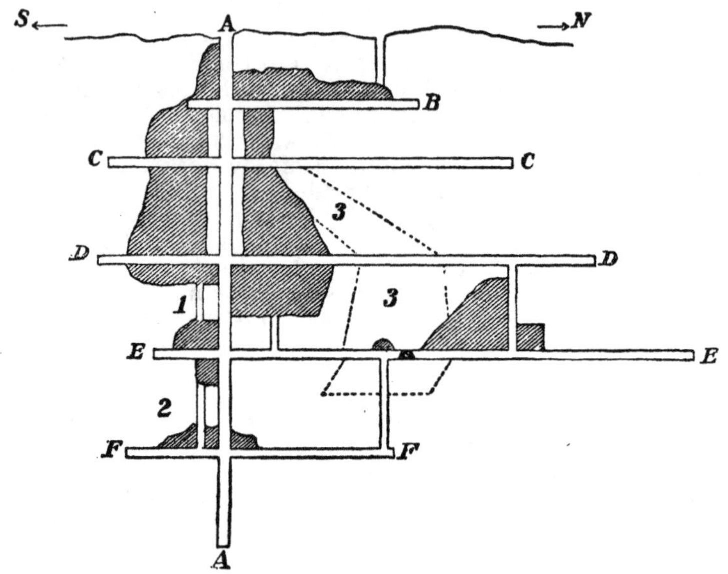

Profile—Scale, 200 feet to the inch.

Course, north and south, (a little west of north;) dip, 45° east; width, 6 inches to 16 feet—average, 4½ feet. Ore, sulphurets of iron, copper, lead and zinc, with a little free gold. A A, main incline, 500 feet deep; B, C, D, E, F—60, 120, 220, 320, and 420-foot levels; 1, vein pinched; 2, vein, 6 feet; 3 3, horse dividing the ledge in two.

At the cross-cut on the 320-foot level these two ledges are 16 feet apart. The reserves in this mine are large and valuable. Water is only troublesome in winter; two 30-horse engines pump and hoist. The shaft-house is on a high hill, and the mill in a ravine, 120 feet below. The ore is let down in cases on a steep surface incline. The mill is run by steam, has 20 stamps, (600 pounds,) and 10 more now erecting. Capacity, 30 tons daily. Fine screens, copper plates, and blankets are used. The blanket washings are worked in Knox pans, with revolving mullers or travellers; the tailings are caught in rockers, in 2,500 feet of sluices and a buddle at the end. Total yield of quartz, $27 50. Immediate concentration and chlorination of sulphurets would be better.

PITTSBURG MINE.

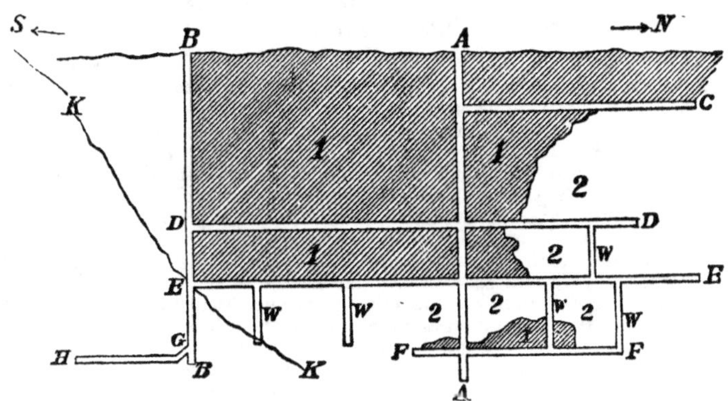

Profile—Scale, 300 feet to the inch.

A A, old shaft, 480 feet deep—lode at bottom 2 feet wide; B B, new shaft, 450 feet deep; C, 80-foot level; D, 260-foot level; E, 330-foot level; F, 430-foot level; G, cross-cut, 33 feet from new shaft to the heaved portion of the vein; H, drift on vein from cross-cut, 130 feet southward; K K, line of a slide, south of which the ledge is heaved forward and eastward; W W, winzes, or interior ladder and air-ways; 1 1, old ground, worked out; 2 2, reserves.

This mine, formerly called the Wigham, is situated some 1½ mile from Nevada City. The works were courteously shown me by Mr. S. D. Merchant, manager and part owner. The vein averages about 2 feet in width, and the claim covers 2,000 feet, or from the new shaft 795 feet north, and 1,205 feet south. The county rock is the peculiar "greenstone" of this county. The ore contains some free gold, and a large amount of sulphurets, of which, say, 1 per cent. is galena. Hanging and foot-wall are both firm, with little fluccan or "gouge." The yield of this mine in June, 1868, was 480 tons, worth $19,260 70, not including the proceeds from sulphurets chlorinated. The expense was about $8,000. Forty men furnish the mill with ore; 36 are engaged on dead work. The whole force in July was 95 men, of whom 5 were Chinamen, employed in surface-work. The mill has 10 stamps, (650 pounds,) and is run at 80 to 85 drops per minute. Its capacity is 22 to 23 tons daily. Sieves No. 5, punched; amalgamation in battery, on copper plates, in Hunter's rubber, (Eureka amalgamator,) copper plates again; tailings caught in vats, concentrated on a rocker, and the sulphurets sent to chlorination works. Tailings from the rocker concentrated in sluices and a large concave buddle. Sulphurets not perfectly clean worked in a Knox pan. I merely put these data upon record, postponing the comparison of them with the processes at other mills of Nevada county and elsewhere to a future report on "Methods and processes." It will be seen that the Pittsburg mill has light stamps and runs rapidly, while the usual practice at Grass Valley is heavy stamps and slow speed. Each style has its partisans, and good millmen do good work with either, which makes it all the harder to decide upon their comparative merits, except by close study and prolonged and exact experiments.

THE DEEP PLACERS OF NEVADA COUNTY, CALIFORNIA.

The following letter was written at my request by Mr. W. A. Skidmore, of San Francisco, an intelligent and experienced observer:

SAN FRANCISCO, July 21, 1868.

DEAR SIR: In accordance with a promise made to you at Grass Valley, I herewith transmit an account of my observations on my return trip to this place through the "Blue Lead" range of Nevada county, Placer county, and the quartz district among the foot-hills near Auburn, Placer county I had only leisure to remain one day at Dutch Flat, one at Gold Run, and one at or near Auburn; and such information as I can communicate is more the result of previous acquaintance with the country than of present research.

Throughout the route traversed as above, I was principally impressed with the decay of the mining towns and the depopulation of the country. If this should continue in the same ratio as it has progressed since my first acquaintance with the part of country referred to, (some five years since,) we will soon have deserted towns and a waste of country torn up by hydraulic washings, far more cheerless in appearance than the primitive wilderness of 1848. The causes for this stagnation and the remedy are subjects for your observation and reflection. I shall proceed to give the simple facts of the condition of the country.

Immediately to the east of the basin in which are situated the towns of Grass Valley and Nevada, is a ridge running nearly north and south, and known as Greenhorn mountain. On the east slope of this mountain we find the ancient channel known as the Blue Lead, and on which are situated the towns of Hunt's Hill, Red Dog, You Bet, and Little York, in Nevada county, and the towns of Dutch Flat and Gold Run, in Placer county. The lead referred to is well defined to the north of Deer creek, Nevada county, and to the south of the North Fork of the American river, in Placer county; but my remarks apply only to that part of it lying between those streams, some 24 miles in length, but embracing at least three-fifths of the mills employed in crushing cement on the Blue Lead.

For convenience of description the mining interests of this section may be classed under three headings, viz: hydraulic mining, cement mining, and river sluicing, the latter referring to the washings of the tailings in the present water courses.

Hydraulic Mining.—The auriferous deposit of this section is from three-fourths of a mile to one mile in width, and the depth of pay dirt varies from 80 to 180 feet from the surface to a bed of hard, cemented gravel, which is not sufficiently rich to crush under stamps, and too hard to be disintegrated by the force of water. This bed of gravel, some fifty feet in thickness, is underlaid by the peculiar blue cement which gives the channel the name of "Blue Lead." Probably no part of this State has yielded as rich returns to the hydraulic miner as the range here described; but this kind of mining is now only systematically carried on in one district on the range, known as Gold Run, Placer county. This district was opened about four years since, and still has enough ground left for two more seasons, exclusive of the present one. The yield for 1866 of this district alone, about two and a-half miles in length, was estimated by the local bankers at $350,000; for 1867, $500,000. The yield of the present year will not probably exceed $400,000; but this is owing to a miners' strike against the ditch companies, which prevented the early opening of the claims, and not to a deterioration of the character of the auriferous deposit. The present price paid for water in Gold Run district is 17 cents per inch for 24 hours, a reduction of nearly 20 per cent. from prices of previous seasons, but still not enough to satisfy the demands of most of the ground owners, who prefer to await a further reduction. These companies use from 350 to 600 inches. This water passes out of the gauge boxes with a pressure of six inches above the feed aperture. The banks here are from 100 to 200 feet in height, and of more uniformly a gold-bearing character than any district now being worked in the State. The tailings from this district run into the North Fork of the American river, and are there lost. In the Nevada county end of the range described, hydraulic mining is still carried on extensively in places, but not with as good results, though water is much cheaper in some cases, being as low as 10 cents per inch for 24 hours. The towns of Hunt's Hill, Red Dog, You Bet, and Little York were formerly the centres of active hydraulic operations; but this kind of mining is now laboring under the depression incidental to this business throughout the State, though there is still a vast field for it.

Cement mining.—The gold-bearing cement lies next to the bed-rock of the ancient stream, and can be worked with profit where the channel has been reached, for a thickness of from 10 to 20 feet, and a width, which varies with the conformation of the channel, of from 20 to 40 feet—the pay being richest where the channel is narrowest, as a general rule. This channel is, doubtless, as continuous as the auriferous deposits above it, but has only been opened at spots which are designated by the location of the towns heretofore named. No branch of mining is attended with more risk and uncertainty than this, but when successful the yield is enormous. This kind of mining will eventually be extensively prosecuted throughout this range, but not until some cheaper process is discovered than the one now in general use—that of crushing with stamps. Whether the "Cox* pan," with some improvements, will

* A new pan, in which the cemented gravel is broken by revolving arms, and the auriferous cement drops through a grating which retains the barren boulders. The object is to avoid the necessity of crushing the whole mass.—R. W. R.

not present the facilities desired, is a question which the experience of this year will decide. It is estimated that a stamp will crush quite as much of the hardest cement as of quartz. The larger boulders are thrown out at the dump-house, where the cement is broken up preparatory to the cement being fed in the batteries. The gold, being mostly free, is caught in the batteries by amalgamation; the pulp thence passes over copper plates and in sluices. Without claiming to be an expert in such matters, I have no hesitation in saying that 20 per cent. at least of the fine gold is *needlessly* wasted and lost, for want of longer sluices and settlers. Probably 33 per cent. of all the gold is lost, as some of it is rusty and needs grinding. Of the 17 mills located on this channel, but two are run by steam, the others having water-power. One of these claims, which I visited two years since, was being run at an expense, for mill and mine, of $500 per week. This claim was open by a bed-rock tunnel 1,000 feet long, with sufficient fall to drain and carry the cement to a ten-stamp mill run by water-power. The receipts of the owners, at that time, were not less than $2,500 per week, and it has steadily paid large profits ever since. An adjoining claim was noted for a production of $60,000 in 90 days, about the year 1865. A few miles above I visited a claim which had cost its owners $30,000 without getting any return. This latter claim took out their cement through a shaft 135 feet deep, and were much troubled with water. This mill, (ten-stamps,) hoisting and pumping works, were run by water-power, which alone cost $25 per 24 hours. I learn that they have struck pay dirt this season. The claims in the vicinity of the town of You Bet have proved the richest on the channel. Two and a-half miles southerly of Gold Run the same channel has been found at a point where it crosses the North Fork of the American, or, more properly speaking, where the North Fork has cut through the ancient channel. At this place (Stone's Mill) the bed-rock terminated abruptly, about 1,000 feet above the present level of the water of the North Fork of the American, and the cemented mass was plainly exposed to view. An eight-stamp mill was erected, and the mass worked by breaking it down, having first loosened it by heavy explosions of powder, in drifts run for the purpose. In consequence of the great facilities thus presented, this claim has steadily paid since the commencement of the enterprise. I visited this ground a few days since, while at Gold Run, and do not think they are in the centre of the channel, but on a shelf of bed-rock. I form this opinion from the absence of the large boulders, petrified trees, brush, sand-banks, &c., usually found in the channel. This channel runs northerly under the Gold Run district to Little York, and perhaps Dutch Flat. Southerly, it makes its appearance at the same elevation on the opposite bank of the North Fork of the American, near Iowa Hill, from whence it is easily traced for many miles. The town of Dutch Flat, which lies to the north of the Gold Run district, is not on the direct north and south line which the channel seems to follow; nevertheless deep explorations there this summer have disclosed the presence of the Blue Lead, but whether on a bend of the main channel, or on a feeder or affluent, cannot be positively known. The following are the number of mills and stamps erected on this part of the Blue Lead:

Locality.	Mills.	Stamps.
Green Mountain	1	10
Hunt's Hill (Gouge-Eye)	3	24
Red Dog	4	36
You Bet	6	56
Little York	3	26
Dutch Flat	1	4
Gold Run	1	8
Totals	19	164

NOTE.—Of these 164 stamps not more than 80 are running this year.

The channel is often said to be "lost," and this accounts for the number of claims lying idle. More properly speaking, they have come upon an unprofitable spot in the channel not favorable to the deposition of gold—though sometimes it meanders out of a particular claim.

River sluicing.—The range I have described presents extraordinary attractions for this class of operations, which are now prosecuted but on a limited scale, but destined to become one of the greatest interests of this part of the country, on account of the number of large streams crossing or running parallel with the best mining ground, and which are filled to a depth of from 30 to 50 feet with the accumulated tailings of 10 years of extensive hydraulic mining. The most prominent of these streams are the Bear river, Steep Hollow creek, and Greenhorn creek; there are, besides, many ravines and cañons, noted for the extent of their accumulations and the former rich character of the adjacent ground. In the early days of hydraulic mining, no allowance was made for the existence of fine gold, and this character of wealth was carried off by the strong and rapid streams of water running over the sluice boxes, which were then of a steeper grade and much shorter than those now used; besides, the advantages of "dumps" and "undercurrents" were then unknown. The result was that a large proportion of the gold was lost—probably one-half—and now lies on the bottom of the streams which were the receptacles of the tailings. A preliminary survey of Bear river was made several years since with a view to the inauguration of an extensive system of tail-sluicing, but the fall of the stream not being sufficient to carry off the tailings, the project was temporarily abandoned. This object can, however, be accomplished by running a tunnel, a mile and a half in length, through the ridge dividing Bear river from the North Fork of the American, which latter stream is several hundred feet lower than Bear river, and laying the sluice boxes in the bottom of this tunnel. Should the project of Sanford & Co., of running off the tailings of Greenhorn creek, prove remunerative, this immense work will doubtless be undertaken. Sanford & Co. have purchased and located ten miles of Greenhorn creek, and commenced putting in their sluice boxes last year. They were much damaged by the extraordinary high waters of last season, and their experiment has not yet demonstrated the profit of this class of operations, but practical men express no doubts of their eventual success.

Present condition and future prospects.—If the condition of the mining towns along the route I have laid out is to be taken as a criterion of the mineral wealth of the country, then a very discouraging picture would be presented. But to do this would be to do an injustice to a district which I believe is yet destined, with the aid of capital, to add millions of dollars to our circulating medium. The causes of the decay of those towns are easily found. The large sums of money which the mines have yielded have not been spent here in making homes and opening new channels of mining enterprise, but in the majority of cases the miner, as soon as he made his "pile," has gone elsewhere to spend it. With the new population which thec ountry requires this will not again occur. The soil, which a few years since was thought worthless except for the gold it contained, is now demonstrated to be productive. if not of all the necessities of life, at least of all that make a home luxurious and pleasant. The grape, fruits, and vegetables of all kinds grow here with a profusion elsewhere unknown, and the new class of miners will learn that here they can provide themselves with homes which will make life endurable without the enormous gains expected in early times. Nearly all these towns have, at some period, been destroyed by fire and rebuilt in a day, but now they are suffering from the equally sure but slower ravages of time The town of Red Dog has not one-half its buildings occupied, and at present none of the cement mills at that place are running. You Bet still retains some of its former prosperity. Little York has deteriorated nearly as much as Red Dog. Dutch Flat, a few years since, had a population of 2,000; at present I should judge the population to be about 1,000. On the main street, here, we find dilapidated sidewalks, vacant hotels and stores, and an occasional ruin of a house which has fallen from the rotting of the timbers which supported it. Hunt's Hill (known in early days as Gouge-Eye) is supported by the cement mills of the Gouge-Eye and eastern companies, whose claims have steadily paid for several years past. Gold Run is the only prosperous town on the part of the Blue Lead range I have visited.

This part of the country is now passing through a crisis. It is an interregnum in which mere labor has nearly exhausted its efforts, and capital has not yet come to its assistance. The gold is in the ground, but not so near the surface as to be extracted by mere labor. Enterprises of great magnitude, requiring capital and engineering skill, must be prosecuted, and when completed this region will enter on a career of prosperity which will last for 20 years or more, and repay their projectors 100-fold. This is not a mere visionary statement, but is founded on observation and an acquaintance of several years with the resources of this range. The tailings of the rivers must be worked over; bed-rock tunnels must be run in the ridges, for the double purpose of drainage and the extraction of the lower deposit. To give a few instances: The hydraulic ground of Dutch Flat, one of the richest localities in the State, is not all washed off, but operations have ceased for want of fall. Let a bed-rock tunnel 2,000 feet in length be run from the level of the Bear river, under the ground to the back of the town, and a new bench, 100 feet in thickness, can be run off over sluice boxes, to be placed in the bottom. The existence of the blue lead under this ground has been demonstrated by the prospecting shaft of Mr. James Taef, of this place. The cement could be taken out through such a tunnel, which would necessarily drain the whole lead; but it lies so deep here that individual enterprise on each claim, in raising and pumping, will not pay. Such a tunnel, by means of drifts, would work the whole lead at this place. There is an abundance of gravel here, and the miners in some cases offer half their claims for machinery to work it. Such machinery, with water power, and including an extra $1,000 for putting the claims in better working order, would not cost more than $4,000—a high estimate. It has been estimated that the main tunnel above referred to would cost $25,000, but I think this too low. Near Gold Run it is contemplated to run a large tunnel, with double set of sluice boxes and tramway for cars, a distance of 5,000 feet. This will not be needed for several years, as there is yet plenty of fall, but it is wisdom for the miners to take time by the forelock. The ground under which this will run is as rich as any in California, and the blue lead is developed both to the north and south of its proposed course. The estimated cost of this project is over $150,000, and work will be commenced this season. This tunnel will begin to pay when the first 1,000 feet is completed, and at 2,000 feet it will strike the channel of the ancient stream, and thence run at right angles parallel with it. Millions of cubic yards of auriferous dirt and gravel must run through this tunnel, which debouches into a deep ravine, from which the tailings will find their way into the North Fork of the American. When it is considered that the usual two weeks' "clean up" on the smaller of these claims, using 350 inches of water, is rarely less than $3,000, can any doubt be felt of the necessity of this work? There are many other projects which could be mentioned, but being of the same nature, these will suffice. The best mining properties in California, at Smartsville, Yuba county, and San Juan, Nevada county, owe their value to extensive works of this nature.

The capital necessary to prosecute these great projects must come from the east or from Europe. Here in California we are accustomed to high rates of interest and punctual payments. No man puts his money out without the expectation of realizing in a few months, by a sale, or getting his interest promptly every month. The capital required here is of that class which can wait patiently for a year or two without a return; but when that return comes it will be nearer ten per cent. per month than one per cent. on the investment.

CHAPTER IV.

GIANT POWDER AND COMMON POWDER.

A ride of eight miles over somewhat steep and stony bridle-paths, from Bear Valley up Mount Oso, over its crest and along the other side, leads from the Mariposa estate to a very interesting mine, in the same county, known as the Oaks and Reese, or Hunter's Valley mine. A vein, bearing the local name of Blue Lead, strikes northwest through Hunter's valley, parallel with the Mariposa veins. It is generally found to yield a low grade of mill-rock; but at various points it is joined by small quartz cross-feeders; and these are often rich, and sometimes appear to "enrich" the main lode. At the junction of one of these, known as Little Lead, with the Blue Lead, the Oaks and Reese mine is situated. The average thickness of the Little Lead in this mine is fourteen inches; that of the Blue Lead, about two feet. Both are very hard quartz, with "greenstone" (probably altered conglomerate) walls. There is no selvage or "gouge" on either wall, of which advantage can be taken in drifting or stoping, and the faces and natural headings of the quartz incline in such a way as to increase the difficulty of back-stoping. Indeed, the stopes in this mine are all underhand. The workings comprise a shaft 233 feet deep on the junction of the veins, levels of 228 and 85 feet, at the depth of 150 and 200 feet respectively from this shaft, west, on the Little Lead, and a level at 130 feet, southeast, on the Blue. As the veins (especially the Little Lead, which has furnished about three-fifths of the quartz sent to the mill) are so narrow, a good deal of hard country rock is blasted in stoping, and besides this it is necessary to keep driving levels and preparing new ground. It is easy to understand that these circumstances make the cost of mining very great. In fact, while the crushing and amalgamation of this quartz are effected in the beautiful ten-stamp mill belonging to the mine, at an expense of about $3 per ton, the extraction costs some $20 per ton. The average yield of the quartz in mill is said to be $30, and the quantity crushed daily is about 15 tons. The mine is owned by a company of San Francisco capitalists, and superintended by Mr. Cassell, an intelligent, enterprising and experienced miner, whose name will be remembered by Washoe or Reese River pioneers.

Mr. Cassell had been using the new Giant powder exclusively, for more than a month, at the time of my visit, in June, and very courteously placed at my disposal the results of his experience with it. To make these results useful to others, they should be accompanied with a description of the conditions under which the work is performed; and hence I have given the above details, which I consider essential to the full statement of the case.

It is evident that this mine is one which would profit largely by a reduction of mining costs, since so large a proportion of its expense lies in that item. At some of the mines on the great Mother Lode, where hundreds of tons are not unfrequently thrown down at a blast, and where a wide, soft "gouge" along one wall enables the miner to keep two or three sides of the rock free, and give the powder the greatest opportunity to "lift" without waste of power, the cost of drilling and blasting per ton is so low that a reduction of one-third, even if it could be made, would not greatly affect the general count; but mines like the one I am describing have comparatively little timbering; and the various expenses of hoisting, transportation, &c., are overshadowed by the great item of labor, which forms, I think, in this case, more than one-third of the cost of extraction.

In the second place, it is in just such hard rock, disadvantageous for common powder, and especially in running levels or sinking shafts, that instantaneous and powerful explosives like nitro-glycerine and Giant powder show their superiority. They never go out of a hole as if it were a gun-bore, or leave a large portion of it standing, so much labor wasted. They tear to the bottom, and act in all directions without waiting, as it were, to find the line of least resistance.

The richness of the ore is another reason for using the new powder, as I shall explain hereafter. The ventilation of the mine is good, and the smoke of the powder soon disappears from the stope. This is a most important consideration, if, as some say, the smoke from nitro-glycerine is injurious to the health. The experiments in which I participated did indeed give me a severe headache; but the blaster who fired the shot, and entered the stope immediately to observe its effect, said that, now he was accustomed to it, he suffered no more inconvenience from it than from common powder. I fancy that the talk to the contrary is inspired by the prejudices of the miners, who are generally hostile to anything new, and have special reason to oppose this material.

Before proceeding now to present the comparative statement of cost and work performed by the two systems, I will mention one interesting fact, for which Mr. Cassell vouches. It is popularly supposed that the Giant powder can only be exploded by means of the fulminating cap. But Mr. Cassell having on one occasion charged a hole with it, and tamped lightly with clay, the charge fired itself in about 15 minutes. On another occasion a hole was charged, and water poured in, as usual. (No tamping is required; the water softens the mass of powder in the hole, and the fuse, with cap attached, is then run down into it, just before firing.) Leaving the place for a few minutes, Mr. Cassell, on his return, found the water boiling. Thinking it best to fire the hole as soon as possible, he inserted and lit the fuse, and retired precipitately. The explosion took place before the fire could have reached the cap in the ordinary way. These facts seem to show that when the powder is confined, it generates a gas which causes sufficient pressure and heat to explode the whole. The powder under water, Mr. C. thinks, would not have exploded without the fuse, as gas was apparently escaping through the water. It is well that persons using Giant powder should take care not to leave loaded holes standing, but, in all cases, load and fire immediately. The true way (adopted at this mine) is to employ for every shift two powder-men, whose business it is to fire the holes and clean out the stope. Meanwhile, the gang of drillers can be putting in new holes in another stope. Where the rock is very rich, there is a great incidental saving in this plan, since no one but the powder-men has any chance to pocket valuable specimens; and these men can be selected for honesty. It is much easier to find two trustworthy men in this respect than twenty or thirty. I saw quartz from this mine so plastered and filled with gold that a single shift of miners, doing their own blasting, on the usual system, could have carried off hundreds of dollars in their pockets, and no one the wiser.

Mr. Cassell has found it most economical to reduce the quantity of the new powder and the size of the drills, keeping the amount of rock moved per foot of drilling as it was before. Increasing the quantity of powder does not increase the effect in the same proportion. This system renders it easier to institute a comparison. I should remark that the most economical point, as to the size of charges, had not yet been reached. There was still powder wasted in the blasts, and it was anticipated that the figures given below would be still further reduced. The results were as follows:

With common powder daily—	
Two shifts, 15 drillers, at $3—15 strikers, at $2 50	$82 50
Two foremen, at $125 and $100 per month	7 50
Powder, one keg, at $3	3 00
Candles	3 60
Total	96 60
Total work, 105 feet drilling, with the large 1½-inch steel—cost per foot	$0 92
With Giant powder daily—the same number of miners—	
Two shifts, 30 drillers, at $3	90 00
Two foremen, as above	7 50
Four powder-men	12 00
Powder, 10 pounds, $1 50, less 5 per cent. for cash	14 25
Candles	3 80
Total	127 55
Total work, 266 feet of small 1-inch drilling—cost per foot	$0 51

Now since the small holes with Giant powder do as much execution as the larger ones with common powder, the comparative cost of using the two materials is as 51 to 92 in favor of the former. This gain arises from the fact that in boring small holes, each man works by himself, and two men drill at this mine in this way 200 inches of small holes in a day, against 84 inches of large holes on the other system, where one holds and the other strikes. It must be borne in mind, also, that in this case the drillers have no time wasted in charging or firing. All that, as well as cleaning out the stope, is done by the powder-men, while the rest are at work drilling elsewhere.

The miners foresee that this change reduces the necessity for skill on their part, and will lead to the introduction of unskilled labor. With only a small drill, a foreman to set the holes and a powder-man to fire them, a Chinaman is as good as anybody, say they, and the skilled drillers and strikers will be superseded. This will not happen while there is so much else for Chinamen to do, and so little desire on their part to engage in underground work. Still our miners would do well to consider that if they persist in demanding of a struggling industry, wages which are (in many parts of the Pacific States) out of proportion to the cost of living, that industry will be revenged upon them by betaking itself to cheaper labor.

In this connection the following account will be ot interest, as showing what can be done with common powder in blasting, when conditions are favorable.

By the courtesy of Colonel George H. Mendell, of the United States engineers, San Francisco, and his assistant, Captain C. W. Raymond, I obtained some facts on this subject, relating to operations last spring in the bay of San Francisco, which are worthy of preservation.

Colonel Mendell is in charge of the government works at Alcatraz island and Lime Point in the harbor of San Francisco, and elsewhere on this coast. In connection more especially with the work of Lime Point, some very successful blasting has been accomplished under his direction. Lime Point and Fort Point are the two side-posts of the Golden Gate, through which the commerce of all nations passing enters the bay. It is intended to occupy these points with twin forts; and Fort Point, as its name implies, is already fortified. At Lime Point, however, there appears, where the fortifications should be, a rocky hill, about 250 feet high, and inclined some 45 degrees. This hill it was necessary to remove in order to prepare a site. The estimate of cost made beforehand demanded a large sum; but the skill and ingenuity of the engineers, and the favorable character of the rock, have already made it evident that the necessary work can be done at comparatively light expense.

About 20 feet above the water a small tunnel was driven into the hill for 60 feet, and from its interior terminus a second gallery at right angles to the first, and parallel with the face of the hill, was driven for a like distance of 60 feet. Two chambers were excavated in the second gallery, one at its extremity and one about 45 feet nearer the corner. These two chambers received charges of 4,000 and 3,500 pounds of blasting powder, manufactured by the California Powder Company. The charges were connected with each other and with Beardslee's magneto-electric apparatus outside, and both tunnels were tamped with clay and sand to the mouth. The tamping was tightly rammed. The effect of such a blast of 7,500 pounds of powder, and the relative economy of the operation as compared with ordinary methods, have as much interest for mining as for military engineers. The state of affairs previous to the blast may be recapitulated thus: The above-named charge of blasting powder, in two portions, occupied a line 50 feet from the face of the hill. Above it was the weight of 250 feet of rock, and behind it a practically immovable mass. The rock is the well known San Francisco slate, considerably contorted, fractured, and decomposed, yet lying on the whole so that when the blast should have thrown out the foundation along the line of least resistance, the superincumbent mass, to an unknown extent, might be expected to tumble into the sea. It should be noted that the line of effective work (50 feet) exceeded the distance between the two charges, (45 feet,) hence the forces of explosion would meet before they could find vent through the lifted rock. The arrangement secured a maximum effect. The sagacity and accuracy of these calculations was confirmed by the thoroughly successful result. The simultaneous explosion of the two charges was perfectly accomplished. There was no violent noise and no scattering of fragments—in other words no power was wasted. A little smoke and flame escaped, and the whole lower face of the hill moved silently and majestically outward, falling down into the sea, and followed by immense portions of the overlying rocks. For several hours the effects of the blast continued, until some 40,000 cubic yards or 80,000 tons of rock had been displaced, and a large portion of it actually rolled into the sea. The entrance tunnel, up to the point of turning, was left intact, with its tamping, so thoroughly had the force of the explosion been utilized. The tunnel being reopened, a short elbow was made on the side opposite to the former gallery, and a chamber constructed for a second blast of 2,650 pounds. The tunnel being tightly tamped as before, the blast was fired with equally favorable results. The rock being considerably disturbed, even where not actually removed by the first blast, there was naturally more noise, and many small fragments were projected a considerable distance; but this incidental waste of power was compensated by the greater ease with which the masses of rock already losened were moved; and the apparent effect of the second blast was even greater than that of the first. Some 20,000 cubic yards were added to the 40,000 already displaced. The economical aspect of the case is conclusive enough. A hundred and twenty thousand tons of rock thrown out with two blasts at a cost somewhat as follows:

For tunnels, powder, and tamping, first blast	$2,000
For reopening tunnel and second blast	500
Total	2,500

Or two and one-twelfth cents per ton! The powder costs 10 cents per pound. Labor about three dollars per day. All these sums are reckoned in coin.

I do not hesitate to say that no other explosive now known would do as well as this under these circumstances. Both nitro-glycerine and dynamid or "Giant powder" are far too rapid in their action to be employed where lifting, and not shattering, is the effect desired. In tunnels and shafts, and frequently in stopes, where there is great tension of surrounding rock, and little working face, these violent agents are more in place. The dynamid is rapidly disarming the feeling of apprehension so generally entertained towards all forms of nitro-glycerine, and coming into extensive use among the mines. The secret of its manufacture is not very profound. The engineers, in opening the tunnels to which we have alluded, employed dynamid which they prepared for themselves, at first by saturating sawdust with nitro-glycerine, and afterwards by substituting for the former material fine sand.

The effect of the mixture is purely mechanical; and this being the case it is much better to employ a substance of indifferent inorganic character, like silica, than to absorb the nitro-glycerine into organic fibres, which may induce a spontaneous decomposition (not to say explosion) analogous to that of gun-cotton. When sand is used, there is no absorption, but an enfilming of the particles with nitro-glycerine, which answers the same purpose.

There is a deposit near San Francisco of infusorial earth, which is sold under the fanciful name of "electro-silicon," as a polishing powder. This fine siliceous earth is admirably calculated for the manufacture of dynamid, and the article, as manufactured by the regular agents there, is apparently (and most probably) nothing more than "electro-silicon," saturated with nitro-glycerine. It is true that the Giant powder has more the appearance of moist sawdust; but the grains are soft and pulverulent, like those of moistened flour. In spite of the high price of a dollar and a half in gold per pound, the new powder is in great demand, and its use in many cases effects a great saving. Half inch bore-holes and single miners are taking the place of the great two-inch drills with "two to strike and one to hold;" and the high cost of dynamid (fifteen times that of powder) does not outweigh the great saving in labor and room which it involves.

SECTION II.

NOTES ON NEVADA.

CHAPTER V.

PRESENT CONDITION AND PROSPECTS OF THE COMSTOCK MINES.

Frequent reports and descriptions contained in pamphlets and periodicals, and the voluminous evidence adduced in numerous litigations, together with the decisions of judges and juries, have given to all persons interested in mining a general notion of the topography and geology of the Washoe country, through which courses the Comstock lode; while the forthcoming work of Mr. Clarence King and his party will doubtless embody the results of patient and thorough scientific research into the details of the character of the vein. I do not know to what conclusion those gentlemen have come, as to the points discussed in this report; but while I willingly leave to them the task of description and discussion, I feel justified in putting forward with some confidence the following opinions as to the present condition and prospects of the mines, based partly upon my own observation, and partly upon the notes of Mr. Cæsar Luckhardt, (author of a valuable paper on the concentration of ores, in the preliminary report of J. Ross Browne,) a mining engineer, whose thorough familiarity with every foot of the Comstock entitles his views to the highest consideration. To explain the sequel I shall premise a partial statement of the

GENERAL CHARACTERISTICS OF THE VEIN.

The Comstock is situated in a heavy belt, consisting principally of metamorphic rocks, but trachyte occurs in many places in the immediate vicinity of the vein. It has a general north and south course and an easterly dip, and has been traced on the surface for more than 27,000 feet. Of this great length about 19,000 feet have been actually explored, and comprise the locations of the principal mines. The western boundary or footwall of the vein consists of a syenitic* rock, which is divided from the vein-matter by a seam of bluish-black crystalline rock, resembling aphanite, and locally termed "black dyke." The eastern boundary, or hanging-wall, is not so well defined. For about 16,000 feet along the most developed† portion of the vein, it consists of a ferruginous felspathic porphyry, in various stages of decomposition, up to that of plastic clay; but both north and south of this, it gradually gives place to diorite, and finally to a syenitic rock which can scarcely be distinguished from the foot-wall. The notion that the Comstock is a "contact vein," between two distinct formations, appears, therefore, to be an erroneous one. The width of the vein, as far as developed, may be said to average about 175 feet. Near the surface it was in places 1,100 feet; and in other parts,

---

* I write this chapter purposely without reference to the masterly essay of Richthofen on the Comstock vein—not because I do not acknowledge its ability, and, in the main, agree with its conclusions; but because an adoption and free use of them would add little to the authority of that work, and detract from the independent value of this.

† Developed, I mean, by mining work.

especially the northern portions of the vein, the walls were found to come very close together—in miners' phrase the vein is "pinched." As the outcrop runs along the steep eastern slope of Mount Davidson, the vein appears, judging from the east wall, to dip under the mountain; and many of the early vertical shafts, sunk to pierce it in depth, were therefore located on the western side, while the true dip is to the east. The popular expression is, that the vein is "overborne" by the mountain and changes its dip near the surface; but this, like almost all the miners' terms in all countries, is the statement of the exact reverse of the truth.* The fact is that the eastern part of the surface, loosened by the formation of the Comstock fissure, slid or subsided, opening a wide gap, into which fragments of the country rock, always from the east, fell. These, acting as wedges, prevented the fissure from closing by the weight of the hanging wall, until it was filled with mineral. There is nothing abstruse in this explanation; but it must be borne in mind that neither the opening of the fissure, the movement of the country rock, nor the deposition of mineral matter were necessarily sudden and violent. Sir Charles Lyell has ably shown that in all probability the most stupendous geological disturbances have been the result of the slowest processes. The only sudden geological operations with which we are familiar are volcanic ones; and these are seldom connected with the immediate production of mineral deposits valuable to man.

The large masses of rock which fell into the fissure all came, as I have said, from the east wall; and this partly explains the irregularity of that wall, while it also produces the appearance of a variable dip, first west, then vertical, and finally east. There was much money lost by the early belief in a west dip, since expensive buildings and machinery were necessarily removed, when the truth was discovered, from the west to the east side of the vein, and much costly excavation was wasted. Whether the ore and gangue of the Comstock came from the east or west, or from immeasurable depths, I shall not discuss. It seems to me that the non-metalliferous portion of the vein matter, near the surface, has been affected more or less by the decomposition and re-crystallization of the constituents of the country rock. But I shall not pause to undertake a discussion for which I do not feel sufficiently prepared. Such suggestions as I may venture will be more appropriate in the sequel.

One very prominent feature in the Comstock is the occurrence of alternate metalliferous and unproductive courses or bodies of ore, imbedded in the matrix. The unproductive masses constitute by far the larger

* It is a curious fact that miners always "put the cart before the horse," in describing the phenomena of their profession. For instance, if a vein, in some rich zone or pocket, is accompanied by side crevices or "stringers," which also carry valuable ore, it is said that the "stringers have enriched the vein;" if a "horse," or mass of country rock lies in the middle of the vein, and the ore continues around both sides reuniting beyond, the vein is said to have split and come together again; if a vein is broken along the line of a cross fissure, and by the slipping of the country rock, one half the vein is moved along, so that it is no longer opposite the other half, and the cross-fissure, afterwards filled with mineral, becomes itself a vein, it is said that the new vein has "heaved" the old one. Veins are talked of as bulging, contracting, changing their strike and dip, as though the intrusion or deposition of their mineral contents were itself an acting cause in determining their form; whereas the form of a vein is generally determined by the previous fissure, and the changes which may take place after the opening of the fissure, but before it is filled with mineral. This way of speaking, however, is convenient, and does no harm, if we bear in mind that it is merely fictionary. I cannot agree with Professor Silliman, who, (if correctly reported,) holding to the theory that many veins are filled by solfataric and thermal-aqueous agencies, nevertheless says that the fissure is frequently widened by the forces of crystallization. The manner in which thermal waters deposit their precipitates, and the phenomena observed in veins themselves, (vugs, empty spaces, and many other things,) as well as the analogies of hot springs, where veins are actually being filled, contradict this hypothesis emphatically.

portion of the whole bulk of the vein. The productive masses (ore-chambers, chimneys, zones, bodies, bonanzas, or what not) are irregular in shape, with a general tendency to a lenticular form, giving a crescent in cross-section, something like a concavo-convex lens. They lie obliquely between the walls, generally originating near the foot-wall, and terminating somewhere in the vicinity of the hanging wall. They appear to be secondary in form to the local influences of the dikes or "horses" of unproductive ground which separate them, and render them wider or narrower as the case may be. While most authorities now agree that the "one ledge theory," famous in the courts, is for all practical purposes the true one, and that the Comstock ledge includes all these bodies of ore, there is still no doubt that *within the limits of the original fissure* these deposits are in a certain sense separate. Doubtless the same thing occurs in many fissure veins; it is the vast proportions of this one which render it difficult to understand. Yet after all, no small fissure vein could produce the same conditions. The very processes which here resulted in the deposition of independent bodies of ore might, in a smaller vein, have produced a continuous "pay-streak," or central zone of ore. The Comstock was begun by nature on a vast scale; but the vehicle (whatever it was) that brought in the ore was not so much more abundant, as the receptacle was more capacious, than in ordinary cases. To illustrate this argument, (which is equally true, whatever be the hypothesis as to the method of filling the fissure,) I will suppose that the gangue and ore were deposited from solution. This process often produces in narrow veins a banded structure. It can be observed in great perfection in many veins of Lander Hill, Reese River district, where there are alternate layers of gangue (quartz, manganese spar) and ore in the veins, parallel with the walls, and symmetrically arranged; showing, for instance, a band of quartz along either wall, then a band of spar, then in the middle of the vein a band or pay-streak or ore. The same vein may, however, have in one part a single central pay streak, and in another wider part two pay-streaks with quartz between. The reason is obvious. If the entrance of metalliferous fluids was abundant enough to fill with its deposit all the space not already occupied by previous deposits of quartz or other gangue along the walls, then a single pay-streak was formed; but in a wider part of the same vein, the deposit of ore merely lined the sides of the fissure, and left room for a subsequent entrance and deposition of quartz. This gave the appearance of two pay-streaks, sometimes erroneously called a double vein.* Now if the ore-bearing solution were not even abundant enough to make a continuous deposit along the walls of the fissure, and its entrances were fitful and comparatively sudden, while the deposition of barren vein matter went steadily on and almost controlled the whole space, the result might resemble the present aspect of the Comstock, and this explanation is equally applicable to the theory of solfataric action. It tends to confirm the belief that the Comstock is a true fissure vein not different in kind, but only in degree, from other fissure-veins; that it will therefore be found to continue in depth, and that, as the fissure in depth contracts its dimensions, the appearance of the ore deposits may change, and new conditions be developed. Perhaps a continuous deposit of low grade ore may be found instead of the present segregated masses.

The 19,000 linear feet along the vein which have been for the past

*A double vein is the result of the reopening of a fissure-vein after it is once filled, and the intrusion of new vein-matter by the side or in the middle of the old.

seven years explored and vigorously attacked, comprise all the locations from the Utah mine to the south part of the Overman, as follows:

	Feet.		Feet.
Utah	1,000	Bacon	45
Allen	1,000	Empire North	55
Sierra Nevada	3,000	Eclipse	30
Union	302	Trench Ground	20
Ophir North	1,200	Empire South	20
Mexican	100	Plato	10
Ophir South	200	Bowers	20
Central	150	Piute	19¾
California	300	Consolidated	51¼
Central No. 2	100	Rice Ground	13⅓
Kinney	50	Imperial South	65⅔
White and Murphy	210	Challenge	50
Sides	500	Confidence	130
Best and Belcher	224½	New York and Washoe	40
Gould and Curry	1,200	Yellow Jacket	1,200
Savage	800	Kentuck	93⅓
Hale and Norcross	400	Crown Point	600⅔
Chollar Potosi	1,434	Belcher	940
Bullion	967	Segregated Belcher	160
Exchequer	400	Overman	1,210
Alpha	278½		
Treglone	31½	Total	18,739½
Imperial North	118		

There are locations both north of the Utah and south of the Overman; but, although many of them have low grade ore near the surface, very little work has, as yet, been done upon them.* The mines enumerated have opened the vein to different depths, varying from 400 to 1,210 feet vertically below the shaft-mouths. The deepest point at present attained is about 1,410 feet below the outcrop of the vein. They have yielded about $80,000,000 since 1862, when work was systematically and vigorously commenced. Some estimates put the total value of bullion, produced since the discovery, at $100,000,000.

As it is my desire to discuss chiefly the possible future productiveness of the Comstock vein, I shall mainly confine myself, in this description, to the ground which has yielded the above enormous product, and to those bodies of ore which are still being worked.

GENERAL DESCRIPTION OF THE ORE-GROUND.

The Comstock vein (by which I mean, at present, the 19,000 feet which have been explored) may be divided into two parts—the northern part, extending from the Utah to the Chollar Potosi inclusive, and the southern, from the Imperial North to the South Overman. Between the two is the ground occupied by the Bullion, Exchequer, Alpha, and Treglone, which is topographically a "divide," the surface sloping away to the north and south on either side. This is on the boundary between Virginia City and Gold Hill; and, what is still more important, it seems to be also a dividing point underground, since it is that portion of the vein which appears to have presented, at the period of the filling of the fissure, sufficient obstacles to prevent a uniform deposit, both north and south

* The Sierra Nevada mill has been, during the summer, successfully reducing the low grade surface ores of the northern end of the Comstock. They contain some gold.

of it, of the siliceous as well as the metalliferous matter of the vein. So far as deep workings have yet penetrated, there is a difference between the northern and southern portions. *The ore bodies north of this division have without exception a southerly pitch, while those immediately south of it stand almost vertically, and those still further south, without exception, pitch northward.* The ores also differ, the vein matter can be in a great many instances distinguished, and even the barren portions of the vein, enclosing and often penetrating the ore bodies, are not the same in character north and south of the point I have mentioned.

DETAILED DESCRIPTION OF THE PRODUCTIVE GROUND.

I. *North portion of the vein.*—We have here four distinctly separate ore bodies.

First body.—This was found to commence near the centre of Cedar Hill, extend southward for about 200 feet, and continue 140 feet below the surface. It carries a great deal of gold, and was formerly worked by hydraulic means, but afterwards abandoned. It is irregular in form, in places 35 feet wide, and pinches out at the vertical depth of 140 feet. It lies in the ground of the Sierra Nevada company, which is now working the ore, with results varying from $3 to $12 per ton. The company has explored the ground for 500 feet vertically below the lowest point of this body, and found the vein to be filled with fragments of country rock from the east wall, clay and clayey matter, and a little quartz in very irregular seams of small dimensions, carrying mere traces of metal.

Second body.—This commenced in the Ophir North, pitched southward into the Mexican, South Ophir, Central, and a portion of the California companies' ground, showing a horizontal extent of about 600 feet of available ore-ground, the whole of which yielded ore abundantly; but especially the portion in the Mexican mine, which displayed in places a breast or width of 59 feet of splendid ore. The body terminated at a vertical depth of 650 feet below the surface. It is practically exhausted, only a little ground, containing ore of very low grade, in the Central mine, being left. Explorations in the Ophir and Central for 200 feet below where the ore gave out failed to discover any other bodies. It is true a northern extension of this large ore-body is still standing in the North Ophir. It has been thoroughly explored in almost every direction, and found to extend 375 feet below the surface, and to contain thousands of tons of ore of low grade; but this ore is mixed with a good many minerals which render it, for the Washoe wet amalgamation process, very refractory, such as zincblende, galena, arsenical pyrites, &c., and manganese ores. It is therefore at present valueless, and will so remain until it can be smelted with the argentiferous galena of Washoe valley. South of this second ore-body there is an interval of 1,384 feet, reaching to the Gould and Curry, and owned by various companies (see catalogue above) which have explored it in an ineffective way, without finding anything, to depths varying from 150 to 400 feet. It is quite possible that the large Ophir–Mexican body may have in this ground some out-runners or "feeders" (as the miners call them) or that there may be a new ore-body in depth; but, thus far, the developments made have not proved the existence of either.

Third ore-body.—This is the largest and best defined yet discovered on the Comstock vein. It commenced at the Gould and Curry claim, and extended through the Savage, Hale, and Norcross and part of the Chollar Potosi, a horizontal distance of 2,700 feet. It was found to be accompanied with many ore-seams and smaller bodies of ore, running parallel with it and sometimes dipping into it. It began to be productive 200 feet south of the north line of the Gould and Curry, and extended 1,200 feet southward along the outcrop, when it descended below the surface, and reappeared again in the Chollar. It has been worked for its whole length in the Gould and Curry, to a depth of 650 feet. In the Savage it "split" into a north and south body, and has thus far been worked in that mine to the depth of 950 feet below the outcrop. It is proved to extend in the Savage at least 1,050 feet vertically below the croppings, and at the deepest point exposed *shows a continuation still deeper*. In the Hale and Norcross, the southern extension of the south branch in the Savage was split again into an east and west body, which descending southward, terminated in that direction, the one 146 feet and the other 310 feet south of the north line of the Chollar, in the Chollar Potosi ground. In the Gould and Curry, this body has been extracted to its lowest line. It was over 60 feet wide in some places. Only some low grade ore is now left near the outcrop; and this the company will, in six months' time, completely exhaust. Explorations have been carried on both east and west of the ore-body, and for 500 feet of vertical depth beneath it, but results have not been encouraging.* The vein is filled with siliceous porphyries and clayey matter, and limestone in various forms begins to show itself through the whole 500 feet of vertical depth above mentioned.

The Savage has produced immense quantities of ore from this body. In this mine it has been exhausted to an average depth of 800 feet below the outcrop, and presented in places a breast, 96 feet wide, of very rich, solid ore. There now remains about 180 feet (vertical) of ground below the 800 feet above named, which has been explored and proved to contain the downward continuation of the ore-body. According to a very careful estimate, this ground will yield over 56,000 tons of $35 mill-ore—that is, ore which will yield by the mill process $35 per ton. As the extraction of ore from the Savage amounted to 87,342 tons during the year ending July 1, 1868, or nearly 250 tons daily, the ground thus measured will be exhausted in less than a year from November, 1868. The latest developments in the Savage, however, show that although the northern branch of the ore-body pinched out at a vertical depth of 850 feet below the outcrop, (or 650 feet below the mouth of the company's new shaft,) the southern branch still continues at a depth of 1,050 feet below the outcrop. The most encouraging fact is the discovery of what is apparently an entirely new body of ore, which was met with in explorations about 100 feet below the termination of the north branch. It sets in near the centre of the mine, has thus far shown a southerly dip, and, if further developments should prove it to be extensive, will most importantly affect the future of both the Savage and the Hale and Norcross.

In the Hale and Norcross, the third ore-body now under discussion is represented by a southern extension from the Savage, split into an east and a west branch. The east branch has been worked to a depth of 1,000 feet below the croppings. At this depth the ore grows narrower and poorer, and divides into separate seams, some of which are more expensive to work than productive. These seams stand more nearly vertical than the body above; and all the surroundings indicate the approach of the southern terminus of the body. The lowest workings in the mine, 1,100 feet below the outcrop, show these seams still, but only close to the Savage line; and as no new deposits of value have been yet

* Since this report was written there has been a little stir about the discovery of a body of ore in depth, by the Bonner shaft. This is a mere quartz body, such as frequently occurs along the wall; and is no proof of the neighborhood of a profitable ore-deposit.

discovered, the quantity of ore now visible in the mine is very small indeed.

In the Chollar-Potosi, as I have said, was found the continuation of the west branch of the south part of the Savage body, which had passed through the entire Hale and Norcross ground. It extended about 560 feet below the outcrop, at which depth it terminated. It has been worked out for about 290 feet horizontally in the Chollar, to its terminus in depth. A small branch of ore, coming from the east branch of the southern part of the Hale and Norcross body, was found in the Chollar about 200 feet east of the continuation just described, as worked out on the west. It seemed as if it had been torn away from the main body; commenced to show itself 342 feet below the surface; was worked for a length of 100 feet; descended along the east wall vertically for 150 feet; and terminated on all sides in small, valueless seams of quartz. It is now entirely exhausted. The company has carried on explorations for 700 feet below the lowest portion of this branch, giving a total depth explored of 1,310 feet below the outcrop. These explorations showed the vein to be filled principally with clayey matter, carrying very little quartz and no ore at all. The absence of quartz at the depth attained is not encouraging.

Fourth ore-body.—This was situated west of the southern portion of the third body, above described. It made its appearance close to the north line of the Chollar, (in what was formerly the Potosi and Bajazetto ground,) at the surface; extended along and near the surface for 900 feet; and found its terminus at the depth of about 500 feet. It varied materially in character from No. 3. Its ores were more highly oxidized and more irregularly distributed. In places it was 125 feet wide; it was often split into three or four parallel courses; and it has yielded immense quantities of ore. In 1867 it yielded for months together from 500 to 550 tons of ore daily. (The company's report for the year ending June 1, 1868, puts the whole amount of ore extracted in twelve months at 70,330 tons; but this was not equally distributed through the year, as the yield from the "Third Santa Fé" station, in the body of ore now under discussion, ceased in February, 1868.) The Chollar-Potosi has been noted, even among the Comstock mines, for the extraordinary rapidity with which its ores have been extracted; but it may fairly be questioned whether the policy pursued has been wise. This ore-body ought to have given the company three years at least of very profitable mining; but the largest and by far the best part of it is already extracted, and a large portion has undoubtedly been wasted by a too speedy extraction. There is enough ore of low grade left to occupy the company nine months more; but the average value has been so reduced by the extraction of the best portions, that the remainder will pay but little more than the cost of mining and milling.

This concludes the description of the northern portion of productive ground on the Comstock vein. The ore-bodies described are distributed through more than 13,000 of the 19,000 linear feet under development.

South of all this occurs an interval of about 2,100 feet of unproductive ground, including part of the Chollar, the whole of the Bullion, and part of the Exchequer claim. The Bullion company has expended, it is said, more than a million dollars, and explored the ground to the depth of 1,210 feet below the surface without finding any ore-bodies.

II. *South portion of the vein.*—Here we meet with seven ore-bodies, much more irregular than those of the north portion, already described.

First ore-body.—This appertains to the outcrop, and commenced at the Alpha mine, extending about 2,300 linear feet into the Crown Point. It lies west of all the bodies to be described hereafter. In no case was it found to extend deeper than 275 feet. It was in places more than 200 feet wide; so that in the exploitation of it the whole side of the mountain, from the Imperial to the Confidence, has been excavated. Its yield of ore has been immense, especially for the last eighteen months, previous to which period its ores were thought to be of too low a grade for profitable extraction. By far the largest portion of the bullion produced in 1867 came from this body; but it may be considered as practically exhausted, only here and there a patch of ore, of very low grade, now remaining.

Second ore-body.—This commenced in the south portion of the Exchequer; passed through the Alpha, Treglone, Imperial, Bacon, Empire, Eclipse, Trench, Empire South, Plato, Bowers, Piute, Consolidated, Rice, and part of the Imperial South, showing a horizontal length of about 810 feet. This body divided into many smaller ones; but the axis of its main bulk stood almost vertical in the vein. In the Imperial North it reached its deepest point, 750 feet below the outcrop, and here it lay pretty close to the west wall, while south of this mine it nowhere extended to so great a depth. Between the Imperial North and the Empire North it attained its maximum width (in places 115 feet) and split into various smaller bodies, some of which, especially those near the surface, still continue to yield ore in the Alpha, Imperial, and some of the smaller claims; but the quantity now remaining is limited, and will not yield great profit. The Imperial and Empire companies, conjointly, have sunk a very large new shaft to explore the vein below the point where the ore terminated. This shaft, with its drifts, has partially explored the ground for 200 feet deeper (in all 900 feet below the surface;) but the work has thus far not given encouraging results in the form of ore, though the quartzose gangue has been discovered at the depth named.

Third ore-body.—This body commenced south of the Imperial South, and extended, with a slightly eastward dip, into the Challenge, Confidence, New York, and Washoe, and the north part of the Yellow Jacket, having thus a horizontal length of about 600 feet; it proved to be very irregular in form and dimensions. Its deepest point was 600 feet below the outcrop in the Confidence; from there it rose to the southward, and in the North Yellow Jacket it proved to extend only 475 feet below the outcrop, where it abutted abruptly against the east wall, which it followed downward for some distance, growing narrow and poor, and finally pinching out. Its heaviest portion lay in the south portion of the North Yellow Jacket, 370 feet below the outcrop. It is now exhausted. Some ore is left near the surface all along the course of the body, but it is of too low a grade to be extracted at present with profit. The Yellow Jacket is the only mine on this body in which explorations have been continued below the terminus of the ore. That company has sunk 450 feet deeper, found some small detached bodies to the east, worked them out, and came finally into entirely barren ground, filling the whole fissure. At the deepest point attained in this mine the vein shows the phenomenon of a dislocation of the vein matter from west to east, which will be discussed further on.

Fourth ore-body.—This commenced in the south portion of the Yellow Jacket, 430 feet south from the one last described. It went through the Kentuck, Crown Point, and part of the Belcher ground, showing a horizontal length of 1,160 feet. It was much more regular than the foregoing, had a general western dip, and proved to be widest in the Yellow Jacket, near the Kentuck line, in places 90 feet. In the Belcher it extended 300 feet vertically, in the Crown Point 400 feet, in the Kentuck 450 feet, and in the Yellow Jacket about 500 feet below the surface, and in all of them it was cut off very abruptly in or near the centre of the vein. It may be said to be entirely exhausted of its ores. (See description of No. 6, below.) The Belcher company explored for 600 feet vertically below the south portion of this body, but so far without successful results; the vein is entirely barren at the depth attained. The explorations of the Crown Point and Yellow Jacket fully demonstrate the "fault" in the vein matter, to be described below.

Fifth ore-body.—In the Segregated Belcher, (south of the Belcher mine,) and about 900 feet south of the southern terminus of ore-body No. 4, commences a piece of ground which extends about 1,100 feet southward, and has contained a series of very irregularly distributed ore-bodies, which have, in places, been very productive. They all had a general incline to the north, and dipped east with the vein. This 1,100 feet of ground has proved remunerative to an average depth of 450 feet below the surface. The outcrop is "blind" or hidden. North of the Segregated Belcher and south of the Overman this ground terminates. The principal portion of it is already worked out; a good deal of low-grade ore still stands along its course, but the only good ore known to remain is in the Overman, where there is enough to occupy the company, at the present rate of extraction, for probably six or eight months. Some small seams and stringers of this great mass extend below the depth at present attained by the Overman; it is quite likely that some of these may widen out at still greater depth; but, as yet, they only contain low-grade ore, and do not exceed six feet in width.

Sixth ore-body.—The large body described as No. 4 of the Yellow Jacket, Kentuck, Crown Point, and Belcher, extended to the depth of 400 to 500 feet vertically below the surface, where a body of clayey matter, originating from a heavy dike of felspathic porphyry, cut it off very abruptly. In the Yellow Jacket, explorations were carried on for 100 feet vertically below this line, but without success in finding ore. In the Crown Point, explorations were made both eastward and downward; and the vein matter to the east of where the ore gave out was found to be replaced, frequently for a horizontal distance (east and west) of 150 feet, with various species of porphyry, of which felspathic porphyry predominated. As the prospecting work advanced eastward, the vein began to carry quartz again, and, about 450 feet east of the place where the ore was abruptly cut off, this quartz began to carry ore. Fifty feet further east, in the 500-foot level of the Crown Point, a very fine body of ore was discovered. West drifts from the first body to the west wall proved the gound to be barren. *This conclusively demonstrated that the vein matter had suffered a dislocation from west to east,* and the ore found east was locally termed the "East Vein." This body has thus far been explored and worked for a horizontal distance of 400 feet. It has its southern terminus about 200 feet south of the north line of the Crown Point; its northern limit has not yet been determined. Its upper edge is 75 feet above the 500-foot level of the Crown Point; it dips with the east wall slightly to the east, and inclines so decidedly to the north in depth, that the 900-foot level of the Crown Point has not a trace of it, even at the Kentuck line. (The ore has therefore made 200 feet "northing" in 400 feet vertical depth.) The terminus of this body in depth has not yet been found. The Yellow Jacket explorations (850 feet vertically below the surface) show it still continuing downward and northward. In the Crown Point it is nearly exhausted. A careful estimate of what is still standing shows about 4,000 tons of ore that will produce $30 per ton by the Washoe wet-crushing and amalgamation. The Kentuck has also extracted a great deal from this body. At the time of my examination of this mine, some 450 tons of ore daily were hoisted from ground not exceeding 93 linear feet upon the vein. The amount of ore standing in the Kentuck is estimated at about 25,000 tons of $35 mill-ore. The Yellow Jacket has extracted large quantities, and still retains in view about 19,000 tons of $36 50 mill-ore. As the lower line of the ore-body has been found in Crown Point, the above estimate for that mine is very nearly correct; but, in Yellow Jacket and Kentuck, the ore extends in depth below the ground included in these estimates; and they are therefore too low.

This completes the description of all the productive ground of the Comstock vein, thus far developed;* summing it up, we have a total of nearly 19,000 feet explored on the vein, and an aggregate length of 5,396 feet of productive ground, viz:

	Whole vein.	Productive ground.
1. In the north portion	12,164 feet.	3,246 feet.
2. In the south portion	6,553 feet.	2,150 feet.

PROSPECTS OF THE MINES.

The foregoing description shows that very little of the productive portion of the vein is now standing. Nearly all the mines contain low-grade ore, some of them even in large quantities; but these ore reserves lie, for the most part, at or near the surface. The Hale and Norcross croppings, for instance, have scarcely been touched. They cannot profitably be worked at the present current expense of beneficiation.

Considering that the average width of the Comstock is 175 feet, and the greatest depth attained is only 1,210 feet below the surface, (Bullion shaft,) while the work of testing the ground in horizontal directions has not kept pace adequately with the depths attained, we may say that explorations have not been very thorough; but the fact remains that, although there is much undeveloped ground on the Comstock vein, the work thus far does not present very encouraging results for the *immediate* future. On the north portion of the vein there are only two mines, (the Savage and the Hale and Norcross,) which show at present a vertical continuation of ore-ground. Many others, as I have said, have con-

* Concerning a more recent discovery in the Yellow Jacket, the Enterprise of December 30 says: "This strike is one of the most important ever made in the mine or upon the great Comstock lode. We say so for the reason that it is the first large deposit of extraordinary rich ore ever found at so great a depth upon the lead. Two big deposits have been found—one in the 900, and one in the 800-foot level, but the former is by far the richest and in every respect the most important. The vein in the lower level is fully nine feet in width, and is composed of what is called 'sacking ore'—ore so rich that it is not rudely shovelled and tumbled about, as is the case with that of a lower grade, but is put up in sacks and tenderly cared for. It is ore that will yield some thousands of dollars per ton, (we don't exactly know how many, as we have seen no assays,) and is just the next thing to finding the silver already moulded into bricks. The ore is composed of both chlorides and sulphurets, and is of a soft and crumbling nature; at least such was the character of all the specimens shown us yesterday. In the 800-foot level, about 90 feet north of the south shaft, has been found a large deposit of very rich ore, though it contains more iron and is not so much like the pure bricks as those below. Let us hope that the barren belt of the Comstock has at length been passed, and that at least one mine has entered upon the rich deposits of a second and more valuable belt than that found near the surface. This strike is certainly most encouraging to all mining companies holding ground on the Comstock, and we hope soon to hear of others striking down into the new White Pine of our own big lode." I confess that I do not share the sanguine expectations above set forth The "strike" in the Yellow Jacket is, I am informed, very important; but later and more detailed accounts must be awaited before any opinion can be formed. In the mean time I see no reason for modifying the views expressed in this chapter.

siderable reserves of low grade; but in every case the limits are known, and are near the surface. On the south portion of the vein the prospects are a little better; yet even here there are only three mines, (Kentuck, Yellow Jacket, and Overman,) which insure us at present a vertical continuation of ore. The low-grade reserves of other mines are considerable; but their limits are known. It is now established that all the ore in this vein exists in zones or bodies which terminate somewhere; and it is impossible to say at what point the descending bodies in the five mines enumerated may find their lower limits. The only hope for the future is the discovery of new bodies of ore, (one such as has been discovered in the Savage; see description above, under ore-body No. 3 of the north portion of the vein.)

Judging from present appearances only, and regardless of probable or possible new developments, I should say that remunerative operations on the Comstock proper* can only continue for a period of eighteen months or two years longer. Of course it is possible that new and brilliant discoveries may at any time completely change the face of affairs. All speculation of this kind is, however, only speculation; and so far as we have any indications afforded, they are, I think, unfavorable to the hope of immediate discoveries of ore. In this connection the following considerations may be of value:

Since the beginning of operations on the Comstock, the ores have diminished in quality and quantity as the work advanced in depth. No later than last year, the waste-piles of 1864 were overhauled, and immense quantities of $40 mill-ore† were obtained. In 1864 this ore was discarded as too poor; now many a mill-owner would be glad to buy a large dump of $15 ore. With one exception, (where the vein-matter has been dislocated from west to east, in Belcher, Crown Point, Kentuck, and Yellow Jacket,) the productive ground has been the downward continuation of the outcrop. The bottom of this outcrop-zone has everywhere been reached, and an unproductive period of vein has been entered, the extent of which is unknown. The explorations in depth are not yet sufficient to lead to any decisive conclusions; but some things there are which seem to indicate that this barren ground will continue further than many suppose. For instance, it has been observed throughout the Comstock that, wherever quartz forms the larger portion of the vein-matter, there the heavier deposits of ore have been found. Now it is found that in depth, especially in the northern portion of the vein, limestone in various forms gradually replaces the quartz; and no traces of metal have yet been found where the limestone predominates. Should limestone eventually form one of the principal constituents of the vein-matrix, it is quite evident that the character of the ores will be changed from that which they bear when accompanied with quartz; and this change or transition in both ore and gangue would be likely to occupy a considerable period of the vein, through which the mines would have to pass, without meeting with much ore-ground of value. On the other hand, should further developments prove the limestone to exist only subordinately and not to interchange with the quartz, then the present barren zone might be regarded as the alternative of the productive ground above; and, *from present appearances*, it is likely to continue in proportion to the amount of the latter.

In the southern portion of the Comstock, the same phenomena have not been met with; and prospects are not quite so discouraging. Here

* For a description of the metalliferous veins of the neighborhood, outside of the Comstock, see below.

† That is, ore that yielded $40 per ton in the mills, not by fire assay merely.

we have a decided dislocation of the vein-matter from west to east, by a dike of porphyry *in the vein.* The west wall, where it has been reached, through this immense dike, which lies immediately upon it, seems not to have been disturbed. The dike consists principally of porphyry of various characters, imbedded in which are smaller bunches of trachyte. It has been explored for 1,300 feet in length, and in places cut across, showing a width of 400 feet and less. Further explorations must prove whether this dike originated before or after the filling of the Comstock fissure, or contemporaneously with that process. It is possible that the first of these will prove to have been the truth—there are so few decisive signs of motion in the vein in this vicinity—and in that case the vein-matter will gradually recede from east to west again; and we may from analogy expect ores in successive bodies until the west wall is reached. But should this dike be of more recent date than the filling of the fissure, or, still worse, of contemporaneous origin; and should its course prove to have been upward between the walls, (which is possible, since it is not known to have broken either wall,) it may have filled the entire vein for a considerable distance; and the chance of immediate discoveries of ore would naturally be very small.

The irregularities and alternations of the Comstock may naturally be expected to occur on a scale proportionate to the magnitude of the vein, and the present barren zone, however extensive, *is no indication that the ore-bodies will not recur in depth.* The great practical question relates to the manner in which prospecting work shall be continued. The present method of isolated shafts and exploring drifts is very expensive; and it is to be feared that, when the ores now in sight shall have been extracted, the perseverance and capital of the companies will not be equal to the task. Besides, the ore may be expected to be more refractory in deeper zones; the large proportion of native gold and silver which forms the chief yield of the simple "Washoe process" of direct amalgamation, and without which that process could not be employed, may give place to the sulphurets, which are now subordinate. The cost of drainage and hoisting will increase with every hundred feet of added depth, and, in many mines, new and more powerful machinery will be required. Ventilation must be improved—a matter which has yet received but little attention. The newspapers lately called attention to the extremely oppressive temperature in some of the deeper workings, and, ascribing it to the internal heat of the earth, expressed apprehension that it might prove a bar to future operations; but the internal heat of the earth will not trouble the mines for many a day, if provision is made for the removal of foul air and the heat of lamps and human bodies. All this entails grave expense, which few of the companies can bear, unless very rich deposits are soon discovered. If, on the other hand, the barren ground to be traversed by vertical workings should be as extensive as those barren intervals which have already occurred on the horizontal course of the vein, (some of them 1,300 feet or more in length,) the outlay required for explorations would be enormous. It is important to bear in mind that, while the discovery of new ore-bodies would postpone the evil day, it would not relieve the mines from the constant expense and burden of the present system of working. The true economy is to open the vein by a deep tunnel and drifts, reduce the number of shafts, and consolidate the management of the mines in many respects. (Ownerships of course may remain as they are, but administration should be modified by association.)

GENERAL DESCRIPTION OF PRODUCTIVE MINING GROUND SITUATED OUTSIDE OF THE COMSTOCK VEIN.

Both east and west of the Comstock many locations have been made, and considerable prospecting has been done. On the west occurs a series of small quartz veins, imbedded in the syenite, and carrying precious metals, principally gold. They run, as a general rule, parallel with the Comstock, but are narrow; and none of them has yet given encouragement for the outlay of time and capital. In the low hills of metamorphic rocks, west of Washoe valley, is a well-defined vein, carrying argentiferous galena, which will undoubtedly, at some future day, become very valuable. Several attempts have been made to work its ores; but want of confidence has prevented adequate investment of capital; and the ill success of the initial operations in treating the ores tended to destroy all faith in the enterprise. It is for the present abandoned.

East of the Comstock, and 1½ or two miles distant, is a "contact-vein," which has been traced for three miles northeast and southwest, and found to vary in width between 10 and 50 feet. The matrix in the north portion is quartz. Near the surface in the south portion occur heavy layers of lime rock, which yield in depth to quartz. The vein dips east, the foot-wall is diorite, and the hanging-wall trachyte and trachitic rocks, separated from the vein by a heavy band of argillaceous matter. A large number of locations, with an aggregate length of about three miles, have been made upon the vein. Many of the companies formerly at work sank shafts and ran prospecting drifts and tunnels, but, finding the ores unremunerative, abandoned operations. Since the cost of milling has been reduced, (it is now $12 per ton, I believe, at the custom mills,) several companies have resumed work. The principal ones are the Lady Bryan, St. George, Occidental, and Metropolitan. The largest developments have been made by the Occidental Company, which has opened the vein to the depth of 600 feet, and is now running a tunnel to cut it at 850 feet. In this mine an enormous body of low-grade ore has been exposed, yielding $17 to $28 per ton, and a large amount of it has been already extracted; but the greater bulk is still standing in the mine, and promises, so far as it is developed, at least two years of profitable mining to the company. The vein has thus far continued productive in depth, and it will not be long before the entire length of the locations will be under active development. One great advantage of this vein is its accessibility in many places by means of cross-tunnels from the slope of the hills, rendering expensive hoisting works unnecessary. Another advantage is the stability of the enclosing rocks, enabling the miners in excavating ore to dispense with the costly item of timbering, which is absolutely required in the Comstock. An estimate shows that for a length of more than 1,000 feet on this vein the ores can be extracted to the depth of 800 feet below the outcrop, at an average cost of $1 75 per ton. In other parts of the vein the conditions are not quite so favorable. In many places this cheap extraction could only be carried 300 feet below the outcrop. The productiveness of this vein is a very fortunate circumstance for the numerous mills which have heretofore reduced the Comstock ores, and are now likely to find employment here for a long time to come.

THE SUTRO TUNNEL.

It is sufficiently evident from the foregoing description that the future of the Comstock mines depends on the discovery and successful exploration of new bodies of ore, and the reduction of expenses so far as to permit the extraction and beneficiation of the low-grade ores which are expected by good judges to predominate in depth. (See report of Baron von Richthofen.)

For both of these results some change in the present system of mining is vitally important. Mr. Sutro's plan for a deep adit, starting near the Carson river, and cutting the vein 1,970 feet below the outcrop, presents one solution of the problem.

The plan for the construction of the Sutro tunnel has been before the country for several years and is sufficiently well known. A full account of it is contained in the two reports of Mr. J. Ross Browne, and I can only say here that the developments of the past year, and the present condition and prospects of the Comstock mines, discussed above, tend to establish more positively than ever the absolute necessity of this great work. The barren ground now presenting itself should be *underrun* with a tunnel, and the necessary dead-work cheapened. A few remarks will show what interest the government possesses in the question:

1. The bullion product of the United States is decreasing every year. There are various reasons for this decrease. Some of them are beyond the reach of legislation, while others are themselves the results of unwise legislation. Everybody admits the decrease to be, especially at this time, a national misfortune.

2. One great cause of trouble is the fact that mining has not on the whole been profitable to individual adventurers. And of this fact the Comstock lode has furnished a striking example. Nearly $100,000,000 have been extracted from that one lode within the past nine years, yet the aggregate cost to owners has been almost as much. The reason is simple. Unnecessary labor has been employed, and vast sums of money wasted in extravagant speculations and litigations; and the root of the whole evil lies in the system of scattered, jealous, individual activity, which has destroyed, by dividing, the resources of the most magnificent ore deposit in the world. Thirty-five or forty companies, each owning from 10 to 1,400 feet along the vein, and each (almost without exception) working its own ground independently; 40 superintendents, 40 presidents, 40 secretaries, 40 boards of directors, all to be supplied with salaries, or, worse yet, with perquisites, or, worst of all, with opportunities to speculate; an army of lawyers and witnesses, peripatetic experts, competing assayers, thousands of miners, uniting to keep up the rate of wages; these things explain the heavy expense of Comstock mining. Aside from this immense drain of money, amounting to 20 per cent. of the whole production, the labor actually performed has been, for want of united action, often useless. There have been tunnels enough run by different companies into the Comstock lode to make, if put together, the whole length of the Sutro tunnel. Hardly one of them is good for anything to-day. The Bullion company, which has the deepest shaft on the lode, never had any ore, but has spent more than a million of dollars in prospecting, while some neighboring mines, like the little Kentuck, have been in *bonanza* for long periods. Now this division of a vein, which gives the rich chimney to one owner and the barren intervals to another, is not conducive to economy. The result has proved to be that both owners waste money. All the explorations in the barren mines of the Comstock could have been executed with the money flung away by the mines that have had, for a time, rich ore.

3. Those errors in legislation, or the want of it, which have permitted the growth of such a condition of things, cannot now be repaired. It is not wise to interfere with existing privileges, even though they have no other foundation in right than a custom of 10 years' standing. The companies on the Comstock lode must be allowed to go on until the stern fact of failure forces them to adopt some system of association.

4. At present, however, the tendency is more than ever the other way. As the prospects of mining on the old wasteful plan grow darker and darker, officers, agents, and stockholders bend their energies to save what they can by speculation out of the approaching wreck. We might well afford to leave them to their fate, but for the fact that the effect of an abandonment of the Comstock lode would be almost fatal to systematic and permanent mining in the Pacific States. It would confirm the mischievous feeling that mining is half grab and half gamble; that the only way to make money at it is to dig out what rich ore you can get, and then find a fool to buy the property; or failing that, to make a fool of that collective individual, the public, and to "unload" yourself of your stock.

5. The Sutro tunnel will do four most important things: it will settle the question of the continuance of the Comstock in depth; it will inevitably unite the mining companies in many respects, and remove much of the expense of separate pumping, hoisting, prospecting, and general administration;* it will render possible the beneficiation of low-grade ores, absolutely the only basis for rational and permanent mining; and, finally, by assuring the future, it will kill that speculation which thrives on ignorance of the future.

6. I do not think the tunnel would prove a total pecuniary loss in the worst event, since it would also explore in depth a country which is very likely to contain other bodies of rich ore. All the indications are *that the origin of the Comstock bodies was east of the vein*, and promising deposits are already known to exist in that direction.

VIRGINIA AND CARSON CITY RAILROAD.

A movement is on foot, looking to the passage of a bill by the present legislature of Nevada in aid of the construction of a railway from Virginia City to the Sierras by way of Carson City. This project is urged by the Milling Association, which owns most of the mills about Virginia. They also expect aid from Comstock and Story counties. Its success will enable them to bring wood in abundance and at low rates to the mills. These will then be arranged to work large quantities of low-grade ores, and the mines will be gutted to supply them. This plan will be beneficial, whether the Sutro tunnel should be run or not. It will primarily facilitate the reduction of the bodies of low-grade ores now exposed in the Comstock vein—all of which are near the surface, and can be more cheaply extracted by shafts than by a deep tunnel. It will also establish a permanent communication between the district and the forests of the Sierra, on which all dependence for fuel must be placed; and it will materially cheapen the cost of all materials and supplies, and place Virginia City *en rapport* with the great Pacific railroad. Finally, it will run by the Spring Valley mines, which will probably be again

* The direct saving in drainage is doubled by the fact that the water now lifted at great expense, by steam, would, if allowed to fall instead, itself generate a motive power, to take the place of steam. Hydraulic engines utilizing this source of power are common in the deep mines of Europe, but have never been introduced in this country. In the case under discussion, the conditions would be extremely favorable, permitting a hydraulic column of 2,000 feet. Fifty gallons of water per second, with a fall of 2,000 feet create a working capacity of 1,800 horse-power. Another way of utilizing the water of drainage would be the erection of water-wheels under ground, by which various operations requiring machinery could be conducted. This, too, is very common in Europe, and, like the use of hydraulic engines, may be introduced with advantage wherever there is deep tunnel-drainage. In the absence of deep drainage, both these economical devices of science are out of the question. If the Sutro tunnel is completed to the lode, and connected with deep shafts, *the conditions for further explorations to still greater depths will be more favorable than they were at the very surface; since the immense power of the hydraulic column will be at the service of the miner.*

opened, and will be likely to furnish a large quantity of rock worth $20 to $25 per ton.

It is evident, however, that nothing but a deep tunnel can secure the future of mining on the Comstock lode. All other plans are merely expedients to save as much as possible from the approaching wreck; and even the discoveries of new bodies of ore by the present deep shafts will but prolong for a time a system of working which has proved in the main, unprofitable.

TAILINGS AND SLIMES AT VIRGINIA CITY.

The tailings are those portions of fine sand and gold, silver and quicksilver which escape from the settlers, suspended in water, and are either allowed to run off entirely, or caught in reservoirs, or concentrated upon sluices. The slimes are finely divided sulphurets, which are even longer in settling than the tailings, and have hitherto not been successfully caught and worked. There are thousands of tons of tailings and slimes in the cañons where the Comstock mills are situated; and their economical treatment is a matter of great importance. I am indebted to Louis Janin, esq., late superintendent of the Gould & Curry, for considerable information on this subject, which will be more appropriately given in a future report on methods and apparatus of American mining. In this place a few remarks will suffice.

The tailings vary in value according to the quality of ores worked in the mills, the economy and thoroughness of the mill treatment, the admixture of slimes in the reservoirs, &c. Twelve assays at different points in the Carson river reservoir gave results varying from $7 68 to $24 31 per ton, the average being $12 79. The richest results were nearest the embankment, where the slimes had settled. The slime pit below the reservoir gave assays of $19 22 per ton. From one-third to one-half the value of bullion is gold. A good deal of amalgam and quicksilver is obtained from tailings in actual re-working; but this is not a constant quantity, and is not included in the results of the above assays, which were made upon samples washed free from quicksilver beforehand. The Gould & Curry reservoir mill worked from July to November, 1867, 861 tons of tailings in Varney and Wakelee pans, with the following results:

	Lot No. 1.	Lot No. 2.
Number of tons	770	91
Quicksilver	387 pounds loss.	43 pounds gain.
Amalgam produced	9,340 troy ounces.	1,250 troy ounces.
Bullion	8,957.90 troy ounces	1,198.50 troy ounces.
Value	$15,202 76	$1,990 25
Assay of tailings	$28 56 per ton.	$33 79 per ton.
Percentage obtained	69.1	64.5

These were evidently concentrated tailings. From the Park reservoir 76½ tons of tailings, worked in the fountain pan, yielded 60 pounds 11 ounces of amalgam, worth about $3 98 per pound or $241 54, making the average yield per ton $3 16.

It is not necessary to point out to the educated engineer that the foregoing data as to the value of tailings and slimes are inconsistent with the popular notion that only 65 per cent. of the silver in the Comstock ore is extracted by the Washoe process.

A loss of 35 per cent. should leave richer tailings. In point of fact, the public has been misled by the circumstance that the Washoe mills guarantee 65 per cent. of the assay, to believe that this is the measure of the accuracy of the process. Dr. J. P. Kimball, of the American Bureau of Mines, speaks* of a loss of $9,000,000 from this source in 1867, and Mr. J. Ross Browne falls into the same error. (Report of 1868, page 364.) The truth is that the assays are made with dry powered samples, and the ore is sent to the mills with more or less moisture, varying, it is said, from three to 10 per cent. Sixty-five per cent. of the assay value per dry ton, applied to the moist ton means therefore, in reality, from 67 to 72 per cent., which is what the mine receives. But besides this, the amalgam caught by simple concentration from the tailings is a perquisite of the mill. In fact, the low rates of custom mills are made possible by the margin of profit left between the 67 to 72 per cent. which the mills guarantee, and the 75 to 80 per cent. which they actually extract. The Washoe process is not a rude and imperfect one in principle; it is scientific and remarkably successful—better for the circumstances than any European process. A little more economy and care in managing the details, and above all such a study of the process itself by the mill-men as would settle its real nature and principles, and lead to some uniform rules as to the management of certain parts of it, would make it a credit to American ingenuity and skill. A great improvement has been made since Mr. Guido Küstel † described the Washoe process, in the introduction of large pans; and the necessity for increased economy is now leading to still other improvements. In this respect the Comstock mining enterprises have nothing to be ashamed of. The comparison often made with the Reese River mills, which charge high prices and guarantee 80 per cent., is thus seen to be based on an apparent, rather than a real difference. No doubt the loss by the Washoe process will be much larger if the proportion of native gold and silver in the ore decreases in depth.

The amount of tailings and slimes collected in various reservoirs, since the practice of saving them was introduced, amounts to many thousand tons. Janin's Dayton mill, which works tailings only, has (or will soon have) a capacity of fifty tons daily, and supplies assured of some 75,000 tons. The large Dayton reservoir contains some 140,000 tons, and the Carson River reservoir (which being furthest from the mills contains most slimes) about 200,000 more. There are numerous others, but the occasional floods in the narrow cañons have carried away a large amount of tailings to the Carson.

*Memoirs of the American Bureau of Mines, 1867.

†Nevada and California processes, &c., San Francisco, 1863.

PRODUCT OF LEADING MINES ON AND NEAR THE COMSTOCK LODE.

First quarter of 1868.

Company.	January.			February.			March.		
	Bullion.	Assessment.	Dividend.	Bullion.	Assessment.	Dividend.	Bullion.	Assessment.	Dividend.
Alpha									
Belcher								$26, 000	
Bullion								25, 000	
Crown Point	$54, 249			$37, 248			$85, 663		
Confidence								15, 600	
Chollar Potosi	45, 682			30, 527	$140,000		34, 798		
Daney					16, 000				
Exchequer		$24, 000							
Empire M. and M. Co.	16, 050			16, 601			16, 627		
Gould and Curry									
Gold Hill Company	6, 838			5, 000			8, 166	10, 000	
Hale and Norcross				5, 418			90, 000		
Imperial	43, 883			63, 028			73, 655		
Justice & Independent		22, 500							
Kentuck	92, 914		$30, 000	69, 526		$30, 000	68, 898		$10, 000
Lady Bryan							20, 000		
Ophir		50, 400							
Overman		48, 000		22, 328			55, 937		
Segregated Belcher									
Savage	151, 400		80, 000	181, 657		80, 000	257, 953		80, 000
Sierra Nevada					30, 000				
Yellow Jacket*		150, 000							
Total in 1868	411, 016	294, 900	110, 000	431, 333	186, 000	110, 000	711, 697	76, 600	90, 000
Total in 1867	1, 022, 378	110, 000	284, 000	1, 014, 238	76, 000	206, 000	728, 916	44, 480	250, 000
Total in 1866	671, 555	62, 000	60, 000	803, 161	299, 000		817, 177	113, 600	30, 000

* The yield of the Yellow Jacket is not given.

Second quarter of 1868.

Company.	April.			May.			June.		
	Bullion.	Assessment.	Dividend.	Bullion.	Assessment.	Dividend.	Bullion.	Assessment.	Dividend.
Alpha								$30, 000	
Belcher									
Bullion					$25, 000				
Crown Point	$169, 074			$168, 677		$60, 000	$116, 000		$90, 000
Confidence							8, 626		
Chollar Potosi	46, 676			64, 839			76, 563		
Daney		$24, 000							
Exchequer									
Empire M. and M. Co.	17, 574			17, 027			20, 659		
Gould and Curry									
Gold Hill M. and M. Co.	9, 787			11, 066			12, 051		3, 750
Hale and Norcross	84, 344			69, 767			38, 244		
Imperial	58, 579			51, 235			65, 607		24, 000
Justice & Independent					15, 000				
Kentuck	110, 517		$20, 000	106, 970		40, 000	120, 766		40, 000
Lady Bryan					60, 000				
Ophir								67, 200	
Overman	37, 353			41, 299	64, 000				
Segregated Belcher					38, 400				
Savage	222, 734		80, 000	329, 760		80, 000	384, 675		160, 000
Sierra Nevada		30, 000							
Yellow Jacket*									
Total in 1868	756, 638	54, 000	100, 000	860, 640	202, 400	180, 000	843, 191	97, 200	317, 750
Total in 1867	1, 262, 937	31, 600	283, 000	1, 599, 797	25, 000	460, 200	1, 436, 388	153, 300	475, 000
Total in 1866	781, 362	140, 000	164, 000	852, 569	44, 800	108, 000	1, 000, 884	28, 000	164, 000

* Product not reported.

PRODUCT OF LEADING MINES, ETC.—Continued.

Third quarter of 1868.

Company.	JULY.			AUGUST.			SEPTEMBER.		
	Bullion.	Assessment.	Dividend.	Bullion.	Assessment.	Dividend.	Bullion.	Assessment.	Dividend.
Alpha									
Belcher		$26,000							
Bullion					$25,000				
Crown Point	$145,923		$90,000	$132,122		$60,000	$44,369		$60,000
Confidence	11,919			17,300			21,280		
Chollar Potosi	86,029			97,993			78,013		
Daney		16,000							
Exchequer									
Empire M. and M. Co.	20,464			20,646			18,837		
Gould and Curry	3,239			1,520			10,195		
Gold Hill Mill & M. Co.	8,899		3,750	8,836			10,318		
Hale and Norcross	19,900	80,000					31,198		
Imperial	69,433			55,627			64,532		
Justice & Independent		15,000							
Kentuck	138,860		50,000	164,550		60,000	132,882		60,000
Lady Bryan		60,000							
Ophir									
Overman	5,415			28,000			33,000		
Segregated Belcher	4,371								
Savage	279,788		240,000	187,141		160,000	140,000		80,000
Sierra Nevada							4,542	$30,000	
Yellow Jacket*									
Total in 1868	794,240	197,000	383,750	713,735	25,000	280,000	589,166	30,000	200,000
Total in 1867	1,379,116	108,570	577,500	1,306,549	6,400	447,500	1,171,327	258,000	370,000
Total in 1866	939,605	80,800	154,000	1,106,896	75,000	154,000	1,054,011		174,000

* The Yellow Jacket produced $676,861 39 bullion during the year ending June 30, 1868; but its monthly product is not reported.

Fourth quarter of 1868.

Company.	OCTOBER.			NOVEMBER.			DECEMBER.		
	Bullion.	Assessment.	Dividend.	Bullion.	Assessment.	Dividend.	Bullion.	Assessment.	Dividend.
Alpha								$60,000	
Belcher		$26,000						26,000	
Bullion								25,000	
Crown Point	$45,670			$51,515			$35,720	90,000	
Confidence	22,832			13,983			14,728		
Chollar Potosi	112,898			102,722			108,336		
Daney									
Exchequer									
Empire M. and M. Co.	16,804			16,908			15,574		
Gould and Curry	5,650			8,953				72,000	
Gold Hill Quartz Mill and Mining Co.	9,104			2,326			11,295		
Hale and Norcross	26,641	80,000		16,013			10,875	40,000	
Imperial	58,229			35,944			44,288	100,000	
Justice & Independent									
Kentuck	69,145		$40,000	86,097		$40,000	98,582		$60,000
Lady Bryan					$30,000				
Ophir					50,400				
Overman	35,000			34,000	64,400		60,258		
Segregated Belcher									
Savage	128,000		80,000	119,760			152,000		64,000
Sierra Nevada	5,191			5,504			7,568		
Yellow Jacket*						360,000			
Total in 1868	535,164	106,000	120,000	493,725	144,000	400,000	559,224	413,000	124,000
Total in 1867	1,079,799	205,000	240,000	894,120	132,000	135,000	646,628	145,600	153,750
Total in 1866	1,032,713	164,620	167,200	1,040,172	34,000	229,200	1,039,537	128,000	370,000

* Product not reported.

Product of the principal mines on the Comstock vein for the year ending December 31, 1868.

Company.	Bullion.	Assessments.	Dividends
Alpha	....	$90,000	....
Belcher	....	104,000	....
Bullion	....	100,000	....
Crown Point	$1,086,230	90,000	$360,000
Confidence	110,668	15,600	....
Chollar Potosi	885,076	140,000	....
Daney	....	56,000	....
Exchequer	....	24,000	....
Empire Mill and Mining Company	213,771	....	....
Gould and Curry	29,557	72,000	....
Gold Hill Quartz Mill and Mining Company	103,686	10,000	7,500
Hale and Norcross	392,400	200,000	....
Imperial	684,040	100,000	24,000
Justice and Independent	....	52,500	....
Kentuck	1,259,707	....	480,000
Lady Bryan	20,000	150,000	....
Ophir	....	167,000	....
Overman	352,590	176,000	....
Segregated Belcher	4,371	38,400	....
Savage	2,534,868	....	1,184,000
Sierra Nevada	22,005	90,000	....
Yellow Jacket*	800,000	150,000	360,000
Total in 1868	8,499,769	1,825,500	2,415,500
Total in 1867	13,626,062	1,296,250	3,991,950
Total in 1866	11,732,100	1,194,820	1,754,400

* Estimated.

Fluctuations in leading mining shares for the six months ending December 30, 1867.

Name of company.	July 10th.	July 20th.	July 30th.	August 10th.	August 20th.	August 30th.	September 10th.	September 20th.	September 30th.	October 10th.	October 21st.	October 30th.	November 11th.	November 20th.	November 30th.	December 10th.	December 20th.	December 30th.
Gould and Curry	725	755	715	600	630	560	325	320	360	275	310	310	375	320	327½	315	350	357½
Ophir	325	235	150	100	102½	117½	87½	78	54	40	37	50	60	62½	62½	50	67½	57½
Savage	4, 950	4, 500	4, 375	210	218½	205	175	146	150	115	129	116	107	102	107	104	122	116½
Chollar Potosi	457½	450	432½	375	447½	420	430	331	355	195	185	202½	130	138	131	135	131½	145
Hale and Norcross	3, 100	......	......	3, 000	......	......	......	1, 100	850	500	745	880	875	810	840	890	1, 160	1, 240
Sheba	......	......	......	......	......	......	......	......	......	......	......	......	......	......	......	......	......	......
Daney	8	19	22	16	20	......	......	......	......	......	9	......	......	......	7	......	8	......
Wide West	......	......	......	......	......	......	......	......	......	......	......	......	......	......	......	......	......	......
Bullion	41	33½	27½	20	35	35	25	21	21	15½	18	15	8	6½	15	17½	19	31
Real del Monte	......	......	......	......	......	......	......	......	......	......	......	......	......	......	......	......	......	......
El Dorado	......	......	......	......	......	......	......	......	......	......	......	......	......	......	......	......	......	......
Overman	220	150	160	85	81	70	62	56	55½	33	56	51	48	49	44	50	78	107
Sierra Nevada	18	16	22	55	36	35	14	7	4	½	13½	9½	......	2½	3⅛	......	12½	15
Yellow Jacket	1, 520	900	980	1, 085	900	695	455	455	465	340	480	340	375	400	524	475	720	790
White and Murphy	......	......	......	......	......	......	......	......	......	......	......	......	......	......	......	......	......	......
Baltic	......	......	......	......	......	......	......	......	......	......	......	......	......	......	......	......	......	......
North American	......	......	......	......	......	......	......	......	......	......	......	......	......	......	......	......	......	......
Baltimore American	......	......	......	......	......	......	......	......	......	......	......	......	......	......	......	......	......	......
Imperial	214	195	210	172½	135	145	143	144	159	112½	127	135	154	158	170	160	172	165
Crown Point	1, 700	1, 225	1, 020	1, 400	1, 150	1, 015	870	715	750	560	890	595	560	665	690	640	690	765
Belcher	460	316	280	275	215	170	115	82½	135	75	110	......	110	......	105	......	120	134
Alpha	......	......	......	......	......	450	450	......	......	......	......	450	......	450	......	......	600	......
Empire Mill and Mining Company	180	180	185	175	......	......	175	......	175	145	......	......	175	175	167½	......	167½	......
Confidence	65	60	57½	62½	72½	80	50	50	......	......	......	......	36	35	......	......	......	......
Justice and Independent	20	15	8	31	13	29	12½	14	8½	3½	2	12	......	......	......	......	......	......
Exchequer	12½	10½	......	11	......	11	9	8	......	9	8½	......	......	8½	11	10	15	16
Kentuck	497½	395	370	360	366	305	200	200	242½	200	234	169	140	160	160	165	226	270
Gold Hill Quartz Mill and Mining Company	210	185	165	140	130	120	......	80	......	......	100	90	90	105	132½	......	76	80
Segregated Belcher	18	11½	8½	8	7	......	......	5	7	5	5½	......	3½	5	4½	7½	......	11

Fluctuations in leading mining shares for the six months ending June 30, 1868.

Name of company.	January 11th.	January 20th.	January 30th.	February 10th.	February 20th.	February 29th.	March 10th.	March 20th.	March 30th.	April 10th.	April 20th.	April 30th.	May 11th.	May 20th.	May 30th.	June 10th.	June 20th.	June 30th.
Gould and Curry	340	390	435	435	850	665	620	670	650	660	560	535	540	420	430	110	112	114
Ophir	60	70	65	55	190	168	195	197⅛	225	245	180	175	167½	167	180	14¾	12¾	13½
Savage	122	128	190	145	190	189	172	170	173⅛	177	156	153	156½	151	150½	163	154½	157½
Chollar Potosi	197½	215	3,400	191	225	210	182½	269	263	337½	250	225	237½	230	246	290	245	255
Hale and Norcross	2,200	2,900	....	4,100	....	....	2,900	2,730	2,350	2,425	2,000	2,000	127½	110	106	117	80	102
Sheba	....	....	11	....	....	....	....	....	....	....	....	....	....	....	....	....	....	....
Daney	....	8	....	10	14	....	27	35	28	20	19	7½	18	14	23	7	7¼	8
Wide West	....	....	....	....	....	....	....	....	....	....	....	....	....	....	....	....	....	....
Bullion	42	37	35	42	70	60	52½	70	131	112½	60	52	70	54	47	37½	23	30
Real del Monte	....	....	....	....	....	....	....	....	....	....	....	....	....	....	....	....	....	....
El Dorado	....	....	....	....	....	....	....	....	....	....	....	....	....	....	....	....	....	....
Overman	86	71	80	93½	200	197½	174	178	185	212	150	122½	127½	74	82	77	77½	82
Sierra Nevada	17	24	15½	12	18⅛	16	24	25	31	30	17	14	18	26	25	31	25	30
Yellow Jacket	675	725	790	830	1,240	1,259	1,220	1,555	1,480	1,520	1,280	1,340	1,430	1,050	1,200	1,205	1,115	1,235
Amador	....	....	....	....	....	....	....	....	....	300	287½	297½	292½	290	....	261	255	245
Lady Bryan	....	....	....	....	....	....	....	....	....	58	38	28	38	29	23½	31	25	32½
North American	....	....	....	....	....	....	....	....	....	....	....	....	....	....	....	....	....	....
Baltimore American	....	....	....	....	....	....	....	....	....	....	....	....	....	....	....	....	....	....
Imperial	175	179	208	205	275	248	265	272½	283	285	243	239	250	292½	208	210	100	140
Crown Point	730	1,000	1,220	1,280	1,900	1,875	1,855	2,450	2,340	2,150	2,175	2,225	2,790	108	117	113½	104	93
Belcher	152½	150	182½	195	360	285	295	425	400	380	325	305	340	302½	301	285	200	190
Alpha	....	700	1,000	1,200	1,475	1,300	1,320	77½	99	100	88	83	88	66	75	72	57½	52
Empire Mill and Mining Company	175	180	187½	197½	275	....	280	....	315	315	260	265	....	200	225	225	....	150
Confidence	50	57½	....	....	....	....	70	90	89	110	....	95	....	62½	....	50	....	....
Justice and Independent	....	....	....	....	....	....	....	....	....	38	21	15	15	....	....	....	....	....
Exchequer	16	19½	29	27	37½	40	41	43	80	79	46	43	57½	35	41	39	31	29
Kentuck	252½	255	262	283	309	285	295	435	435	477½	445	450	477½	410	417	385	380	372½
Gold Hill Quartz Mill and Mining Company	77	80	92½	95	100	95½	125	95	99	122½	125	120	125	112	....	117½	82½	100
Segregated Belcher	10	8½	9	9	14	19	17	22	21	25½	17½	15	18	11	9½	8½	11¼	10

Fluctuations in leading mining shares for the six months ending November 30, 1868.

Name of company.	June 10th.	June 20th.	June 30th.	July 10th.	July 20th.	July 30th.	August 10th.	August 20th.	August 30th.	September 10th.	September 20th.	September 30th.	October 10th.	October 20th.	October 30th.	November 10th.	November 20th.	November 30th.
Gould and Curry	110	112	114	100	103	105	91	88	106	94	84	109	100	96	89	70	82½	108
Ophir	14¾	12¾	13	15½	22½	21	20½	32	21	18	17	17	19½	19	19	19	23	38
Savage	163	154½	157	136	138¾	132½	129	113	118¾	91½	90	105	110½	82½	75	60	70½	75
Chollar Potosi	290	245	255½	214	181	138	138	162	183½	153	149	158	155	146½	136½	126	143½	175
Hale and Norcross	117	80	102½	71	65	79	74½	77	93	53½	48½	49	49½	44	44¾	38½	63	76
Sheba	......	......	......	......	......	......	......	......	......	......	......	......	......	......	......	......	......	......
Daney	7	7¼	8	7¼	......	3½	......	......	......	......	3½	6¼	6½	5	6	4	5	6¼
Wide West	......	......	......	......	......	......	......	......	......	......	......	......	......	......	......	......	......	......
Bullion	37½	23	30	26	23	21	17½	22	20	15	16	18½	15	......	14	12	16	18
Real del Monte	......	......	......	......	......	......	......	......	......	......	......	......	......	......	......	......	......	......
El Dorado	......	......	......	......	......	......	......	......	......	......	......	......	......	......	......	......	......	......
Overman	77	77½	82	69	82	78	78	110	88	83½	81	83	89½	81¾	70½	46	46	51
Sierra Nevada	31	25	30	27	29	32	38¼	37	27	27	20	16½	20	18½	29	22½	16	......
Yellow Jacket	1,205	1,115	1,235	1,240	1,230	1,185	1,135	1,220	1,400	1,270	1,190	1,400	1,580	1,490	1,409½	925	1,210	1,705
Amador	261	255	245	225	255	265	260	237½	242½	253	240	240	229	230	207	215	217¼	227½
Lady Bryan	31	25	32	27	23	14	15	15	21	16	12	16	14	10	10½	10	6	19
North American	......	......	......	......	......	......	......	......	......	......	......	......	......	......	......	......	......	......
Baltimore American	......	......	......	......	......	......	......	......	......	......	......	......	......	......	......	......	......	......
Imperial	210	160	140	130	118	103	111	118½	114	108	97	108	112	112	101	89	100	136
Crown Point	113½	104	93	88½	94	88	87½	87	84	68	44½	47	45	44½	43	33	44	49
Belcher	285	200	190	172½	152¼	115	122¼	140	160	160	125	135	152½	140	127½	125	140	180
Alpha	72	57½	52	47½	44½	41	51	50	51½	51	45½	47	54	42½	39	27	36½	48
Empire Mill and Mining Company	225	......	150	......	135	120	115	115	120	115	......	101	100	......	105	......	90	113
Confidence	50	......	......	38	38	35	......	......	35	......	30	......	......	......	......	......	28	60
Justice and Independent	......	......	......	8	6	5	......	......	......	......	......	6	......	......	4¼	......	3	......
Exchequer	39	31	29	25	24	20	19	19	19	......	12	14½	15	14¾	14	14	17½	28
Kentuck	385	380	372	392½	387½	382½	350	450	425	411	295	288	262	280	262½	180	247½	280
Gold Hill Quartz Mill and Mining Company	117½	82½	100	85	70	69	65	......	60	62	......	......	......	......	50	......	......	52
Segregated Belcher	8½	11¼	10	10	13½	11½	11¼	13¾	11¼	10½	9	9¾	9½	8¾	8¼	5½	5½	7¾

[From the San Francisco Weekly Stock Circular, January 2, 1869.]

QUOTATIONS OF MINING STOCKS.

Name of company.	No. of feet in mine.	Shares, per foot.	Total No. of shares.	Incorporate value.	Bid.	Asked.	Last monthly dividend.	Last assessment, per share.	When delinquent.
Alpha (consolidated)	300	20	6,000	$250 00	$41 50 per share	$42 00 per share		Dec. 3, $10 00	Jan. 2, 1869.
Bacon Mill and Mining Company	45		4,000	200 00			June 19, 1868, $2 00	Nov. 7, 10 00	Dec. 11, 1866.
Baltimore American	2,600	1	2,600	500 00				Jan. 12, 2 00	Feb. 18, 1867.
Belcher	1,040	10	10,400	100 00	162 00 per share	165 00 per share		Oct. 6, 25 00	Nov. 5, 1868.
Bullion, G. H	2,500	1	2,500	400 00	14 50 per share	15 00 per share		Dec. 7, 10 00	Jan. 6, 1869.
Central	150	12	1,800	390 00					
Crown Point	600	20	12,000	250 00	52 50 per share	53 00 per share	Sept. 12, 1868, 5 00	Dec. 18, 7 50	Jan. 17, 1869.
Cole, (Va.)	3,000		3,000	500 00	8 00 per share	11 00 per share			
Confidence	130	12	1,560	500 00	36 00 per share	39 00 per share		Mar. 26, 10 00	Apr. 25, 1868.
Consolidated Virginia	1,160	10	11,600	300 00	9 00 psr share	11 00 per share			
Chollar Potosi	2,800	1	2,800	2,000 00	153 00 per share	155 00 per share	Oct. 15, 1867, 25 00	Feb. 10, 50 00	Mar. 11, 1868.
Daney	2,000	4	8,000	60 00	3 00 per share	3 50 per share		July 27, 2 00	Aug. 26, 1868.
Exchequer	400	20	8,000	300 00	25 00 per share	26 00 per share		Jan. 30, 3 00	Feb. 29, 1868.
Empire Mill and Mining Company	75	16	1,200	833 00	125 00 per share	126 00 per share	May 15, 1867, 6 00		
Gould and Curry	1,200	4	4,800	500 00	99 00 per share	100 00 per share		Dec. 5, 15 00	Jan. 4, 1869.
Gold Hill Quartz M. and M. Company	13⅛		500	500 00	65 00 per share	75 00 per share	July 13, 1868, 7 50	Mar. 13, 20 00	Apr. 12, 1868.
Hale and Norcross	400	20	8,000	200 00	44 50 per share	45 00 per share	Sept. 16, 1867, 125 00	Dec. 12, 5 00	Jan. 11, 1869.
Imperial	184		4,000	500 00	109 00 per share	110 00 per share	June 20, 1868, 6 00	Dec. 15, 25 00	Jan. 14, 1869.
Julia	2,000	1	2,000	200 00	3 00 per share	3 50 per share		Oct. 22, 1 50	Nov. 21, 1868.
Justice and Independent			3,000	100 00	8 00 per share	8 50 per share		July 28, 5 00	Aug. 27, 1868.
Kentuck	95		2,000		255 00 per share	270 00 per share	Dec. 10, 1868, 30 00		
Lady Bryan	5,900		6,000	300 00	19 50	20 00 per share		Nov. 24, 5 00	Aug. 24, 1868.
North American	4,100	1	4,100	300 00	2 00	5 00 per share			
Occidental M. and M. Company			10,000	100 00	22 00 per share	23 00 per share			
Ophir	1,400	12	16,800	300 00	37 00 per share	40 00 per share		Nov. 9, 3 00	Dec. 8, 1868.
Overman	1,200		3,200	500 00	85 00 per share	88 00 per share		Nov. 13, 20 00	Dec. 13, 1868.
Segregated Belcher	160	40	6,400	300 00	8 00 per share	8 50 per share		May 15, 6 00	June 14, 1868.
Savage	800	20	16,000	200 00	78 00 per share	7 090 per share	Dec. 12, 1868, 4 00		
Sierra Nevada	3,000	1	3,000	500 00	19 00 per share			Nov. 16, 12 50	Dec. 16, 1868.
Union	302		1,200	100 00				June 2, 5 00	July 2, 1868.
United States	1,600		4,000	500 00				Oct. 15, 1 00	Nov. 14, 1868.
Yellow Jacket	1,200	1	1,200	1,000 00	1445 00 per share	1450 00 per share	Nov. 10, 1868, 300 00	Jan. 22, 125 00	Feb. 21, 1868.
Amador Mining Company, California	1,850	2	3,700	400 00	235 00 per share	240 00 per share	Dec. 19, 1868, 6 00		
Aurora, White Pine	800	20	16,000	100 00	25 00 per share				
Eureka Mining Company, California			4,000	300 00	210 00 per share		Dec. 19, 1868, 7 50		
Silver Hill, Esmeralda	3,000	1	3,000	500 00					
De Soto, Humboldt	1,980	2	1,900	100 00		2 00 per share			
Golden Rule, California	3,000	1	3,000	100 00	5 00 per share		Dec. 26, 1868, 0 50		
Mohawk, California	1,200	2	2,400	100 00				Dec. 7, 1868, $3	Jan. 6, 1869.

Report of the Savage Company for the year ending June 30, 1868.

RECEIPTS.

On hand July 10, 1867	$77,715 58
Bullion	3,484,185 72
Ore sold	21,897 25
Premiums	9,999 91
Other receipts	14,751 54
Total	3,608,550 00

DISBURSEMENTS.

Dividends	$1,548,500 00
Custom mills	1,006,628 61
Reduction, &c., company's mills	226,150 21
Labor	311,277 74
Timber and lumber	102,107 52
Fuel	50,366 98
Taxes	40,635 13
Legal expenses	46,169 40
Salaries	20,650 00
Supplies, &c	52,268 45
Freight on bullion	27,857 66
Other disbursements	69,618 80
Cash on hand July 11, 1868	106,319 50
Total	3,608,550 00
Assets, exclusive of mine and mills	223,403 00
Liabilities	29,358 00
Surplus	194,045 00

	Tons.	
Ore on hand July 1, 1867	2,865	
Extracted during the year	87,342	
		90,207
Reduced	84,627	
Sold	3,897	
		88,524
On hand July 1, 1868		1,683

Average yield: first class, $359 52; second class, $78 16; third class, $37 41. Total average, $40 84. Cost of extraction, $7 21; of reduction, $13 74. Total cost per ton, $20 95. Average profit per ton, $19 89.

Total ore product from date of organization, nearly seven years, 270,521 tons; yield n bullion, &c., $11,327,700; assessments, $188,000; dividends, $3,560,000.

Report of the Ophir Company for the year ending December 18, 1868.

RECEIPTS.

From mine	$3,558 00
Woodworth mill	3,017 00
Reduction works	3,341 00
Bridge and road tolls, Washoe Valley	1,372 00
Lands in Washoe Valley	2,502 00
Sale of bridge over lake and road	3,000 00
Toll road—dividends four months	4,586 00
Toll road—cash portion sale money	7,500 00
Assessment account	149,065 00
Miscellaneous	750 00
Total receipts	178,691 00
Cash on hand December 18, 1867	11,811 00
Total	190,502 00

DISBURSEMENTS.

For mine	$1,028 00
Woodworth mill	5,279 00
Reduction works	1,689 00
Bridge and road, Washoe Valley	1,166 00
Land in Washoe Valley	2,179 00
Office expenses, San Francisco	1,655 00
General expenses of mine	9,668 00
Buck's shaft—construction	93,819 00
Buck's shaft—machinery	32,878 00
Buck's shaft—timber, &c	2,092 00
Buck's shaft—ground	329 00
Legal expenses	6,414 00
Salary account, San Francisco	2,233 00
Miscellaneous items	3,267 00
Total disbursements	165,696 00
Cash balance December 18, 1868	24,806 00
Total	190,502 00

The company have levied three assessments during the year, amounting to $168,000, as follows:

Assessment.	When levied.	Per share.	Amount.
Number 6	January 20	$3 00	$50,400
Number 7	June 15	4 00	67,200
Number 8	November 2	3 00	50,400
Total		10 00	168,000

On the last assessment there still remains unpaid the sum of $18,935. In all, the company have levied eight assessments, amounting to $593,000, or about $424 per foot. There have been no dividends since March, 1864. The first dividend paid was on the 17th of July, 1860. During this interval there were 22 disbursements, amounting in the aggregate to $1,394,400, being equal to $83 per share, or $996 per foot. The Ophir Silver Mining Company was incorporated on the 28th of April, 1860, with a capital of $5,040,000, divided into 16,800 shares of the par value $300 each. The total bullion product up to the close of the fiscal year ending December 12, 1867, was $5,286,639. The old mine and shaft were abandoned about 16 months ago, since which time work has been progressing on the new shaft, without, however, striking ore. This shaft is now down 585 feet, of which 573 feet is timbered. At a depth of 300 feet hard rock was encountered, which continued 200 feet; since then the rock has been changeable and the sinking more rapid, two and a half feet per day being accomplished. The water at the bottom of the shaft has diminished four inches, ditch measurement. At the annual meeting to-day 11,638 shares of 16,800 were represented. The stock was first introduced in the market October, 1860. The highest price ever reached was $3,800 per foot, and the lowest $37.

Report of the Empire Company for the year ending November 30, 1868.

RECEIPTS.

From bullion account	$215,866 00
From mine account	4,842 00
From mill account	700 00
Assets November 30, 1867	15,963 00
Liabilities November 30, 1868	26,794 00
Total	264,165 00

DISBURSEMENTS.

Indebtedness November 30, 1867	$5,617 00
For mill	119,925 00
For mine	72,779 00
Miscellaneous	52,729 00
Total	251,050 00
Assets November 30, 1868	13,115 00
Total	264,465 00

The amount of liabilities above the assets on the 30th of November, 1868, was $13,679. The Empire Mill and Mining Company was incorporated in March, 1863, with a capital of $999,600, divided into 1,200 shares, of the par value of $833 each. The first recorded sales of stock were in June, 1864, when 20 shares were sold at $800. The operations of the company for the past year have been largely confined to work on the Imperial Empire shaft, which is down 1,100 feet. It is expected that by the 1st of January drifts will be commenced from the 1,000-foot and 1,100-foot levels. The amount disbursed on account of the shaft for the past year is $28,946. The extractión of the ore for the past year has been restricted to the upper portion of the mine, say from the surface to the 330-foot level; from that section 11,028 tons of low-grade ore has been raised, averaging $29 54 per ton. The amount of ore reduced for the year is 10,724 tons, yielding $205,055 in bullion.

Report of the Gould and Curry Company for the year ending December 1, 1868.

RECEIPTS.

Cash on hand, December 1, 1867	$147,944 15
Ores sold	43,959 29
Bullion account—Company mill	29,127 67
Bullion account—Custom mill	22,198 56
Materials sold	16,226 76
Tolls on Virginia and Carson river road	4,130 43
Ore scales at mine	147 72
Interest	249 17
Bills payable	3,875 90
Cash indebtedness	33,822 09
Total	301,680 24

DISBURSEMENTS.

Mine account	$180,108 52
Mill account	50,925 39
Dividend account	3,165 00
General expense account	17,737 37
Reduction of ores at Custom mills	15,510 82
Mill repairs	9,072 57
Taxes	5,851 38
Legal expenses	3,368 50
Bills receivable	8,559 46
Virginia and Carson river road	4,371 19
Sundries	3,010 04
Total	301,680 24

The assets and liabilities of the company at the close of the fiscal year are as follows:

ASSETS.

Bills receivable	$18,613 29
Ores, tailings, &c., on hand	51,500 00
Real and personal property—mine	156,823 92
Real and personal property—mill	218,896 27
Boarding-house at mine	3,750 00
Reservoir tailings' mill	22,884 61
Assay office, &c	7,711 68
Virginia and Carson River toll road	6,750 00
Office in San Francisco	1,000 00
Total	487,929 77

LIABILITIES.

Cash indebtedness, &c	$29,532 31
Bills payable	3,875 00
Dividends uncalled for	535 00
Total	33,942 31

Report of the Gold Hill Quartz Mill and Mining Company for year ending January 1, 1869.

RECEIPTS.

Supplies on hand January 1, 1868	$8,670 00
Bullion product	101,563 00
Premium and discount	742 00
Mill account	1,598 00
Assessment	10,000 00
Book accounts	9,123 00
Rent and expense account	203 00
Total	131,899 00

DISBURSEMENTS.

Book account	$7,036 00
Mine account	28,599 00
Mill account	66 946 00
Bullion and exchange	2,058 00
Dividends Nos. 7 and 8	7,500 00
General expenses	5,859 00
Miscellaneous items	11,667 00
Due from sundry debtors	2,232 00
Total	131,899 00

The above receipts include the March assessment of $20 per share. Two dividends, of $7 50 per share each, were disbursed during the year. The disbursements on mill account include $17,563 for labor and $19,000 for wood. The assets of the company on the first instant amounted to $13,038; liabilities, $9,123—leaving a surplus above assets of $3,915. On the first of January, 1868, there was 124 tons ore on the dumps; amount raised during the year, 6,295 tons; amount crushed, 6,080 tons; on the dumps on the first instant, 339 tons. The amount of bullion produced from the above ore was upwards of 40,000 ounces. The average cost of raising the ore was $4 93 per ton; average cost of crushing, $10 65; average yield per ton, $16 70. The superintendent thinks 2,000 tons of pay ore can yet be taken from the upper chambers, and that by the time this ore is worked up deeper levels will be available.

Report of the Yellow Jacket Company for the year ending June 30, 1868.

RECEIPTS.

Balance at last annual report	$116,086 54
Assessments—No. 9, October, 1867	120,000 00
No. 10, November, 1867	120,000 00
No. 11, January, 1868	150,000 00
Bullion 34,718 tons of ore, averaging $19 50	676,861 39
Ores sold	5,142 51
Profits of Morgan mill	40,821 98
Hoisting ore for Kentuck company	10,896 90
Cash received for advertising assessments	776 02
Total	1,240,585 34

DISBURSEMENTS.

Dividend No. 13	$90,000 00
Labor at mine	294,833 02
Reduction—Outside mills	254,228 16
Reduction—Company's mill	263,415 42
Legal expenses	14,848 88
Wood for mine	45,431 72

Timber and lagging	$62,070 10
Improvements at south hoisting works	45,368 26
Assay fees, discounts, and bullion tax	21,801 51
Salaries of officers	20,303 33
Mine supplies, candles, oil, iron, &c.	38,717 08
General expenses	29,142 36
Sundries	11,176 37
Balance to credit of company over all liabilities	49,249 13
Total	1,240,585 34

LIABILITIES.

Bills payable	$38,671 86
Dividends uncalled for	2,575 00
Balance due mills	23,179 12
Sundry accounts	2,396 01
Balance to credit of company	49,249 13
Total	116,071 12

ASSETS.

Cash in Bank of California	$104,724 17
Sundry accounts	7,314 80
Morgan mill supplies	2,904 18
Mine supplies	302 97
Assessment on one foot unissued stock	825 00
Total	116,071 12

Report of the Hale and Norcross Company for the year ending February 29, 1868.

RECEIPTS.

Cash on hand March 31, 1867	$133,288 99
Assessment No. 30	60,000 00
Ore account, 25,546 tons	865,925 45
Premium on bullion	6,826 46
Other receipts	82,483 71
Total	1,148,524 61

DISBURSEMENTS.

Ore account—reduction	$360,105 63
Dividend account	300,000 00
Fair shaft	212,684 85
Mine account	207,654 92
Sundry accounts	67,895 28
Cash on hand	183 93
Total	1,148,524 61

ASSETS.

Cash, net value of ore on hand, &c.	$16,907 88
Property	172,458 16
Total	189,366 04
Liabilities	69,960 38
Excess over liabilities	119,405 66

The average product of ore reduced up to the first of February was $34 14 per ton, or 65⅛ per cent. of the mine assay.

Report of the Kentuck Company for the year ending November 21, 1868.

RECEIPTS.

Cash on hand November 21, 1867	$20,365 03
Bullion	1,255,485 54
Premium on bullion	4,232 45
Total	1,280,083 02

DISBURSEMENTS.

Dividends, Nos. 15 to 26	450,000 00
Crushing ores	448,323 60
Labor	161,203 62
Timber	54,378 55
Wood	12,114 05
Mine expenses and supplies	25,194 45
Assays	12,979 75
Hoisting ores	17,544 46
Other expenses	34,122 33
Cash on hand November 21, 1868	63,862 21
Total	1,280,083 02

From November 1, 1867, to November 1, 1868, 31,390¼ tons of ore were reduced, showing an average yield of $40 06 per ton. The average cost per ton was $23 65, showing a net yield of $16 41.

Report of the Crown Point Company for the year ending May 1, 1868.

RECEIPTS.

Cash on hand May 1, 1867	$57,051 30
Bullion	866,028 60
Assessments	60,000 00
Other receipts	25,115 14
Total	1,008,195 04

DISBURSEMENTS.

Dividends	48,000 00
Mining expense	256,744 34
Milling expense—company	162,116 27
Milling expense—outside mills	175,941 57
Legal expense	75,994 18
Mill and mine improvement	104,064 00
Salaries, rent, &c.	22,573 06
Taxes, assaying, &c.	31,479 07
Cash in treasury May 1, 1868	127,082 55
Total	1,008,195 04

The assets of the company are stated at $294,765. The following is a comparison of this and the previous year:

Year ending—	Tons mined.	Cost of mining.	Cost of milling.	Bullion receipts.	Dividends.
May 1, 1868	25,964	$9 85	$11 82 (company.) 14 90 (custom.)	$866,028 60	$48,000
May 1, 1867	34,750	7 50	....	1,247,938 47	372,000

Report of the Imperial Company for the year ending May 31, 1868.

RECEIPTS.

Cash on hand May 31, 1867	$36,606 62
Bullion	893,554 27
Tailings, &c.	3,553 75
Sundries	39,664 74
Total	973,379 38

DISBURSEMENTS.

Dividend	120,000 00
Alta mine	170,840 74
Holmes mine	42,039 08
Rock Point mill	299,800 82
Imperial Empire shaft	107,907 24
Rock Point mill-dam	94,506 85
Sundries	21,486 74
Cash on hand May 31, 1868	83,835 40
Total	973,379 38

From the date of incorporation, March, 1863, to the close of this fiscal year the receipts of the company have amounted to $4,625,069 33, of which $4,535,388 26 was for ores and sundries sold. The dividends amount in all to $1,043,500, and the assessments to $50,000.

Report of the Chollar-Potosi Company for the year ending May 31, 1868.

Amount of ore extracted from the mine, 70,330½ tons, of which 29,792 tons came from the third Santa Fé station, and 15,671 from the Blue Wing. The total quantity of ore milled was 77,957¼ tons, and the following figures will illustrate the cost of production:

Average yield per ton		$24 14
Cost of milling per ton	$14 75	
Actual cost of extracting per ton	4 24	
Filling mine and dead work per ton extracted	33⅓	
Taxes per ton	22½	
Expenses at new works per ton	1 87	
Incidentals per ton	26	
		21 68
Net yield per ton		2 46

The amount expended for account of new shaft was $131,835 86. In the old mine, as nearly as can be calculated, there are 33,000 tons of ore that will afford a small margin over expense of mining and milling. The new shaft penetrated the west wall at a depth of 913 feet from the surface. Here a station has been made, and an incline at an angle of 45° has been driven to the extent of 266 feet. Two stations have been made in the incline—one at 1,000 and the other at 1,100 feet, leaving 247 feet of unprospected ground overhead. They are about to drift east from the 1,100 level, and the incline will be continued down to another station. These deep driftings are of great importance, as upon their favorable development depends the success of the company in the future.

RECEIPTS.

Balance on hand per last statement	$108,947 21
Bullion product	1,873,306 18
Ore sold	32,115 31
Assessment account	182,000 00
Sundries	5,259 36
Total	2,201,628 06

DISBURSEMENTS.

Dividends	$353,200 00
Labor	320,821 07
Timber and lumber	109,723 91
Taxes	19,268 69
Reduction	1,135,203 96
Freight account	22,259 60
Sundries	131,002 48
Cash on hand at date	110,148 35
Total	2,201,628 06

As a fair specimen of the general rates of expense in mining items, I present this company's condensed statement of production, expenses, work, &c., for the fiscal year ending May 31, 1868:

	First class.	Third class.	Total.
Ore produced—	*Tons.*	*Tons.*	*Tons.*
Extracted by company	9.36	70,330.9	
Extracted by Lynch and Eureka mill		16,125.3	
Extracted from croppings and waste dumps		9,528.8	
	9.36	95,985.0	95,994 36
Ore reduced for company's account		77,957.28	
Ore sold		15,173.39	
Ore remaining on hand May 31, 1868		555.97	93,686.64
Cost per ton of ore extracted—			
Extracting ore	$4 24.0		
New shaft, sinking, repairing, &c	1 29.6		
Prospecting	75.8		
Filling mine	15.4		
Incidentals	48.2	$6 93	
Reduction		14 75	$21 68
Average yield of ore worked			24 14
	Gold.	*Silver.*	*Total.*
Average value of bullion per ounce	0 73.52	1 24.15	1 97.67
Average fineness of bullion	0 35.5	0.960.24	995.74
Average proportion of metals per cent.	37.2	62.8	100.00

Drifts, winzes, &c., run, or sunk—
New works—278½ feet shaft sunk—total depth 930 feet.
241 feet incline sunk.
106 feet winze sunk.
1,278 feet drift run.
Old works—3,083 feet drift run.
188 feet winze sunk.

Work of assay office—

Ounces of bullion assayed before melting	673,595.82
Ounces of bullion assayed after melting	744,848.57
Average loss in melting	2.95
Number of ore assays made	2,567

Cost of assaying, excluding all returns from ashes, sweepings, and slag—

Gold per bar	$2 00
Silver per centum	357-1000 per cent
Gold and silver per centum	3-10 per cent.
Ore assays	50 cents.

Materials purchased and consumed from July 1, 1867, to May 1, 1868.

Articles.	Stock.		Consumed.		Average per ton of ore extracted.	Quantity sold.	Stock on hand May 31, 1868.*
	On hand July 1, 1867.	Purchased.	Quantity.	Value.			
Timber ....feet..	171,000	2,736,892	2,212,902	$61,483 60	1.06	192,820	501,170
Candles ....boxes..	225	1,085	1,218	6,495 50	.112	44	48
Wood ....cords..	150	1,138½	946⅝	13,108 08	.226	14 9-16	327 9-16
Charcoal ....bushels..	3,700	7,060	10,361	3,768 85	.065	50	349
Coal....pounds..	....	8,140	7,803	345 99	.005	....	337
Iron ....do....	18,000	22,133	32,853	4,134 88	.071	....	7,280
Steel....do....	2,000	1,943	2,989	988 56	.017	....	954
Powder ....kegs..	39	106	132	617 12	.011	....	13
Pick handles	178	988	1,039	612 58	.011	....	127
Sledge handles....	96	222	316	176 25	.003	2	....
Shovels	170	233	381	663 84	.011	15	7
Sledges	12	4	16	84 00	.012	....	....
Fuze ....feet..	5,000	14,000	18,600	532 21	.002	....	1,000
Nails ....pounds..	1,000	15,816	15,886	1,498 12	.026	300	630
Files, assorted	26	411	417	211 26	.004	2	18
Axes	9	44	49	112 75	.002	1	4
Saws, assorted....	2	15	17	80 25	....	....	....
Wheelbarrows....	4	29	33	328 00	.005	....	....
Brooms....	19	30	46	42 75	....	....	3
Leather ....pounds..	35	128	107	33 25	....	....	56
Canvas ....yards..	65	213½	246½	246 50	.004	....	32
Lard oil ....gallons..	60	360	415	691 17	.012	....	5
Car oil ....do....	70	405	315	349 70	.006	....	160
Coal oil ....do....	50	695	730	626 46	.011	....	15
Nut oil....do....	....	100	100	130 00	.002	....	....
Tallow ....pounds..	300	3,256	2,476	298 97	.005	....	1,080
Car wheels....sets..	4	1	5	....	....	....	....
Car axles ....do....	4	1	5	154 00	.003	....	....
Gum packing ....pounds..	....	328	281	408 40	.007	....	47
Tar ....gallons..	10	265	265	319 50	.005	....	10
Rope, Manilla....pounds..	....	10,150½	10,150½	2,077 67	.04	....	....
Rope, wire....feet..	....	4,800	4,800	6,689 09	....	....	....
Rope, bell-wire....do....	....	4,000	4,000	93 80	....	....	....
Sundries	$948 50	$8,366 54	$8,975 46	8,975 46	.155	....	$587 00
Total....	....	....	....	116,378 56	1.893		

* Value, $26,083 66.

General expenses.

Month.	Extracting ore.	New shaft.		Old works.		Incidentals.*	Third class ore produce.		Average cost per ton, gross expense.	Paid for milling.	Third class ore worked.		Average cost per ton, milling.
		Sinking and repairing.	Prospecting.	Filling mine.	Dead work.		Tons.	lbs.			Tons.	lbs.	
June, 1867	$40, 498 19	$3, 685 75	$4, 462 40	....	....	$54, 635 41	12, 077	1, 430	$4 52	$185, 242 50	12, 349	1, 900	$15 00
July, 1867	36, 049 79	4, 951 31	3, 563 52	....	....	50, 153 00	9, 222	1, 430	5 43	168, 317 85	11, 220	1, 750	15 00
August, 1867	40, 078 31	4, 605 42	5, 348 34	$2, 876 00	....	61, 929 22	9, 994	1, 620	6 19	186, 215 47	12, 414	710	15 00
September, 1867	38, 343 12	3, 644 22	5, 499 29	....	$1, 322 50	58, 012 46	10, 497	1, 980	5 52	169, 308 57	11, 287	630	15 00
October, 1867	32, 110 06	4, 305 70	5, 673 37	269 50	....	52, 575 33	7, 151	430	7 35	122, 733 02	8, 182	430	15 00
November, 1867	28, 250 08	3, 089 63	5, 936 55	1, 335 00	....	42, 113 74	6, 631	160	6 35	108, 725 10	7, 248	690	15 00
December, 1867	28, 227 80	4, 475 72	5, 923 79	5, 923 00	3, 682 00	53, 087 97	5, 762	140	9 21	45, 996 40	3, 538	370	13 00
January, 1868	15, 693 42	4, 884 46	4, 366 00	440 00	1, 220 00	29, 024 93	2, 164	1, 890	13 41	40, 313 40	2, 849	1, 610	14 14
February, 1868	8, 169 12	6, 046 45	....	....	1, 800 00	17, 003 46	574	570	29 60	31, 224 75	2, 081	1, 300	15 00
March, 1868	7, 466 23	10, 661 47	....	....	2, 642 00	24, 966 28	847	1, 740	29 47	18, 300 00	1, 220		15 00
April, 1868	10, 933 91	8, 798 23	....	....	1, 854 00	23, 433 66	2, 176	1, 730	10 81	32, 817 15	2, 397	1, 620	13 68
May, 1868	12, 502 05	7, 038 97	....	....	112 00	20, 848 47	3, 229	680	6 46	40, 991 15	3, 167	450	12 94
Total	298, 322 08	66, 187 33	40, 773 26	10, 843 50	12, 632 50	487, 783 93	70, 330	1, 800	....	1, 150, 185 36	77, 957	560	....
Average per ton of ore	4 24	94	58	15. 4	18	....	....		6 93	....	....		14 75

* Analyzed below.

Analysis of the items included under incidentals.

Months.	Machinery and repairs.	Freight.	Legal.	Surveying.	Stable.	Taxes.	Exchange.	Office and house repairs.	Sundries.
1867.									
June	$511 54	$310 23	$110 50	$100 00	$146 38	$3,537 97	$467 45	$133 25	$671 75
July	36 64	980 85	....	100 00	269 00	2,740 74	472 50	637 40	351 25
August	2,659 19	210 00	20 00	100 00	129 70	3,088 98	427 50	527 07	1,858 71
September	5,556 77	18 85	15 00	100 00	119 50	1,861 96	461 25	57 00	1,013 00
October	5,783 62	1,462 00	97 60	100 00	273 05	1,010 74	348 75	71 20	1,069 74
November	906 15	18 30	5 50	100 00	30 90	1,919 07	331 16	150 90	40 50
December	3,373 43	21 75	7 50	100 00	369 16	459 00	281 25	117 27	126 30
1868.									
January	878 27	500 70	....	100 00	....	245 88	236 25	127 95	332 00
February	62 00	....	....	100 00	66 45	201 07	146 25	25 37	380 75
March	2,024 17	....	1,507 50	100 00	35 45	178 01	157 50	174 03	19 62
April	1,063 72	267 27	85 00	100 00	....	74 82	185 62	11 59	59 50
May	....	167 40	150 00	100 00	16 00	565 12	56 25	....	140 68
Total	22,855 50	3,957 35	4,998 60	1,200 00	1,455 89	15,884 36	3,571 73	2,033 03	6,069 80
Average per ton of ore	$0 32.5	$0 05.6	$0 02.8	$0 01.7	$0 02	$0 22.6	$0 05	$0 03	$0 08.5

Statement showing cost of reducing ore and bullion produced from June 1, 1867, to May 31, 1868.

Months.	Ore, third class, worked.		Cost of producing bullion.				Returns from ore worked.				Net returns of bullion.	Average per ton of third class ore.			
			Milling.	Internal revenue tax, (bullion.)	State and county taxes, (ore.)	Total.	Third class ore, bullion.	Net returns, first class ore.	Reclamation.	Total.		Cost of milling.	Taxes.	Gross yield.	Net yield.
1867.	*Tons.*	*lbs.*													
June	12, 349	1, 000	$185, 242 50	$1, 651 87	$1, 508 70	$188, 403 07	$345, 991 89	$5, 551 78	....	$351, 543 67	$163, 140 60	$15 00	22c.	$28 01	$12 79
July	11, 220	1, 750	168, 317 85	1, 537 48	1, 197 87	171, 053 20	310, 917 47	....	$750 00	311, 667 47	140, 614 27	15 00	24	27 78	12 54
August	12, 414	710	186, 215 47	1, 676 57	1, 386 09	189, 278 13	349, 286 00	....	5, 600 15	354, 886 15	165, 608 02	15 00	25	28 57	13 32
September	11, 287	630	169, 308 57	1, 261 09	520 08	171, 089 74	252, 258 34	....	1, 410 00	253, 668 34	82, 578 60	15 00	16	22 47	7 31
October	8, 182	430	122, 733 02	809 66	180 20	123, 723 18	164, 976 67	....	2 294 00	167, 270 67	43, 547 49	15 00	12	20 04	5 32
November	7, 248	690	108, 725, 10	720 10	122 54	109, 567 74	142, 724 29	....	3, 696 25	146, 420 54	36, 852 80	15 09	11¼	20 20	5 09
December	3, 534	370	45, 996 40	345 75	84 25	46, 426 40	71, 446 17	634 45	....	72, 080 62	25, 654 22	13 00	12	20 22	7 10
1868.															
January	2, 849	1, 610	40, 313 40	227 11	....	40, 540 51	46, 282 10	....	572 90	46, 855 00	6, 314 49	14 14	08	16 44	2 36
February	2, 081	1, 300	31, 224 75	148 29	9 60	31, 382 84	38, 690 28	....	21 75	38, 715 03	7, 332 19	15 00	08	18 58	3 50
March	1, 220	......	18, 300 00	167 87	....	18, 467 87	26, 634 99	....	....	26, 634 99	8, 167 12	15 00	14	21 83	6 69
April	2, 397	1, 620	32, 817 15	....	44 78	32, 861 93	46, 676 05	....	465 35	47, 141 40	14, 279 47	13 68	02	19 66	5 96
May	3, 167	450	40, 991 15	....	86 80	41, 077 95	64, 818 75	....	....	64, 818 75	23, 740 80	12 94	02¾	20 47	7 50
Total	77, 957	560	1, 150, 185 36	8, 545 79	5, 141 41	1, 163, 872 56	1, 860, 703 00	6, 186 23	14, 813 40	1, 881, 702 63	717, 830 07	14 75	19	24 07	9 13

Analysis of mine costs and returns, as paid and received at the Virginia office, June 1 1867, to May 31, 1868.

Month.	MINE COST.												
	Milling ore.	Wages.	Timber and lumber.	Firewood.	Charcoal.	Miscellaneous supplies.	Machinery and repairs.	Taxes.	Water.	Surveying.	Freight.	Assay office.	Exchange.
June, 1867	$185, 242 50	$33, 204 24	$14, 215 89	$2, 075 62	$841 40	$1, 167 28	$511 54	$1, 696 78	$307 50	$100 00	$310 23	$839 16	$467 45
July, 1867	168, 317 85	31, 054 85	15, 522 33	2, 072 00	802 20	1, 766 38	36 64	2, 029 27	307 50	100 00	980 85	888 15	472 50
August, 1867	186, 215 47	36, 155 75	22, 152 66		348 60	2, 382 56	39 50	5, 143 26	307 50	100 00	210 00	951 77	427 50
September, 1867	154, 331 32	33, 652 62	23, 321 71	9, 547 11	350 00	1, 943 48	220 20	1, 682 89	307 50	100 00	18 85	933 72	461 25
October, 1867	137, 710 27	28, 600 12	9, 453 48	3, 224 09	399 00	3, 269 87	529 13	1, 266 88	307 50	100 00	1, 462 00	711 32	348 75
November, 1867	108, 725 10	26, 196 62	9, 339 38	1, 612 59	443 80	1, 918 95	574 00	4, 918 42	307 50	100 00	18 30	829 10	331 16
December, 1867	45, 596 40	26, 755 36	1 395 59	366 87		1, 779 94	168 10	732 30	307 50	100 00	21 75	425 00	281 25
January, 1868	33, 484 40	18, 347 60	110 71	73 00		1, 740 77	878 27	345 75	307 50	100 00	500 70	425 00	236 25
February, 1868	28, 510 00	13, 050 00	68 78			1, 491 95	62 00	227 11	307 50	100 00		360 00	146 25
March, 1868	28, 243 75	14, 869 24	165 89			1, 238 99	194 10	626 92	307 50	100 00		226 88	157 50
April, 1868	32, 817 15	15, 671 08	601 71			1, 171 14	690 72	167 24	307 50	100 00	267 27	205 00	185 62
May, 1868	40, 991 15	14, 748 87	3, 084 03		127 40	1, 091 15		431 87	307 50	100 00	167 40	224 00	56 25
Total	1, 150, 185 36	292, 306 35	99, 432 15	18, 971 28	3, 312 40	20, 962 46	4, 904 20	19, 278 69	3, 690 00	1, 200 00	3, 957 35	7, 019 10	3, 571 73
Average per ton	$14 75	$4 14	$1 40	27 cts.	4 cts.	27 cts.	7 cts.	27 cts.	5 cts.	1¼ ct.	5 cts.	10 cts.	5 cts.

Month.	MINE COST—Continued.							MINE RETURNS.						
	Stationery & reven'e stamps.	Repairs of house.	Filling mine.	Horse keeping.	Legal.	Sundries.	Total.	Bullion.	Reclamation.	Ore sales.	Timber.	House rent.	Sundries.	Total.
June, 1867	$30 25	$103 00		$146 38	$110 50	$671 75	$242, 041 47	$351, 543 67				$75 00	$359 63	$351, 978 30
July, 1867	55 65	581 75		269 00		351 25	225, 608 17	311, 681 17	$750 00	$1, 500 00	$1, 038 41		304 25	315, 273 83
August, 1867	66 45	460 62		129 70	20 00	414 95	255, 526 29	350, 599 62	5, 600 15	548 00		150 00	91 50	356, 989 27
September, 1867		57 00		119 50	15 00	1, 013 00	228, 075 15	253, 866 89	1, 410 00	1, 906 05				257, 183 94
October, 1867	71 20		$269 50	273 05	97 60	1, 069 74	190, 163 50	164, 976 67	2, 294 02	2, 392 36		75 00	10, 150 00	179, 888 03
November, 1867	43 91	106 99	1, 335 00	30 90	5 50	40 50	156, 877 72	145, 977 49	3, 696 25	3, 551 78	580 96	75 00	411 68	154, 293 16
December, 1867	17 27	100 00	5, 411 00	369 16	7 50	126 30	83, 961 29	72, 080 62		2, 482 99	518 04	150 00	195 50	75, 427 15
January, 1868	36 20	91 75	440 00	66 45		332 00	57, 449 89	46, 436 10	572 90	1, 668 45	504 36		164 50	49, 346 31
February, 1868	25 37			35 75		386 75	44, 802 16	38, 690 28	24 75	2, 931 58	532 96	125 00	277 50	42. 582 07
March, 1868	26 38	147 65			1, 507 50	19 62	47, 867 67	26, 634 99		905 02	890 40	50 00	348 50	28, 828 91
April, 1868	11 59				85 00	59 50	52, 340 52	46, 676 05	465 35	2, 670 39			94 48	49, 906 27
May, 1868	37 02			16 00	150 00	140 68	61, 673 32	64, 818 75		6, 707 56	2, 225 09		621 44	74, 402 84
Total	421 29	1, 648 76	7, 455 50	1, 455 89	1, 998 60	4, 626 04	1, 646, 386 15	1, 873, 982 30	14, 813 40	27, 264 18	6, 320 22	700 00	13, 018 98	1, 936, 099 08
Average per ton		2 cts.	10 cts.	2 cts.	2 cts.	6 cts.								

EXTRACTING ORE.

Month.	Ore, third class, extracted.		Wages.	Miscellaneous supplies.	Timber and lumber.	Firewood.	Charcoal.	Water.	Ore assays.	Total.	Average cost.	
	Tons.	Pounds.									Per ton of ore extracted.	Per cent. of yield of rock.
June, 1867	1,277	1,430	$27,737 19	$2,560 00	$8,749 00	$1,170 00	$127 00	$155 00	....	$40,498 19	$3 35	11.96
July, 1867	9,222	1,430	25,191 87	2,327 47	7,210 95	1,087 50	....	155 00	$77 00	36,049 79	3 90	14.05
August, 1867	9,994	1,620	25,915 75	2,560 00	10,290 06	1,000 00	....	155 00	157 50	40,078 31	4 01	14.05
September, 1867	10,497	1,980	26,962 12	2,313 76	7,410 99	1,200 00	211 25	157 50	87 50	38,342 12	3 66	16.29
October, 1867	7,151	430	22,880 62	2,199 50	5,602 44	980 00	200 00	157 50	90 00	32,110 06	4 51	20.08
November, 1867	6,631	160	20,614 87	1,621 50	4,608 71	1,050 00	100 00	157 50	97 50	28,250 08	4 26	20.89
December, 1867	5,762	140	16,808 11	4,103 30	6,051 39	877 50	140 00	157 50	90 00	28,227 80	4 89	24.18
January, 1868	2,164	1,890	10,636 00	1,111 13	2,648 79	945 00	105 00	157 50	90 00	15,693 42	7 26	44.16
February, 1868	574	570	5,912 00	637 72	941 40	308 00	105 00	157 50	107 50	8,169 12	14 23	76.54
March, 1868	847	1,740	5,046 49	622 42	899 82	450 00	175 00	157 50	115 00	7,466 23	8 80	40.31
April, 1868	2,176	1,730	8,040 33	577 66	1,588 92	180 00	280 00	157 50	109 55	10,913 91	5 01	25.49
May, 1868	3,229	680	9,509 87	445 45	2,187 23	*	70 00	157 50	132 50	12,502 05	3 87	18.91
Total	70,330	1,800	205,255 22	21,079 91	58,189 70	9,248 00	1,513 25	1,882 50	1,153 50	298,322 08	4 24	17.58
Average per ton of ore extracted	....	....	$2 92	$0 30	$0 83	$0 13	$0 02	$0 02½	$0 01½	....	$4 24	17.58

* All ore run out by way of tunnel.

CHAPTER VI.

ORMSBY, WASHOE AND CHURCHILL COUNTIES.

The following letters, addressed to Surveyor General A. P. R. Safford, of Virginia City, who kindly made inquiries for me, will show the condition of mining for the year in the counties above mentioned:

OFFICE OF THE COUNTY ASSESSOR, ORMSBY COUNTY,
Nevada, Carson City, August 24, 1868.

DEAR SIR: Your communication of the 24th instant is before me, and contents noted. In reply I have to say that at present there are no producing mines in Ormsby county. All the ores worked in this county are from mines situated in Storey county, of which there is no such statistical information as you desire in this office.

During the years 1865 and 1866 some work was done upon the Athens mine, owned by the Athens Company, and situated in the foot-hills about three miles west of Carson City. Some 20 or 30 tons of ore were extracted from the mine and reduced at the Carson mill situated near by. Of the amount of the precious metals produced therefrom I am not informed, but believe it was not sufficient to warrant the further prosecution of work upon the mine, as since that date no work has been done.

I am, sir, very respectfully, your obedient servant,

GEORGE W. CHEDIC, *County Assessor.*
By H. H. BENCE, *Deputy.*

WASHOE, *September* 16, 1868.

DEAR SIR: Yours of August 21 came during my absence, and was mislaid and not discovered until yesterday. In reply I will state that there are no paying mines in this county. A great many experiments have been made with some galena found near the town of Washoe City, but with poor success, and no work is being done at present. In what is known as the Peavine district there is copper ore, but it has never been worked successfully, and is pretty much abandoned. No returns have been made from any mines in this county.

Yours, respectfully,

T. A. READ,
Assessor of Washoe County, Nevada.

ST. CLAIR'S STATION, CHURCHILL COUNTY, NEVADA,
September 14, 1868.

DEAR SIR: Your note of inquiry came to hand. I will say, in answer, that there are no mines working in this county this year. The report of 1866 will give you all the information that I can in regard to mines and mills in this county, except one small five-stamp mill near New Pass, in the east end of the county. The company is prospecting its ledges with favorable results. There are no quarterly reports to be made this year. The mills are all lying idle.

Yours, with respect,

C. ALLEN, *County Assessor.*

The New Pass mill, to which allusion is made in the foregoing letter, was formerly the Ware mill of Austin, and has been purchased and removed by Mr. Slauson and others, to work the ores of the New Pass district. This district, situated about 22 miles west of Austin, but on the other side of the county line, and in Churchill county, is remarkable for containing gold instead of silver ores, and for certain beds of fossiliferous limestone which I believe to be of jurassic age. The Shoshone range, forming the western boundary of Reese River valley, divides south of New Pass into two chains, which unite again north of the district. The eastern chain is called Mt. Airy, and the western New Pass. The district is not large, but very diversified in surface, and remarkably abundant in springs, timber, fine grass, and arable land. The rock is porphyry of different characters, with the beds of fossiliferous limestone above mentioned, which are broken through and underlaid by gabbro. A still more recent outbreak of pitchstone-porphyry adds another element of variety. The outcrops of gabbro are generally elliptical in form, and these contain the veins, which mostly strike north 30° to 45° west, and dip 60° to 80° northeast, are six inches to six feet wide, and have as gangue exclusively quartz, carrying native gold (very fine-grained,) argentiferous galena, enclosing native gold, and iron pyrites, sulphuret of copper, malachite and azurite, all containing gold. The lodes consist of the Golden Belt series; the Lake series (including the Superior, Ontario, Huron, and Erie,) the Ingoldsby, the Central, the Churchill, and the Oriental. I visited the district last summer, and was much impressed with its advantages. I have not since heard of the results of the treatment of the ores in the mill. All or nearly all the veins above named belong to the same company.

CHAPTER VI.

LANDER COUNTY.

Reese River district.—This district has been frequently and fully described, and I propose to offer, not a detailed account of the different mines, but a few general remarks concerning the results of seven years' experience. Having been familiar with the history of the district, I can speak with greater confidence.

The rich veins of Lander Hill have always been known to be very narrow, rarely more than two feet in width, and only in brilliant instances carrying a "pay-streak" of more than six inches. At the same time they are unmistakably fissure-veins—perhaps the most distinct specimens of that class in all the west. They show very clearly the manner in which their fissures were filled, by successive depositions of quartz, manganese spar, silver ore, &c., along their walls. The seams in the granite of Lander Hill are very numerous and very close together; and on the surface one looks as promising as another. Almost all of the thousands of outcrops which have been located here carried rich chloride ore in pockets or streaks. It was inevitable, therefore, that in the beginning both the miners and experts sent to examine the veins should consider them as generally of equal value. Some praised them all alike; others condemned them all alike. The first step of progress was the distinction made between the veins in granite and those in slate, and between the northwest and southeast veins and the north and south ones. The veins running northwest and southeast were pronounced by experts the most valuable system. The developments of actual working have since determined several highly important facts, among which are the following:

1. It is found that the mines on the western half of Lander Hill contain in depth large quantities of base metals, which render the profitable reduction of their ores at present rates impossible. This is the case with mines which, on the surface, produced chloride of silver of great purity and richness. The Diana is an example.

2. It is found that many of the outcrops on Lander Hill do not continue as independent veins in depth. At least, in one or two instances, deep cross-cuts, underrunning the outcrops, have not exposed the veins. I believe this is owing either to the fact that these surface veins are merely spurs of persistent fissures, with which, at no great depth, they unite themselves, or to the closing of the small fissures by the weight of the hanging wall, and the partial or total obliteration of the seam by infiltration and slight decomposition of the granite. The latter seems to me most probable. The flat dip of most of the veins makes a

permanent unsupported open fissure impossible; and all the signs show that the fissures of Lander Hill, subsequent to their formation, and previous to their filling, closed up wherever it was possible, and only remained open where fragments or projecting points of the wall-rock prevented them from closing.

3. It is found that all the veins of the eastern and richer part of Lander Hill have been obliquely cut off in depth by cross-seams, and that the whole country rock, above these seams, has slid southward carrying with it the upper portions of the veins. It seems likely that there are one or two great slides common to all the mines of this group; but this point is not fully established. It is certain, however, that the veins are cut off at various depths, and must be sought again by northeastward cross-cuts, below the faults.

4. It is believed that the distance to which the upper portion of a vein has been heaved is often greater than the distance on the surface between the outcrops of two veins; consequently, when the miner drives his cross-tunnel to find again the downward continuation of his vein, he may strike first the vein of a neighbor; and it is extremely difficult, in view of the great similarity mineralogically, and the great variability in size, of the Lander Hill veins, to decide which is the continuation in depth of a given vein, cut off by a cross-seam. This difficulty can be illustrated to every mind by a simple experiment. Take a card and draw across it several parallel oblique lines, not of uniform thickness, but bulging and narrowing, as when the pressure upon the pen is made alternately heavy and light. Let the lines be, say, half an inch apart. They will then answer to represent cross-sections of different parallel veins. Now cut the card in two, along an oblique line nearer to the horizontal than that of the veins, and slide the upper half of the card down hill, as it were, for one inch. The new position of the lines will represent a section of the veins after the slide; and the difficulty of deciding (without knowing exactly how far the upper portion has moved) "which is which," is sufficiently evident. This is the precise nature of the difficulty on Lander Hill. There is scarcely a producing mine on the hill which is not working a vein claimed by some one else; and the question of title is generally settled by the financial position of the parties. Rich and prosperous companies hold their ground. In cases where both parties have capital, the struggle is likely to be prolonged unless they wisely compromise at the outset. The root of the trouble is the absurd and unreasonable nearness to one another of the Lander Hill locations. The United States law can scarcely be applied, and if it could, would not help the matter. There is no help for it, except the gradual acquirement, by a few strong companies, of the whole of the hill. These companies should then unite to construct a tunnel from Clifton to Mount Prometheus, cutting their veins at a depth of 1,000 or more feet. The tunnel scheme is now in the hands of energetic men, who, if they carry it through, will claim all the veins they cut, and thus a new element of chaos will be added.

The foregoing remarks as to the nearness of locations and the slides in the veins, are partially illustrated by the rough sketch here given of the portion of Lander Hill now producing ore. But a very small portion of the locations is shown on the sketch. They are frequently only 50 feet apart. The distance between the two shafts of the Manhattan (about 500 feet) shows how far the North Star and Oregon ledges of that company have been thrown by the slide. The North Star is cut by the lower shaft at the depth of 310 feet, and it is supposed to cross the upper at not more than 460 feet. If the vein were restored to its original position, the two shafts cutting it would probably be less than 200 feet apart.

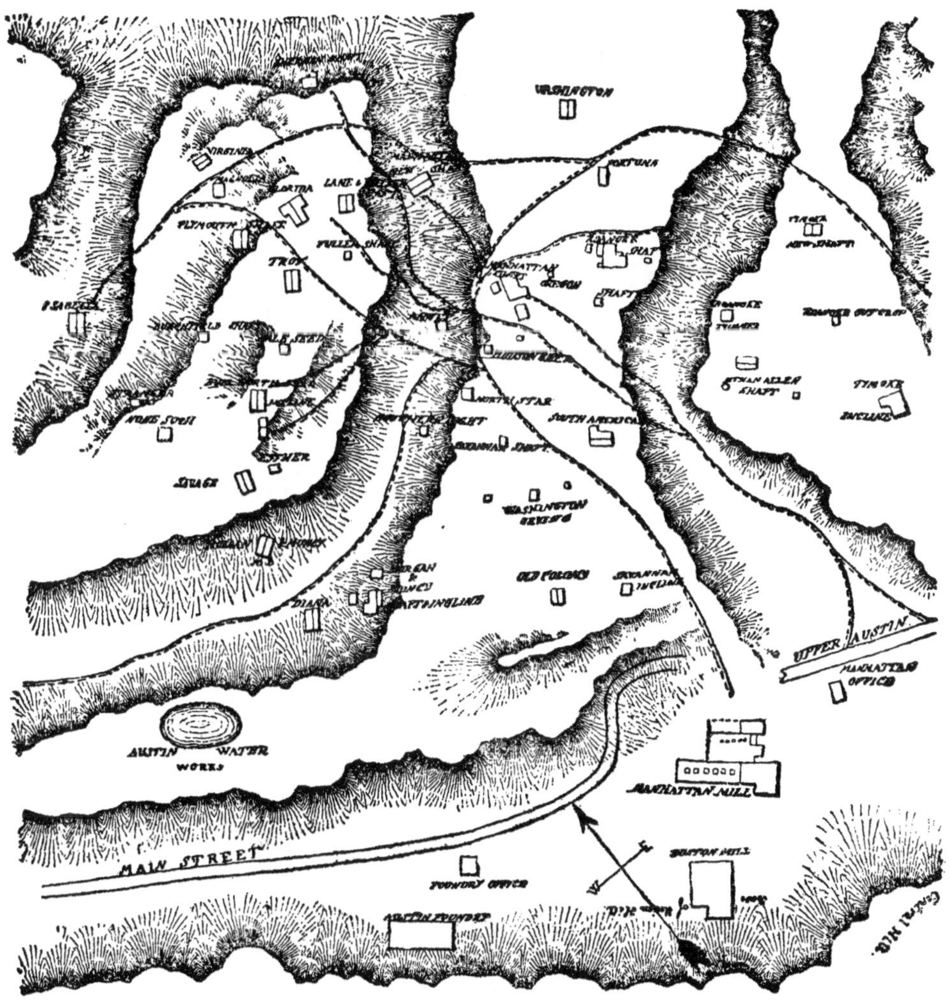

Topographical sketch showing the locations of the principal mines of that portion of Lander Hill now producing ore

5. It is found that the veins of Lander Hill frequently "pinch," and contain large barren intervals, sometimes only showing a clay seam where the vein should be. This is a disastrous peculiarity *for mining on the present system of small ownerships.* The profits of the bonanza are wasted in the administration of the mine, and there is nothing saved for the period of dead work in exploration. None of the mines have extensive reserves. But on the other hand, these narrow but persistent veins may be followed in the firm faith that they will widen again and contain ore. What is needed is a proper system for prospecting work, reducing it to its lowest cost.

6. There is a great deal of low-grade ore not sent to mill. Small as the veins are, their product is still further reduced by wasteful sorting. The rich ore only is sent to mill, and has, therefore, to bear the cost of the whole extraction. Of course the second class ore is made all the poorer by such handling, (the average of the whole being reduced,) and is less likely than ever to be profitably reduced. Concentration of the dry pulp, so as to give a rich product for roasting and amalgamation, if it could be successfully carried out, would work a great and beneficial change in the management of the mines. A great many persons (see Mr. Browne's last report, page 401, note) seem to think the *cost* of the ordinary concentration is what prevents its use in Reese river, and not to be aware that it is the actual loss of silver ore in the operation which renders the use of concentration by water impossible. This loss sometimes amounts to 80 per cent. At the Comstock mines there are extensive sluices and other apparatus for catching and concentrating tailings, but the lightest portion of all, which floats further than the tailings themselves, is the sulphurets of silver. The desideratum is a dry concentrator. The particles of sulphurets are specifically heavier than quartz; it is their shape and fineness which make them float in water. But the thinner medium, air, if properly employed, might give better results. I have never heard of dry concentrators being tested in Nevada, but I presume they will be tried before long.

7. The necessity of roasting the ores with salt before amalgamation is a serious addition to the cost of treatment. Mining and milling cost subtracted, there is no margin of profit, in most cases, on ore which assays less than $75. This is the real secret of the high milling results from Reese River ores, so often boastingly compared with those of Washoe. Mining is never on a sound and prosperous footing until low-grade ores are successfully reduced. Even on the Comstock vein, as I have shown, this is not the case to such an extent as might be wished; but in eastern Nevada the waste of low-grade ores is still greater. In a certain sense the high yield per ton reported from these districts is a measure of the wastefulness of mining. It represents, *not the average quality of the vein-matter, but the quality of that portion of it which is rich enough to pay for milling.* These remarks do not at present apply to White Pine; but there is little doubt that, sooner or later, the profits of mining, even there, will depend upon the cost of reduction and the treatment of low-grade ores. I have already spoken of concentration as a possible cure for this evil; and it remains to be added that any reduction of mining or milling cost will sensibly increase the amount of ore reduced in Reese River and similar districts. The gradual fall in wages and living expenses will do something; and among inventions for the saving of expense the new chloridizing furnace of Mr. Stetefeldt promises to be highly beneficial. It saves a great deal of the cost of roasting, and, what is even more important, a part of the saving is in fuel—the scarcity of which in Nevada, and the disastrous consequences of its exhaustion, are not to be measured by its present money value.

8. I do not see any reason to believe that the resources of Reese River district are exhausted. On the contrary, they have but just been skimmed. Not a single mine is deep enough to be upon the undisturbed and settled portion of its vein. At the same time, it is evident that a consolidation of properties and a new and more economical system of mining will be required for the adequate future development of the district.

The principal producing mines at the present time are the Manhattan North Star, the Buel North Star, the South American, and one or two others. The old Yankee Blade, in Yankee Blade cañon, three miles north of Austin, has been reopened with success; and the Chase mine, one mile further north, supposed to be the same as the Tuolumne vein in Yankee Blade cañon, is producing rich ore in small quantities, and is being gradually developed for systematic working.

The valleys of Nevada.—Like a great many other so-called deserts, the great American desert is not so bad as it is painted. There are spots in it which seem to be forsaken alike of nature and of man; but a greater part of the sage-brush country—even the alkali country—is inhabitable, and capable of sustaining a rural population. Nevada, in an agricultural point of view, perhaps at present the most forbidding of all the States, will ere long supply her own people with the necessaries of life.

The lands of Nevada may be divided into three classes—those which are absolutely worthless, (say one-third of the whole area;) those which could be made productive by irrigation; and those which may be occupied as ranches without irrigation. The latter class is far more abundant than a casual observer might suppose. The history of eastern Nevada furnishes a curious illustration of this fact. For the first year or two after the country was opened by the pioneers it was thought impossible to keep stock in these mountains and valleys through the winter. Now horses and cattle of all kinds are turned out for the winter, and actually fatten on the white sage and the "bunch grass." The latter is a product remarkably adapted to this climate. It starts very early—as soon as the snow disappears from the valleys—comes speedily to maturity, and, when the rains cease, wisely dries up and turns into a nutritious, standing hay. Its most useful peculiarity is the tenacity with which it clings to its seeds, which (in the variety known as sand-grass) are small, dark grains, which the Indians thresh out and convert into bread, and which cattle devour with avidity, even digging in the snow, sometimes, to obtain them. This grass grows in bunches, almost as if planted in hills; and the traveller may frequently discern at a great distance patches of these bunches, sometimes several square miles in extent, contesting with the sage-brush the occupation of the arid soil, and forming, with their light straw-color, a striking contrast to the dusty green and gray of the latter. I should think this grass might be cultivated with success on many sandy soils of the east, and would convert useless waste lands into valuable pastures. On the other hand, it is likely that winter wheat and barley would do pretty well on some of the land here, even without artificial irrigation, since they would escape the destructive effects of the dryest season. At present there are many ranches in the valleys of Nevada where stock-raising, haying, a little cultivation of grains, and a little dairy-work are carried on with success.

The topography of eastern Nevada is formed by a succession of valleys, separated by meridional ranges of mountains. In travelling eastward from Virginia City, by the overland road, the stage, for days together, alternately climbs over these ranges, or traverses, often enveloped in clouds of irritating and suffocating alkaline dust, the level lands between.

A remarkable peculiarity of these valleys is that they are not connected with one another. Each has its own water-system and its own level. Smoky valley lies much lower than Reese River valley, yet there is no water flowing from one into the other. They are rather like terraces than ordinary river valleys. Frequently they do not contain any main streams at all; when they do, it is merely the snow-water from the mountains which unites in the centre of the lower lands. All the rivers, creeks, brooks, and springs finally stop short, and "sink"—that is, spread into pools, and disappear, partly by absorption into the porous soil, and partly by the rapid co-operation induced by this dry and ever-shifting air. That evaporation has a great deal to do with this phenomenon may easily be proved. In Smoky valley, for instance, which has no river, almost all the tributaries from the mountains "sink" before they can find their way to the middle of the vast plain. One or two attain the barren honor of reaching the goal, and ignominiously disappearing in a puddle there. But riding along the road in the early morning, one will find many a musical brook of clear, cold water, rippling across the way, and, with vain ambition, attempting the passage through the desert, through which one can trace its path for miles by the livelier green of the brush, or perhaps by a scanty fringe of willows along its banks. Return in the afternoon, and the same channel will be as dry as though it had forgotten the taste of water; yet the snows above are melting abundantly, and the soil cannot absorb more at one time than another. It is the evaporation which makes the difference. The ground is covered in many places with efflorescence of alkaline salts, formerly in solution in the springs. These alkaline deposits have not been utilized, except in Humboldt county, where they furnish soda and lime fluxes for smelting. The salt-marshes, however, which are formed by the evaporation of saline springs, are eagerly occupied, and the salt is collected and sold to the quartz mills, where it is used in chloridizing the sulphuretted silver ores to prepare them for amalgamation. The manner of obtaining the salt is very simple. It is *shaved* from the smoothed surface of the ground, and packed in sacks for transportation. In a short time there is a new coating of salt on the same ground. Experience has shown that more is obtained by frequent gathering in this manner than by waiting for a greater depth of salt to accumulate. The product is, of course, not pure. It contains many alkaline salts; and, from the color which I observed in some of the flames of the reverberatories, I believe that considerable chloride of potassium is mixed with the chloride of sodium. In purchasing salt, however, the mill-men only care to know what proportion of chlorine it contains, and on this basis the price is regulated. Some of the marsh-owners, I believe, have attempted to refine their salt by boiling or by re-solution and evaporation—but I doubt whether the manufacture could be made profitable. The impurities in the salt are not known to be greatly injurious in the furnaces; and the mills would hardly be willing to pay more *in proportion* for their chlorides for the sake of getting them pure.

Cortez district lies about 60 miles northeast of Austin. In topographical and geological features, it strongly resembles Reveille district. The principal mountain chain runs north and south. It is the range east of the Toiyabe and comprises the high peak of Tenabo. The western declivity is a steep cliff of granular dolomite. Near the summit is an intercalation of quartzite more than 300 feet thick, and stretching along the range for miles. This quartzite belt was considered to be a vein by the first discoverers, and christened the Nevada Giant. It carries no ore, but both above and below it are found masses of ore similar to those of Reveille district, but on the whole not so rich in silver, and more debased with zinc, blende, galena, iron and copper pyrites. Neither are the ore masses in Cortez district so numerous. They seem to be more confined to certain zones of the dolomite. (This has hitherto been the case also in White Pine.) These bodies of ore, like those of Reveille, and, I think, of White Pine also, probably owe their origin to the formation of cavities in the dolomite, and the subsequent filling of these cavities with ore by means of mineral springs. The formation of the cavities, a frequent phenomenon in dolomite and limestone, might take place in several ways, as, for instance, through the action of carbonic acid waters, which carried away the lime as bicarbonate in solution; or by the contraction of the dolomite itself, in changing from its sedimentary to its crystalline form; or finally, by the penetration of the same solfataric (sulphurous acid) currents which began the metamorphosis of the porphyry. These gases, piercing the dolomite, may have converted portions of it into gypsum and sulphate of magnesia; and these being washed away the cavities remained. A change of conditions then took place, and while gases and silicious waters completed the transformation of the porphyry into quartzite, similar, but metalliferous, springs found their way into the cavities of the dolomite or limestone, and deposited there the metallic ores. This theory is strongly confirmed by the actual process now going on at the many hot springs of Nevada. But a thorough discussion of it would lead me too far.

The mining operations in Cortez district have not been carried on with much wisdom or economy. The Cortez company, owning some of the best deposits, has made thus far a partial failure. The district is nearly but not quite abandoned. A few men are still at work, and doubtless the completion of the railroad, which passes within some 25 miles, will stimulate a renewal of operations. There is a steady, though limited, transportation of rich ore from Cortez to Austin for reduction. As the hauling costs some $45 per ton, and the milling about $45 more, it is evident that only rich ore can be profitably handled in this way. The Saint Louis mine, next north of the Cortez, on the Nevada Giant, is steadily worked; and the ore sent to mill has regularly increased in value and quantity during the present year, as appears from the assessor's reports, according to which there were reduced in Austin, from this mine—

During the quarter ending—	Amount of ore.		Yielding in currency.
	Tons.	*pounds.*	
March 31, 1868	12	919	$4,976 37
June 30, 1868	21	1,108	10,808 90
September 30, 1868	28	162	21,214 60

It is such formations as Hot Creek, Reveille, Cortez, and White Pine, that require skilful miners, and certainly revenge themselves upon the ignorance and carelessness of those who treat the irregular ore deposits as if they were simply fissure veins. The management of mines which show at one time rich bonanza, and at another time, nothing at all, is a matter of difficulty; and when to this is added the small proprietorship of mines without capital, each man working with mingled extravagance and penuriousness his own petty claim, the certain result is disappointment.

Big Smoky district, about 12 miles from Austin, (five miles by air-line,) in a southerly direction, and in the Toiyabe range. The veins occur mainly in an apparently recent granite-porphyry, with coarse felspathic structure. They stick fast to the country rock, without selvages, so that the latter breaks out with the quartz rather than separates. There is no banded structure in the veins, or at least a very indistinct one. The silver ores are silver-copper-glance and native silver. In contact veins, between the granite-porphyry and belts of metamorphosed slates, occurs gold also, both free in the ferruginous outcrops and with pyrites in depth. Some veins in the slates, as for instance, the Big Smoky, appear to me to be merely large segregations of quartzite. Southward, towards Santa Fé, there is a zone of very steeply dipping sedimentary strata, comprising lime, dolomite, and slate. The slates contain faint remains of corals, the age of which cannot, on present evidence, be determined. The limestone contains caves of considerable size, some of which can be entered from the deep cañons which here intersect the mountains. Small crevices, one or two inches wide, in these caves contain a white or yellowish crystalline salt, soluble in water and containing nitrates of potassa, soda, and lime, and chloride of sodium. The largest streams in the Toiyabe flow through this district, and fine wood is abundant, (white pine and cedar, as well as nut pine.) No ore has yet been obtained in the district that will pay for milling at present rates. A New York company, owning the Big Smoky mine, erected at great cost a handsome 20-stamp mill at the mouth of the Birch Creek cañon, in Smoky valley. There were many tons of ore taken from the mine, (the estimate was 4,000 tons,) and supposed to be rich. If this was really the belief of the superintendent, he must have been deceived by spots of graphite in the quartz, mistaking them for silver glance. The mill has no roasting furnaces, and has never run but a few days, as the ore extracted at so much cost, and in such great quantity, was found to contain but $10 or $12 per ton. The Commercial company are at work with a long tunnel, which is to cross-cut the same ledge at a considerable depth. Of many mines which have been begun in the district, the Commercial is the only one now being worked. The rest are for the present abandoned.

Santa Fé district, about 20 miles in a direct line, south of Austin, and in the Toiyabe range, which is here very precipitous, and rises some 5,000 feet above the level of Smoky valley. The formation is slate, much broken and disturbed by dikes and masses of greenstone, basalt, and porphyry. The principal vein of the district lies in the slate, to which it conforms in dip and strike. It is a porous mass of quartz, showing no banded structure whatever, and, although cubes of iron pyrites have apparently been washed out of the outcrop by snows and rains, yet the mass is not at all ferruginous. One would hardly call such a deposit a vein. Yet this nondescript shows here and there handsome selvages and casings, and even "slickensides."* The vein matter contains fragments of slate, which often usurp the whole width of the vein. The ore of this "Veta Madre," or mother lode, as it was called, contains only gold as obtainable metal. Wonderful specimens are said to have been discovered on the surface; but they have never been found in depth. The vein outcrop is distinct for several veins, and can be seen from the stage-road in the valley below, some five miles distant. It is the only vein ever worked in the district, and, so far as I know, the only one ever discovered. (Mr. Browne's report alludes—page 414—in a general way to numerous ledges, perhaps meaning different parts of the same outcrop of the Veta Madre.)

This vein was opened by the Centenary (afterwards wittily converted by the miners into the Nary Cent) company, which also built a mill in Kingston cañon to work the ore. I am informed that the average yield

* Polished surfaces, formed by the movement of one rock upon another, and generally an indication of fissure-formation in a vein.

obtained was not more than $10 per ton, while the hauling from the mine to the mill cost about that sum. A splendid road was cut along the face of the mountain to the mine; but the ore still continued to yield less than expenses, and the company finally abandoned the mine and, I believe, removed the mill to Newark, where it has recently produced a good deal of bullion from White Pine ore. Santa Fé district contains fine timber and water. The saw-mill formerly there furnished excellent lumber. The natural advantages of the location are such that some good mining engineers do not hesitate to say the Veta Madre may yet be worked with success, the ores being reduced in Kingston cañon. Perhaps this will be the case when labor and provisions shall have grown cheaper.

Bunker Hill and Summit districts are situated on the eastern slope of the Toiyabe range, about 25 miles south of Austin, and on both sides of Big Smoky creek, which flows into Smoky valley. The geological formation is argillaceous slates, interstratified with calcareous and graphitic slates, the whole being broken and uplifted in many places by dikes of greenstone and diorite. The ledges occur in the slates, or between them and the diorite, and generally coincide with the slates in dip and strike. A few ledges run across the course of the country rock, but these are poorer in precious minerals than the others. There appears to be one mother lode in the district, with several subordinate ones parallel or only slightly divergent in course. The ores are antimonial sulphurets, chlorides, &c., combined with considerable quantities of copper and lead minerals, such as malachite, azurite, and silicate of copper, and carbonate, chloride, and sulphate of lead, with occasionally some galena. Gold occurs native in most of the ledges, and in some forms the most important constituent. Among the principal mines are the Victorine, Real del Monte, Gold Point, Phœnician, Brown, and Jackson. Much of the ore, especially in the first two, is stained with copper minerals. The porous ore from the Gold Point assays high in gold. A selected sample from this vein yielded by assay $226 12 per ton in silver, and $886 29 in gold. There is abundance of fuel in the district, and the stream flowing through the cañon on both slopes of which the mines are situated is one of the largest that enter Smoky valley.

The Sterling Silver Mining Company constructed a handsome twenty-stamp mill, run by a turbine wheel, in the mining town of Kingston, in this district. The battery is one of the best in the State, and the capacity of the reverberatories is sufficient for the stamps. This enterprise was ruined by the failure of the mines on which it was based, and the company's mill is now owned by its creditors. Half a mile below the Sterling mill is the twenty-stamp mill erected by an eastern company for the treatment of the ore from the mother-lode in the neighboring Santa Fé district. This mill also failed on account of the poverty of the ore. C. Coover, a practical mill-man, in company with others, under the name of the Bunker Hill Mining Company, afterwards erected a five-stamp mill, run by water-power, for wet crushing, without roasting. In this mill 1,000 tons of unassorted Victorine ore were worked, with an aggregate yield of $19,500. This mill has now been moved to White Pine. The ore of these districts is generally of low grade; but the large quantity in sight, and the ease with which, by means of tunnels, etc., it can be extracted, render inevitable a future recovery of the lost activity and the inauguration of a new prosperity.

Northumberland district.—This district lies in the Mootay range, which lies opposite and parallel to the Toiyabe, forming the eastern boundary of Smoky valley. The district is about 25 miles south of the overland road, and the same distance north of Belmont. The principal rocks are granite, (chloritic and syenitic,) porphyry, (generally much decomposed,) and lime. The mines occur almost exclusively in porphyry. The ores are sulphantimoniurets, (ruby silver, etc.,) with the usual products of decomposition, (chlorides, etc.,) and occasionally copper minerals, such as malachite and azurite. The principal veins are the Northumberland, Lady Cummings, and Detroit; but there are, as usual, numerous locations the value of which is unknown as yet. From the Northumberland and Lady Cummings some 20 tons of ore were sent to Austin last year, and yielded, it is said,* from $70 to $150 per ton. The Quintero Company have recently erected a ten-stamp mill, with roasting furnaces, to work ore from the Northumberland vein. The machinery was obtained by dismantling Hunt's mill at San Antonio. Considerable money was expended in miners' dwellings, etc., and the mill closed soon after starting, on account of financial embarrassments. The Northumberland is a large vein, but the ore is of low grade. Wood is abundant in this district, and water is supplied by several springs.

White Pine district was organized in 1865, but did not become the scene of successful operations until the fall and winter of 1867, when the rich mines of Treasure Hill were located. Previous to that time a company, called the Monte Cristo, was engaged, with no very flattering prospects, in the development of certain mineral veins on White Pine mountain, from which the district derives its name. It is said that an Indian, seeing the ore piled in the Monte Cristo mill, offered to make known a place where there was plenty of such material, and guided a party to Treasure Hill, sixteen miles distant, where the Hidden Treasure mine was located September 14, 1867.

The White Pine mountain, so called from the species of timber with which it is abundantly covered, is about 120 miles south of east from Austin, and 60 miles southwest from Egan cañon, a station on the overland road. It is said to be situated in latitude 39° 10′ north, and longitude 38° 30′ west. The mountain is ten or twelve miles long, and rises boldly some 2,000 feet above the level valleys, having a total altitude of perhaps 10,000 feet above the sea. On the western slope are the veins first discovered, some of which were worked by the Monte Christo Company above mentioned. They are said to have been tolerably rich, but small. Parallel with White Pine mountain, on the east, is a ridge some 1,500 feet lower, and five or six miles long, in which mineral veins occur carrying ores of silver considerably contaminated with baser metals. This is called the Base Range. Still farther east is the mountain known as Treasure Hill. It is comparatively bare of timber, about 9,000 feet above the sea, and separated by deep cañons on every side from surrounding ranges. All these mountains have a generally north and south course.

The geological formation of the district is extremely simple, resembling that of all the so-called limestone districts of Nevada. An upheaval of limestone strata by porphyry, and a subsequent metamorphosis of structure by solfataric and thermal-aqueous action, is evidently indicated. My brief examination did not extend to the minute local details of the formation, but I believe this neighborhood, when thoroughly studied, will throw much light on the geology of other districts, where the effects of these agencies are more obscure and the exposures of rock less extensive and distinct.

The limestone strata of Treasure Hill have been tilted from the east,

*See J. Ross Browne's last report, page 423.

and have a general course north and south, and a dip of about 20° west. The uppermost layers now remaining from the extensive denudation which has degraded all the mountains of Nevada form a rugged summit of limited area, which has been (strangely enough) described as "trap, but consists of highly fossiliferous limestone, containing mainly crinoids. Below this is a thin stratum of calcareous shales, colored yellow and red with iron, and beneath these again is the limestone stratum in which the rich deposits of silver ore occur. This limestone is highly siliceous, and contains little or no traces of fossils so far as I can learn at present. The eastern side of Treasure Hill is precipitous, and exposes the outcrops of successive strata; and here it may be seen that fossiliferous limestone appears again beneath the metalliferous layers. It is believed by many that a second stratum of ore-bearing rock will be found beneath the lower fossiliferous limestone, but this has not been proved. Across the cañon to the eastward the precipitous face of a parallel range shows the continuations of the limestone strata; but the range is of inferior height, and the upper metalliferous layer is consequently wanting, having probably been carried away by denudation. This range dips eastward, and the cañon between it and Treasure Hill probably occupies an anticlinal axis.

"The formation of the White Pine district," says an otherwise intelligent correspondent, "is an anomaly, and sets at defiance all known laws and rules of geology." This is the common expression of miners and tourists, readily adopted by speculators, who have learned by experience that "anomalies" sell best in the market. The truth is, there is nothing unusual in the formation of the district, except the enormous value of its ores. These occur in irregular masses and impregnations throughout a certain stratum of the limestone, and, fortunately for the miners, this stratum is the very one which the processes of disintegration and denudation have left uppermost. The ore consists of chloride of silver, with some enargite and stetefeldtite, and (in rare instances) native silver in capillary form. Of the extent of the deposits nothing can be said at present. They are probably bounded above and below by the planes of stratification, but laterally they seem scarcely to be separated from one another—what has been considered barren rock between them being mainly low-grade ore, which will hereafter be extracted like the rest. The accompanying minerals are quartz and calc-spar. The copper-stains upon most of the ore show that this metal was a constituent of the original deposits; and I conclude that the remarkable purity of the chloride ore of the Treasure Hill mines is the result of chemical changes subsequent to their original formation, in the course of which soluble chlorides, sulphates, and bicarbonates have been removed. It is possible, therefore, that the ore deposits of Treasure Hill have a common origin with those of the Base Range, and that the present differences are due to the concentrating and purifying action of thermal waters carrying chemical reagents in solution. There is no radical distinction in nature between the filling of a fissure and that of a cavity in limestone. The metalliferous fluids, whether solfataric gases, aqueous solutions, or molten masses, find their way wherever an opening is offered, and leave their deposits wherever they are checked for a sufficient time to cool or evaporate, or wherever they meet with chemical agencies which produce in them insoluble precipitates. Experience has shown that upheavals of stratified limestone do not generally produce fissures so extensive and well-defined as occur in some other kinds of rock. The solubility of the limestone itself in carbonated waters, especially under high heat and pressure, tends both to fill up the fissure with calc-spar and to open outlets from it into irregular cavities, and, finally, to cause a general alteration (silicification, often) of the country rock, and its impregnation with the metallic contents of mineral waters. Hence the miner's maxim, that lime is a "good gangue, but a poor country."

The ore deposits of Treasure Hill are richer than any that have been discovered during the present century; but, according to all the data that have yet been collected, they are not fissure veins. These data, though they all point one way, are necessarily incomplete, since no shaft on the hill is deeper than 60 feet, and no horizontal drift longer than 100 feet.

Not long before my visit, the miners of the district held a meeting, at which they were strongly urged to adopt at once the system of "square locations," and abandon the farce of staking out claims on ledges which do not exist. This proposition was defeated; and every man on Treasure Hill now claims so many feet of a vein, running, he does not specify in what direction, and dipping, he cannot tell at what angle, from a hole which he has made at random in the neighborhood of some already exposed body of ore. If he gets down to the ore, all the better; he can then work night and day, extract a large quantity of rich chloride, and send it away, before the neighbor, who has a prior location, can prove the identity of the deposit. In the utter absence of any real distinctive features of lodes, the principle has been set up by the White-Piners, that proof of such identity must consist in absolute continuity of chloride of silver from the working of the prior locator to those of the alleged trespasser. In one case, that of the Eberhardt and Blue Bell, this astounding demand was satisfied. A drift from the Eberhardt opening 30 feet to the Blue Bell shaft, passed through a mass of horn-silver, such as human eyes have rarely looked upon; and, as a consequence, the Blue Bell was united to the Eberhardt. The Keystone is, without the shadow of a doubt, on the same deposit as the Eberhardt. There is only a wall of two feet between them; but this wall is amicably let alone, and the "two veins" are therefore held by miners' law to be distinct! In another case which came to our knowledge, a claimant was endeavoring to protect himself from robbery, by tracing the ore into the works of a new-comer, close by, and had successfully arrived within a yard of his object, when the occurrence of a piece of calc-spar across his path defeated him. The intruder, protected by that bulwark, laughed his claims to scorn, and continued to extract and carry away the ore, which was, under miners' law, in a distinct vein, separated from the other by a "wall." All the "walls" thus far discovered on Treasure Hill are of this wholly indefinite and untrustworthy character—mere seams of calc-spar in limestone; and, under the present regulations, there is no such thing as security of title. Even if one had a regular fissure vein, he might be cheated out of all but a few feet of it by some accidental shoot of calc-spar across it; and when we consider that calc and limestone are chemically the same, and that a little trickling of water might deposit one of these so-called walls anywhere, we shall see what protection is offered to capital by such a rule as has been adopted in White Pine.

This is an instance of the danger of allowing the first miners in any district to make, without limitation, such laws as they please, governing the rights of property. This splendid district is now subjected to two styles of operations—grabbing on the spot, and gambling away from it. A great many worthy, honest, and industrious men are at work there; but they will acknowledge that they are merely putting off the evil day of litigation and chaos. Others are interested in claims, which they want to sell to capitalists; and they may sincerely believe their claims to be valid and well-defined. No one is accused of intentional deception in the matter; it is only to be lamented that the inhabitants did not, by adopting at once a rational basis for mining titles, introduce order among conflicting claims. To their credit be it spoken, there has been thus far little quarrelling among them. White Pine has been notably a quiet, industrious, and good-natured mining camp. But that is because there was room for all, and profitable work for all. Unless some radical change, of which I have now no knowledge, has taken place since my visit in September, White Pine is a good place for men who live there, and can watch and defend their own interests, and for custom-mills, which will doubtless do a good business for months to come, in reducing the marvellously rich ores of the different deposits; but I must again repeat that I cannot find in the circumstances of the case any protection for permanent investment of capital. Some of the mines, as for instance the Hidden Treasure and the Virginia, standing a little apart from the great crowd, already extensively worked, and having moreover a semblance at least of definiteness in their deposits, are better off than others; but they all suffer under the absurd regulations of the miners.

It is the natural tendency, when men with nothing but their own industry to depend upon gather in a new district, that they should make such laws as will favor industry, and that only. When I was in White Pine, many a man with pick and shovel, and now and then a little gunpowder, was making good wages out of his small prospecting shaft. The retail mining business suited him well enough; but capital must work on a larger scale. Insecurity of title is no trouble to one who, if he is ejected to-day, can pack up his tools, move away a rod or two, and have a new mine in full blast to-morrow; but capital requires a certain basis for the investment of its thousands in permanent works. The only cure for this evil now possible, is that which the inhabitants may themselves supply, by uniting conflicting claims, and arranging amicably their boundaries. Perhaps it is not too late to establish square locations by general agreement, and to adjust the claims for damages that may arise from such a change by means of a commission elected by the citizens.

I adopt, with such alterations and additions as my notes of personal observation suggest, the following account of different mines, &c., from the letter of a San Francisco Alta California correspondent, who visited the district in November, two months after I left it:

The mines from which nine-tenths of the treasure now being produced in the White Pine district is being taken are located along the broken edge of the dolomite formation, in a line running southwards from the town of Hamilton up to the summit of Treasure Hill, and thence in the same direction over the declivity on the other side. The length of this lode or line of deposits is, so far as is known, between two and three miles—say about that of the Comstock; the Virginia at the northern end answering, for the purpose of illustration, for the Ophir and Gould and Curry, and the Aurora, Keystone, and Eberhardt, near the south, for the Crown Point, Kentuck, and Yellow Jacket. The principal claims thus far opened along this line of deposits are located in succession, as follows, commencing at the northern end: Virginia, Mammoth, Ellersly, north of the crest of Treasure Hill; Hidden Treasure, near the summit; South Extension of Hidden Treasure, North Aurora, South Aurora, Keystone, and Eberhardt. There are numerous other localities along this line, or nearly parallel with it on the west, but these are the principal claims opened. There is an apparent break in the line of deposits, as evinced by the croppings at the crest of the hill, south of the Hidden Treasure and north of the Aurora; but from that point south the deposits crop out so near together that they may practically be said to be continuous.

Virginia.—Located at the northern end of the Treasure Hill belt, or line of deposits, half a mile south of Hamilton, and 500 feet higher. This claim is situated on the eastern side of a ravine near the top of a ridge, running north and south. It includes 600 feet north and south, and 200 feet in width from east to west. It has been but partially opened, but the ore crops out nearly its whole length, at points from 40 to 60 feet apart, east and west, and at a depth of 20 feet, solid rock, with a large, well-defined pay streak of *bonanza*, has been exposed. On the top of the ridge, above the Virginia shaft, a claim was located, and called the Aladdin's Lamp. This claim ran directly across the Virginia, and though the prior claim exhibited no evidence of a ledge, excavations on the Aladdin's Lamp ground soon disclosed rich ore in detached masses, and the whole hill appears to be full of it. The Virginia ore, though not so exceedingly rich as that of the Eberhardt and Keystone, which is so near pure silver as to be hardly describable as ore, runs from $100 to $2,000 per ton, the average being probably not under $225. Sixteen tons recently crushed and worked yielded $226 net per ton.

Hidden Treasure.—This mine was discovered by an Indian, who guided white men to it, September 14, 1867. There was considerable secrecy maintained for a time, but the facts which were attempted to be suppressed soon leaked out, and the result led to the discovery of the great Keystone and Eberhardt deposits, lower down the hill, on the south, and the sudden development of the whole district. The present owners are T. J. Murphy and J. E. Marchand. It includes 600 feet. The line of deposits has been stripped for nearly the entire length of the claim, and in places to a depth of 20 feet. The lode, if such it may be called, pitches westward at an angle of 20 degrees, and its thickness has not yet been clearly determined. Three hundred tons of the ore—no rich specimens included—hauled to the Monte Cristo mill, on the west side of White Pine mountain, 16 miles by the road via Hamilton, yielded $160 per ton. The cost of reducing it was $65 per ton. Next year it will cost not over $20 per ton to reduce the same ore. The owners now have 100 tons of ore of superior quality out ready for crushing, and the lode is increasing in richness. The mine is entirely uncovered, and no work will be done on it after the heavy snows fall, until next spring. Picked specimens show horn-silver in abundance, worth $1,000 per ton and upwards.

Aurora.—This mine is located on the south of the crest of Treasure Hill—the Hidden Treasure being on the north—and just east of the town of Treasure Hill. This is properly the South Aurora, the North Aurora being above it, near the summit of the hill, and being but little developed. Work was commenced on it with two men, September 22, 1868; 30 men are now worked. One hundred and fifty tons of rock from this mine, worked at the Newark mill, in the Diamond range, 90 miles to the northwest of Hamilton, yielded an average of $185 per ton—the highest being $202, and the lowest $155. The cost of hauling was $20 per ton, and of working $35. There is more quartz here than lower down the hill on either side, and the indications of a regularly defined deposit are better than elsewhere. The shaft is 20 feet deep, and the drift westward 60 feet. The entrance to the mine is roofed over, and work can be carried on all winter.

Keystone.—Descending the hill southward past a number of claims, we come upon the Keystone, which is situated some distance below the edge of the dolomite croppings, on the eastern face of the hill. Here the chloride deposit crops out in almost incredible richness, and the developments are astonishing. The claim covers 800 feet, and the deposit was discovered by a party following "float" ore up the hill from the ravine below. At the point where the shaft now is, one of the party, a mere lad, named John Turner, struck a pick into what seemed to be a mass of dried putty. This proved to be pure chloride of silver, worth $15,000 to $25,000 per ton, and under it was found more of the same sort, and masses of almost pure metallic silver. The original location was mixed up with that of the Eberhardt, but a compromise has been effected; a neutral line, beyond which neither is to pass, has been agreed on, and on the 1st of August next the two claims are to be consolidated. At present each company works its own ground. The amount already taken out of the Keystone is not stated by the owners, but it is very large, and all came out of an opening in the hill, not more than 50 feet long horizontally, and 20 feet deep. A shaft has been sunk 60 feet through successive layers of dolomite, at the entrance of this open cut, and ore is said to have been found at the bottom. Much of the wealth of this mine consists of dull yellowish brown colored dust, which is run through screens to free it from rock, and placed in bags. This is clear chloride of silver. One piece of this chloride, shown me while at the mine, weighed 143 pounds and was worth, as it lay on the ground, over $1,500 in coin. In one pile were 100 tons of ore which will work $300 per ton; in another, 150 tons which will yield $300 to $500 per ton; in another, 600 tons which will yield $100 and upwards; in another a large pile of chloride dust in bags, worth—one hesitates to say how much. Two lots of the ore from this mine, worked at the Newark mill and the Manhattan mill, at Austin, yielded an average of $1,000 per ton, or $100,000 in the aggregate.

Eberhardt.—Next south, and adjoining the Keystone, is the most celebrated of all—the Eberhardt. So rich is this mine that its name has become almost synonymous with that of the cave entered by Aladdin. The location was made in December, 1867, and covers 800 feet, north and south.* At a depth of 20 or 30 feet from the surface drifts have been run in several directions through solid masses of chlorides, and other ores of silver for 20 to 50 feet, and the end is not yet reached. The entrance of the tunnel has been closed, and admission to the mine can now only be gained by descending the vertical shaft in the company's building. Descending the shaft on a rope, we found ourselves among men engaged in breaking down silver by the ton. The light of our candles disclosed great black sparkling masses of silver ore on every side. The walls were silver, the roof over our heads silver, the very dust which filled our lungs and covered our boots and clothing was a gray coating of fine silver.

From a chimney in the Eberhardt ground $85,000 worth of silver was taken in a few days, and the party taking it out then compromised with the company, being allowed to hold all he had taken out and release to the Eberhardt company the ground in dispute. The silver is now piled up in a cabin at Treasure Hill. The proprietors have $50,000 worth of similar specimens piled up in another place. One of the owners of the Eberhardt, but recently a poor man, values his interest at $1,000,000, and we presume the others would refuse to sell for less money.

Down the long cañon a road leads to Silver Springs, where the Oasis mill, now owned and run by the Eberhardt company is situated. This is the old Keystone mill, which was burned at Austin last summer. Mr. Page, after settling with the underwriters, took the machinery to this place and rebuilt it. It has ten stamps, eight Varney pans, and three settlers. No roasting, chlorination, or other expensive process is employed; the wet process of crushing and direct amalgamation, known as the Washoe process, being found for the present sufficiently remunera-

* Or, according to White Pine law, in any other direction which the locators may subsequently choose. The present assumed course is nearly east and west, I believe.—R. W. R

tive. Mr. Page erected the mill on a contract to work the Eberhardt and other ores; but the company soon found it for their advantage to purchase the establishment. The mill cost $30,000, and the mill and contract were sold to the company for $75,000.

Chloride Flat is a slope comprising from five to ten acres on the western side of the hill, adjoining the town of Treasure Hill. It is perforated like a sieve with shafts, sunk often within from 10 to 30 feet of each other. The holders claim 400, 600, or 1,000 feet each, and the claims, being located on the old ledge theory, run into each other, cross and interlace in every direction. At present the lucky holders of claims in which metal has been struck are too busy getting out rich horn silver and other forms of the metal to quarrel with each other, but as soon as they work out the horizontal deposits, and run into each others' claims, as they soon will, shooting and lawsuits will be the order of the day in what is now a peaceful and highly prosperous community. The great mistake of organizing the district on the perpendicular ledge theory—each claimant being allowed 200 feet on the ledge, "with all his dips, spurs, and angles," and the discoverer 200 feet in addition—was made at the outset, and it is now too late to remedy it. Had the location been made by the square yard it would have been all right, and many a lawsuit and shooting affray saved. Already difficulties are arising in the vicinity of the Eberhardt, and more must follow. From 10 to 30 feet through the limestone brings the prospector on Chloride Flat to his deposit of silver, or to the certainty that he has missed it and must seek elsewhere. The owners of the Robert Emmet mine, on Chloride Flat, who are taking out rich horn silver, reject as base rock, unworthy of being worked, all yielding less than $50 per ton. This deposit is at least seven feet thick, and not yet worked through. The Genesee, Stonewall, Delmonico and other mines in the vicinity, are among the richest on the Flat. There are 1,500 locations recorded in this district, and of this number 500 at least are within rifle shot of the above named mines.

There are three towns in the district, Hamilton, north of Treasure Hill; Silver Springs or Shermantown, south of the hill, and Treasure City in the midst of the mines upon the hill itself. Chloride City is a part, I believe, of Treasure City.

Hamilton, the town which has grown up in the cañon at the entrance of the hills on the north, contains perhaps 600 inhabitants. From thence a graded road winds up the hill to Treasure City, which stands below the crest of Treasure Hill, within the line of rich mines named on the east and Chloride Flat on the west. Here the principal mining population is congregated, the inhabitants (regular and transitory) numbering from 800 to 1,000. The distance from Hamilton to Treasure City is not over one and one-half miles in a direct line, though two and one-half by the toll road, and the difference in altitude is estimated at from 1,000 to 1,200 eet. The town of Silver Springs, sometimes called Shermantown, is located at the southern end of the Base Metal Range, two miles southwest of Treasure Hill, the road winding down a deep cañon to reach it. It is probably 1,500 feet lower than the town of Treasure City, or 7,500 feet above the level of the sea, and containing 400 or 500 people.

Hamilton has a supply of water, and is the stage and express depot, and the primary depot for supplies for the district. Treasure Hill is exposed to the full sweep of the winds on the summit of the mountain, and has no water save what is hauled up there from Hamilton or Silver Springs and sold at eight cents per gallon, but it is in the heart of the mineral deposits, and must be an important place despite its unpleasant ocation.

Silver Springs is sheltered from the winds, and is the more desirable—rather endurable—place of residence. Hamilton was first called Cave City, from a number of caves below the town in which the people first found shelter. It consists of board and cloth shanties, tents, and brush, rock and earth cabins. Treasure Hill ditto. Silver Spring has two or three good brick buildings, and is generally better built than either of the others. There is a saw mill, quartz mill, brick yard, (not now in operation,) and large slaughter-house, at Hamilton; two banks and several assay offices at Treasure Hill; and a quartz mill, smelting furnaces, assay office, and saw mill at Silver Springs. The entire population of the district may be put down at 2,500 or 3,000 at this time, and increasing at the rate of 50 per day. A very few women have found their way into the district, but as yet there can hardly be said to be anything like female society there. The wages paid in the mines are $5 per day, coin, and those not at work for themselves get employment easily at something, if so disposed. Lots which sold at $25 in Hamilton and Treasure Hill two or three months since are now in many cases worth $600 to $1,200, and "jumping" is as lively as in San Francisco, though attended as yet by no bloodshed. Nearly every building spot along the road, from Hamilton up to and through Treasure Hill and down to Silver Springs, is already claimed by somebody, and holders always ask an advance on yesterday's prices.

The climate—Necessary outfit.—The peculiarities of the climate of White Pine are not so well known as they will be when the district shall have been inhabited for a few years, instead of less than a year. Treasure Hill is from 8,000 to 9,000 feet above the level of the sea, and exposed to the full sweep of the winter winds, which are fearfully severe at times between the Rocky mountains and Sierra Nevada. Spring is late, cold, and wet; summer short, dry, and tolerably pleasant; autumn long and pleasant, with fine days and cold, frosty, freezing nights. It is reported that snow falls to a depth of 15 feet on the White Pine range in winter, but this story is not well authenticated, and the vegetation and general appearance of the country would lead to the belief that the annual fall is not extremely large. Up to the 20th instant there were but a few inches of snow on the highest peak of the White Pine mountains, and only an inch or two, in scattered patches, on Treasure Hill and the Base Range. It was snowing on the 20th and 21st on the Toiyabe and other ranges south and southeast of Austin, and probably also at White Pine, but the storm did not appear to be of long duration. The winter, however, must be intensely cold, and those who propose to remain there until spring must be well provided with good heavy woollen underclothing, heavy pilot, beaver or blanket cloth outer-clothing, and at least two pairs of the heaviest and best San Francisco or Oregon blankets—the best are the cheapest in the end, and will always find ready sale.

It is difficult to get goods over the railroad at this time promptly, owing to the pressure of material for extending the line, which must go forward whether or no; but parties intending wintering in the mines must either take over a stock of provisions, and have them hauled from Argenta, or go provided with means to purchase them at Hamilton day by day for four or five months, probably at an advance on the prices quoted below as the present ruling rates. The climate appears to be exceedingly healthy, but owing to the great elevation of the country, and consequent rarefaction of the atmosphere, no person with weak lungs should attempt to winter there. Colds, rheumatism, and fevers will doubtless prevail to some extent before spring, as the result of exposure, neglect, and carelessness.

*Present cost of living.**—At present the necessaries of life are high-priced, but of good quality and abundant. At Hamilton and Treasure Hill are quite a number of restaurants at which a tolerably good meal may be obtained. The price per meal is $1, and board by the week is $12. There is no hotel in the district, and but one or two places where a bunk to sleep in can be rented. The price of a single bunk bed, with a mattrass and blankets, at the store of Wakefield & Wheeler, in which Wells, Fargo & Co.'s office is kept, in Hamilton, is $1 per night. This is the general resort of all new-comers, and a man who is in season to be booked for a bunk is looked upon as a favored mortal. Others, less fortunate, sleep in their blankets on the floor of the store, in saloons, restaurants, tents, hovels, or in the open air, as they can catch it. The prices of various articles of food for man and beast are as follows: Flour, $16 per hundred pounds; potatoes, (grown in Nevada and of superior quality,) 12½ cents per pound; onions, 15 cents per pound; sugar, (brown,) 3½ pounds for $1; crushed sugar, 3 pounds for $1; coffee, (ground,) 75 cents per pound—(no facilities for grinding it in the district;) bacon, (sides,) 37½ cents; hams, 37½ and 40 cents; shoulders, 35 cents per pound; beef, fresh and of good quality, 25 cents; pork, 37½@50 cents per pound; eggs, from Salt Lake, (so-soish,) $1@$1 25 per dozen; eggs, (fresh,) $2 per dozen; tea, $1 25 per pound; candles, 35 cents per pound; barley, 10@12½ cents per pound; hay, $150 per ton; drinks, 25 cents each, and no credit at the bar.

Wood of good quality is abundant, and can be had for the cost of cutting and hauling. All the wood land in the vicinity is being claimed by parties who propose to cut wood for the mills and to supply the miners. Lumber costs $150 per 1,000 feet for ordinary, $175 per 1,000 feet for choice at Hamilton, where there is a little steam saw-mill with a single circular saw constantly engaged in cutting lumber from the "bull pine," (or "nigger pine," as it would be termed in the south,) which grows on the White Pine mountain proper, in considerable quantities, and of sufficient size to afford saw logs 20 to 25 feet in length and two feet thick. At Treasure Hill $200 and upwards per 1,000 feet is charged for boards, which are hauled from Hamilton or Silver Springs, or from remote districts by heavy teams. Half a dozen men clubbing together could in a few days put up a shanty of cedar posts chinked with stones and mud, and roofed with cedar boughs and earth, which would afford comparatively comfortable quarters for the party through the winter. Those erecting buildings of sawed lumber at present line them with cotton cloth to exclude the wind, then shingle or tin the roofs. A horse will "eat his head off" in a week or two, and parties coming into the district at this time will do well to send them off to the lower valleys, 20 to 50 miles away, where they can winter on bunch grass and white sage in the open air, only requiring the attention of a herder. Clothing and blankets cost about 50 per cent. more than in San Francisco.

There are, as yet, no agricultural developments in the district itself. Some fine ranches on the road to Austin produce hay and grain, and considerable coarse hay is cut in the next valley eastward. Teams from Salt Lake via Egan cañon have found their way in great numbers to the White Pine cities, and their owners have done a flourishing business in grain, vegetables, etc.

Mills and reduction works.—The Oasis mill at Silver Springs, (10 stamps,) the White Pine mill at Hamilton, (10 stamps,) and the Monte Cristo,

---

* Since this chapter was written, in November, 1868. the great influx of prospectors and speculators into White Pine may have enhanced these prices still further.

(5 stamps,) are, I believe, all running. The old Butte mill, (5 stamps,) from San Francisco cañon, Reese River district, has been transported to White Pine, and will soon be in operation. There are also two smelting furnaces, which will start in the spring, for the treatment of the richest ores, and of the ores from the Base range. The product of White Pine for 1868, including the value of the ore extracted, but not yet reduced, may fairly be estimated at a million dollars, perhaps more.

At present there is but one route by which the White Pine district can be reached from San Francisco, viz: via the Central Pacific railroad, Argenta and Austin. The distance from San Francisco in round figures is about as follows: San Francisco to Sacramento, by rail or steamer, 100 miles; Sacramento to Argenta, by rail 400 miles; Argenta to Austin, by stage, 97 miles; Austin to Hamilton, by stage, 120 miles—total, 717 miles. The cost of the trip for passage alone, only 25 pounds of baggage being allowed, is as follows: To Sacramento $5, to Argenta $40, to Austin $15, to Hamilton $25—total, $85. After passing Reno, meals are $1 each along the whole route, and $15 is a moderate allowance for the expense of eating on the way, which would bring the cost of the trip to $100 in round figures, providing one has no extra baggage, does not stop to sleep on the way, and indulges in no luxuries. By purchasing a through ticket at Sacramento for Austin $10 can be saved on the above estimate, but the stage by which one engages passage from Argenta to Austin may be filled in advance, in which case it may be necessary to remain for days at the former point. If no detention occurs, and travelling is kept up night and day, the trip through from San Francisco to Hamilton may be made in five days. There are two regular stage lines, Wells, Fargo & Co.'s mail line and Miller, Wadleigh & Co.'s passenger and fast freight line, running between Argenta and Austin. Between Austin and Hamilton there are two regular stage lines, viz: Len Wine's (connecting with Wells, Fargo & Co.) and Shannon's and half a dozen guerilla lines, which make about half as good time as a man can make on foot. Fare the same all round.

In a few weeks—the weather permitting—it will be possible to reduce the staging on the trip by one-half. From Hamilton to the nearest point at which the railroad can be reached—near Fort Halleck, east of Gravelly Ford—the distance is not over 110 miles, possibly not more than 100. The new road will leave Austin far to the westward, and passing down an open valley country directly northwards, will present no heavy grades. It can be constructed cheaply, and must be opened immediately. It may run through Ruby valley, or it may leave it to the right, and pass to the westward. There are now probably 3,000 people in White Pine district and vicinity wholly without mail facilities, and dependent solely on Wells, Fargo & Co., for their letters, papers, &c. A mail route should and probably will be opened between the railroad, near Fort Halleck, and Hamilton immediately on the cars reaching the former point.

The future productiveness and importance of this district cannot now be foreseen; but much may be expected from the active explorations of next season, in a broad belt of country as yet comparatively unknown. As for the deposits of Treasure Hill, they are certain to yield large amounts of silver before they are exhausted; and the prospects of the mines would be most encouraging, but for the confusion and waste which an injudicious system of titles will be certain to generate.

SOCIAL AND STEPTOE MINE, EGAN CAÑON.

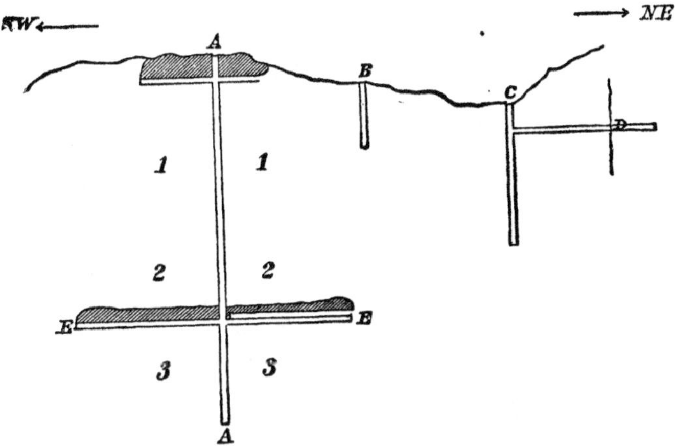

Social and Steptoe mine, Egan cañon, Nevada. Profile, 100 feet to the inch.

Course of the vein, northeast and southwest magnetic, (variation 16° east,) and dip 50° to 60° northwest; A A, main incline; B, prospecting shaft; C, shaft in ravine, to be connected as air-shaft with the mine; D, drift northeast on the vein, cut off at D by a greenstone dike, beyond which the vein has not yet been found; 1 1, 2 2, workable ground, computed to contain 20,200 tons of ore, worth $60 per ton and upwards; 3 3, reserves containing within the length of E E and depth of A, 6,800 tons of ore. The vein has been stripped and distinctly shown along the outcrop for 500 to 600 feet southwest of incline A.

Egan cañon is a pass of great natural beauty, traversed by the overland road, about 250 miles west of Salt lake, and half as far east of Austin. I believe the name of the mining district here organized is Gold cañon. It has been the scene of some mining "excitement," but operations are at present confined to a small arastra gold mill, which is said to be paying on a limited scale, and the mine of the Social and Steptoe Consolidated Company, on the Gilligan vein. The mountain range through which Egan cañon runs has a north and south course, and consists of slates, quartzite, and porphyry, (or altered sandstone,) which is highly ferruginous. On the east side there is a kind of trap, and running north and south through the centre a greenstone dike; the strata dip west being apparently tilted by the trappean rocks. The Gilligan vein shows itself along the northern mountain side in the cañon. It has been traced on the surface, or in depth, for more than 1,000 feet horizontally, and the mine workings have attained a depth of 400 feet. Everywhere there is a ledge of four to five and more feet, averaging four and one-half feet, carrying quartz with some calcspar and decomposed auriferous silver ore. The ore originally contained, probably, argentiferous galena and antimonial sulphurets. It has been tested for four years past in a little five-stamp mill belonging to the company, which has produced in all some $80,000 bullion from ore running from $50 to $150 per ton. The superintendent, Mr. O'Dougherty, and Judge Riley, estimate that 3,000 tons are now lying on the dumps, which will yield $50 per ton. The bullion from this ore is worth $2 per ounce, on account of its gold contents. The mine is an excellent one and remarkably well opened. The reserves of 27,000 tons above calculated do not include the ground outside of the 300 feet opened by the level E. By drifting along the whole length of the lode traced, (1,000 feet,) ground of great extent and value will be opened at little expense. This enterprise is ripe for a good mill; and the company are taking steps to put up one. The development of the mine has been slow but sure, and now the harvest may be gathered. If the rich mines of Reese river, Twin river, and some other districts, had been opened to the depth of 400 feet, and all necessary levels run, before actual exploitation on a large scale was begun, they would have realized much greater profit, and for a longer time. Premature extraction of ore has well-nigh ruined some of the best mines in Nevada. Mr. O'Dougherty is to be congratulated on having pursued a contrary course.

Egan cañon being in Lander county, the yield of the mines is reported to the assessor at Austin.

Product of mines.—The only means for arriving at the product of the mines of Nevada, outside of the Comstock, is afforded by the returns of the county assessors; these are unfortunately made out with considerable irregularity, and are especially liable to error from the fact that all values are calculated in currency, according to the State law, for purposes of taxation. I applied for these returns to all the assessors in the State, but was only able to obtain in time those of Lander county for the first three quarters of 1868. The tables subjoined have been partly copied and partly calculated, by myself, from the memoranda furnished. The grand totals are correct, and the different items approximately so. The designation "chloriders" is given to parties who bring in small lots of ore, without reporting the mine from which they obtained it. In the second quarter there were 109 of these, but they are now considerably diminished in Reese River district, by the stampede to White Pine.

ASSESSOR'S RETURNS OF BULLION-PRODUCING MINES OF LANDER COUNTY.

For the quarter ending March 31, 1868.

Mine.	Location.	Ore reduced.		Average per ton.		Yield.	
		Tons.	*lbs.*				
Aurora	White Pine	7	1,478	$255	75	$1,979	25
Buel North Star	Reese River district.	6	327	219	85	1,355	15
Chase	Yankee Blade	14	1,510	124	94	1,849	11
Fortuna	Reese River district.	26	1,496	130	29	3,485	26
Harding and Dickman	....do	13	973	233	50	3,148	98
Isabella	....do	2	1,734	821	60	2,355	53
Magnolia	....do	98	669	243	19	23,913	68
Macey's	....do	4	468	125	55	531	58
Morse	....do	7		250	43	1,752	81
Manhattan Company	....do	761	347	154	36	117,495	26
Niagara	....do	1	372	140	71	166	88
New York and Austin, (Florida)	....do	210	1,627	361	24	76,154	08
New York Company, (Troy)	....do	28	1,358	264	44	7,583	88
Posey	....do	3	1,348	145	99	532	77
Social and Steptoe	Egan cañon	217		66	49	14,428	33
Sam. Brannan	Reese River district.	1	884	122	83	177	12
Silver Parlor	....do	2	1,144	71	75	183	53
Semanthe	....do	3	690	253	93	849	40
South American	....do	3	738	100	45	338	42
Savage Consol	....do	17	1,534	245	11	4,356	75
St. Louis	Cortez district	12	919	399	50	4,977	79
Shoshone Company, (Great Eastern)	Reese River district.	105	1,412	105	81	11,184	94
Timoke	....do	79	1,199	222	83	17,735	05
Vedder Company	Amador district	5	798	307	07	1,657	87
Wisner		2	1,072	106	25	269	45
Washington		6	297	286	07	1,759	04
Yosemite		1	1,111	120	10	186	75
46 "Chloriders"		107	1,194	171	20	18,420	83
Total		1,753		181	87	318,825	29

For the quarter ending June 30, 1868.

Mine.	Location.	Ore reduced.		Average per ton.	Yield.
		Tons.	*lbs.*		
Aurora	Reese River district.	2	1,704	$287 11	$818 84
Buel North Star	....do	126	1,000	425 12	53,777 68
Buckeye		16	218	276 72	4,457 68
Cedar Point		2	1,628	153 19	431 08
Chase	Yankee Blade	7	90	414 09	2,917 26
Comet		2	1,104	198 54	506 77
Centenary Company	Newark	392		98 82	38,737 44
Diana	Reese River district.	71	1,134	190 46	13,630 65
Eliza Anderson		2	1,760	79 59	229 22
Eberhardt, South	White Pine	2	748	271 26	643 97
East Oregon	Reese River district.	1	536	283 20	359 09
Florida	....do	150	1,885	370 00	55,848 72
Fortuna	....do	11	1,206	270 27	3,135 94
Featherstone Company	White Pine	1	366	514 10	608 16
Girard		3	1,908	332 91	1,316 33
Great Eastern	Reese River district.	30	307	303 10	9,139 51
Hidden Treasure	White Pine	73	930	179 14	13,615 19
Hunchback		11	1,888	114 45	1,365 31
Keystone Company	Reese River district.	11	156	190 07	2,105 59
Kaleseed	....do	1	126	153 20	162 85
Keystone Company	White Pine	4	675	994 77	4,314 81
Magnolia	Reese River district.	16	906	464 91	7,649 16
North Star	....do	575	1,339	144 09	82,947 49
Navarette		5	1,846	101 74	602 60
New York	Reese River district.	1	1,700	78 12	144 52
Old Colony	....do	4	788	135 04	593 37
Silver Chamber	....do	16	36	144 26	2,310 75
Silver Belt	....do	4	1,058	346 85	1,570 88
Santa Fé	Santa Fé	2	664	88 62	206 67
St. Louis	Cortez	21	1,108	501 48	10,759 92
Semanthe	Cabaley	2	1,465	455 28	1,244 05
Do	Craycroft	9	944	240 09	2,274 13
Sam Brannan		5	538	175 53	924 87
South America	Reese River district.	3	574	202 64	683 69
Savage	....do	3	1,768	354 34	1,376 26
Timoke	....do	118	1,252	269 74	31,998 17
Troy	....do	92		363 19	33,413 48
Vineyard		3	1,704	251 77	969 82
Washington		30	736	97 68	2,966 33
Yaqui		6	952	113 94	737 87
Yellow Jacket		4	116	269 02	1,091 68
106 "Chloriders"		337	247	84 51	28,492 38
Total		2,173	1,000	188 50	410,110 48

The increase in the product of the Buel North Star is a noticeable feature of the quarter. There is also an increase in the Timoke, while the Manhattan North Star, Florida, and Magnolia show a falling off. The Timoke was doing its best in this quarter, and, having exhausted the ore-body in view, was abandoned in the following quarter. The celebrated Great Eastern mine makes its last appearance in the quarter ending with March 31. It has since been entirely abandoned, and the timbers withdrawn. It will be seen that the ores of White Pine begin to show themselves in the above table. The principal developments in White Pine occurred, however, after this quarter.

For the quarter ending September 30, 1868.

Mine.	Location.	Ore reduced.		Yield.
		Tons.	*lbs.*	
Aurora	White Pine	14	1,926	$3,123 13
Aurora, (S. Ext.)	......do.	2	1,782	750 72
Aurora, (Western Company)	......do.	1	1,655	289 05
Aurora	Reese river	2	1,194	715 79
Blair	White Pine	5	400	477 86
Buel North Star	Reese river	343	866	122,113 28
Chihuahua	Newark	109	1,000	7,626 66
D. A Cleavenger	Yankee Blade	1	1,645	369 04
Chase	Reese river	5	1,494	2,806 63
Double Eagle	White Pine	3	1,731	957 66
Diana	Reese river	7	1,650	1,267 25
Empire	White Pine	3	1,302	435 30
Eberhardt	......do.	141	765	188,207 58
Eclipse	......do.	1	352	663 84
Featherstone	......do.	21	1,543	1,714 02
Fortuna	Reese river	4	970	1,004 92
Genessee	White Pine	79	369	13,186 26
Green Mountain		3	450	3,027 68
Grinnell	Chase, Reese river	2	850	385 89
Hidden Treasure	White Pine	211	637	24,103 06
Hidden Treasure, (S. Ext.)	......do.	2	500	1,275 88
Hart and Harps	......do.		1,674	282 45
Iceberg	......do.	5	1,155	1,298 93
Indiana	......do.	12	1,947	1,459 00
Keystone	......do.	56	1,938	64,808 61
Last Chance	......do.	12	1,332	2,320 32
Mississippi	......do.	1	1,926	489 94
Magnolia	Reese river	43	1,502	14,875 73
Manhattan Company	North Star, Reese river	320	1,592	52,493 96
Napier	White Pine	1	663	274 37
Florida	Reese river	97	446	27,246 42
Owens & Jones	Yankee Blade	1	888	359 55
Patriot	......do.	1	1,456	231 36
Plymouth	Reese river	7	1,894	2,926 05
Romulus	White Pine	10	1,977	3,420 74
Ross & Taylor	Cortez	8	648	1,963 29
S. B. Ross	......do.	4	1,918	996 69
Sumott & Casey	Yankee Blade	14	1,496	5,322 76
South American	Reese river	58	198	19,503 63
Silver Chamber	......do.	12	464	5,876 29
St. Louis	Cortez	28	162	21,214 60
Savannah	White Pine	1	1,824	505 66
Timoke	Reese river	11	948	2,882 16
Turner & Co	......do.	17	1,558	5,442 00
John Traverse	......do.	4	1,650	428 39
Vedder Company	......do.	1	346	146 32
Virginia	White Pine	3	1,987	724 80
Virginia, (S. Ext.)	......do.	2	265	91 00
Virginia, (Float Rock)	......do.	2	551	418 47
G. B. Wilson	Cortez	2	84	1,122 83
I. H. Walker	......do.	6	340	1,073 12
Willard & Osborne	White Pine	9	580	10,110 54
J. R. Williamson	......do.		1,892	2,513 91
Wabash	......do.	2	192	450 88
Total		1,739	1,574	627,767 27

To this must be added 202 tons 564 pounds of ore brought in by "chloriders" in small lots, and yielding $92,806 98, making the total for the quarter 1,941 tons 1,138 pounds, yielding $720,574 25—a general average of $371 13 per ton. This high average is due in part to the extraordinary richness of the ore from the new district of White Pine. The returns for the quarter ending December 31, 1868, (not yet made out,) will show still greater improvements from this source.

The product of Lander county for the year 1868 may be estimated from these data as follows:

	In currency.
First quarter	$318,825 29
Second quarter	410,110 48
Third quarter	720,574 25
Fourth quarter (estimate)	900,000 00
	2,349,510 02

The shipments of bullion through Austin for the year amount to $3,000,000, gold, as reported by Wells, Fargo & Company. This sum includes the bullion of Nye county, and possibly of some other localities.

Railroads.—The great benefits which Humboldt and the northern part of Lander county have experienced already from the construction of the Pacific railroad naturally indicate a most important means of developing and maintaining the industry of central Nevada. Nature has provided, in the series of magnificent level valleys which stretch from north to south through the State, a system of highways unequalled in the world. Reese River, Smoky, Steptoe, and other valleys, along the sides of which are located numerous mining districts, offer extraordinary facilities for the laying of railroads, and at no distant day, when the supply of fuel has become in many localities insufficient, no doubt the ores will have to be transported to the more favored localities on the Pacific railroad for reduction. Reno, on the Truckee river, is expected to become an important centre for operations of this kind, and the Central railroad is extending every facility to those who desire to ship ores for treatment. The route for a cross railroad must be determined by more careful examinations hereafter. In some respects an oblique route, traversing the mountain ranges by the low passes which abound in most of them, would be the most beneficial. At all events, it seems advisable that such a road should terminate, if possible, in an agricultural district. I am inclined to believe that a road might easily be constructed, say through Reese River valley, and through a pass in Esmeralda county, into the Owens River valley, California. This is, at least, the opinion of intelligent men, and I have examined a part of the route and found it quite feasible.

Probably the first step towards a cross-railroad system will be the construction of short branches from the Pacific railroad to the nearest mining districts. The railroad proposed to Virginia City is an example; and if the developments at White Pine increase in importance, the connection of that district with the Pacific road at Gravelly Ford (110 miles) may be undertaken, as the road would lead through a level valley most of the way. One such road, reaching into the heart of the silver-mining districts of Nevada, would effect wonders for their future prosperity.

The same may be said of the proposed northern lines, connecting Idaho and Montana with the Pacific railroad. An interesting discussion of this subject will be found in the section on Montana.

The policy of granting land in aid of such enterprises is heartily to be recommended. The government is not only enabled to double the price of the alternate sections which it retains, but to sell them at that double price; whereas, without the railroads, such lands are of no value to anybody.

CHAPTER VIII.

NYE COUNTY.

Mammoth district, situated about 60 miles west of south from Austin, and 12 miles west of the Union district, on the Mammoth range of mountains. The district has been known for some years, and the Mount Vernon company in particular expended considerable money there; but the ore, though abundant, seemed to be of low grade, and the mines declined in the estimation of the population. The company alluded to stopped work early in 1868. During the summer, however, discoveries have been made which promise a bright future. The ledges formerly known lie in granite, characterized by unusually large and regular crystals of felspar, sometimes several inches in length, generally twins, but occasionally single. The old claims in this district are fine specimens of fissure-veins, regular, well-defined, and dipping steeply. They are from two or three inches to as many feet in width, and contain a good deal of antimony, in silver ores of medium grade. The new discoveries are several miles west of the old Mammoth silver-belt, in limestone, which in some places passes over to a kind of greenstone. These claims are remarkable for containing gold, as well as silver. The Marble Falls, owned by Hatch & Company, located April 25, 1868, is a very large lode (10 feet wide) and shows native gold throughout nearly its whole extent. The gold is light-colored, evidently being alloyed with silver, in what proportions is not yet made public. The owners are shipping the ore in sacks to San Francisco.

Union district.—This district is situated in the Shoshone range of mountains, about 50 miles south of Austin. The Shoshone mountains are parallel with the Toiyabe, and form the western boundary of Reese River valley. Union district was organized in 1863, and the town of Ione, then commenced, was for some time a flourishing settlement. In the geological formation porphyritic rocks predominate, and occur in great variety of form, color, and texture. In many places the porphyry appears to be stratified, and this, with other indications, leads to the inference that it is not a true eruptive or igneous porphyry, but rather a metamorphosed sandstone. A kind of gabbro also occurs, enclosed with porphyry. The veins are in the porphyry, which in their immediate neighborhood assumes a closer texture and shows few or no crystals. They vary from a few inches to two or three feet in width, and are in some places considerably broken. The minerals occurring in the veins are native gold and silver, horn-silver, (chloride) antimonial sulphurets of silver, copper and lead, with carbonate and silicate of copper and carbonate of lead. Galena, very rich in silver, is also frequent. Among the principal mines are the Mountain Brow, Yolo, Pleiades, Stonewall, Franklin, Revenue, Andrew Jackson, Hobart, and others. In the Mountain Brow an exceedingly rich galena has been found, while handsome gold specimens have been taken from the Franklin. About 12 miles south of the town of Ione is the mining camp of Grantville, now nearly deserted. Here are several large ledges which have been considerably prospected. The Great Eastern is situated on a hill north of the camp, and consists of several parallel locations on what appears to be one large outcrop. The ore is porous, and contains some gold with its silver. The ledge is much broken, and the explorations on it have not, on the whole, resulted favorably. Union district has an abundance of fuel and water.

The Pioneer mill at Ione has ten stamps and four roasting furnaces. It formerly worked the ores of the neighborhood, but is now closed. A few miles south of Ione is the Knickerbocker mill, of twenty stamps, owned by a New York company. It was employed in working the ore of the Great Eastern, but has recently been run as a custom mill. In the spring and early summer its yield of bullion was quite regular, and the owners of some ten mines were kept at work to supply it. It is said that the Indianapolis, a mine belonging to the company which owns the mill, contained no water at the depth of 240 feet—a phenomenon remarkable in mining generally, but not very uncommon in eastern Nevada. It is observable in San Antonio, Trinity, and other districts. Ione, like other towns, will suffer from the excitement now drawing thousands to White Pine.

TWIN RIVER DISTRICT, (see report of J. Ross Browne, 1868, page 414.)

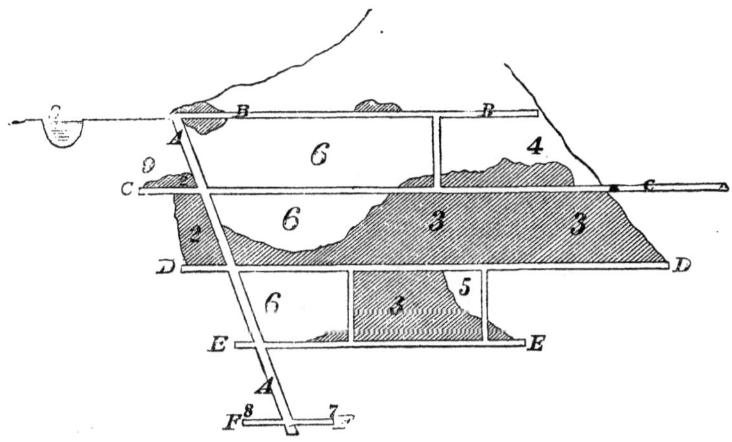

(Twin River Mine, Ophir Cañon, Nevada.—Profile, 150 feet to the inch.)

Course, north and south; dip, 46° east; AA, main incline; BB, tunnel run northward into the hill; CC, 10-fathom level, (60 feet vertical depth;) DD, 20-fathom level; EE, 30-fathom level; FF, 40-fathom level; MM, south boundary, or Macdonald line; S, Ophir creek; 1, 1, irregular workings in the tunnel, from which rich ore was taken, previous to the sale of the mine; 2, 2, old stopes, from which much valuable ore was taken in 1866 and 1867; 3, 3, stopes of 1867 and 1868, in which an immense body of very rich ore was found; 4, ground still standing, of medium grade, the ore containing considerable pyrites, and the vein six to eight feet wide; 5, a small portion of ground, containing about 400 tons of quartz, (say 100 tons $100 ore) in a vein 15 feet wide; (this was the principal stope in August, 1868;) 6, 6, low grade, still standing, too poor for extraction at present rates; 7, vein at north end of 40-fathom level, looks poor, being still in the zone of low grade which separates the two ore courses thus far discovered; 8, vein at south end of 40-fathom level, 100 feet from Macdonald line, looks very well, promising productive ground south, as the upper level showed; 9, broken ground, the filling of the cañon.

The vein is cut off, as the sketch shows, in the 10-fathom level at 320 feet north of the incline; in the 20-fathom at 346 feet, by a slide, coursing north 75 east, and dipping about 60 north. The indications are that the continuation of the vein will be found to the west, but this should be done once for all on the 30-fathom level, as a re-discovery in the 10-fathom would not open any great amount of ground. Two hundred feet and more of drifting and cross-cutting have been done on this upper level, in the dead rock, to satisfy the anxious desire of the stockholders to find the vein again as soon as possible. As the sketch shows, the immediate reserves of the mine are small, (4 and 5 of the sketch,) but the completion of the 30 and 40 fathom levels to the Macdonald line on one side, and to the line of the slide on the other, would give an amount of productive ground larger than that already worked out. A great difficulty in this mine has been the extraordinary density and hardness of the rock. Eighteen thousand drills are sharpened monthly for less than 40 men. In sinking the incline, three shifts of three men each, or nine men daily in all, have sometimes not made ten feet in depth in a month. It is, therefore, impossible for the mine to be worked to the best advantage, and to supply the large 20-stamp mill of the company, (see J. Ross Browne's report, 1868, page 416,) unless a considerable amount of ground is first opened in advance. True economy requires that the levels should be 120 instead of 60 feet apart, and that a new level should be completely open before the one above it is exhausted of its ore ground. The mining work of the Twin River has been thoroughly well done, and the mine is in good condition, and one of the most valuable which I have seen during the year. It is proposed to stop the mill and open mining ground for six months. Giant powder and the diamond drill will be tried, and Stetefeldt's roasting furnace, which has been tried here and found successful, will replace the reverberatories in future. I think the rock of the Twin River mine would give good results with the giant powder, but experiments only can decide.

Since the above notes were collected, during a personal examination, the company has gone into bankruptcy, with property amounting to $300,000 outside of its mine, and a debt of some $60,000 covered by the cost of winter supplies on hand. This remarkable proceeding is said to be owing to the discouragement of the stockholders, who have received no dividends, although its mine has produced more than three-quarters of a million of dollars. My opinion of the mine, expressed above, remains unaltered; nor do I perceive any ground for such a feeling as is said to exist among the stockholders. If the property is sacrificed, it will perhaps fall into the hands of a set of proprietors who understand its nature and value.*

The Twin River mill reduced in 1867 and 1868 ore as follows:

Quarter ending March 31, 1867, 1,161½ tons, yielding per ton .... $84 18 coin.
Quarter ending June 30, 1868, 805½ tons, yielding per ton .... 92 94 coin.
Quarter ending September 30, 1867, 800 tons, yielding per ton .... 179 24 coin.
Quarter ending December 31, 1867, 1,080½ tons, yielding per ton .... 181 97 currency.
Quarter ending March 31, 1868, 664½ tons, yielding per ton .... 127 16 currency.
Quarter ending June 30, 1868, 838 tons, yielding per ton .... 116 17 coin.

The assessors began in the latter part of 1867 to reckon their returns in currency. The usual rate assumed is 75 cents gold per $1 currency; but I do not know positively that all the assessors invariably adhere to it. I obtained the last item in the above table from the assessor of Nye county, before the calculation of currency value had been made. The following table of production is compiled and calculated from the books of the company, and has reference only to coin:

Month.	Bullion.	Number of days' run.	Average number of stamps per day.	Days' work at full capacity calculated.	Value of ore per ton.	Remarks.
January, 1868 ..	$12,075	13	13.23	8.57	$80 50	Stopped for repairs.
February, 1868 .	22,856	20	14.25	14.25	122 00	Short of salt.
March, 1868	28,443	22	16.32	17.95	86 00	
April, 1868	35,595	24	17.89	21.47	104 00	
May, 1868......	42,190	23	14.44	16.60	120 00	
June, 1868......	19,578	13	12.75	8.28	....	Short of ore.
July, 1868	16,439	22¼	10.13	11.39	....	Short of ore.
Total	177,176	137¼	14.33	98.51	....	

* The above account of the present condition of the Twin River mine must be understood as an addition to the account in Mr. Browne's report. I do not go over the ground to repeat what he has said, unless for some correction or explanation.

The stamps are 850 pounds in weight, lift 8–12 inches, and drop 70–72 per minute. The average of pay-rock last year was about 2 feet, out of an average of 6 feet vein-thickness. The ore was sorted one in three; and for every ton worked, two were mined and not worked. The dumps of low grade ore at the mine are very large. The average cost of running the mine is $10,000 per month, and the mill $15,000. When the mill runs virtually at half capacity, as for several months in the above table, it loses money.

San Antonio district.—This district lies across the southern portion of Smoky valley. The settlement is called Indian Springs, and its position relative to other well-known points will be seen from the following:

TABLE OF DISTANCES.

Direction.	
E.	From Austin to Smoky valley, 12 miles, road hilly.
S.	From Entrance into S. valley to Minium's R., 16 miles, road fine and level.
S. & W.	From Minium's to mouth of Ophir Cañon, 20 miles, road fine, 4 miles rising.
S. & E.	From Ophir Cañon to Shay's Cold Spr. R., 12 miles, road fine, 3 m. descending.
S.	From Minium's to Shay's ranch direct, 30 miles, road fine and level.
S.	From Shay's to Indian Springs, 25 miles, road fine and level.
E. & S.	From Austin to Indian Springs, 83 miles, 71 on level.
N.	From Shay's to Hot Springs, 2 miles.
N. E.	From Indian Springs to Belmont, 30 miles, road good, some hills.
S.	From Indian Springs to Lone Mt. Salt M., 30 miles, road level and sandy.
S. & W.	From Lone Mt. Marsh to Silver Peak, 30 miles, road tolerable.
S.	From Indian Springs to silver Peak, 60 miles.
S. S. E.	From Indian Springs to Montezuma, 60 miles, road dusty, mostly level, with one ridge.
E.	From Silver Peak to Montezuma, 20 miles, road—mountains.

The San Antonio district is a very large one; it stretches from the southern line of the Marysville district nearly one hundred and fifty miles southward, and extends from a point fifty miles east of Indian Springs to a point a hundred miles west of that place, covering, therefore, an area of almost 150 miles square. Of course, surveys have never been thought of; and, in point of fact, I have no doubt that this vast and vague district, if its limits were once determined, would be found to overlap a good many others of later date. Whatever its real boundaries may be, it is certain that it contains the short range called San Antonio mountain, about eight miles southeast of Indian Springs. The district was regularly organized November 1, 1863. There is a provision in the mining laws of San Antonio district, according to which any claim opened to a certain extent (expressed in the number of feet of drifting or shafting—and I think the number is fifteen!) remains forever the property of the claimant, and can never be relocated on account of subsequent abandonment. This provision is highly absurd and detrimental to the general interests of the district, which is full of claims, abandoned (for a time, at least) by their locators, who were without capital to work them, and yet completely shut out from development by other hands. The Toiyabe range of mountains, separating Reese River and Smoky valleys, consists of slate, quartzite, granite, porphyry, greenstone, and trachyte, the mere enumeration of which is sufficient to prove that the formation is the product of different ages, and the structure by no means regular. The San Antonio mountain, which may be regarded as a southern extension of the first range east of the Toiyabe, seems to contain no granite, but to consist mainly of slate, quartzite, porphyry, greenstone and volcanic rock. Obsidian, which is an unmistakable volcanic product, is found on the mountain. Judging from the character of the *débris* on the southern and western sides, where the Liberty and other mines are situated, I should think the predominant rock of that flank to be porphyry. The evidences of disturbance are quite sufficient to account for the numerous fissure-veins found in this locality.

Liberty mine, belonging to the Rigby Silver Mining Company, of New York; length of claim 2,400 feet.

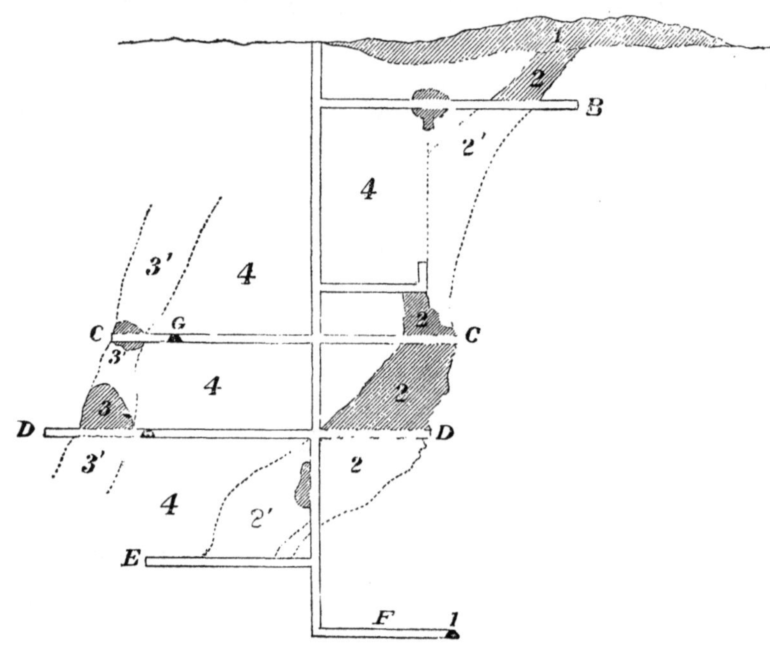

Incline of the Liberty mine, San Antonio, Nevada. Profile 100 feet to the inch.

Course of the vein at this point northwest and southeast, dip 40° northeast. A, incline, 300 feet deep: B, first level northwest, 30 feet below surface; C, 150-foot level; D, 200-foot level; E, 270-foot level; F, 300-foot level; G and H, turns or cross cuts southward, in the levels, the vein being faulted and thrown about 30 feet; I, cross cut northeast 136 feet, the vein having been underrun by the incline. At the end of this cross cut, not shown on the sketch, is a winze about 20 feet deep. The vein is 30 feet wide in the cross cut, and filled at that point with low-grade quartz. 1, surface working; 2, 2, ground partially worked out on a supposed course of very rich ore; 2′ 2′, portions of the said course not yet worked; 3, 3, ground worked on a second course of rich ore, southeast of the incline; 3′ 3′, supposed continuations of the said course; 4 4, ground containing, so far as explored, second and third class ore, with $40 to $75 per ton.

The Liberty vein lies in the foot-hills on the southwest side of San Antonio mountain, about twelve miles from Indian Springs. Its general course is northwest and southeast, and the dip, as measured in the incline, is 43° northeast for the first hundred feet in depth, and 56° northeast below that point. At the lowest workings the vein stands yet steeper, according to the measurement of Mr. Rigby. The outcrop may be traced on the surface, with an insignificant "heave" of about 20 feet, occurring some 50 feet southeast of the incline, for a distance of 700 or 800 feet. The company's claim includes the whole of the visible outcrop. Northwest of the incline the vein sweeps towards the west, describing a curve of some 45°. The fissure varies from four feet in width upwards. Two or three hundred feet northwest from the main incline, at the end of the curve alluded to, it is 80 feet wide, as shown by a cross cut, connecting a shaft and incline on opposite sides of the vein, at the depth of some 70 feet. Excluding this extraordinary and local development from the calculation, I should put the average width of the vein at 8 to 10 feet. The country rock on both walls is porphyry. The walls are tolerably well defined, the hanging-wall being on the whole the most regular and distinct. It is my impression that the change of course above alluded to, being accompanied with a widening of the vein, and a decrease of dip to 30° north, is largely a superficial matter, and that in depth both the course, dip and width of the fissure will be more nearly uniform. This notion may be illustrated by taking a pamphlet and holding it with the back downwards, inclined so as to represent the average dip of the vein. The edges of the leaves, opposite the back, will represent the outcrop of the vein. If now the pamphlet be bent with thumb and finger at one of the upper corners, three results will follow. The dip of the whole upper edge will be decreased, especially near the corner bent; the course of the edge will be deflected at that corner; and the leaves will spread under the thumb and finger, thus widening the outcrop. Precisely these phenomena are observable in the Liberty mine, and this is my reason for the theory above advanced. The vein-matter of the Liberty is mainly clay, porphyry and quartz—the latter being accompanied with ores of silver. The rich ores are distributed in pockets and chimneys, but a good deal of the vein around and between these pockets is ore of the second and third class. The lowest quartz found is a little damp; but there never has been a drop of water struck, thus far in the mine. Probably the next 100 feet in depth will bring water. With this will come sulphuretted ores, without doubt, and the vein may be expected to show its permanent structure and character. Hitherto all the ore extracted has been chloride (and other haloids) of silver, native silver, and oxidized metals, together with disintegrated sulphurets.

The Rigby mill (four stamps) is at Indian Springs. The stamps weigh about 700 pounds each, and are run at 85 to 100 drops per minute. A reverberatory and two Varney pans complete the apparatus of reduction. The stamps and pans are run by means of a small upright engine of about 15-horse power, receiving steam from a 30-flue tubular boiler. The maximum capacity of the battery and pans is probably greater than that of the furnace; but, as it does not equal that of two furnaces, there is no economical way of increasing the yield of the mill beyond the two tons daily which can be roasted by the present apparatus. The actual operations of the last year show that one and three-quarters to two tons of ore have been the average quantity treated daily, when the mill was running—that is, from April 1, 1867, to July 10, and from the middle of October of the same year (with a loss of more than a month for repairs, last spring,) to the present time—or rather the 1st of September—about a twelve-month in all. The amount of ore reduced, and its yield, may be found in the following statement. The tailings are not subjected to further treatment. No doubt, in working on a larger scale, they could be saved and profitably treated.

Statement of bullion produced by the Rigby mill up to August 1, 1868.

ACTUAL RUNNING TIME ABOUT ONE YEAR.

Mine.	Tons ore.	Oz. crude B.	Oz. bar B.	Fineness.	Value.
Liberty	536	71, 694	67, 030. 30	Av. 710. 50	$62, 048 66
Phœnix	4	1, 027	990. 00	774. 00	990 69
Potomac (estimated)	10	900	873. 30	653. 00	737 33
Revenue	1½	....	398. 00	775. 00	398 70
Karrick	2¾	....	1, 986. 00	449. 00	1, 152 93
Silver Peak	1¼	....	193. 00	635. 00	323 18
Totals	555½	....	72, 270. 60	....	66, 251 09

Average yield of Liberty ore, per ton, $116 87.

The high yield of the Liberty ore is not a measure of the profit of the company, but (as I have remarked in speaking of Reese River ores) an indication of the high cost of mining, transportation, and reduction. The attempt of the company to carry on this enterprise by skimming the richest ore out of their splendid mine lasted about one year, and has been wisely abandoned. The mill has been stopped, and the mine is now being thoroughly opened, so that when reduction of ore is resumed, it may be upon a scale large and certain enough to allow expenses per ton to be decreased, and ore of average richness ($60) to be worked with profit. In this way a large and prosperous business will doubtless be established on the only sound mining basis—reduction of ore in great quantities at low rates. As an illustration of this, I have prepared the following statements, the fundamental principle of which is applicable to many other companies:

Memorandum of daily expense of running the present four-stamp mill at San Antonio, and of working the mine on present system.

RIGBY MILL.

	Gold.	
Wages—2 engineers, at $4 50	$9 00	
3 roasters, $4	12 00	
2 battery hands, at $4	8 00	
1 mechanic, at $4 50	4 50	
1 blacksmith, half time, at $4	2 00	
Wood, 3½ cords, at $10	35 00	
Salt, 300 pounds, per cwt. $3 50	10 50	
Transportation of ore to mill, two tons, at $13	26 00	
Loss of quicksilver (overestimated)	1 50	
Loss on board of eight men	1 15	
General expenses, covering coal, oil, and repairs	6 00	
Interest on $20,000, at 7 per cent. per annum	3 85	
		$119 50

LIBERTY MINE.

Wages—16 men, (average number,) at $4	64 00	
1 foreman, board and $5	6 30	
1 cook, board and $2	3 30	
Loss on board of 16 men	2 30	
Powder, fuze, and candles	5 60	
General expenses, covering feed, timber, &c	3 25	
		84 75

GENERAL EXPENSES OF COMPANY.

Bookkeeper, (board and $1,000 per annum)	4 00	
Stable boy	3 00	
Feed of two buggy horses	3 00	
Taxes, United States and State, about $1,600 per annum	4 38	
Interest on amounts overdrawn at Austin, for current expenses, about $3,000 per annum	8 21	
Exchange, say 1 per cent. on $136,558 53 per annum	3 74	
Assay fees, bullion charges, &c., $1,000 per annum	2 74	
		29 07
Total daily expense of R. S. M. Co		233 32

Estimated cost (daily expense) of running a ten-stamp mill, (heavy stamps.)

	Gold.
Wages—2 engineers, first-class, at $5	$10 00
2 battery feeders, at $4	8 00
12 roasters, (4 furnaces,) at $4	48 00
1 mechanic, at $5	5 00
1 blacksmith, at $5	5 00

Cost of bringing eight tons ore to mill, at $13 per ton	$104 00	
Wood, nine cords, at $8 per cord	72 00	
Salt, 1,200 lbs., at $2 50 per cwt.	30 00	
Quicksilver, one pound per ton of ore, at 72 cents	6 00	
General expense	15 00	
Interest on $43,000, at 7 per cent.	8 25	
		$311 25
Daily expense		311 25

PROBABLE REDUCTION OF THE ABOVE EXPENSES.

On transportation of ore by using oxen	$72 00	
On wood, by bringing wood from Peavine	27 00	
On quicksilver, reduced freights	40	
		99 40
Minimum expense		211 85

N. B.—A still further reduction may confidently be expected in the item of wages, which will gradually fall as the completion of the railroad and the settlement of the country increase the supply of labor and reduce the cost of living. The amount of saving from this source I am, of course, unable to calculate at present, and I have there excluded it from the above estimates.

Comparison between the foregoing statements.

The present four-stamp mill reduces daily 2 tons of ore, average yield,	$116 87	$233 74
Total daily expense, (see VII)		119 50
Net earning, per ton $57 12		114 24

A ten-stamp mill, with steady supply of ore, would reduce daily 8 tons, at $116 87			934 96
Total daily expense, (see VIII,) max.	$311 25	min.	211 85
Net earnings per day, min.	623 71	max.	723 11
Net earnings per ton, min	77 96	max.	90 39
Saving per ton of ten-stamp over four-stamp mill, min.	20 84	max.	33 27
Saving on 536 tons worked to August, 1868, min.	11,170 24	max.	17,832 72

The Potomac, and other mines in San Antonio district, are not sufficiently developed to prove their value. The Potomac looks promising, and has furnished some rich ore.

Reveille district is in Nye county, about 130 miles south-southeast of Austin. In order to reach it from the latter place five ranges of mountains must be crossed, viz: the Toiyabe, Smoky Valley, (or Mootay,) Monitor, Hot creek, and Reveille ranges. From Hot creek to Reveille is about 40 miles. The journey from Austin requires three days for a horseman and six for a loaded wagon. The geological character of the district is that of a steep dolomitic range, forming the western side of the Reveille mountains. The surrounding porphyritic mountains, and many of the sloping foot-hills, are wooded. In the valley is an extensive salt marsh. The supply of water is poor, there being no running streams. Water is obtained, however, by wells in the porphyry. Six miles from the mines it is abundant. The dolomite range above mentioned is not continuous, but is divided into a northern and a southern portion by a wedge-like body of porphyry, and this rock also constitutes the mass of the mountain range on the eastern side, which doubtless caused the upheaval of the dolomite. The processes and products of metamorphosis can be here studied to great advantage. The porphyry in the neighborhood of the dolomite loses its solidity; the crystals of felspar are altered to kaoline; the color of the rock changes or disappears; efflorescenses of alum occur; in short, there are many evidences that the alteration of the rock was begun by *solfataras*, or springs of sulphurous acid gas. The metamorphosis has, however, gone still further. After the solfataras had transformed to sulphates the iron, alkalies, and the greater part of the alumina in the porphyry, and these had been washed away, mineral springs began the work of silicifying and otherwise solidifying the decomposed mass. In this way it comes to pass that the porphyry apparently passes over into dense, colorless rock, in which the original structure is no longer visible. Even the quartz granules have become indistinguishable in the mass, and one observes only here and there pseudomorphs of felspar. Even this feature vanishes at last, and fine-grained sandstones are formed, now colorless as white marble, now striped with red and yellow; and these finally pass into hard quartzite. All these stages of metamorphosis may frequently be observed within a limited space. A fine opportunity to study them is afforded by a cañon in Atlantic mountain, in this district. It should be added that the porphyry had not merely lifted the dolomite, but also broken through between its layers, and separated some portions of it from the rest. The foregoing description will apply with general accuracy as an explanation of the apparently chaotic variety and confusion of the so-called porphyries, quartzites, greenstones, granites, limestones, &c., of the Nevada mountains. The full understanding of these phenomena is to be sought by careful and detailed stratigraphical studies with the key afforded by the known results of solfataric action, and that of thermal and mineral springs. I am indebted for much information on this point to Mr. Stetefeldt, whose ideas have been almost invariably confirmed by my personal observations. The full report on Reveille district from his pen is one of the ablest papers on the geology of Nevada which I have ever seen.

The dolomite of this district is the country rock of the ore deposits. It is granular, white, or gray, devoid of stratification, and, as far as is yet known, of fossils. It contains a little quartz in fine particles and, in some places, carbonate of iron. The silver ores occur in it neither as veins nor as beds, but as irregular masses quite distinctly separated from the country rock. These masses crop out even above the dolomite, sometimes standing like walls on the side of the mountain. They vary in size from a few inches to many feet. The gangue is exclusively quartz, containing silver copper glance, and silver glance, altered on the surface to native silver, horn silver, and carbonates of copper. Antimony glance is rare. Sulphurets of iron, copper, zinc, and lead, have not been found. A more favorable ore for amalgamation could scarcely be sought. The contents in silver, especially in the masses which do not crop out very widely, are extremely large. Pulp assays run from $200 to $1,647 per ton; and quartz assays of selected samples might attain almost any figures, up to the chemical limits. The masses referred to were erroneously held to be the outcrops of veins, and much disappointment has resulted from failure in some cases to find their continuance in depth. Among the mines, or rather claims, may be named the Fisherman, Crescent, August, Adriatic, Garden City, Highbridge, Aurora, Bolivia, Ottawa, Mediterranean, Baltic, and Indian Queen mines. Considerable ore has been hauled to the Old Dominion mill at Hot creek, 40 miles distant. To pay expenses of mining and transportation, the ore must be worth more than $100 per ton. The Rutland mill (five stamps) was refitted in April last, and set to work in May. I have no recent reports from it; but I am under the impression that the district has been partially abandoned, the idea having obtained currency among the miners that deposits in limestone are not permanent. This is in a certain sense true of this and similar districts; but the real difficulty is one of ownership and management. I believe that claims on "lodes" where there are no lodes cannot be profitably worked; and Reveille, like Cortez district, has suffered from the attempt to apply to it a system of vein mining which could not be carried out. The same danger threatens White Pine, which in many respects resembles both the districts named. Companies owning a sufficient area in square locations, to include many of these ore masses, might yet achieve in Reveille a brilliant success.

Hot Creek district lies 90 or 100 miles southeast of Austin, and about 40 miles by air-line almost due east of Belmont. The district lies in a colossal mass of porphyry, 20 miles wide and 50 miles long, which includes in several places large bodies of limestone, or rather dolomite, forming precipitous and irregular cappings along the highest points of the mountain range. It is not easy, under such circumstances, in advance of more thorough geological surveys, to say whether the porphyry has upheaved these sedimentary masses, or is itself a metamorphosed sedimentary rock in place beneath them. The porphyritic ranges of Nevada frequently exhibit these limestone caps; and the latter are accompanied with belts of quartzite, or "quartz veins," often of incredible extent. The explanations given in the account of Reveille district may apply here. The great quartzite belt of this district (similar to the Nevada Giant in Cortez) is in some places three-quarters of a mile wide, and may be followed for 10 miles, while its continuations in other dolomitic islands appear throughout the whole length of the porphyritic range. The quartz of this belt is often white as snow. It never shows any ore; but ore is found in the neighborhood of its course, in the dolomite. The manner of occurrence can scarcely be classified among the usual general terms as vein, bed, mass, pocket, or impregnation. It might be called a segregation, since that may mean anything. There are some features of almost every class presented. Most frequently the ore deposit consists of a vein-like zone of the limestone, highly silicified, (cherty,) which contains in spots a little horn silver, and at greater depth silver copper glance, but very irregularly and sparingly. The Indian Jim and Old Dominion are examples. Other deposits are more massive, but retain the form of veins. Those most resembling veins have, however, neither selvages nor slickensides. The Keystone is an example. On the other hand some small bunches, like the Pennsylvania, show very distinct slickensides. The cañon of Hot Creek is very precipitous. The hot springs appear to break out from the border between limestone and porphyry. In the bed of the stream there are steam springs, which for a distance of 2,000 feet keep the water boiling. It is remarkable that the finest springs of cold water occur close by the hot ones. The Hot Creek company (or Old Dominion) had a 10-stamp mill here, which was supplied from these springs with hot and cold water. This company owned the Norfolk, Merrimac, Old Dominion, and other claims. After a brief success with the surface ore of the latter vein the mill failed, was partly burnt down, rebuilt, and set at work upon ore from Morey district. Afterwards it stopped again; and I am told it has been removed to White Pine. Three or four settlers still maintain the town of Hot Creek with the perseverance of despair—unless they, too, since my last advics, have gone to White Pine.

Philadelphia district.—This district, known also as Silver Bend, is described in Mr. Browne's last report, page 420. I visited Belmont, its mining town, (and the county-seat of Nye county,) in August, and found mining operations rather depressed. The Combination Company's splendid 40-stamp mill was about to be shut down for want of ore. This was done in a day or two after; and the company is now proceeding to open the mining ground in depth which will enable them to run the mill. But the latter is too large. Buel's Belmont Silver Mining Company was extracting good ore on a small scale, and the vein (the celebrated Transylvania) had been worked by open cuts and other expedients almost as far as practicable, without machinery, from the surface downward. The Buel mill, 10 stamps, was idle, or only running now and then on tailings, or custom-ore. I hear it has since been started up with success. The Buel and the Combination are both properties that will probably be found very valuable when once thoroughly opened. The only mine I saw on the Transylvania* which contains any considerable portion of ore in sight ready for stoping down is the Silver Bend Company's, a sketch of which is here given, as showing the general features of that famous deposit.

SILVER BEND COMPANY'S MINE, BELMONT.

[Profile, 100 feet to the inch.]

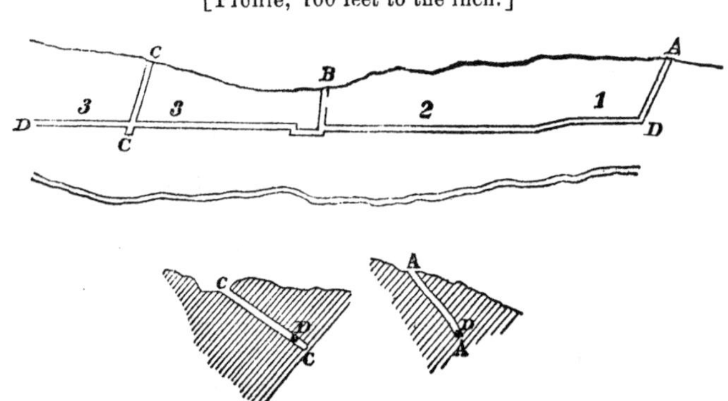

Silver Bend Company's Mine. Profile, ground plan of outcrop and cross-sections of shafts. Scale, 200 feet to the inch.

Course of vein north 30° west, south 30° east, (true course, magnetic declination 16° east;) near the north incline, and south of south incline, nearly north by south. The outcrop turns south up the hill, at the south incline. Dip, 40° to 60° and upwards, easterly. Thickness of vein, 0 to 8 feet and more. A, north incline; B, vertical shaft; C, south incline; D, level connecting the three shafts; 1, vein 5 to 8½ feet wide; 2, vein pinched to a clay seam; 3, vein on the average 3 to 3½ feet wide. Only 200 tons have been extracted in surface works, and in the running of shafts and level. Reserves 1 and 3 3 I estimate to contain about 1,500 tons of $100 ore, consisting of stetefeldtite and sulphurets, chloridized at and near the surface. The average width of the Transylvania ledge in the Buel and Combination mines seems to be 6 or 8 feet.

Combination mill.—The following notes upon this mill will be interesting to mill-men. There are 40 stamps, weight 720 pounds; drop, 80 per minute; 24 smooth-bottom pans for amalgamation, and 12 settlers. A Corlie's engine (125-horse power) runs the pans, and a Todd & Rafferty (75-horse power) the stamps. This arrangement is unfortunate, since the mill cannot be run at all without keeping both engines in motion; running at half capacity on custom work is therefore not profitable. There are 10 reverberatories for roasting ore. At the time of my visit, 20 stamps were crushing wet, for direct amalgamation, (Washoe process,) and 20 dry, for roasting, (Reese River process.) Ore yielding $25 to $30 was being worked by wet crushing; and 700 to 800 pounds of concentrated tailings were obtained from the 20 stamps daily, assaying $200

* I regard the Transylvania and Highbridge as one and the same vein.

per ton. These were roasted. There appears to be little loss in "slimes," as the ore is soft, and the sulphurets do not get too finely ground. Assays in the reservoir show, at the end of sluice, $21 99 per ton; 15 feet further, $15 71; 15 feet still further, $12 56. The tailings from roasted ores assay at the end of the sluice $20 41, indicating a yield by the process of about 80 per cent. of the silver in the ore. The mill guaranteed 80 per cent., but could do better on uniform ores than on the small lots of custom-work it was obliged to accept. Ore worth more than $80 per ton is roasted.

The cost of the wet process is estimated at $7 50 per ton only; but this figure is, in my opinion, too low. It can only be maintained, at any rate, by steadily running the mill at full capacity, when the cheapness of fuel ($5 per cord) will give a certain advantage over the mills of the Comstock mines, which employ the same process, at a cost of $10 to $12 per ton.

The Combination mill produced bullion as follows:

For the quarter ending—	Ore.		Process.	Yield.
	Tons.	*Pounds.*		*Coin.*
March 31, 1868	730	1, 308		$84, 755 80
June 30, 1868	450	710	Roasted	36, 168 07
June 30, 1868	688	97	Wet	17, 045 51
September 30, 1868, custom work, &c., in July, estimated				15, 000 00
December 31, 1868, mill idle				
Total				152, 969 38

Eldorado.—The Transylvania lode, as I have said, turns south, at the south incline on the Silver Bend location. How far it continues in that direction is not known; but further south, and separated from this point by two ridges, crops out the Eldorado vein, running north and south with the slate-country rock. The vein carries a body of quartz, nearly barren, 4 feet in thickness, to the depth thus far explored, (120 feet on the incline,) and in the hanging wall a magnificent mass of rich chloride ore, of unknown extent. The ore gives (first-class) $200, $300, and even $500 per ton. It contains much visible horn-silver. The owners of the Eldorado south were simply "gouging the outcrop" at the time of my visit.

Manhattan district.—This district lies in the Mootay or Smoky range, (the eastern boundary of Smoky valley,) about 15 miles south of Belmont. It was not mentioned in Mr. Browne's report; and not much can be said about it now. The principal rocks are granite, argillaceous and calcareous slates, and some limestone. The ores are the usual antimonial sulphurets, peculiar to eastern Nevada, with their decompositions, such as chloride of silver, &c. The Ophir mine has been opened to a depth of about 50 feet, and shows some very rich ore. A test working of 2,500 pounds, made at one of the Austin mills last summer, is reported to have yielded by pulp assay* $230 per ton.

This district is abundantly supplied with nut-pine, suitable for fuel and mining timbers, and contains several springs.

* The pulp assay is the assay made upon a carefully taken average sample of the crushed ore from the batteries. It is generally higher than the actual mill-product by a small amount.

Quarterly return of the assessor of Nye county, for the quarter ending March 31, 1868.

Mine.	Ore reduced.		Average per ton.
	Tons.	*lbs.*	
Murphy	664	1,000	$127 16
Transylvania	289		26 72
El Dorado, North	7	1,000	84 76
Highbridge	730	1,308	154 66
El Dorado, South	18	1,059	160 58
Reveille, Mitchell	9	92	177 19
Reveille, Prometheus Company	1	60	160 77
Reveille, Tennant		912	182 60
Hot Creek, Gally		1,300	81 47
Hot Creek, Old Dominion Company	6	1,740	70 00
Hall & Emerson, Morey district	12	1,650	162 92
Liberty, San Antonio	114	1,404	122 97
Revenue, San Antonio	1	949	360 25
McMasters, Union district	6	310	74 26
Savage, Union district	13	541	125 72
Alice Wright, Union district	13	15	57 41
Pleiades, Union District		1,142	252 03
Victor, Union district	11	1,660	152 84
Astoria, Union district	1	258	140 46

These returns are calculated in currency. The assessor of Nye county kindly promised to forward subsequent reports to me, but as he shortly after emigrated to White Pine, I suppose he must have resigned his office, and I have been unable to communicate with his successor in time to obtain the desired statistics.

CHAPTER IX.

LINCOLN COUNTY.

Pahranagat district.—In addition to the description of this district contained in Mr. Browne's last report (Mineral Resources, &c., 1868, p. 426,) the following statements are offered, based upon a more recent and careful examination.

The Pahranagat mines are situated in a chain of mountains, mainly composed of limestone and porphyry, which forms the western slope of the head of Pahranagat valley. The highest ridge of this chain, Mt. Irish, is the centre of the mineral belt of Pahranagat district. This belt extends north and south about five miles, and has a width of from half a mile to two miles. Almost everywhere the mountains are well covered, as compared with other ranges of their class, with nut-pine and cedar; and on the western slope of Mt. Irish, near the summit, there is abundance of pine timber, many of the trees measuring two feet, and a few over three feet in diameter. This timber is, however, not of superior quality, being very brittle on account of the extreme dryness of the soil. There is plenty of water in Pahranagat valley, 12 miles from the principal mines, but it is very scarce near the mines themselves. The principal mining camp, Silver City, is compelled to haul its supply from a spring two or three miles distant. For this reason mills must either be built in Pahranagat valley, involving a heavy expense for transportation of ores, or they must rely upon the mines for their supply of water. The latter source is extremely unreliable, as the water-line in the mines seems to lie very deep. The great distance of Pahranagat from commercial centres (the route to Austin is nearly 200 miles, and all other lines of communication are much longer) considerably enhances the cost of materials and supplies.

The geological features of the district are analogous to those of Cortez, Reveille, and Hot Creek. The base of Mt. Irish, and the ridges which emanate from it, are composed of gray crystalline limestone, here almost entirely without fossils and stratification. Further north, and outside of the metalliferous belt, the limestone abounds in fossils, and is distinctly stratified. Above the limestone lies an immense stratum of quartzite, 300 to 400 feet in thickness, which forms the precipitous eastern slope of Mt. Irish, and is again overlaid with limestone. There is also a huge quartzite dike which cuts, with a westerly dip, nearly north and south through the ridges and cañons of the eastern slope of Mt. Irish, forming a barrier beyond which the mineral veins do not extend, and no mineral deposits have been found. A similar dike runs northeast and southwest with northwestern dip through the limestone, near its southern terminus in Crescent cañon. The upheaval of the limestone formation has been effected by eruptions of quartz porphyry, which forms the foot-hills of the eastern branches of Mt. Irish, and rises in bold mountains south of Logan and Crescent. It is again found west of Mt. Irish, and almost surrounds the whole limestone formation. In Crescent cañon the decomposed *débris* of this rock form a tolerable clay for bricks, the best material for this purpose in the district, from which were manufactured the bricks for the new furnaces of the mill in Hiko. Near Logan the porphyry is much decomposed, as shown by white zones running through the rock. The *débris* of this decomposed porphyry have formed a white conglomerate, which is a good building stone. As I have remarked, these features are common to many districts of Nevada, though it is usual with prospectors to pronounce every new district discovered a *lusus naturæ*, "baffling the knowledge of the geologist and setting all preconceived notions of science at fault." (This sort of talk is now current about White Pine, a district the geological formation of which is singularly clear and simple.) The principal source of difficulty in the study of such formations is the extent and variety of the metamorphosis of the porphyry. In many places it is evident that the quartzite which is found in connection with the crystalline limestone and porphyry is but a highly altered form of the latter. (For a discussion of this point see description of Reveille district.) The gangue accompanying the Pahranagat ores is an extremely hard and solid quartz, either white or stained with iron; calcspar appears subordinately. The silver-bearing minerals are galena and stetefeldtite. The latter is the principal silver ore in all the mining districts of southeastern Nevada.* It contains from 2 to 13 per cent. of silver, according to locality, in combination with sulphur; also oxides of iron, lead, and copper, combined with antimonic acid and water. Near the surface these minerals are, of course, more or less decomposed.

In most mining districts of Nevada, where limestone forms the country rock, no mineral veins are found, but only deposits of very irregular shape; but the mineral belt of Pahranagat is traversed by innumerable fissures, running in all directions. Some of these appear to form permanent veins; some are only superficial; while others enclose wedge-shaped deposits of ore, the walls of which meet at various angles; and still others are only slides and breaks in the mountains. The limestone overlying the quartzite is, so far as known, barren of metalliferous ores.

*This mineral (probably the same as the partzite of Esmeralda) was established as a species two or three years ago by Mr. C. A. Stetefeldt, of Austin, whose name it bears. The remarks of Adelberg and Raymond, quoted on page 426 of Mr. Browne's report, were made previous to this identification of the species. From assays (not analysis) and general appearances we supposed it to be polybasite, and alluded to it as such.

There are some mineral-bearing fissures in the quartzite itself, near the summit of Mt. Irish, but the principal mineral belt is the limestone underlying it. The walls of these fissures are sometimes, where they have been filled with quartz, extremely smooth and highly polished.

The mineral deposits of Pahranagat may be classified as follows:

1. A system of veins running nearly northeast and southwest; examples, List, Ulrich Dahlgren, Illinois.
2. A system running east and west, with more or less variation to the south and north; examples, Juniper, Springer, Utah, and Nevada.
3. Veins running northeast and southwest in the quartzite; examples, Green Monster, Penobscot.
4. Superficial veins; examples—it is probable that most of the east and west veins belong to this class.
5. Deposits; examples, Diana, lower workings of Indiana.

The northeast and southwest veins must be considered as the main lodes of the district. They have a steep dip of about 75° southeast, and are distinguished by their huge croppings, often more than 20 feet in width. The quartz has a dull color, resembles quartzite, and is mostly barren; but in places chimneys of rich ore have been found. In the List and Illinois, the two most developed mines, it was found that these bodies of pay-ore only extended some 40 feet below the croppings, and thus far, down to 180 feet, no more material has been found which will pay either mining or milling expenses.

The east and west veins have mostly a northern dip, from 35° to 75°. Their croppings are not so prominent as those of the first class. The quartz is mostly porous, and colored with oxide of iron. There is sometimes good ore in sight at the surface. The width of these veins varies from two inches to two feet. The narrower ones are mainly found near the northeast and southwest main ledges, and can only be considered as spurs. Although some of them, like the Nora, carry extraordinarily rich ore, they cannot be worked with profit on account of their small size. Only one of the east and west veins, the Springer, has been developed to any considerable depth. The Springer incline is 115 feet deep, and the vein at the bottom is about one foot wide, white quartz, with cubes of coarse galena. The Juniper, one of the larger veins of this group, can be traced for a long distance, and has been worked at the surface, yielding an ore containing galena, and a very plumbiferous variety of stetefeldtite, and averaging $80 to $90 silver per ton.

The veins in quartzite are narrow, and resemble the foregoing. Several tons of ore have been extracted from the Green Monster, and are said to have yielded $150 silver per ton; but there is hardly any ore now in sight. It is not known whether these veins in quartzite descend into the underlying limestone.

In several places irregular masses of ore, sometimes of very high grade, have been segregated in the limestone, generally at the intersection of two or three fissures, not belonging to the main systems. Such is the case with the Diana, which has been entirely dug out, and vainly sought for at greater depth by means of a long tunnel. Many other locations in the district, which have no signs of true veins, are doubtless similar to this.

The developments in this district are both costly and extensive, but have been conducted with such conspicuous absence of skill and common sense, that they may be said to have produced hardly any results whatever. On the one hand, no mine has yet been made productive; and on the other hand, scarcely any have been so thoroughly explored as to render their unproductiveness a matter of certainty. But few companies are now at work; and it is to be hoped that these will persevere until the actual value of the district is ascertained. The sums expended in Pahranagat are estimated as follows:

Companies or mines.	Amount.
Alameda and Crescent	*$180,000
Montauk	33,323
Pioneer, Pahranagat Valley, and Hiko	†400,000
Globe and International	20,000
Vance and Livingston	50,000
Pro Rata Company	20,000
Gould and Sherwood	30,000
Other companies	100,000
Individual labor	100,000
	933,323

The amount of bullion extracted in the district up to July, 1868, is about $20,000.

CHAPTER X.

ESMERALDA COUNTY.

Columbus district lies in Esmeralda county, about 60 miles east-southeast of Aurora, 140 miles southwest of Austin, and 35 miles northwest of Silver Peak. It was discovered in 1864. The town of Columbus is situated on the western edge of an alkaline flat, designated on some of the maps as "Great Soda Lagoon." Two miles north of the town and on the edge of the same flat is a salt marsh of considerable extent. The hills of which the district is composed are spurs or offshoots of the White Mountain range, and generally almost barren of wood. The rocks of the district are granite, metamorphic slates and sandstones, and trachyte. The veins may be divided into two classes, the one lying generally in the granite, and the other in the metamorphic rocks. The first class is highly cupriferous, and carries horn-silver, stetefeldtite and other kindred silver minerals, combined with malachite, azurite and other common products from the decomposition of copper-bearing minerals. These veins are generally from one to two or three feet in width, and their ore is of high grade. The Balnarte is a good example of the first class. The second class occurs generally in slate, more or less metamorphosed, and the ore contains much carbonate, antimoniate, and other salts, of lead. The veins are broader than those of the first class, and the ore is more uniform, but of lower grade. The Potosi group, Northern Belle and Ural, are good examples. The Northern Belle is more than 15 feet wide, and crops out distinctly for several hundred feet. About 25 tons of the ore are said to have been worked at the Knickerbocker mill, at Jones's, 90 miles distant, and to have yielded by pulp assay $123 per ton. Until recently, Columbus district has been without reduction works of any kind, but during the past year A. J. Holmes and others have put up a small mill (four stamps, I believe,) which will soon commence, if it has

* One 10-stamp mill.
† One 5 and one 10-stamp mill.

not by this time already commenced, to work the ores of the neighborhood. Water is found by sinking a few feet in the alkaline flat above-mentioned, and an abundance of wood is obtained from hills 10 or 12 miles distant.

About 18 miles northwest of Columbus is the Virginia salt marsh, well known as one of the largest and best ever discovered in Nevada. For some time it supplied the mills of Virginia City; but upon the discovery of salt marshes nearer to that town this one was abandoned. I think it is only occasionally worked, to fill special contracts. The salt is collected by excavating in the loose soil of the marsh vats, in which water accumulates, and dissolves the salt from the surrounding earth. The subsequent evaporation of the water under the heat of the sun, the dry air and almost constant wind, leaves a thick crust of pure and excellent crystalline salt, which is gathered with shovels and thrown into heaps to await wagon transportation to the mills.

The Red Mountain gold mines, near Silver Peak, 90 miles southeast of Aurora and 140 miles south of Austin, are being successfully developed by a New York company. The improvements mentioned in the report of my predecessor (1868, page 339) have been completed; the mines are connected with the mill by a skilfully constructed railway, 1½ mile in length, and a fine wagon road 6½ miles in length, having so uniform a grade that a team of eight mules can haul 15 to 20 tons at a load down the mountain, making one trip in two-thirds of a day. The transportation of the ore does not exceed $2 per ton in cost, the mining $1 50 to $2 per ton, and the working in mill $4 to $5. These extraordinarily low rates arise from the natural advantages of the location as well as the skilful use that has been made of them. The principal gold-bearing veins of the company lie on the side of a high mountain, dipping with the slope of the surface, and they have been stripped of large portions of the hanging wall by natural denudation and deeply cross-cut by several cañons. In other words, nature has laid bare the veins to the depth of hundreds of feet below their highest outcrops, and mining is mere quarrying. This fact, and the wise liberality of the company in providing—at a cost of more than $20,000—cheap transportation for its ores, will enable it to work low-grade quartz, of which it possesses an immense quantity, together with much that will yield $50 and upwards per ton. The 20-stamp mill of the company at Silver Peak is now running; but I have no results as yet. The current year will probably witness a large production of bullion from this locality.

Colonel Catherwood, of a New York company, is working some very promising mines in Palmetto district, 20 miles from Silver Peak. The mill under his charge is said to have started recently, but I have not received any returns. The ore from the mines is often very rich, indeed, containing stetefeldtite, native silver and chloride.

Pine Grove district.—This district is situated in Esmeralda county, Nevada, at the southwest end of the great basin which terminates northward in the sink of Carson river. The district is in a range of hills east of the Washoe range, and about 30 miles in direct line, or 63 to 65 miles by wagon road, from Carson and Virginia Cities. These pine grove hills are in many places densely covered with nut pines or piñons, and consist principally of syenite, which is traversed by gabbro. In the latter rock occur most of the auriferous quartz veins. The inhabitants believe that the numerous outcrops, which course generally north and south and vary in width from 20 feet downward, (the average is much less than 20 feet,) are all parts of a mammoth fissure vein 200 feet thick. It is quite likely, however, that these constitute only a vein system of gash-veins, caused by the breaking through the granite of the gabbro. The vein matter is principally quartz, carrying, near the surface, free gold, oxides of iron, decomposed copper pyrites and galena. Near the surface the quartz is very porous and the ores are richer than they have hitherto been found in depth, where the quartz becomes more solid, and crystalline, and galena, copper ore, and iron pyrites predominate, while free gold begins to disappear. The deepest mining work, however, is only 80 feet underground, and the only indications as to the character of the veins at greater depth are afforded by wells, which have been dug 150 to 200 feet below the surface. At this point is the water level, and it is possible that below that level the ores will be principally of lead and copper, poor in silver, while the gold will be found in the iron pyrites. Some of the pyrites already mined contain gold at the rate of $5 to $7 per ton.

The principal mines are the Wilson or Himalaya, (1,000 feet,) the Midas, (1,000 feet,) the Central, (1,000 feet,) and the Wheeler, (1,200 feet.) These are all situated on the main vein of the district, having a general course north 60° east and a dip of 27° to 43° northwest. This vein has an average width of 17 feet and carries ore from 4 to 7 feet in width. It has casings of greenstone, which on the hanging wall is in places not more than three inches thick, and beyond which is the syenitic granite of the country. Ore has been extracted from the surface downward. Some very rich pockets have been met with, and the four mines above named yield from 50 to 70 tons of ore daily, yielding in mill an average of about $25 per ton. The cost of mining and milling, including all expenses, is probably not more than $17 per ton. There are two mills in the district, which are kept constantly employed. They have ten stamps each, crush wet, amalgamate in the battery, and have no pans.

The assessor of Esmeralda reports for the quarter ending August 1, 1868, (July?) 2,681 tons of assessable ore, valued at more than $18 per ton, and 135 tons of an inferior grade, yielding in the aggregate over $95,000. Further returns not received.

CHAPTER XI.

HUMBOLDT COUNTY.

This county having been treated very briefly and unsatisfactorily in the report of the mining commissioner last year, I felt the more desirous of visiting it in person and collecting more definite and detailed information concerning its resources. It was my good fortune to meet a number of the most respectable and substantial citizens, among them Judge E. F. Dunn, of Unionville, to whom I am indebted for much of the following description. The most important localities in the county I visited myself.

Humboldt county has an area of about 16,000 square miles, nearly in the form of a square. Like Lander and other counties, it is divided into independent, narrow, parallel valleys by ranges of mountains, which have a general north and south course, and an altitude varying from 3,000 to 8,000 feet. Star Peak, the highest point, is 10,000 feet high. The Humboldt river separates the southeast quarter of the county from the rest, running as it does across the eastern line to the centre, and then almost due south to Humboldt lake, on the southern boundary. Humboldt lake is about 16 miles long by 12 wide. It has not the beauty of

Pyramid or Bigler. The eastern part of the county is the most elevated. West of 116° west of Greenwich, the country sinks gradually, until at about 118° 30′ west it subsides into sandy plains and alkali flats, barren of vegetation, dry and parched in summer, half covered with water in winter. In the centre of the county sparkling mountain streams abound, and cedar, mountain mahogany, and pine are found. East and north of this, it is well adapted for grazing and some branches of agriculture. Here, as elsewhere in Nevada, cattle are kept on range the whole year, without shelter, and are able to grow fat on the white sage and bunch-grass. A large portion of the southern half of the county is sandy and alkaline valleys, one of which includes the dreaded Forty Mile desert, once the terror of emigrants, but now traversed by the railroad, and, so far as it was a barrier to the westward flowing stream of travel, quite annihilated.

Humboldt has had a remarkably speculative and fluctuating history. It has been the scene of higher hopes and more bitter disappointments than almost any other region. In the early days of silver mining in the State, Humboldt shared in the furor of prospecting and exploring and investing; but the difficulty, mechanical, metallurgical, or merely economical, of treating the ores, the lack of ores in many veins in depth, the effect of hasty and ill-considered local regulations, and other agencies, brought about a revulsion akin to a panic. Populous towns were deserted, whole districts abandoned, and mines upon which large sums had been expended were forsaken as worthless. It is usually a long time before one of our mining districts recovers from such a reaction. They are always, so to speak, prematurely settled. The enterprise of the miner precedes all others, and when he fails there is nothing left for the community to fall back upon, and it disappears as swiftly as it was gathered. Humboldt county might have waited long for the renewed attention of labor and capital, but for the fortunate fact that the Pacific railroad was located through its territory and very near some of its most metalliferous ranges. The immediate result was an influx of visitors from California, looking for good mines, or making contracts to purchase ore. The forests of the Sierra are now made available for fuel and lumber; labor is decreasing in price; and, in a word, Humboldt is "looking up." The principal districts in the county will be described in alphabetical order.

Battle Mountain district.—With the exception of a central meridional portion, the general course of the Humboldt is from east to west. It cuts across the ends of the long, flat valleys to the south. These valleys, divided by high ranges, are about 15 miles wide. Reese River valley is one of them, and opens out on the Humboldt at a point 380 miles by rail east of Sacramento, or 226 from Reno. The range on the west side of Reese River valley at this point is the Battle Mountain range, and the very point of it at the northern end, where it begins to slope down towards the Humboldt, is the high peak of Battle Mountain, named from an early Indian fight. At the base of Battle Mountain runs the Pacific railroad, and here will doubtless be located the railway station with which the southern trade and freight for Austin and other points must connect. Austin is 85 miles south by the new wagon-road through Reese River valley. The probable point of junction with the Idaho travel is also in this neighborhood, so that the prospects of Battle Mountain for easy communications and even commercial importance are not to be despised.

The mines are situated in the cañons around Battle Mountain, and have been located since the summer of 1866. The district was organized in the spring of 1867. The ledge upon which most work had been done up to August last was the Little Giant, running north and south across the summit of Little Giant hill, and dipping 35° west. The width of the vein is four to six feet; the country rock quartzite; the ore concentrated in one pay-streak about 20 inches wide. The ore on the surface, from the decomposition of compounds of lead or antimony, has acquired a yellow, ocherous appearance, and is soft and crumbling. The gangue is not distinguishable in this yellow mass. This is true of all the surface ore of the district, except that of the Caledonia mine, which looks like broken steel. At a little depth the ore of the Little Giant grows darker in color, some of it being black and soft, but on exposure to the air it hardens and changes to the color of mispickel. The workings are not deep. From the summit to the northern end of the location—that is, for half the claim—the ledge has been stripped wherever it did not already crop out on the surface, and at intervals it has been opened with shallow shafts. The prospecting has, therefore, been pretty thorough, except in depth. The south half of the Little Giant is owned by Mr. John Atchison, and has not been worked to any extent. The black ore from the workings (just described) of Fox and Macbeth assayed as high as $500 to the ton; and a lot of 22 tons, hauled to mill, is said to have yielded $269 per ton. Next on the north is the location of the Monitor company, 600 feet. This was the original location on the Little Giant, Fox and Macbeth having, in reality, the first southern extension. Still further north is the Santa Clara, supposed to be still an extension, and beyond this, in the same direction across an intervening cañon, is the St. Helena, which is claimed as another extension of the Little Giant on the evidence of similarity in the general appearance of its mineral. The Montrose, three-fourths mile north of this, is a ledge of which high expectations are entertained. It is cased in talcose slate, and begins handsomely at the top with six feet of ore—how rich or how permanent was not yet known in August. Above the Montrose lies the Idaho, and above the Idaho the Caledonia, a fine-looking, with heavy, not decomposed ores, assaying $90. Mr. Atchison has put up in Fox cañon a ten-stamp mill which was moved over from Black Rock. There is plenty of water in the district for steam-mills, and wood is abundant within ten miles. The district is ten miles from the Humboldt and seven or eight from the railroad.

Besides the silver-bearing veins already mentioned, this district is distinguished, like some others in Humboldt county, for its veins of copper ore. These are in copper cañons, some eight miles from Fox cañon, and are very numerous and rich, though their true character is scarcely determined. They vary in thickness from a few inches to several feet. The rock is talcose slate, dipping west, and overlying the quartzite in which most of the silver veins are enclosed. My authority for this observation is Judge Dunn, a keen observer by nature as well as education. I do not, however, attach any significance, in a region where the geological formation is so broken and irregular, to the local superposition of strata. The occurrence of veins of baser metals, or the admixture of such metals in silver ores, has not been very welcome to the Nevada miners hitherto, since nothing but the most precious metals would bear the cost of mining, reduction, and transportation; but the construction of the railroad puts an entirely new face on the matter, and mines that would not formerly pay on silver alone have suddenly become profitable by virtue of their base metals. These, however, cannot be utilized except by smelting. In my observations on Trinity district, below, more will be said on this subject.

Since my return to the east it is reported from this district that the Battle Mountain mill, owned by Macbeth, Atchison & Co., is a perfect success. If this be the case, we may naturally look for a very rapid development of the district, as the result of all the concurring circumstances above described.

Black Rock district.—This district, comprising a large portion of the northwestern quarter of Humboldt county, has been the scene of hopes as wild and disappointments as overwhelming as any recorded in the history of American mines. As early as 1859 the notice of acute, but ignorant observers was attracted by a dark-colored rock, occurring in heavy masses in that region, about a hundred miles from Unionville. It was a bituminous clay, and the associated rocks were almost without exception volcanic, giving no encouragement for the discovery of precious metals. But the waxy texture of the clay, doubtless being compared to that of the rich silver ore known as horn-silver, (chloride of silver,) was considered a "good indication," and it was not long before the story found credence that a new ore of silver had been discovered in the "black wax" of Humboldt county. Respectable assayers in the Pacific States, and, to my knowledge, also in New York, flatly contradicted the popular delusion. But the Black Rock people had an assayer of their own—a man by the name of Isenbeck—who claimed that no one but himself could extract the silver from these peculiar ores. He worked by what he called the Freiberg process, and made use of a peculiar flux. It seems strange that intelligent men could believe such trash. Of course Mr. Isenbeck's secret flux contained a compound of silver. Six or seven years passed away in experiments and explorations. The people of the Pacific coast were the victims far more than eastern capitalists. They wanted to keep the good thing to themselves. At last, in 1867, Mr. Isenbeck announced that he was ready to work the rock on a large scale, and 13 tons were hauled for him from different ledges to Dall's mill, in Washoe county. The result announced was $70 to $400 per ton. A renewed excitement was the consequence. A mill was built in the Black Rock country, to be managed by Isenbeck. Two others were put in active preparation. But Mr. Isenbeck could not afford to use his flux on a large scale; and, before operations commenced, he disappeared from the public eye. The Black Rock miners, who had shown for more than six years a grim determination and perseverance worthy of respect, though they had been credulous as children of the stories of this charlatan, abandoned their mines in despair. Houses, mills, everything was left as it stood, and in the summer of 1868 there was not a human being in the district. Even thieves would not go there to steal the abandoned property. An expedition sent to the region by Mr. Clarence King confirmed the opinion of all scientific men from the beginning, that "Black Rock was a swindle."

I have related this story at some length, partly because my predecessor, unable to visit the district in person, was misled into expressing a favorable opinion of it, although by the time his report was in print the bubble had long been dissipated and the scheme forsaken. It is an unfortunate accident that, after this great fraud had been branded by the public press and public opinion, it should receive its last word of praise in a "public document." The accident is due, as I have pointed out, to the lapse of many months between the writing and the printing of the paragraph referred to. A second and still more important reason for dwelling on this history at the present time is the light which it throws on the knowledge and temperament of our mining population. A geologist would have condemned the Black Rock mines in the beginning; every chemist and metallurgist did declare the ores to be worthless; yet, on the word of a single pretender, hundreds of thousands of dollars were expended by men who believed that their black wax contained silver and gold in such a form that no ordinary assay could extract them. It was not for lack of scientific men, but for lack of faith in science, that these victims floundered on to their fate. This shows the insufficiency of imported science in a community uneducated to value it aright. It is true, as some western journal has remarked, that we can bring over from Europe scientific men enough; but what we need is a mining science at home, which will raise the tone of the whole community. But this theme will find separate consideration in the sequel. I would remark, in closing this description of Black Rock, that miners in general cannot follow a safer course than to condemn instantly as a swindle any process which is declared to extract more gold and silver from any or every ore than can be extracted by an experienced assayer. We can, by quantitative chemical analysis, account for every atom of the weight of the substance analyzed; we can check and prove our assays by various means, which approximate our certainty to the absolute; we have studied for years the nature and the combinations of the elemental substances; and now it may indeed be possible that gold and silver exist in forms and conditions hitherto unsuspected—imponderable, insoluble, infusible, intangible—but it is not likely; and the man who asserts it may claim the ear of the chemist, but he has no right to ask attention of the capitalist. The chances of the truth of such an alleged discovery are in inverse proportion to the number of men who have been busy with the subject, with all the light of modern science, without making the discovery—say as one to a thousand. Now, one to a thousand is a probability quite sufficient to deserve the respect of scientific inquirers; it is, in fact, as great an authority as most new doctrines can claim; but men investing money in matters of which they personally know nothing should look for better security.

I have alluded to this whole region as the Black Rock district. Strictly speaking it comprised several districts, viz: Hardin, Black Rock, Pinte, Fireman, Chico, and High Rock, of which Hardin was the most important, and contained the Black Rock Co.'s mill, (four stamps,) now remaining idle on the spot; the Goodwin Co.'s mill, (four stamps,) fate unknown; and the mill of Mr. Atchison, (five stamps,) now in operation in Battle Mountain district.

Buena Vista district.—This district lies for about eight miles along Buena Vista cañon, one of the side cañons of a large desert valley parallel with the Humboldt and eastward of it. A fine stream of water flows through this cañon and "sinks" in the great valley three miles below. By utilizing the fall of this stream a good many stamps could be driven by its power. This is only done at one mill at present. The district contains numerous locations on which a good deal of work has been performed; but few are now under active development. The country rock is mainly quartzite and porphyry, but the tops of the mountains are capped with limestone and calcareous shales. It has been the complaint of the miners here that their veins were "bottom up," *i. e.*, that instead of increasing in width and value with depth, they narrowed or "petered out." This has been in fact the experience of many of the locators. The explanation I conceive to be this: First, there is no law that causes fissure-veins to increase or improve in depth. Experience gives as many examples on one side as the other. Secondly, the veins of Buena Vista occur parallel to each other, and in groups. Every main fissure has subordinate fissures by its side, and the latter, at some comparatively slight depth, pinch together to a mere seam, and probably join the master-lode. Unfortunately, however, it is not easy to decide at the outcrop which is the permanent lode; and as the mining law allows every outcrop to receive a separate location, several owners must be disappointed for every one that succeeds. There are a number of well-opened and evidently permanent veins in the district, and many more which have "given out" and are abandoned. This and Star district, near by, afford a good illustration of the unwisdom of our United States mining law, which forbids the obtaining of more than the right to one outcrop under one patent—a point to be hereafter discussed.

Buena Vista district was organized in 1861. But few of the mines have been worked since 1865, yet operations have never been allowed to entirely die out. Unionville, the county seat of Humboldt, is in this cañon. The hills around have some fine grass, and the whole cañon wears an appearance of verdure and beauty most refreshing. Among the mines I can only mention a few. On the north side of the cañon is located the Persia series, comprising the National, Governor Downey, and Alba Nueva ledges. A tunnel 100 feet long exposes the latter, a fine-looking vein, two or three feet thick, with north and south course, well-defined walls, and dip east 50°. Next above, and parallel, is the Downey, opened with a pit of 25 feet, and remarkable for containing free gold. The ledge is narrower than the former. Still further up the hill a shaft of 85 feet shows the National to be a well-defined vein, about as large as the Alba Nueva, and dipping east 75°. The county assessor reports that several tons of ore from this vein, worked at the Pioneer mill, yielded $150 per ton in gold. No work has been done on the Persia series since 1865. On the south side of Eagle cañon, one of three forks into which Buena Vista cañon divides, a little above the mines just described, lies the property of the Seminole company, comprising the Cass, Joe Pickering, Halleck, Seminole, and Eagle ledges. The first and last of these show well in shafts 40 or 50 feet deep, and the ores contain gold as well as silver. At the time of my visit, I believe work was still going on in a tunnel cross-cutting the whole series. The first ledge was expected to be reached in 325 feet from daylight, and considerably more than half this distance had been accomplished. On the other side of Eagle cañon there is a tunnel about 100 feet long, intended to cut a lode called the Leroy, the cropping of which was very encouraging. There are no mines of importance beyond this to the north and west boundary lines of the district, the ground being occupied with what is called in that country a "thick growth" of cedar and mountain mahogany, from which wood (at $10 per cord for cedar, and $15 for mahogany) is supplied at Unionville. Another and more important group of mines is found southwest of the Pioneer mill, which stands on Buena Vista creek, just below Unionville. About a mile distant, on the north side of Peru gulch, is the Agamemnon ledge, coursing west of north, dipping east 75°, exposed by a shaft 50 feet deep in a width of five feet. Assays have been high. A tunnel is being run to cut the ledge at a depth of 200 feet. The Champion and Cedar Hill claims, on the Champion ledge, are parallel with the Agamemnon, and a little further south. They have been considerably talked about as very rich, especially in gold; but the evidence is not quite clear. The Agamemnon bestrides the high divide between Peru gulch and Buena Vista cañon. On the west of that divide occurs the Manitowoc, a remarkable vein, encased in calcareous shales which cap the hill, and striking north 37° west, with a dip nearly horizontal. The width varies from six inches to four feet, averaging two and a half or three feet. The shales seem to have nearly or quite the same strike and dip as the vein. But the remarkable feature of this deposit is its continuity with two others, one northeast and the other southwest of the works on the Manitowoc. These are not "extensions," in the ordinary sense, but outcrops of the same claim. The vein begins to pitch about 45° southwest, but at 25 feet it breaks to the almost horizontal position shown in the Manitowoc, and maintains this position for nearly 300 feet, when it suddenly resumes again its original dip of 45° southwest. I think this broken dip is the result of a slip of part of the mountain. The slates enclosing the vein appear to follow its changes; and this excludes the idea of an original irregularity of the fissure. On the three portions of the vein thus divided, these locations have been made. The upper one is at present a mere pit; the middle one is the Manitowoc; and the third is the Arizona. The workings on the two latter are somewhat extensive. The incline winze of the Arizona is nearly 80 feet deep. At the time of my visit, (August, 1868,) the daily production of ore was about 12 tons; the mining cost was $8 or $10 per ton; but this was considered temporarily high; hauling to mill, down a very steep road, $4 per ton. The ore consists of chloride of silver, with various salts of lead, and some sulphuret of silver, with traces of copper. It is worked in two mills, one belonging to the Pioneer company, and one to Fall & Temple, who own the mines. At the former mill, the pulp assays have averaged $97 per ton; at the latter, $110. The difference is due to the fact that the former mill has been running a much longer time. The bullion is very fine, and worth, I am told, some $20 per pound, owing to the presence of gold in the silver. The shipments of bullion by J. C. Fall and Fall & Temple, given in this chapter, from October 13, 1867, when the Pioneer mill started, to August 20, 1868, were from the mines just described. The North Star and Atlas are claimed as southern extensions of the Manitowoc. The southern boundary of Buena Vista district is formed by Cottonwood creek, which might furnish water-power for mills, but has not yet been utilized. The cost of tunnelling in this district ranges from $8 to $20 per running foot; shafting costs from $15 to $30.

There are two stamp mills in the district, the names of which we have given above. The upper one is the Pioneer, a small, old-fashioned, eight-stamp mill with double stems, run by water-power. Screens used, No. 50. There are eight small Knox pans, with a total daily capacity to amalgamate four or five tons of pulp. As the stamps could crush more than this, they are only run half the time. No roasting is practiced, and considerable loss is the natural result, the pulp assaying $97 and the tailings $40. This loss is not absolute, however, for the tailings are caught in a large reservoir, where they rapidly dry, and are preserved for future treatment. At present it will not pay to work them over.

The lower mill is Fall and Temple's. It is driven by steam, sage brush and grease wood being the fuel under the boiler. There are ten stamps, six Varney, and two large Wheeler pans; all flat-bottomed. The stamps weigh about 800 pounds, and are run at about 75 drops to the minute; screens, No. 40. This is a new mill, and was not adjusted to successful running at the time of my visit. It was producing very fine bullion, but at a very great loss, the pulp assaying $110 and the tailings $66. Capacity, 14 tons daily. The shipments of bullion from Unionville from October 13, 1867, to August 20, 1868, amount to some $90,000, and I estimate the total shipments for 1868 at $150,000, mostly the product of the two mills just mentioned.

Central district.—The reappearance of the Humboldt range, on the north side of the river, is called Eugene mountain, and the south end of this mountain is Central district. The famous mine known as the "56" is in this district, scarcely half a mile from the bank of the Humboldt.

The vein is generally supposed to be about 50 feet wide; the lode strikes north and south, along the western slope of the low foot hills. It is easily accessible by wagon road. The ore seems thus far to occur in bands from one to four feet thick, very rich in copper, and worth, it is said, some $50 and upwards per ton in silver. About 150 feet of tunnel and 60 feet of shaft constituted the workings up to September. The Unionville Register, October 24, says that the owners of the 56 mine have made arrangements to ship by the Central Pacific railroad 10 tons of ore to San Francisco. This will be the first shipment of ore made by the railroad company, but it is anticipated that a large business will be done in the way of back freights, as it is understood that the company will offer great inducements to parties owning low grade or refractory ores which cannot be worked with profit at the mines. This mine, in particular, is very favorably located for such shipments, and the percentage of copper in the ore is an element of profit at San Francisco, though entirely worthless at the mine, inasmuch as it cannot be extracted by the ordinary mill process. The sudden opening of a market for base-metal ores is producing in many districts a revolution in the notions of miners, and Humboldt county in particular, which has suffered heretofore in comparison with the pure ruby ores of districts further south, is beginning to find advantage in the copper, lead, and antimony for which it has hitherto been scorned. This will be more strikingly illustrated in the sequel by the experience of the Montezuma company, in Trinity district. Central district contains, besides the mine already alluded to, a number of outcrops of argentiferous galena, which will, doubtless, for the reasons just mentioned, soon receive the attention of miners. This district was organized in 1862.

Eldorado district.—This district is also one of the early ones, having been organized in 1862. It is situated nearly under Star Peak, on the western side of the Humboldt range. I believe there is nothing doing in the district at present. The Banner mine, owned by the Eldorado company, has been developed at an expense of about $10,000 in coin. It has about 250 feet of tunnel, and 80 feet of inclined shaft. The results of these explorations have been highly encouraging, but the owners resolved, some three years ago, to wait for the railroad to cheapen the cost of work. As the whole body of the ledge is considered to yield an average of $90 per ton, it is to be expected that operations will soon be resumed upon it, since the railroad is finished within a short distance. Other mines in this district are the Corinth series, the New England series, the Mount Carmel, &c. All the veins of the district have limestone for the country rock, a fact which, in view of frequent experience in Nevada, may throw some doubt on their character as true fissures, permanent in depth.

Gold Run district.—This is one of the recent discoveries, organized in 1866. The principal mines are the Golconda, Cumberland, and Jefferson. The Golconda is an immense mass of ore, whether a fissure vein or not does not yet clearly appear. A shaft 80 feet deep has been sunk in a solid bed of ore, which is further exposed by a large open excavation. There is, consequently, a great deal of milling rock in sight. This mine is an acknowledged success. I believe there are two mills running on the ore; Negus's mill, 8 stamps and 13 pans, 7 miles from the mine, and Holt's Winnemucca mill, just moved over to Golconda. The Cumberland, one and a half mile south of the Golconda, a well-defined vein 10 feet wide, striking north and south, dipping west 45°, has been developed by a shaft some 50 feet deep, and prospecting is still going on. The ore assays well, and the outcrop of the vein is prominent for 1,000 feet. A half mile further south is the Jefferson, also a promising mine, but at present lying idle for want of means. The railroad, which passes within seven miles, and the Humboldt canal, which already brings water 40 miles to Winnemacca, will be of benefit to Gold Run district.

Humboldt district.—The oldest in the county, organized 1860; lies on the west slope of Star mountains, five miles from the Humboldt, two and a half miles from the railroad, 16 miles from Unionville, and 175 miles from Virginia City; contains Humboldt City, the first settlement in the county. There is an immense bed of sulphur near the town, and a good deal of fine agricultural land along the Humboldt creek and river. The veins of the district are mostly in the quartzite or siliceous porphyry of the Star range. The Starlight, Calaveras, Sigel, Adriatic, Winnemucca, Washington, and San Bernard and others have been prospected. The Calaveras is said to carry black sulphuret of silver; the Sigel, gold; the rest, argentiferous galena. None of these mines are producing, but renewed activity is expected now that the railroad has reached them, and ores of galena, in particular, have acquired a market value.

Oro Fino district.—Organized 1863. Situated in the first east range beyond that which contains Humboldt City, Star City, and Unionville. Starting from a point on the Humboldt river, about 25 miles above Humboldt City, and running south along the range, the first ten miles constitute Sierra district, and the next eight, including both sides of the range, Oro Fino. The geological features of both districts are westward dipping beds of quartzites, with limestone overlying, which latter, cropping on the eastern side of the mountains at the summit, and dipping west, makes the western slope appear to be entirely lime, and the eastern slope, until the summit be reached, entirely quartzite. A landmark in Oro Fino district is an immense ledge of brilliant, opaque white quartz, coursing and dipping with the rocks, and from 6 to 30 feet in width. It is called the Great Eastern, and located as a mine; but it appears to be barren. The Natchez and Yosemite are more promising. The latter vein is now considered the principal ore in the district, and owned by the California Navigation Company, who propose to work it.

Sacramento district.—About 15 miles south of Unionville, on the stage road. The outcrops are large and prominent. The Montana ledge is owned by the Nevada company, which has also a fine mill on the Humboldt seven miles away. Mine and mill are now idle, but the company has applied for a United States patent on the vein. The Rochester company on the same ledge, south, appear to work by fits and starts. The Sacramento and Bullion properties are highly spoken of, but not now actively worked. Here, too, people were last summer waiting for the railroad.

Sierra district.—Situation defined above, under the Oro Fino. The town of Dun Glen in the centre of the district, is about 25 miles northeast of Unionville, 20 miles from Star, seven miles from Mill City, and five miles from the Humboldt river. A small but constant stream runs through the town. The Tallulah mines, on the Neptune series of ledges, a mile and a half northwest of Dun Glen, has been opened by a tunnel of 500 feet, cutting three of the parallel veins into an average depth of 200 feet. These veins are said to be each three feet wide, coursing north and south, and pitching west 45°. The ore assays high, but a small lot, tried in the Essex mill, did not give satisfactory results by the ordinary Washoe process, without roasting. It is probably antimonial sulphurets of silver. Nothing of importance has been done on the mine since November, 1865. On the same series, apparently, are located the Empire and Essex claims. The ledges in these are also well defined, with polished walls, and sulphureted ores of silver. Drifts and inclines, besides a tunnel of 630 feet cross-cutting the Essex, and a tunnel of 320 feet in the Empire, cross-cutting the Ophir ledge, have been opened. Expectations were very high at one time; but the Essex mill is now idle for want of ore. The Gem of Sierra, five miles from Dun Glen, is in limestone country rock, is 22 inches wide, runs east and west, dips south 70°, and contains sulphuret and chloride of silver, with a little carbonate of copper. The decomposed condition of the ore makes it easy to work. Over $40,000 in bullion, 984-1000ths fine, have been taken from this ore at Fall's Pioneer mill, Unionville, 26 miles from the mine. The average yield is said to have been $175 per ton. Yet the mine was not being worked when I visited Humboldt county, and there was a rumor that the vein had been lost. A large vein of similar ore to that of the Montezuma in Trinity district, described below, has been found in the eastern slope of the mountain, four miles from Dun Glen. It is called the Chattanooga. The ore contains about 50 per cent. of lead, (and antimony?) and is said to yield by common pan process $40 per ton, silver. The Chrysopolis is half-way between the Gem and Dun Glen. It is a vein of brilliant white quartz, in state, with defined walls, striking north 38° west, and dipping northeast 48°. This mine belonged to what is now the Montezuma company, formerly, I believe, the Trinity and Sacramento. The company had a mill at Etna, which has since been removed to Oreana, and the Chrysopolis, after having been considerably worked, has been temporarily, at least, abandoned. The Monroe series of ledges, one mile southeast of Dun Glen, is different from the rest of the district in bearing, not silver, but gold—free, and in sulphurets. The returns made to the county assessor for the first two quarters of 1866, state the average yield of ores reduced from January 1 to April 1 to be $526 29 per ton; from April 1 to July 2, $279 05 per ton. These were small lots of selected ore, hauled to Winnemacca, 50 miles, and worked in Holt's mill, which is now moved to Golconda. An attempt to reduce Monroe gold ore in the Essex silver mill, nearer home, resulted in the extraction of $12 16 per ton. The working of the mine on a regular scale has not yet proved successful; but the proprietors are still persevering, and profess great faith in the value of the property. Besides the mining operations above mentioned, Sierra district contains the usual quantity of "locations," not sufficiently developed to warrant further notice. The district was organized in 1863.

Star district is one of the most celebrated in the county, and perhaps the one which has experienced the most sudden transition from a condition of enterprise, hope, and even actual prosperity, to abandonment and despair. It was organized in 1861, and lies immediately north of Buena Vista district, Star City being 12 miles from Unionville. The mountain range here runs north and south, and attains in Star Peak its greatest altitude—11,000 feet. The distance from the foot-hills to the summit, on the eastern slope, is about four miles, and this is the width of the district, which is about six miles long from north to south. A deep and wide cañon, dropping suddenly from the very summit-ridge and running east to the valley, bisects the district, and gathers all its waters into Star creek, a stream of more than ordinary size and permanence for this region, carrying 70 miners' inches in the driest summer months, and swelling to 200 or 300 inches in the early summer, after the melting of the snows. As rain is almost unknown here, the creek is fed entirely from the accumulated snow in the mountains; and its size and extraordinary permanence are due to the great area drained by the Star cañon, which collects a vast quantity of snow in the winter, and to the unusual height of the range at this point, which allows this snow to melt slowly, and preserves some patches of it till winter comes again. In the latter part of August, I found snow still lying several thousand feet below the summit of Star Peak. The result of this topographical peculiarity of the district is a much more verdant and fertile cañon than the traveller ordinarily finds in this region. Star City, two and a half miles up the cañon, has a pretty location, and has been a flourishing town, with two hotels, post office, and daily United States mail, a Wells-Fargo express office, a telegraph office, connected by a special line with Virginia City, and a population of more than 1,000 souls. So sudden has been its decline that the daily mail, the express office, and the telegraph office are all in operation yet, though the entire population consists of a single family, the head of which is mayor, constable, postmaster, express agent, telegraph operator, and, I believe, sole and unanimous voter! The city was built of adobe, stone, and wood. Whatever was movable has been carried away; but the adobe and stone houses, outlasting the industry that created them, are still in tolerable condition, and it would require nothing but the resumption of work on one or two of the mines to call back to Star City its former glory. The proprietors of some of the best mines intend to renew working soon, it is said; but in this case I do not feel so confident of their immediate activity as in others, for the district is on the opposite side of the mountains from the Humboldt valley, and consequently from the railroad. It will not be so quick to feel the stimulus which the completion of the road imparts to the regions traversed by it. Still, it is certain that sooner or later this district will receive attention once more; and this fact, together with the great fame which it formerly enjoyed, will warrant a description of its principal features.

The strata of the country rock dip west, into the mountain. In ascending the cañon, the first formation crossed is that which has frequently been called "quartzite," for want of a better name. It is a highly silicous, metamorphosed rock, and probably the same, essentially, as a good deal of the "porphyry" of Humboldt county. In Star cañon, this rock, when freshly broken, is gray, but changes on exposure to brown. The next layer above is a gray limestone, dipping west about 60°, bedded in layers of a few inches' thickness, the whole group being about 100 yards thick. Next above this rock, and still more extensively displayed, is a black limestone, in which several silver-bearing veins have been discovered. The black limestone is succeeded by a hard, bluish rock, and this again by what appears to be black slate. Between the last two formations occurs the famous Sheba belt, or ore-channel, which is claimed to be 150 feet wide. Both the geological indications of the spot nd the history of the mine favor the opinion that the Sheba is not a fissure vein. If it is so, then it is one of those immense veins which, like the Comstock, contains a great many other things besides ore. The special deposit or chamber in the Sheba is all worked out. The mine is not in operation; but the De Soto, directly across the cañon, contains some of the same rich ore as was formerly found in the Sheba; and it will be operated, I am told, by a San Francisco company. A union of the two claims would be a good thing for both. The Sheba mill, of 10 stamps, four reverberatories, six pans, two settlers, steam power, &c., is situated in the large valley at the mouth of the cañon. It is in good condition, and is said to have reduced quite satisfactorily (with the aid of roasting) the refractory ores of the district. The "pulp" from dry crushing is drawn up by means of fans from the battery-screens into an elevated bin, and by this means a space is left in which the usual sluices can be set for wet crushing. The mill is thus made available for either process.

No work has been done on the Sheba mine for more than 18 months, though previous to that time several hundred thousand dollars were expended. The ore is an antimonial sulphuret of silver and baser metals, (a peculiar fahlerz,) and occurs in chambers, of which it is highly probable that more remain in the mine, besides the one or two already exhausted. The temporary failure of the enterprise is due, partly, to extravagant management while the rich ore continued, and partly to the lack of a proper system of economical and judicious prospecting. There is no test of skill in mining more severe than the management of a mine in such ground. Anybody can work a "bonanza;" the large profits cover all mistakes, and the happy stockholders make no inquiries. But the science at which lucky miners are accustomed to sneer, is invoked by them, often too late, when they have wasted their luck, and the dark day of "dead work," for which they made no provision, has come upon them.

An interesting commentary upon miners' law is the fact that the Sheba mine and mill were both "jumped" during the last year; that is, re-located and claimed as a new discovery, under the laws of the Star district. It seems that the miners of that district, anxious to "keep things lively," made it necessary for every claimant to do a certain amount of work annually, or forfeit his claim. As the Sheba had lain idle for a year, some enterprising parties from a neighboring district thought they would appropriate mine, mill, and all; and certainly they would have good standing in "law," if not in equity, but for another peculiarity in the wonderful code which still holds sway in the now all but uninhabited district. For, in their laudable desire to push things, the miners of Star once on a time passed an amendment to their law providing that if any person would do in one year the "assessment work" of two, his title should be secure for three years without further performance. Afterwards, changing their minds, they repealed this provision, but not until the Sheba mine had more than satisfied its requirements. As all these matters are to be proved, not by legal records, but by newspaper extracts and the memory of witnesses now scattered in other districts, the affair is a promising one for the lawyers. Those who profess to wonder why capital is not more freely invested in property, the very title to which is at the mercy of a mass-meeting of temporary colonists, may perhaps find food for reflection in this incident.

Opposite the Sheba, on the south side of Star creek, is the De Soto, already alluded to. The location comprises 2,100 feet, and its southern extension, the Whitmore, is 1,500 feet long, followed by the American Basin, 1,800 feet. The Whitmore, owned by a London company, has a tunnel of 500 feet, and the American Basin, owned principally by a New York company, has a tunnel of 1,000 feet. The former is not yet near the line of the vein, and the latter is supposed to be near it, but has not cut it. All the tunnelling is in very hard rock, and cost at least $25 gold per linear foot.

Above the Sheba belt the black slate, interstratified with gray limestone, extends up the mountain for three-fourths of a mile, when it changes to quartzite. In this rock are the Mammoth series of veins, carrying hard, brittle quartz, with disseminated galena. The ore is argentiferous. Above this series, and almost at the summit of the ridge, is the Mountain Top series, containing the great San Bernard ledge—a wall of brilliant, white, barren quartz, striking northeast and southwest, and visible from a distance of 10 miles. This ledge, coursing as it does across, not with, the strata, is the only unmistakable fissure vein in the district, but unfortunately that is its sole merit. It has been but little worked, and offers no encouragement to mining. In former times the Perigard Tunnel Company proposed to run a tunnel through the mountain into the Humboldt valley, a distance of two miles, and the work was said to be under way, but I found no traces of it.

Trinity district.—This is one of the most interesting localities to the mining engineer and metallurgist in all the west. It is the seat of the famous Oreana smelting works. The district was organized in June, 1863. It is situated on the west bank of the Humboldt, 25 miles north of Humboldt lake, and 30 miles southwest of Unionville. A small portion of the district, in a projecting group of the Trinity mountains, is known as Arabia, and comprises the most noted mines—the Montezuma, Jersey, Savannah, Sultana series, Chloride, Guatimozin, Tontine, Eagle, Dunderberg, Ne Plus, Bald Hornet, Daisy, and Oxide. In these veins the same phenomenon has been observed as in other districts of Humboldt county. They occur in groups of parallel course, and some of them pinch out to a mere seam at no great depth. This is the reason why so many locations in Humboldt county cover, not single veins, but series. The miners found that it was necessary to allow such locations, as no man could be sure of an independent vein in a single outcrop. The application of the United States law, forbidding the grant of more than one outcrop within the space covered by the patent, would work mischief here.

The Montezuma mine was the only one actively worked at the time of my visit. The vein crops out on the south side of a shallow cañon, while most of the neighboring mines are on the north slope. Their course is north 10° east, while that of the Montezuma is nearly east and west, and the cañon runs nearly northeast and southwest. The country rock is porphyry, and the ledge dips north between well-marked casings, at an angle of 45°. The outcrop is 11 feet wide, and the vein in depth averages seven feet. At the lowest point exposed, (150 feet on the incline, at the bottom of a prospecting shaft,) there is still a vein of six feet. The longitudinal extent of the workings is about 500 feet; the whole claim covers 2,000 feet. As the mine is at least 500 feet above the Humboldt, and the vein-matter exceedingly decomposed, it is not surprising that it contains no water. This and the Liberty mine, in San Antonio district, Nye county, are the driest I have visited. The workings on the Montezuma consist of a deep open cut, and inclines to a depth of 80 feet, opening good ground, besides the 150 feet exploring shaft already mentioned. About 1,500 tons of ore have been already extracted, and I estimate the reserves in sight at 1,200 tons more. The ore is very friable, consisting of salts of lead and antimony, (cerussite, antimony spar, antimonic oxide,) in a gangue of quartz and felspar. The value in silver ranges from $60 per ton upwards. The present average yield at the works is $80. The Jersey ledge, which strikes north-northeast and intersects (as is supposed) the Montezuma, answers to the same description, except that the average width is three feet, and the average yield of silver per ton $40. This would not pay for working, nor indeed does the $80 of Montezuma ore leave a very large margin; but both these mines are enhanced in value to a remarkable degree by the railroad, which now passes within sight of them. Their base metal, amounting to 40 or 50 per cent. of the ore, is now worth as much as the silver, as will be seen presently. The Jersey has been well opened by inclines to the depth of 60, 800, and 100 feet, and drifts connecting them. There are at least 2,000 tons of ore exposed. The claim is 1,200 feet, for 1,000 of which the outcrop has been traced. The mine has been idle, waiting for the railroad, but the work will soon be actively prosecuted.

Mr. Nason, the energetic and skilful superintendent of the Montezuma company, deserves the highest praise for the perseverance and talent with which he has redeemed what was at the outset as decided a failure as any in Nevada. I do not mean to enter upon the history of the enterprise in which he was at first engaged, further than to say that the removal of the company's original mill from Etna to Oreana, the acquisition of the Montezuma mine, the bold plan of erecting furnaces and smelting the ore in a region so destitute of fuel, and in the absence of all precedent or experience of the kind in Nevada—these are all parts of a Napoleonic policy by which one man was able to wrest victory from disaster. I wish such cases were more numerous; but, in general, the despair and apathy of American capitalists at their first discouragement are equal to their credulity and extravagant expectation at the outset; and their agents are not able to rescue them from the consequences of their first blunders.

Mr. Nason's works at Oreana are in some respects quite original. Mr. Clarence King's exploring party have drawings of them, which will doubtless be published; and I shall confine myself to a brief description.

The works stand on the bank of the Humboldt, about a mile from the Central Pacific railroad. The custom department contains five light stamps, three flat-bottomed pans, and one settler. This machinery, used for reducing such ores as can be treated by the Washoe process, is driven by an engine of about 25 horse-power, which keeps in motion, also, the blower for the shaft furnace. The process employed for the Montezuma ore is direct smelting with fluxes, and subsequent calcination and cupellation. The ore contains about 50 per cent. of lead and antimony, and $80 of silver to the ton. The method of treatment is as follows:

The ore, reduced to about egg-size with a Blake crusher, is mixed on the charging floor with a flux consisting of 20 parts of soda and 80 of lime. The materials for this flux are gatherèd from the alkaline deposits of the valley and foot-hills. The most desolate and forbidding feature of the country thus turns out to be an important element of future wealth. The flux is added to the ore generally in equal weight, and the whole is charged with charcoal into the furnace. About once in seven minutes two shovelfuls of charcoal and four of the mixed ore and flux are charged. This represents about 12 bushels of charcoal, or 225 pounds, per ton of ore. Considering that Mr. Nason has paid as much as 65 cents a bushel for charcoal, and that he can now obtain it for 25 cents, by means of the railroad, the economy in this one item is evidently enough to pay a handsome profit to the company. The furnace will melt about 12 tons of ore daily, producing 30 to 35 pigs of metal every shift, or about 10,000 pounds in 24 hours. The discharge of cinder is continuous; but the metal is drawn off once in an hour and a half or two hours, when from four to six pigs, or 300 to 450 pounds, are obtained. This metal is an alloy of antimony and lead, containing about $200 per ton in silver. There are two furnaces in the works for the production of the crude metal, but only one was running at the time of my visit. There are also four large reverberatories, in which the crude metal was formerly calcined and purified of antimony. These furnaces were able to calcine a charge of 16 tons in 14 days. They are now superseded by the arrangement which the railroad has enabled the company to make with parties in San Francisco. The same is true, also, of the cupelling-furnace, a very neat structure, with movable test, raised or lowered with screws. The silver produced from this establishment was 997 and 998 thousandths fine. The antimony was formerly thrown away as refuse, but has become valuable for type-metal, Babbitt's metal, &c. Still the prices of transportation were such previous to the completion of the railroad that the lead and antimony produced could scarcely be said to find a profitable market, and the silver had to pay all costs. All this is now bravely changed. The operations of calcination and cupellation are no longer carried on; the crude pigs from the shaft-furnace are sold directly to Selby and Co., of San Francisco, who pay $100 per ton for the base metal, and $1 per ounce for the silver it contains. The favorable effect thus produced upon the business of the Montezuma company is typical of the good results which will follow the introduction of the railroad in all our mining districts. The running expenses and profits of the Oreana works may be sketched as follows, on the basis of the single shaft furnace in operation at the time of my visit:

MINING COST.

Twelve tons of ore daily, mined and hauled to mill	$84

REDUCTION COST, 12 TONS DAILY.

Four smelters, two at $5, and two at $2 50	15
Two engineers, at $4	8
Five laborers, feeders, &c., at $3	15
Two cords of wood, at $15	30
Limestone, iron, horse feed, &c	10
Charcoal, 144 bushels, at 25 cents	36
Total daily labor and material	198
Add for superintendence, office, &c	25
Transportation 4.8 tons metal to San Francisco	144
Total cost of metal from 12 tons ore	367

VALUE OF METAL IN SAN FRANCISCO.

Four and eight-tenths tons lead and antimony, at $100	$480
Three hundred and sixty ounces silver, (the average contents) at $1	360
Total	840
Subtract cost of production, &c	367
	473

Any error of under-estimate on the above expenses will be more than counterbalanced by the fact that labor is reckoned at former rates, and that a great reduction might be effected in that item, especially by the employment of Chinamen. Of their capacity I have not the slightest doubt. Indeed, the most faithful and skilful workman that Mr. Nason ever had at his reverberatories was a Chinaman; and a metallurgist will understand that if a Chinaman can be trusted to manage a reverberatory furnace, there is nothing which he may not, under proper direction and supervision, be trusted to do in the whole field of the reduction of ores. I incline strongly to the opinion that our much needed supply of skilled labor in metallurgy is to come, in the Pacific States, from the patient and imitative Chinese.

An inspection of the figures above given shows the interesting fact that the silver alone does not quite pay the expense of working. In point of fact, when the silver was produced at Oreana, there was no transportation of base metal to be paid, so that item of $144 falls away; but, on the other hand, there was a heavy expense for calcination and cupillation, which was not balanced by the fact that, when the silver was at last refined, the company received $1 30 per ounce for it, instead of $1 as now. In a word, the railroad has made all the difference between paying expenses merely, and paying 100 per cent. profit over expenses, in this one representative case. The Oreana enterprise is one of the few which rest upon a sound economical basis, comprising the utilization of all the valuable ingredients contained in its raw material.

Winnemucca district, about 40 miles north of Oreana, on the west side of the Humboldt, comprises the Winnemucca, a large vein, owned by eastern capitalists, but not yet developed; the Union series, now owned and worked by a New York company, and said to be valuable; the Pride of the Mountain, belonging to a French company, (the owner of the Humboldt canal,) which is still experimenting upon the refractory ore; and a hundred other locations not yet developed.

Bullion shipments from Unionville, Humboldt county, Nevada.—These shipments were made through the express office of Wells, Fargo & Co., and, as the express charges were generally very high, (to cover the risk as well as cost of transportation,) being frequently three per cent. on the amount declared, it was customary for shippers of bullion to assume part of the risk themselves, by declaring at the office an amount less than was actually delivered. The excess of actual over reported value is at least 33⅓ per cent., and sometimes more. I have added a column with this correction:

Shipments of bullion from Unionville, Humboldt county, Nevada.

Date.	Name.	Amount.		Date.	Name.	Amount.	
		Decla'd.	Real.			Decla'd.	Real.
1867.		*Coin.*	*Coin.*	1868.		*Coin.*	*Coin.*
Oct. 13	J. C. Fall	$600	$800	Mar. 17	J. C. Fall	750	1,000
Oct. 17	......do	200	266	Mar. 25	......do	585	780
Oct. 25	......do	800	1,066	Apr. 1	......do	675	900
Oct. 31	......do	600	800	Apr. 6	......do	330	440
Nov. 6	......do	870	1,160	Apr. 14	......do	750	1,000
Nov. 10	Gold Dust	875	1,167	Apr. 18	......do	825	1,100
Nov. 12	F. G. Negus	3,000	4,000	Apr. 21	......do	750	1,000
Nov. 12	J. C. Fall	1,395	1,860	Apr. 23	......do	870	1,160
Nov. 18	......do	570	760	Apr. 27	......do	350	466
Nov. 23	......do	750	1,000	Apr. 27	......do	510	680
Nov. 26	F. G. Negus	....	2,666	Apr. 29	......do	825	1,100
Nov. 31	J. C. Fall	900	1,200	Apr. 31	......do	375	500
Dec. 7	......do	700	933	May 5	......do	780	1,040
Dec. 11	......do	1,125	1,500	May 8	......do	$750	$1,000
Dec. 15	......do	1,020	1,360	May 11	......do	900	1,200
Dec. 19	......do	700	933	May 15	......do	750	1,000
Dec. 21	......do	750	1,000	May 18	......do	825	1,100
Dec. 25	......do	8.0	1,080	May 21	......do	810	1,080
				May 23	......do	750	1,000
1868.				May 27	......do	525	700
Jan. 5	J. C. Fall	600	800	May 29	......do	750	1,000
Jan. 11	......do	540	720	May 31	......do	750	1,000
Jan. 15	......do	720	960	June 3	......do	675	900
Jan. 20	......do	615	820	June 6	......do	650	866
Jan. 22	......do	420	560	June 10	......do	675	900
Feb. 1	......do	690	920	June 13	......do	675	900
Feb. 4	......do	840	1,120	June 15	......do	480	640
Feb. 6	......do	675	900	June 17	......do	931	1,241
Feb. 9	......do	750	1,000	June 20	......do	825	1,100
Feb. 18	......do	855	1,140	June 23	......do	675	900
Feb. 20	......do	750	1,000	June 25	......do	750	1,000
Mar. 5	......do	975	1,300	June 28	......do	780	1,040
Mar. 11	......do	600	800	July 1	......do	975	1,300

Shipments of bullion from Unionville, Humboldt county, Nevada—Continued.

Date.	Name.	Amount.		Date.	Name.	Amount.	
		Decla'd.	Real.			Decla'd.	Real.
1868.		*Coin.*	*Coin.*	1868.		*Coin.*	*Coin.*
July 2	J. C. Fall	600	800	July 26	J. C. Fall	600	800
July 4	......do	825	1,100	July 27	Fall & Temple	450	600
July 9	......do	750	1,000	July 29	J. C. Fall	675	900
July 11	......do	750	1,000	Aug. 4	......do	975	1,300
July 13	......do	630	840	Aug. 4	Fall & Temple	600	800
July 15	......do	1,050	1,400	Aug. 6	......do	540	727
July 17	......do	630	840	Aug. 10	J. C. Fall	360	480
July 17	John S. Northup, gold from Dun Glen.	250	300	Aug. 10	Fall & Temple	630	840
				Aug. 20	......do	1,380	1,840
July 20	J. C. Fall	675	900	Estimated shipments to Oct. 14		....	20,000
July 23	......do	600	800				
July 25	Macbeth & Fox, Battle mountain.	4,000	6,000	Total for one year		....	109,884

SECTION III.

NOTES ON MONTANA.

BY PROFESSOR A. K. EATON, ASSISTED BY W. S. KEYES, ESQ., CAPTAIN W. W. DE LACY, AND OTHERS.

CHAPTER XII.

GENERAL GEOLOGICAL FEATURES OF THE TERRITORY.

Rocks, representing the three grand divisions of geological time, are more equally distributed in the Territory of Montana, perhaps, than in any other part of the continent.

Granite and other arzoic rocks, secondary limestones and sandstones, and extensive tertiary deposits lie literally side by side in nearly every part of the Territory as yet examined.

The azoic rocks are represented by granite, gneiss, and trappean rocks, the latter principally dioritic in their character, but sometimes assuming the trachytic, amygdaloid or basaltic characteristics.

Owing to the partially metamorphic condition of the secondary rocks, their relative age cannot at present be determined. Very few fossils are found in them, and those usually quite indistinct. The tertiary deposits are very distinctly marked, and generally quite undisturbed, showing no marks of metamorphic action.

If we should say that granite accompanied the anticlinal axes of the main mountain ranges, secondary rocks covering the slopes, and tertiary deposits lying horizontally in the valleys, it would express with accuracy the geological character of much of the Territory, especially that portion lying above the forks of the Missouri river. It is true that granite does not form uninterruptedly the crests of the mountain ranges, but its frequent appearance at their higher points strongly suggests continuity along the whole axis of elevation, though concealed beneath secondary rocks that often cover the mountains to their summits.

To the subordinate ranges and spars the rule does not so generally apply, many of the latter especially showing only secondary rocks, or, as is frequently the case, showing gneiss or granite at the point where they leave the main range only secondary rocks at their lower elevations.

The following are the more marked localities in the occupied portions of the Territory when the azoic rocks predominate.

On entering the Territory by the west from Salt Lake, we find a broken mountain range, lying between the Beaver Head and Black Tail Deer creeks. This is mainly gneiss, so far as examined, but showing occasional masses of trap. As there have been no mines of value developed in this range, comparatively little can be said of it.

About 50 miles northwest of this range is Bald mountain, the most prominent and picturesque peak in Beaver Head county. Though covered on the southerly slope with secondary rock to the very summit, it is a mountain of true granite. Its altitude, determined both by triangulation and by barometric measurement, is about 4,500 feet above the valley of the Grasshopper creek, but though apparently the most prominent peak in the vicinity, and so considered by the inhabitants, a visit to the summit will discover a still higher peak about 12 miles northwest, probably having an altitude of 1,000 feet greater than Bald mountain. This has been named Torrey's peak, but so far as is known has never been ascended.

These, with their smaller associates, form an interesting cluster of granite mountain peaks, and so far as has been discovered furnish the only instance of the existence of true granite within the limits of Beaver Head county, with the exception of its occasional appearance upon the crest of the main range, the latter forming the boundary of the county on three sides. Crossing the Black Tail Deer in the direction of Virginia City, we strike a mountain spur extending northward from the main chain, this exhibits gneiss near its junction with the main range, but the northerly portion, lying west of the Stinking-water river, is wholly secondary in its character.

The Tobacco Route range, as it is sometimes called, lying between the Madison river and the Stinking-water, exhibits mainly rocks of the azoic age, principally gneiss interupted by trappean masses, but sometimes showing true granite.

This range, above or north of Virginia City, on Alder gulch, is principally gneissoid in its character, but at the point where the city is located the range is cut by an extensive mass of trap, stretching from the hill east of the town nearly to the Eight-mile house at the eastern foot of the range, and having a breadth of three or four miles.

Following the range northerly for many miles, we find on the west side gneiss only, cut, however, by dikes of trap, but as we approach the Jefferson river the range changes in its character, the rocks becoming mostly secondary.

Examining the range along its eastern slope, the gneiss changes to granite proper, as we approach the town of Sterling, but is still bounded by gneiss further east. The formation where the town is located and the mountain side west of it is granite, but following the Hot Spring creek easterly to the old crossing we find an abrupt change to gneiss. Near this point we find an eruptive mass of trap of peculiar form, known as Flat Top Butte.

Situated near this butte is the hot spring from which the stream derives its name. There are many of a similar character in the Territory, and a general description of this will apply to nearly all. The water, which issues in considerable volume, is almost perfectly pure, quite as much so as the water of the purest cold springs. The temperature, varying but slightly through the different seasons of the year, is about 133° Fahrenheit in this and the majority of springs examined, but in rare instances it is as high as 160° Fahrenheit. The purity of the water is not, however, common to all these things, without exception; the water of the hot spring of Deer Lodge valley being charged with carbonic acid gas, and holding considerable carbonate of lime in solution. The rapid escape of the gas in this case gives an appearance of ebullition, and the carbonate of lime, no longer capable of being held in solution by the decarbonated water, is deposited. Thus an incrustation of carbonate of lime has been formed by the water, until a hemispherical mound about 30 feet in height has been formed, to the top of which the water rises in its central well. The only peculiarity observed in connection with the hot springs of *pure* water is the unusual vegetable growth upon the grounds watered by them, including a rapid propagation of water plants proper. The latter effect is demonstrated whenever the water is allowed to run through open troughs of wood, the whole surface of the troughs beneath the water being covered, in a few days, with a rich green confervoid growth.

These springs, so far as examined, are found near the juncture of granite and sedimentary rocks. If it were not already sufficiently proven by other facts, the character of purity exhibited by these thermal waters would demonstrate that this heat is derived from deep subterranean channels of high temperature, through which the water passed before reaching the surface, rather than from any chemical reaction of water upon mineral matter. The bearing of the study of thermal springs upon the later theories, with regard to the origin of metalliferous veins, makes all facts touching the character of such waters of importance.

Passing northward across the Jefferson, by the route from Virginia City to Helena, we find in the Silver Star district an exposure of granite proper in Hell cañon, which changes to hornblendic gneiss, as we go east toward the Jefferson river. The gneiss continues nearly to the level country bordering the river, where a secondary limestone makes its appearance, but is quite limited in extent.

Moving northward to the Boulder valley, we find the range lying west and north of the valley at that point wholly granitic; while easterly and southerly we see ranges that show secondary rocks only.

Still further north the town of Jefferson lies between ranges both of which are essentially azoic. The granite range dividing the waters of Prickley Pear from those of Crow creek shows an extensive mass of greenstone trap at the summit. In the vicinity of Helena granite makes its appearance about three miles above the town. Its line of junction with the limestone and sandstone of the secondary can be readily traced in a southeasterly direction until it crosses the Prickley Pear above Prickley Pear city. The auriferous veins of the vicinity lie in the granite, and generally near the line of change of formation referred to.

In addition to the localities already mentioned, the trappean rocks make their appearance at many points, and are often intimately associated with the metalliferous deposits. They break through the secondary deposits at several points in Beaver Head county, as in the Horse Prairie, Bannock, Blue Wing, and Rattle Snake districts, and show themselves conspicuously in the northern portion of Edgerton county in large tabular masses, or characteristic shapes, like the well-known "Birdtail rock."

These masses are more generally dioritic, but sometimes exhibit several different varieties in the same immediate vicinity, as, for instance, the extensive formation that underlies Virginia City, and cuts the range west of it. This shows, near the town, two distinct and well-marked varieties, the trachytic and amygdaloid; but as we cross the range and begin to descend on the eastern slope by the toll road, we find the trap assuming the basaltic character, showing distinct grains of olivine.

The most interesting feature connected with the trappean rocks of the Territory is that arising from their association with certain metalliferous deposits. The auriferous veins of Bannock are wholly *contact veins*, lying between the secondary rocks and the erupted trap; and the argentiferous veins of the Blue Wing district, as well as those of Argenta, are intimately associated with the trappean masses, being wholly in the adjoining limestone, but evidently having as their starting point the dividing line between the different formations. The secondary rocks of the Territory are found upon the slopes of most of the mountain ranges, and many of the subordinate ranges and spurs show this formation almost exclusively. It is rarely that a valley is bounded on both sides by rocks of the same age. The Madison valley, bounded on the west, as we have already seen, mostly by azoic rocks, shows an eastern boundary of sedimentary rocks of the secondary age. These rocks are, in all parts of the Territory, very greatly disturbed, in some cases highly metamorphic, and in all cases more or less so.

The obliteration of fossil indication by metamorphic action precludes the possibility, at present, of determining the exact geological period to which to refer the different deposits of this age. The secondary limestone at the point of contact with the trappean masses referred to becomes white crystalline marble, but the effect is limited to the immediate neighborhood of the line of contact.

The tertiary deposits of the Territory are extensive and widely distributed, being found in almost every portion occupied, from Fort Union to the head-waters of the Missouri.

The lignite group, lying about Fort Union, at the eastern limit of the Territory, is 2,000 feet thick, and extends over an immense area. This group is tertiary, probably of the eocene age. The same group makes its appearance at different points in the Territory, and at no point is its occurrence more clearly marked than at the head-waters of the Missouri. We may say that the level or gently undulating plateaux of all the valleys above the confluence of the Jefferson, Madison, and Gallatin rivers are underlaid by lignite or other beds of the same age. They are made up of deposits of sand, clay, and friable sandstone, with beds of lignite, gypsum, fire-clay, &c.

In some localities fossil trees are found in abundance; as, for instance, in the tertiary near Gallatin. Silica is the fossilizing agent.

If we examine the present conformation of this portion of the Territory we shall readily discover the origin of the tertiary seas in which these deposits were formed. We find the mingled waters of the Jefferson, Madison, and Gallatin sweeping through an abrupt cañon, where once an uninterrupted rocky barrier was presented to the northward flow of these waters. This caused the water to overflow all the comparatively level land south and west of the present "forks" of the Missouri, forming an extensive inland sea, which was afterward drained by the cutting through of the present cañon. At the same epoch the different cañons on the upper waters of the same streams and their tributaries were also closed, causing the existence of other and smaller inland seas.

The beautiful valley of the Madison river was then one magnificent sheet of water, extending from the mouth of the present cañon southward as far as the eye could reach, and even far up on the very sources of the Missouri; as, for instance, above the cañon at Bannock smaller tertiary seas existed. Beneath these seas the lignite clays and soft sandstone of the present valleys were formed during the lapse of tertiary age.

The Madison valley, with its broad and beautiful plateaux, underlaid by undisturbed tertiary deposits, is perhaps the best illustration of the formation of this age in the Territory.

Though as yet undeveloped, the lignites of this formation are doubtless destined to furnish fuel in sufficient abundance to meet the requirements of the Territory.

A bed of lignite has been worked to a slight extent near Bannock with fair promise, it is said, of success. Beds have been discovered in various points of the Territory, and the coal rudely tested with varied results. As in other sections, we shall doubtless find many of the lignite seams unfit for use; but, long before the forests fail to furnish a supply of fuel, veins of good lignite will doubtless be developed in different parts of the Territory.

From the tertiary beds above Bannock, gypsum may be obtained in large quantities, and probably from similar beds in other valleys. The clays of some of these beds are of a very refractory character, and are destined to furnish material for the construction of smelting furnaces, &c.

CHAPTER XIII.

POPULATION, ASSESSMENTS, IMPORTATIONS, WAGES, COST OF MATERIAL, CHINESE, PACIFIC RAILROAD, ETC.

Population.—The present year has been a period of very general prosperity. Emigration from the Territory is far less observable than last fall.

Farming has become a settled pursuit.

The quartz mines are building up around them permanent towns, and families are becoming more common in the community.

For the above reasons it is probable that the population has increased to somewhat over 28,000 souls, not including the Indians.

Territorial assessment.—The assessment of the different counties, as filed in the auditor's office, September 1, 1868, is as follows:

Madison county	$2,259,238
Lewis & Clarke county	*2,343,453
Deer Lodge county	957,920
Beaver Head county	453,608
Chouteau county	438,907
Gallatin county	438,139
Missoula county	$407,216
Meagher county	357,405
Jefferson county	257,284
Total	7,903,170

List of steamboats arrived at Fort Benton in 1868.†

1. Success, 150 tons freight; arrived May 13, 10 a. m.
2. Cora, 150 tons freight; arrived May 15, 5 p. m.
3. Deer Lodge, 130 tons freight; arrived May 19, 10½ a. m.
4. Nile, 130 tons freight; arrived May 21, 6 p. m.
5. Miner, 80 tons freight; arrived May 25, 8 a. m.
6. Only Chance, 170 tons freight; arrived May 25, 11 a. m.
7. Sally, 208 tons freight; arrived May 25, 9 p. m.
8. St. Luke, 200 tons freight; arrived May 28, 4½ p. m.
9. Henry Adkins, 150 tons freight; arrived May 30, 1¼ p. m.
10. Mountaineer, 205 tons freight; arrived May 30, 10 p. m.
11. Octavia, 175 tons freight; arrived May 31, 8 a. m.
12. Ida Stockdale, 170 tons freight; arrived May 31, 11 a. m.
13. Peninah, 50 tons freight; arrived May 31, 8 p. m.
14. Antelope, 180 tons freight; arrived June 1, 2 p. m.
15. Huntsville, 170 tons freight; arrived June 1, 9½ p. m.
16. Bertha, 150 tons freight; arrived June 2, 3 p. m.
17. Lacon, 150 tons freight; arrived June 8, 7 a. m.
18. Guidon, 125 tons freight; arrived June 8, 7¼ a. m.
19. Benton, 125 tons freight; arrived June 13, 4 p. m.
20. Yorktown, 125 tons freight; arrived June 14, 7 a. m.
21. Importer, 100 tons freight; arrived June 15, 5¾ p. m.
22. Ida Rees, 100 tons freight; arrived June 16, 1 p. m.
23. Andrew Ackley, 175 tons freight; arrived June 17, 7 a. m.
24. North Alabama, 150 tons freight; arrived June 19, 12 m.

---

* A supplemental list, now making, will add largely to the sum total of this, the most flourishing and populous county of the Territory.

† I am indebted for the above list to Messrs. Basset and Magee, compilers of the forthcoming Montana Statistical Almanac.

25. Fanny Barker, 140 tons freight; arrived June 20, 7 a. m.
26. Hiram Woods, 80 tons freight; arrived June 23, 4 p. m.
27. Viola Belle, 175 tons freight; arrived June 26, 4 p. m.
28. Columbia, 175 tons freight; arrived June 27, 6 p. m.
29. Urilda, 130 tons freight; arrived June 28, 5 p. m.
30. Deer Lodge, (second trip,) 75 tons freight; July 4, 10 a. m.
31. Tom Stevens, 100 tons freight; arrived July 7, 11 a. m.
32. Silver Lake, 100 tons freight; arrived July 7, 2 p. m.
33. Andrew Ackley, (from Dauphan's rapids,) 50 tons freight; arrived July 23, a. m.
34. Leni Leoti, 180 tons freight; arrived July 26, 9 p. m.
35. Success, 100 tons freight; arrived August 4, 10½ a. m.

The Only Chance, Lacon, Bertha, Fanny Barker, and North Alabama discharged cargo below, but delivered it at Fort Benton.

The Amelia Poe was lost at a point a short distance above Milk river.

Latterly, owing to the close of navigation on the Missouri, and the near approach to Salt Lake of the Union Pacific railroad, small lots of the more valuable goods have been shipped hither by car and wagon.

During the summer many pack trains cross the mountains from Oregon, bringing clothing, blankets, and similar goods from the Pacific slope.

I think it would not be out of the way to put the amount of imported freights at a grand total of 6,000 tons for the entire country.

Labor.—In order to a correct conclusion in regard to the relations of labor and capital, as expressed in the term wages, we must bear in mind the general principle that, where capital is abundant, interest is low and labor likewise; on the other hand where capital is scarce interest is high and labor likewise. In the first case the laborer is, so to speak, at the mercy of capital; in the latter he is free and independent. In all long settled countries we find examples of the first condition, and in all new countries of the second. And it is to escape this pressure, or supposed pressure, that our American population, or at least the discontented and ambitious portion, seeks the frontier where capital is scarce, and the remuneration of the laborer high.

Montana, with the other new Territories, and the older States to the east, exemplify the above enunciated proposition. The price of labor here, as elsewhere, is governed by the general law of supply and demand.

Wages reach their maximum in summer, and minimum in winter; and for the following reasons: During part of the spring, summer, and early fall, the placers offer a ready field for labor, and wages are, consequently, at their height. The price varies from $2 50 to $8 (gold dust) per day, equal to $3 to $10 currency; the last figure being the exceptional remuneration of first class "drifters." It is quite improbable that less than the former price will be paid for many years to come, for the simple reason that there are still thousands of acres whereon a man may, by his own unaided labor, obtain that amount as a daily minimum. Indeed, such placers are denominated by the miners "China diggings," *i. e.*, fit only for the Chinese, and are now passed by without a second thought. The average miner of all the new Territories is far superior, both in natural intelligence and acquired knowledge, to the laborers of the older States. He requires a large income, and, owing to a chronic habit of improvidence, is often in actual want.

In ordinary years the placer miner can count upon eight months, during which the streams are not frozen, and hence he must earn enough during two-thirds of the year to support him during a twelvemonth.

Amongst the entire population of the mining Territories there is, in reality, no laboring class. The man who gives his services for hire to-day may be the employer to-morrow; and it is this uncertainty of fortune which insures mutual consideration, self-respect, and a spirit of independence.

Such as are unwilling to work in the placers find employment, during the summer, in haymaking and general farm labor. The usual rate of wages for such labor is $60, currency, per month and board. Teamsters receive $40 to $50, currency, per month and board.

During the winter season placer mining is impossible, or at best the miner can only hoist the pay gravel to the surface, so as to be ready for the spring washing. Hence a large number of men are thrown out of employment, and many who, through ill fortune or improvidence, have not sufficient funds to bridge over the winter, must perforce seek a living otherwise.

This state of affairs conduces greatly to the advantage of the quartz claims, and good miners are readily attainable at rates varying from $40 to $60, currency, per month, and board. Prudent managers often extract, during the winter, ore in sufficient quantity to keep their mills employed far into the summer, so that the major portion of the hands may, with the opening spring, be released to work in the placers. Good carpenters and machinists receive $6 to $8 per day; boiler makers and master builders often as high as $12 to $15 per day. Employment of all kinds is remunerated far in excess of the simple cost of living; the uncertainty, however, of steady occupation, not only renders these high prices necessary, but still further tends to unsettle the laborer. In cases where hands are employed under an agreement that board be furnished them, it is usual to rate this outlay as equivalent to an addition to the wages of $1, currency, per day. In the towns the cost of living is much greater; ordinary board, without lodging, varies from $12 to $18, currency, per week.

With every season, however, we find a gradual diminution in the cost of the necessaries of life. The Territory is, as concerns agricultural products, very nearly self-supporting; and as the farmers cannot rely upon any other than the home market, their increasing production will year by year lower the cost of living. Good flour now ranges from $8 to $15 per sack of 100 pounds; whereas formerly it often cost from $50 to $120 for a like amount. Potatoes have fallen from 80 cents to 2 cents per pound; barley and wheat from 30 cents to 6 cents per pound.

Cost of materials.—Sawed lumber costs from $25 to $50 per thousand; cord wood from $4 to $8 per cord; brick from $30 to $35 per thousand; charcoal, 20 to 35 cents per bushel.

Chinese.—This people are but just now beginning to form an appreciable proportion of the population. I estimate their number at about 800, of whom two-thirds are engaged in washing over the placers abandoned by the whites; the remaining third find employment as washers and ironers, as cooks, and keepers of small shops.

As a class in the community, they are quiet, orderly and peaceable. Their mutual quarrels seldom or never require the arbitrament of the courts, and during the past year there has been among them but one arrest and conviction, on a charge of manslaughter.

As far as my observation extends, public opinion seems, in regard to this people, to be apathetic and seldom demonstrative either for or against them; that there exists, however, a latent prejudice against them is highly probable. From time to time, it is true, we hear of outrages inflicted upon some one of them in the same manner, and perhaps as frequently, as dogs or cattle are maltreated. Otherwise they are as free from annoyance as any other class in the community. They do not compete with the whites, and, when mining, either buy claims, thus acquiring rights which are respected, or take up abandoned ground. I am unacquainted with any locality, either placer or vein mine, where the Chinese are hired by the whites.

Northern Pacific railroad.—The question as to the most feasible route for the construction of the proposed Northern Pacific railroad is one of vital importance in its bearing upon the interests of the Territory. Hitherto the cost of transportation of machinery and supplies, and the uncertainty attending their transit either by the plains or by river, has been a most serious obstacle to the success of all enterprises in the Territory, especially those connected with mining operations. Some of the larger stamp mills of the Territory were freighted across the plains, at an expense of 37 cents per pound, and the first outlay for freight, in many cases, has been so great as to dishearten the proprietors, and stop the further prosecution of the enterprise. Freights by river have not, of late, been extravagantly high, but the uncertainty attending river navigation makes it very desirable, and in the end will make it imperatively necessary, that some more rapid and reliable mode of transportation be adopted. This will doubtless be effected eventually by the construction of the proposed Northern Pacific road; but in the interval of delay arising from the want of aid from a government already heavily burdened, it is hoped that a branch connection with the present Union Pacific may be constructed to meet the present wants of the inhabitants. In this connection the following letter from Captain W. W. De Lacy—who, from his ability as an engineer, as well as his long experience in the Territory, is entitled to the confidence of all—will give reliable data as to the more practicable routes for each of these roads.

DEAR SIR: In answer to your inquiries as to the most desirable routes for the Northern Pacific, and the proposed branch to connect with the Union Pacific roads, I make the following statements: I will take as the basis of my remarks the line laid down on the map which accompanies the report of Edwin F. Johnson, esq., chief engineer of the Northern Pacific railroad, dated November, 1867.

This map, in all essential points, is very correct. The line of the projected railroad is represented as crossing the Yellowstone river at Onahtaroup (or Coal) creek, going up the river some distance; thence crossing to the head of the Musselshell river; thence down Deep creek to its mouth on the Missouri river; thence crossing the Rocky mountains at Lewis and Clarke's, or Cadotte's Pass, both on the head of the Dearborn river; thence proceeding down the Big Blackfoot to the Hellgate, and thence down the Clarke's Fork of the Columbia, where it passes without the boundaries of the Territory. I would remark, briefly, that I am personally acquainted with almost the whole of this route, except the extensive eastern section on the Yellowstone river, and that it is remarkably favorable for a railroad.

There are no heavy mountains between the Yellowstone and Musselshell, the country partaking rather of a high rolling plateau. There is a very low open pass at the head of the Musselshell river, and the passes of the Rocky mountains are not above 6,500 feet high. The approach to these passes is not generally difficult, and timber of fine quality, (chiefly pine,) water, and fine building-stone, abound.

There is another route which would go down the Yellowstone to the Big Bend, cross over by the Boseman Pass to the Three Forks of the Missouri river; thence up the Jefferson to the Big Hole, or Wisdom river, cross the Rocky mountains at the Deer Lodge Pass, which is about two miles wide, and thence down the Deer Lodge and Hellgate rivers to the mouth of the Big Blackfoot, where it would intersect the line previously spoken of. This route would be longer than the one by the head of the Musselshell, and longer than that north of the Missouri surveyed by Governor Stevens; but it would have the advantage of passing through some of the finest agricultural valleys of the Territories; also through some of the richest mineral districts. The difficulties of construction would be less, and the grades easier, than on any other route with which I am acquainted. Coal has been found in many places on or near both of the lines spoken of, such as on the Yellowstone, in several places, the Musselshell river, and also the Judith at Boseman's Pass, and on the Dearborn. These deposits are more properly lignites. Two of them have been tried; one of them, at Boseman's Pass, in making gas, and the other at the Dearborn, in a grate. Both succeeded well. I have been informed that the lignites from the neighborhood of Mount Diablo, in California, are used with success on board the coast steamers.

There is a great deal of excellent land along the Yellowstone, and on the large tributaries emptying into it from the south, such as the Powder, Tongue, Rosebud, Big Horn, Clarke's Fork, and many smaller streams. To the north are the valleys of the Musselshell, Judith, Deep creek, and Missouri. In western Montana the road would pass through mineral districts of known richness. In eastern Montana the country, in consequence of the hostility of the Indians, has not been very thoroughly prospected; but enough has been done to prove that the country is rich in the precious metals. As the questions of climate and depth of snow have a very important bearing on the practicability of the road, I will simply give the general results of years of travel and observation in these mountains. During all of these years I have had occasion to travel in one part or another of the country during the winter, and generally on horseback.

I would say, therefore, that in open valleys, such as that near Helena, the Deer Lodge valley, &c., the snow seldom becomes deeper than one foot, and that in deep, narrow gorges, where the sun cannot reach it, or where the timber may be thick, the depth of snow generally reaches from two to two and a-half feet. In ascending the hills, particularly on their northern slopes, the snow becomes deeper, but I doubt whether, even at the highest summits, it ever reaches the depth of 10 feet, judging by the trees. The southern slopes of the hills, or those opposed to the sun, are generally bare, and horses and cattle there pick up a comfortable subsistence. The winter does not become severe, nor does much snow fall until after the first of January. During that month there are generally ten days or two weeks when the thermometer ranges from zero to 30°, and even 40° below. The rest of the season is not generally as severe as in the northern parts of Maine, Vermont, or Massachusetts. I would further add, that once in about 10 or 12 years, according to the observations of old mountaineers, there comes an extraordinary winter, when a much greater quantity of snow falls than usual. Such a one was the winter of 1860–61, when vast numbers of horses and cattle perished in consequence of the depth of the snow. This occurs, however, in all northern countries.

In further elucidation of the matter I will state that, on the 23d and 24th of December, 1867, I crossed the Belt mountains, east of the Missouri, twice; once at the head of Confederate gulch, and again at the head of the Musselshell river, and returned about the 1st of January. The utmost depth of snow that I found on either summit was about one foot. In going the cold was very severe, but on my return the weather was mild and pleasant.

In the spring, on the 15th of March, I crossed the Rocky mountains at what is called the Frenchman's Pass, within about 15 miles of Helena City, finding about two feet of snow on the summit. There was no snow in the valleys on either side, and but little on the side hills. I passed the range 10 days after at Mullan's Pass, and found but little snow, the ground being bare in many places.

You ask, "What line would be best for a railroad connecting with the Union Pacific?"

This question does not state what point is intended to be connected, but, as Helena is now the commercial center of the Territory, I will take it for granted it is meant as the objective point.

I would state, therefore, in my opinion, the shortest and best line could be obtained by starting from the crossing of Green river, following up the stream or some of its branches to the head of either Salt river or John Gray's river (branches of the South Snake river) to the junction with that river, which takes place where that stream turns from north to southwest; thence the road could go up the South Snake, (in a northerly course,) to the large lake at its head, could cross the mountains there and follow down the south branch of the Madison, and the Madison itself, to the three forks of the Missouri; down the Missouri and up Ten-mile creek to Helena The general direction of this route is a little west of north. The length would be about 350 miles; and it offers the most direct and practicable solution of the problem that I know of.

There is a portion of this route that I am not personally acquainted with. I know nothing of Green river, or of the heads of Salt river, or John Gray's river, but I am well acquainted with the South Snake river, which I explored from its mouth to its head in 1863, and with the Madison, Missouri, and neighborhood of Helena, and these present no serious difficulties.

The worst part would be at the bend of the South Snake river, where it turns at right angles to its former course. Here there is a precipitous cañon, which lasts for several miles. There is an Indian trail on the western side, that being more favorable than its opposite. Above this point there is one other cañon, not nearly as difficult as this one, and the rest of the way is comparatively easy. The river heads in a large lake some 12 or 15 miles long, and flows into another large lake called Jackson's lake, of about the same length.

At the head of the South Snake, and also on the south fork of the Madison, there are hundreds of hot springs, many of which are "geysers."

There are two large prairies, or "holes," in mountain parlance, on the South Snake, which could be cultivated. The whole country is remarkably well watered, and abounds in timber. The mineral indications are numerous, and I have no doubt that, as in the adjacent Territories, the precious metals will be found. Coal was discovered by the party that I was with. The climate, I think, is not severe. It was then in the first half of October, at which time the weather was very mild, and no snow had fallen. This was at an altitude of 6,000 or 7,000 feet. There is a route still further to the west which would pass down the South Snake river from the bend to its mouth, and thence turning northerly cross the divide at the head of Red Rock creek, and follow down the Beaver Head below the mouth of Black Tail Deer creek, thence cross over to the Wisdom or Big Hole river, (there are no mountains in the way,) cross the Rocky mountains at the low and open Deer Lodge pass, and proceed down the Deer Lodge river to the Hellgate, the probable location of the prospective Northern Pacific railroad.

The most difficult portion of the route would be down the South Snake river, which, like the main Snake river, abounds in basaltic precipices. The Rocky mountains, in consequence of a remarkable turn which they make, would have to be passed twice, but both passes are wide and open, and neither are over 100 feet in altitude. Timber and water abound on this route.

W. W. DE LACY.

Professor A. K. EATON.

CHAPTER XIV.

PLACER MINES.

Bannack Placers.—The first placers successfully worked in the territory were those of Bannack, discovered in the summer of 1862.

The yield was at first large and the gold of high grade, but owing to want of capital, only those portions of the gulch were worked that did not involve any considerable expenditure.

The discovery of Alder gulch, in July of the following year, immediately attracted most of the miners to that point, so that by the spring of 1864 Bannack was almost entirely deserted by the active placer mining portion of its population. In 1866 it again began to show signs of activity, and has been steadily increasing its productions since.

The completion of a long ditch by Smith & Graeter, bringing the waters of the Horse Prairie creek into the gulch, has been the principal occasion of an increase in the yield of the gulch the present year.

Enterprising capitalists have long looked upon this gulch as exceedingly rich, especially at certain points, inaccessible except by the expenditure of considerable capital; and preliminary steps have been taken to organize companies for the purpose of working the gulch, or a considerable portion of it, by a thorough system of hydraulic working and bed-rock fluming; but the difficulty involved in securing consecutive claims, and more especially the impossibility of holding the property securely until their arrangements were completed for practically working the claims, have prevented the success of these schemes.

There is little doubt that the gold hitherto taken from the gulch is but a tithe of that now inaccessible for want of capital, but that capital cannot be commanded so long as the statutes do not give ample protection to mining property once acquired, and enable capitalists to hold claims without interference sufficiently long to put a systematic method of mining into actual operation.

The same is true of many other localities, where, as in this case, the conformation of the ground and other difficulties involve the necessity of a great expenditure of money, before remunerative returns could be realized.

Alder Gulch.—This gulch, second in point of discovery in the Territory, and in yield the first, perhaps, in the world, is still being worked at certain points successfully, but those portions that can be worked profitably by individuals with limited means are few, and like most of the older diggings it is awaiting the influx of capital.

The introduction of water from the headwaters of the Madison river has been long contemplated, and a survey of the most practicable course has demonstrated its feasibility, but the great expense of the undertaking—not less than $75,000—precludes the probability of its completion at present.

Alder Gulch has already yielded a fabulous amount of gold, which it would doubtless duplicate if thoroughly worked by a systematic method of bed-rock fluming and hydraulics.

The successful working of claims at the head of the gulch was somewhat interrupted, early in September, by a destructive water spout. Butcher and French gulches were deluged with water, which, sweeping down through the main gulch, buried flumes, shafts, and machinery beneath a mass of sand, gravel and boulders. The effects of the tornado, however, rapidly disappeared before the energy of the miners, and probably did not seriously affect the yield of the gulch for the present season; these water spouts, though not usual, may be considered as part of the "institutions" of the country, as more or less of them are experienced every year.

The introduction of the waters of the Madison would doubtless restore to Alder gulch its former activity and profitableness. Wigwam, a gulch tributary to Alder, is reported to have yielded largely.

Ram's Horn, an old gulch north of Virginia City, and according to common report worked out, has given rise to considerable excitement, based upon the report that valuable deposits have been uncovered beneath the old bed-rock flume.

The Radersbury and Crow Creek diggings, 45 miles east of Helena, have yielded moderately.

Last Chance gulch, one of the most remarkable in the Territory, still continues to be successfully worked, and at some points more profitably than ever. This is especially true of the exterior deposits of pay gravel below the town of Helena; the claims, for instance, of Taylor, Thomson & Company.

In the summer of 1865 these claims were worked only to the depth of a few feet, by stripping the surface to the "pay streak;" it was then supposed that the ground below would not pay. They are now working the deposits to the depth of from 40 to 50 feet, with very remunerative results. The success of operations at this locality has induced parties to search for similar deposits at a point further below the town.

On the slope of Ten-mile creek, below Helena, a number of shafts have been sunk in search of the supposed continuation of the valuable deposit brought to light in the claims of Taylor, Thomson & Company, Getchell & Company, &c., in Last Chance gulch. In the confident belief that such a channel really exists, Colonel Kieler and his associates have commenced a deep drain near the Jewish cemetery on Ten-mile creek. Their ditch has already been dug a distance of 1,500 feet, and a large volume of water has been struck in it.

The majority of the gulches in the vicinity of Helena have been worked more or less steadily and productively. Silver creek, Trinity, and Piegan to the north, have yielded moderately well.

In Ten-mile creek, to the west of Helena, a prospecting company has been formed to test the bed of the gulch, which is believed to be rich. A deep shaft has been sunk and a Woodworth pump capable of raising some hundreds of gallons per minute has been put in. The prospects are reported to be encouraging.

The more economically directed claims in Last Chance expend, on the average, 50 per cent. of the gross yield for running expenses; the others about 75 per cent.

The chief item of outlay is the payment of water money, viz: 50 cents per inch miner's measurement, *i. e.*, for such a volume of water as is discharged through an orifice one inch square, under a six-inch pressure.

Originally but little water flowed down Last Chance. To supply this want a long line of ditches was constructed by Messrs. Truett, Dahler and Atchison. Through the flumes and ditches built by these gentlemen several thousand inches of water have been brought in from Tenmile creek.

Should a bed-rock flume be built through the gulch, this water may be at once turned on; whereby it will be possible to rework not only the great heaps of tailings already washed once, but also to extract the gold from a considerable stretch of ground too poor to return a profit under present conditions.

The early spring and summer have not been marked by any general exodus nor stampede. Momentary excitements, so to speak, have been caused by the boulder gulches, known as Peter's, Galena, and Boomerang, which have yielded nothing or only moderately. More recently, Basin gulch, 35 miles west of Jefferson City, Wilson gulch, 10 miles east of the same town, and Tyser gulch, still further to the southeast, have enlisted some attention, and each, with the coming season, bids fair to be reasonably productive.

To the east of the Missouri river, 16 miles by trail and 26 miles by coach-road from Diamond City, lies Thomson gulch; here three hydraulics have been running successfully on Morgan bar, below Eagle City. The Deep creek country, in the same vicinity, lying between Diamond City and the Musselshell, has during the summer attracted some attention. The diggings are very extensive, but only moderately rich.

Amongst the older and well-known gulches to the east of the Rocky mountains, several have produced far more gold than last year; as an example we may cite the claims of Colonel Head & Company, in Confederate gulch. This gulch, it will be remembered, is the locality where, two seasons ago, the gold dust was collected by the hundred-weight; its product this year, from Montana bar especially, will almost equal the highest yield of the past.

Messrs. King and Gillette, of Helena, have constructed in Confederate gulch a bed-rock flume nearly a half a mile in length. The major portion of the present season having been consumed in the work, it cannot be expected to yield largely until the coming summer. At El Dorado bar on the Missouri river, a locality prolific of fine sapphires, there has recently been completed a long ditch, which was carried over Loup creek through a lofty flume.

The bar has not this season turned out as favorably as had been anticipated. There is, however, reason to hope that better results will be obtained during the next summer.

West of the main range of the Rocky mountains, the placers have, on the average, been far more productive than during the last year. The older gulches—Blackfoot, Confederate bar, German gulch, Elk, Bear, and Lincoln gulches—have been worked steadily, and many of them yielded largely.

Of particularly flattering yields we may instance the placers of Silver Bin and vicinity, and of Gold creek and its neighborhood, famous as the locality where gold was first discovered in the Territory. Among the recent developments we may mention Uncle Ben's gulch, 20 miles southwest of Deer Lodge City, discovered during the past summer, and reported to be yielding satisfactorily. Pioneer gulch, some three miles distant from Gold creek, likewise yielding well. Prairie Diggings, likewise southwest of Silver Bin; Henderson, near Emmetsburg, and Harvey creek, 18 miles above, have all paid moderately. Modesty and Last creeks, to the east of Deer Lodge City, have attracted some notice.

But one "stampede" of any magnitude is to be chronicled west of the range. This was caused by a report of fabulously rich diggings in the Clear Water country, in the Cœur D'Alène range. These placers are situated some 45 miles southeast of the famous Florence, in Idaho. Quite a number of stampeders started thither, but the tide turned, and little has since been heard of the locality. It is reported that 40 men will winter there, so that the country will be thoroughly prospected the coming summer.

In general terms, it may stated that the placers of the entire Territory have yielded, on the average, fully 20 per cent. more than last year. Confederate, Silver Bin, and German gulches excepted, we find a less number of brilliant individual yields, but as an offset we have had a more general well-doing. Among the best indications of uniform prosperity is the fact that but few stampedes have taken place. This gives the assurance that the miners generally have accepted the conclusion that ordinary paying placers near home are far preferable to diggings at a distance, whose only evidence of value is common report. Again, the search for deep placers, similar to the Blue lead of California, has already begun. Should the investigations below Helena prove successful, they will unearth a species of placers which will be prolific for years.

Montana is pre-eminently a "wash" country, and it is impossible to resist the conclusion that the secondary outflows have covered up, to a great depth, diggings far richer than any heretofore discovered on or near the surface.

The importance of such diggings will be better appreciated from a statement of the fact that two-thirds of the gross gold product of California is due to the deep placers. It is improbable, however, that we shall find in Montana any lava-covered localities similar to the Tuolumne table mountain.

CHAPTER XV.

QUARTZ MINES.

The product of bullion from the quartz lodes of the Territory, though small compared to that of the placer mines, shows a very great increase over that of any previous year from the same source. Hitherto, through lack of systematic development, the mines have not generally furnished ore in sufficient quantity to keep the mills continually supplied. This difficulty is fast being obviated and many mills are running uninteruptedly, and with the most satisfactory results. One element of success of late has been the enlistment of *home capital.* The prominent business men of the Territory—merchants, bankers, &c.—have been of late engaging in quartz mining enterprises, and their confidence has been rewarded by success. The increased facilities for the manufacture and repairs of mining machinery have also contributed not a little to this great production of bullion from quartz.

The Unionville mines.—The quartz lodes of Unionville, four miles south of Helena, are first in point of interest in the Territory, since they are the most thoroughly developed, and have produced at least one-half of the whole gross gold product from quartz during the last year. This statement applies more particularly to the property known as the Whitlatch Union vein, which is owned and worked by several different companies. Of them the National Mining and Exploring Company was the first in the field and has been the most successful. The lode has a general course, accepting the angle given by the United States deputy mineral land surveyor, Captain DeLacy, of south 84° 24′ east. It was discovered in the winter of 1864, and work was actively begun the ensuing spring. The country rock is granite and the lode is found a short distance south of a wide belt of limestone. In width the vein varies from 20 inches to 11 feet and upwards, having, in the better portions of the pay chimney, an average width of five to six feet. The gangue is quartzy in the superior portions, and below seems to assume the character of a quartziferous syenite. The minor minerals in the vein are iron pyrites, increasing as the excavation extends; telluret of gold in considerable quantity; copper pyrites in small amounts and occasional markings of carbonate and silicate of copper. Crystals of hornblende are now and then found with adhering particles of native gold.

The ownerships on the lode, commencing at the Discovery claim, are as follows:

Discovery, owned by Whitlatch Union Mining Company.

No. 1 east, owned by Whitlatch Union Mining Company.

West half No. 2 east, owned by Whitlatch Union Mining Company.

East half No. 2 east, owned by Mansfield and Hodson.

No. 3 east, owned by Columbia Mining Company.

No. 4 east, owned by Columbia Mining Company and Mansfield and Hodson.

No. 5 east, owned by Whitlatch Union Mining Company.

No. 1 west, owned by I X L Mining Company.

No. 2 west, owned by National Mining and Exploring Company.

No. 3 west, owned by Columbia Mining Company.

No. 4 west, owned by National Mining and Exploring Company.

East half No. 5 west, owned by National Mining and Exploring Company.

West half No. 5 west, in dispute.

No. 6 west, (called also Owyhee,) owned by Parkison and Whitlatch.

No. 7 west, (called also Owyhee,) owned by Parkison and Whitlatch.

Remaining claims on Owhyee owned by Parkison.

The depths reached on the lode are as follows:

On Discovery claim, 200 feet.

On I X L claim, 380 feet.

On National Mining and Exploring Company claim, 345 feet.

On Columbia Mining Company claim, 340 feet.

On Parkison and Whitlatch claim, 130 feet.

The working of the various claims on this lode have built up and maintained a considerable village. The employés and people directly or indirectly dependent on the mines number between 800 and 1,000 souls. The vein has given employment to three proprietary mills, aggregating 74 stamps, and occasionally to two custom mills of 10 stamps each. The former have been in operation almost uninterruptedly, and have produced a very large sum total in gold bullion.

The average yield of the ore cannot have been far short of $20 to $25 coin per ton of 2,000 pounds. The highest yield from any portion of the mine consisted of an average of $80 coin per ton from 300 tons of selected ore.

The vein near the surface is quite irregular; runs flat in many places, but in depth seems inclined to keep a more constant dip. It is possible that these variations may continue until the limestone belt be reached, from whence the vein would, in all probability, follow the line of demarcation between the two rocks.

In the lowest levels the water-line has been reached, and it is proposed to put in three pumps some time during the coming spring.

Connections have been made on the vein a distance of 1,300 feet, thus facilitating ventilation.

Towards the west the supposed continuation of the Union has received the name of the Park lode. It differs from the Union in so far as larger masses of iron and copper pyrites are found near the surface. This ore is in such abundance that it is advisable to erect chlorination works for its reduction. A number of shafts have been sunk and are now sinking on the lode.

The books of one of the companies working the ores of the Union lode show the receipts during the year ending October 31, 1868, of $136,900. As they work about 600 tons of ore per month, these receipts indicate an average yield of $19 per ton. The cost of mining and milling these ores varies, according to different statistics, from $7 50 to $12 per ton.

The Laramie mines.—The lodes of the Laramie district, south of Virginia City, have proved difficult of development; and most of the mills have been idle much of the year for a want of a supply of quartz. They have recently shown increased activity; and there is little doubt that the district will eventually prove one of the best in the Territory. The gold of this district is, much of it, of very high grade, and occurs in pockets of great richness. The irregularity of the deposits, however, is the occasion of great discouragement; and the difficulties of development are greatly enhanced by the fact that the valuable lodes are owned by many different parties, one owning 100 feet, another 50 feet, &c., making the risk and expense of development too great for any one of the various owners. This difficulty will correct itself in time, by means of combinations that will secure systematic development.

The Bannock mines.—The mines in the vicinity of Bannock have been worked most of the year, but not with sufficient success to furnish a full supply of ore to the mills erected. The mill of the Mineral Land Mining Company has crushed the ores of the Dakota lode as fast as mined, but has probably run but two or three months during the year. A small mill in the vicinity has been running most of the time, principally upon ores from the Cherokee lode. From the Dakota about 1,200 tons only have been crushed during the last year, yielding an average of $18 per ton.

The difficulties connected with the development of the Dakota arise in part from the character of the vein, and in part from divided ownership and disputed titles. The Dakota, like all the auriferous veins about Bannock, is a *contact vein* lying between the dioritic trap, or granite, as the miners term it, and limestone veins of this kind, which conform to the broken outlines of a disrupted formation, are, of necessity, very irregular, especially near the surface; hence the ever-varying character of the Dakota. The trappean mass, in connection with which the Dakota vein occurs, lies in a kind of irregular circle in that part of the cañon, and all the indications of gold in veins are upon the outer limits of this mass.

The Hot Spring mines.—The mines of the Hot Spring, or Sterling, district have not, as yet, proved remunerative. Five mills were erected, but, in all cases, previous to any considerable development of the lodes upon which the hopes of the proprietors were based. One mill, that of the New York and Montana M. & D. Company, has been running with little interruption during the last summer and fall. The ores of the district, *i. e.*, those worked, average probably about the same as in other portions of the Territory—from $18 to $20 per ton. The gold, with few exceptions, is of low grade throughout the district, ranging from $\frac{550}{1000}$ to $\frac{720}{1000}$ fine. This increases materially the difficulty of amalgamation.

Perhaps no district in the Territory showed stronger indications of rich auriferous deposits than this when first examined. The veins are numerous, but many are small, and all irregular at the present stage of development. Deeper workings will doubtless secure greater uniformity. The veins in the upper district lie wholly in granite; those of the lower, in gneiss. The lower district has of late appeared the most promising.

Rochester Gulch and Silver Star district.—The Woodworth and Hendrie mill at Rochester, finished in June last, has run uninterruptedly, and with large profit. The mill has ten stamps. The total expenditure up to the time of starting the stamps is reported to have been $34,000. Of this amount, $6,700 is charged to the mine, and $1,500 for the purchase of teams. The total running outlay is stated to be $560 per week. Within nine weeks after the mill was fairly in operation there was reported a yield of $15,286. The gross yield ranged from 110 ounces to 136 ounces per week. The gold is of a low grade, being largely made up of silver. Further exploration is necessary in order to determine whether the gold or silver will ultimately predominate. Encouraged by the success of Captain Hendrie, several additional mills are in contemplation in the same district; that of Mr. Warren is reported to be nearly completed. At Silver Star, near the Jefferson, we hear of two successful enterprises, viz: the Everett mill of 10 stamps, to work the ores of the Green Campbell lode, and the Stevens & Turitt mill of 12 stamps, to work the ore of the Iron Rod lode; both are reported to be yielding well.

The mills in the New York gulch, east of the Missouri, are all at a stand-still; also the Allen mill on Ten-mile.

It is in contemplation to erect near Diamond the mill of an Indiana company, formerly standing in Clark's gulch, near Helena.

In the Blue Cloud district, west of Helena, there are two mills, one in successful operation, and a second in progress of erection.

A 30-stamp mill is on its way from Fort Benton, which will probably be erected the coming spring on Mitchell's or McClellan's gulch, some 12 miles east of Helena.

West of the main range of the Rocky mountains, we have the mill of Prof. Swallow, at Highland, of 24 stamps. It has recently started up, and is reported to have made a successful run.

The mill of the St. Louis and Montana Mining Company, at Philipsburg, the only silver amalgamation mill in the Territory, has been running more or less constantly the entire year.

Two mills have been erected at Georgetown, 12 miles from Philipsburg, for gold ores; they started, and stopped for reasons unknown.

At Cable City, two miles further on, two mills have been built; the one to work the ores of the Atlantic Cable mine, and the other that of the Thomas lode. Both, and particularly the former, have been crushing successfully.

The Atlantic cable lode seems to be an enormous limestone dike, intercalated between granite walls. And in the limestone are found bands and bunches of ore, often of great extent and value.

The ore consists of some quartz, carbonate of copper, copper pyrites, and a very large amount black and reddish oxides of iron.

Table of quartz mills.

Name of mill.	Number of stamps.	County.	Quartz district.
Philadelphia Enterprise Co	30	Lewis and Clarke	Unionville.
Nat. M. & Ex. Co	20	do	Do.
I. X. L	24	do	Do.
Addis	10	do	Do.
Turnley	10	do	Park.
Gormleys	15	do	Do.
Allen	10	do	Ten-mile.
Blue Cloud	15	do	Blue Cloud.
Plymouth	10	do	Greenhorn.
Postlewaite	15	Madison	Summit.
John How	20	do	Do.
Lucas	20	do	Do.
McClure's Chili mills	5	do	Do.
Midas	15	do	Sterling.
New York & M. M. & D. Co	20	do	Do.
Hall & Spalding	15	do	Do.
Atkins	10	do	Do.
Cope	15	do	Do.
Hobart & Co	6	do	Do.
Upson & Clarks	12	do	Do.
Stevens & Trivett	12	do	Silver Star.
Everett	10	do	Do.
Hendrie	10	do	Rochester.
M. L. & M. Co	15	Beaver Head	Bannack.
Swallow	24	Deer Lodge	Highland.
St. Louis & Montana Mining Co	10	do	Philipsburg.
Herney	10	do	Georgetown.
Ewing	8	do	Do.
Hanans	20	do	Cable City.
Nowlan & Plaistead	20	do	Do.
Vantilburgh	5	Meagher	New York.

In addition to the above-mentioned, there are in the Territory between 40 and 60 stamps which will be erected the coming spring, or as soon as the developments on the respective leads shall warrant. Further, there are some 20 odd stamps erected in different localities, which have returned no profit, and which are now standing idle.

We may estimate the total number of stamps erected in the Territory at about 500. Of these not more than 150 were kept more or less regularly in operation at the beginning of the year. In the month of July the gold interest began to yield brilliantly, and the number of stamps running, including those of new and old mills, could not have been less than 225. At present it is fair to estimate that 275 stamps are working successfully. The failures and disastrous results of the past have yielded an amount of experience by which like errors may be avoided in the future. The principle is beginning to be understood that the mine should be opened before a mill be erected, and that the costs, and not the profits, should form the basis on which to make an estimate.

Ten stamps for gold ores may be erected at a cost of $2,000 to $2,500 per stamp. A yield of $15 to $18 (coin) in free gold, per ton of 2,000 pounds will, at present prices of labor and materials, pay from 20 to 50 per cent. profit, according to the amount crushed and favorable or unfavorable general conditions.

The silver amalgamating mill of the St. Louis and Montana Mining Company, of Philipsburg, is reported to reduce the ores of Flint creek for $30 in silver bullion per ton.

Smelting furnaces.—The earliest discoveries of ore at Argenta, in Beaver Head county, were of such a character as to admit of reduction only by the process of smelting; a small furnace was erected at Bannock and a large double German cupola at Argenta. Neither are now in operation. From the latter, erected by a St. Louis company, there was extracted a considerable amount of silver, which did not, however, yield a profit, and in consequence the company suspended operations. A smaller furnace was subsequently built in the same town, under the direction of Mr. Rompf, an accomplished German metallurgist. According to common report, the furnace ran to a profit. For reasons, however, unknown to the public, the works passed into second hands and were closed for some time. Recently it is reported that this furnace is again in operation.

Smelting operations, excepting only an experimental furnace erected at Butte City to reduce the surface carbonates of copper, have been confined to the mines of the eastern slopes of the main range.

Relying upon the best information at our disposal, there are now in the Territory the following smelting works: One furnace, situated one mile above Bannock, to smelt ores from the Blue Wing district; at Argenta, four furnaces, viz: that erected by the St. Louis and Montana Mining Company; the Esler furnace; a furnace built by Messrs. Tootle, Leach & Co., and one erected by A. Murray, esq.

Proceeding northwards, we find one furnace at Mill Creek, north of Virginia City; and still further north, at Jefferson City, we find two furnaces; the one built by the O. M. G. & S. Co., and the other owned by Mr. Rutan.

It is claimed that the last mentioned has run to a profit. There is reported a second furnace in process of erection at Butte City, west of the mountains.

Smelting is, beyond question, a process whereby a larger percentage of the contained gold and silver can be extracted than by the amalgamation. It differs from amalgamation in so far that amalgamable ores may be smelted, whereas lead-bearing smelting ores cannot be amalgamated. Copper-bearing ores, it is true, may either be amalgamated or smelted. The great advantage of the one process over the other is due to the fact that the amalgamation is brought about by machinery, is soon finished, and leaves no by-products to be reworked, unless we consider as such the pyritiferous tailings; smelting, on the other hand, is performed mainly by manual labor and is complicated with a number of by-products which require a reworking. Moreover, there is required a large percentage of lead to collect the silver scattered through the rock and galena; if the ore itself does not contain a sufficiency of that metal it must be added along with the fluxes. The non-metallic and the valueless metallic portion of the ore must be disposed of in the form of a slag, which must be of such a consistency as to admit of an easy separation therefrom of the argentiferous lead. If the ore does not itself contain the elements requisite to the formation of a proper slag, such fluxes must be added as will make up the deficiency. Owing to the rarity of finding a single ore combining all these advantages it is usual, in England and on the continent of Europe, where smelting is profitably carried on, to combine the ores of the different mines in such a manner that the valueless gangue of the one shall act as a flux to that of the other. In this way smelting is robbed of half its difficulty. Moreover, the mines and smelting works are rarely if ever the property of the same parties. The mine-owner raises his ores, dresses them, and sells them to the furnace-owner. In early times both pursuits were combined, but all recent experience teaches that it is far preferable to keep them separate. What is needed to make smelting an attractive and profitable pursuit here in Montana is—1st, a separation of mine and furnace ownership; 2d, a market for the lead, which at the present rates of transportation is practically valueless; 3d, cheap labor, and 4th, the discovery of a variety of coal susceptible of being coked. At present no other fuel than wood and charcoal can be obtained.

The time will most assuredly come when the large amount of smelting ores in the Territory can be reduced to a profit. Some central location will be selected on one of the great rivers and in the vicinity of a coal bed, the blast will be driven by water power, and every unnecessary pair of hands dispensed with. Under such conditions smelting will be very profitable; the country will have been settled, and the present annual home consumption of lead will be increased an hundred fold. Even under present conditions an abundance of reasonably rich ores, water-power, and other natural facilities, combined with the strictest economy and prudent management, may realize a small profit.

Export of ores.—Owing to the difficulty of obtaining economically favorable results from the lead and copper bearing ores of the Territory, small lots have, from time to time, been exported from the Territory to the eastern States and to Europe. Among the lots so shipped may be enumerated 1½ ton of black copper from the experimental furnace at Butte City. This metal was shipped by Captain Hendrie, of the Helena foundry, and was reported to contain a high percentage of gold. Further, 1,000 pounds of argentiferous galena, from the Ten-mile district, was shipped by Messrs. T. E. and D. G. Tutt, and 20 tons of rich silver ores from the Poor Man's Joy lode, of Philipsburg, by Mr. Cole Saunders.

The costs of shipment may be estimated as follows: $20, currency, per ton to Fort Benton, the head of steamboat navigation on the Missouri river; $20, currency, per ton to St. Louis, by water, and $10 to $15, currency per ton to the seabord. From thence to foreign ports about $15 currency per ton; making in all a grand total of $65 to $70 currency per ton of 2,000 pounds. Hence ores yielding $100 coined value per ton may be, even at present rates, raised and shipped with a small profit.

The tendency of prices in Montana is steadily downward, and as the population becomes more stable and compact, whereby the costs of labor and of the necessaries of life are diminished, these shipments of ore will increase in volume and will yield a much greater profit. Under such conditions, however, it would probably be more advisable to reduce the ores on the spot.

Production.—The production of bullion from Montana for the year 1868, judging from the most reliable estimates obtainable, probably reached $15,000,000, of which about $1,000,000 was the product of the quartz mines. The amount of silver produced was about $100,000.

CHAPTER XVI.

REMARKS ON THE OPERATION IN MONTANA OF THE UNITED STATES MINERAL LAND ACT OF JULY 26, 1866, BY W. S. KEYES, MINING ENGINEER, HELENA.*

In order to have a clear understanding of the provisions of this law, as applied to Montana, it is necessary to bear in mind the territorial enactments governing the location and tenure of lode claims. These were two, as follows: The first, consisting of 12 sections, entitled "An act relating to the discovery of gold and silver quartz leads, lodes, or ledges, and of the manner of their location," was approved December 26, 1864.

*I do not entirely agree with Mr. Keyes in his unqualified condemnation of the United States law of 1866. My own opinion will be found in Part II of this report.—R. W. R.

The second became law January 17, 1865. Without repeating here the text of the first law, which is found entire in my report of last year to the United States commissioner of mining, to which reference is made, it will suffice to touch upon its peculiarities. This law differs from the local laws and customs of other mining districts, in so far as only 50 feet are allowed on each side of the respective claims, and each mine is limited in length to 2,200 feet, including discovery claim, and to 200 feet for each name. The second law gives absolute title as against the Territory, and by making the quartz claims a matter of county record, places them upon the same footing as other real property.

In Montana, therefore, as compared with other mining regions, we find an anomalous condition of the quartz titles, and the incubus of a rigid, ill-considered, and hastily adopted mining code. The Territory, unlike a concourse of miners, cannot enact retroactive laws, and hence a mistake, once made, cannot be remedied, and improvement can only be applied to new districts.

The mining customs east of the Rocky mountains are very different from those of the west. The latter were colored by the spirit of the Mexican Ordenanzas de Mineria, and took form and substance from the customs of a people accustomed to mines and mining for centuries. The former, born in Colorado and transplanted to Montana, are the product of the crude theories of an agricultural, and not of a mining, people. As a result of these laws I have found much complaint, among such mine owners as have themselves had faith enough to explore their own lodes, founded upon the fact that many claims are held totally untouched for years, and by an absentee ownership, which will neither develope nor sell. All these peculiarities combined render the application of the law of 1866 exceedingly unsatisfactory. And, further, in the light of the past two years, and in view of its practical working, at least in Montana, I am constrained to characterize the law a failure.

My objections in detail are as follows: 1st. It is tedious and vexatious. 2d. It is excessively costly. 3d. Even the issuance of a patent does not materially diminish the probability of litigation; and 4th. It has brought and can bring but little revenue to the government.

First. It is tedious and vexatious. I can offer no stronger proof under this head than the appended letters of Mr. O. B. O'Bannon, the register of the United States land office, to whom all applications for patent must be made, and of Mr. G. B. Foote, deputy mineral land surveyor. The opinions of each of these gentlemen merit careful attention, and particularly those of Mr. O'Bannon, who, besides having a thorough acquaintance with the details of the law, is himself a practical quartz-miner of several years' experience in Nevada. I addressed to Mr. O'Bannon the following interrogatories:

1st. How many applications for mineral land have been made?

2d. How many have been contested?

3d. How many have been withdrawn?

4th. How many certificates of final entry have been issued, and for what claims?

5th. How many patents have you received, and for what claims?

6th. As far as your observation extends, what is your opinion of the practical working of the United States mineral land act of July 26, 1866?

7th. Would patents under this law serve to quiet title and prevent litigation?

8th. What are the defects in the law, and, if any, what remedies would you suggest?

To all of which Mr. O'Bannon made reply, as follows:

UNITED STATES LAND OFFICE,
Helena, M. T., November 21, 1868.

DEAR SIR: Your note of the 12th instant, containing certain interrogatories in regard to the mineral act of July 26, 1866, is before me. In reply I would state:

1st. That 30 applications for patent under the said act have been made at this office.

2d. That seven of these applications have been contested. In two cases the applicants did not appear, and seem to have abandoned their applications. In one case the contestants withdrew his objections; and the remaining cases have been referred to the courts of the Territory for adjudication.

3d. Six applications have been withdrawn.

4th. Certificates of patent have been issued by me for nine mining claims, to wit: to Whitlatch Union Mining Company, for claims on Union No. 2 lode; to McIntyre Mining Company, for claims on McIntyre lode; to James W. Whitlatch, for discovery claims on Park lode; to Turnley Mining Company, for claims on Park lode; to Ten-mile Mining Company, (three certificates,) for claims on Douglas, Roderick Dhu, and Ivanhoe lodes; to Granite Mountain Company, for claims on Granite Mountain No. 2 lode; to Essex Mining Company, for claims on Parkison lode: all situate in Lewis and Clarke county. In the case of the Whitlatch Union Mining Company, above referred to, the papers were returned from the General Land Office for irregularities, and the application was abandoned by the company.

5th. No patents for mineral lands have ever been received at this office; and, except in the case of the Whitlatch Union, above referred to, I am not advised of any action at the General Land Office in regard to any of the mineral applications forwarded from this office.

6th. The "practical working" of the act in question, so far as I can judge, has from various causes, some of them general and some purely local, not been satisfactory.

This mineral act seems to have been gotten up with direct and special reference "to the rules and customs of the miners" of California and Nevada. Here there are, strictly speaking, no local rules and customs relating to quartz or "lode" property. The whole matter is regulated by the territorial legislature, and the act of the legislative assembly of the Territory of Montana, entitled "An act relating to the discovery of gold and silver quartz lodes, leads, or ledges, and the manner of their location" approved December 26, 1864, is universally recognized by the miners of the Territory. This act differs in many essential particulars from the mining rules and customs which obtain on the Pacific coast, and which form the basis of the act of Congress of July 26, 1866. Many of the difficulties encountered by applicants for patent to mineral lands in this Territory arise from this fact.

Among other serious obstacles and drawbacks, I would enumerate the inadequacy of the compensation allowed to the deputy surveyors of mineral lands, and the requirement that the estimated cost of survey and publication of notice shall be placed by the applicant in a government depository "in favor of the United States Treasurer, to be passed to the credit of the fund created by individual depositors for surveys of the public lands." This latter has been a peculiar, and, it seems to me, unnecessary hardship in this region so remote from the seat of government; as an evidence of which I cite the fact that much of the money thus deposited has lain idle in the vaults for nearly a year before it was paid over to the deputy surveyors and publishers to whom it rightfully belonged.

I see no reason why it might not be so arranged that deputy surveyors could be paid as soon as their services are rendered, or why applicants might not be permitted to make their own terms with publishers.

Without further particularizing, I would state generally, under this head, that proceedings under this law here are tedious, vexatious, and expensive; that miners seeking patents have generally become discouraged, and that mineral applications have well nigh ceased at this office.

Commissioner Wilson, judging from some of his recent rulings, seems disposed to relieve the law of its harsher features, so far as this can be done, by the most liberal construction of its provisions; and even if some of the details of the law are not modified by Congress, I doubt not that proceedings under it will eventually be greatly simplified by the Commissioner, and the attainment of mineral patents rendered reasonably certain to all meritorious applicants, even in Montana.

7th. So far as I am able to judge it is not the wish of any considerable portion of the mining population of the country that government should dispose of any large part of its lands containing precious metals; and there is nothing the miners would probably ask in relation thereto, except to have an assurance from government that they should be permitted to hold undisturbed such titles as they now enjoy, and that the paramount title of government to such lands should never be enforced.

But conceding the point, so stoutly contested by the miners, that it is the true policy of the general government to dispose of all its mineral lands, I must say, after considerable reflection upon the subject, that, aside from the very trifling revenue which would accrue to the government therefrom, I cannot see how matters can be materially improved by the final disposition of the whole, or any large part of them, under the act of July 26, 1866.

If the precious metals were always found in regular and well defined veins, which, after the expenditure thereon of labor of the value of $1,000, could always be traced with tolerable certainty for a distance of 3,000 feet; if there were no "faults," or bifurcations, or short curves, or sharp angles, I should grant that patents under this law would have the effect of quieting title, and ordinarily prove a sufficient safeguard and protection to the patentees. But my observation is that auriferous, argentiferous, or copper-bearing veins, that are regular and well defined, and which, after the expenditure of $1,000 in development, can be traced with any degree of accuracy for a distance of 3,000, or even 1,000, feet, are rare exceptions; that off-sets, curves, angles, &c., frequently occur, and often when least expected; that in numerous instances, as in the mines of Cerro de Pasco, in Peru, of Santa Eulalia, near the city of Chihuahua, in northern Mexico, and in the recent remarkable discoveries at White Pine, in central Nevada, ores of immense value are found in beds, or irregular masses, where such a thing as a vein or lode cannot, properly speaking, be said to exist; that sometimes, as in the Winnemucca district, in Humboldt county, Nevada, the precious metals are found in a net-work of innumerable small veins, intersecting at all angles over an area of several hundred acres. In none of these cases cited am I able to perceive how patents under this law can protect the holders against litigation, or even materially diminish the chances of dispute, or give to the miner any better security than he already enjoys under his "local rules and customs."

In my humble opinion this whole idea of giving patents to leads or lodes, as such, is erroneous, and can give to patentees no compensating advantages for the trouble and expense necessary under the present law. If the mineral lands must be sold, I would suggest the ollowing as the only plan which has ever occurred to me by which an unassailable title can be secured to the patentee. When a valuable mine is proven to exist, whether of gold, silver, cinnabar, or copper, and whether found in a vein, lode, bed, or deposit, upon proper application of the owner thereof, and his compliance with such necessary rules as may be prescribed, let patent issue to him for a certain amount of land, including his mine. Whether there be one lode or ten, or no lode at all, let the patentee have absolute title to everything contained in the land for which his patent calls, but nothing more. Let him work his mine or mines to any depth, but give him no reserved right to follow his vein or lode, "although it may enter the land adjoining." Let it be his misfortune if his land has not been properly located so as to cover and include his mine.

Under such a system there would, doubtless, be cases of individual hardship, such as cannot be guarded against in the framing of any general law; but the patentee would be effectually protected against all the ordinary chances of ordinary litigation and dispute. There would be no controversy likely to arise between him and an adjoining claimant which could not be readily decided upon the testimony of a competent engineer.

I am, very respectfully, your obedient servant,

O. B. O'BANNAN, *Register*.

W. S. KEYES,
Mining Engineer, Helena, Montana Territory.

The following is communicated by Mr. Foote:

HELENA, MONTANA, *November* 26, 1868.

SIR: Yours of the 24th instant has been duly received. I regret exceedingly that I cannot devote as much time to the subject as its importance requires. My duties and engagements occupy so great a share of my time that any remarks I can make in regard to the practical workings of the mineral land act will necessarily be brief and imperfect. It would afford me great pleasure to make a careful and detailed statement of my observations and notes upon the subject, but the time given me for their preparation is too short to be as explicit as I could wish. The act of Congress of July 26, 1866, generally known as the mineral land act, was looked upon with favor by the miners, and was hailed as one that would inure to their benefit, and I will add that so far as my observations extend, the act itself is still regarded with great favor by a majority of the miners; the general dissatisfaction that seems to exist is based on the fact that the act has been in force nearly three years, and as yet no patent has been granted or issued on any lode. It is true that rumors have been circulated that one patent has been issued on a tract of mineral land in California, covering an area of between 300 and 400 acres, but this is not regarded as a patent on a lode.

Numerous applications for patent have been made in this Territory, and quite a number of final surveys have been made. Among those who have completed their applications and made their entries there seems to be general dissatisfaction, many of them expressing the opinion that their time and money have been thrown away, thus discouraging others and preventing many applications being made. There are hundreds of miners who are desirous of availing themselves of the benefit of the act, but they are discouraged by those who have tried to obtain a government title. Could one patent to a lode mine issue to any person in this Territory, it would cause hundreds to take the initiatory steps to secure patents to their mines. There are but few miners who are acquainted with the manner of doing business in the General Land Office, and it does not appear to them that the certificate which they receive from the local land office is their evidence of title. Until the patent is issued they remain in doubt whether the patent will issue for so many feet on their lode, or for so many acres of land, leaving them still a contestable title to their lode or vein. This doubt seems to arise from the fact that the first surveys which were made in this Territory, and which were made in accordance with the mineral instructions of January 14, 1867, the instructions of the surveyor general, and the local rules, regulations, and customs of miners, *i. e.*, by surveying and marking the required number of feet along the apparent general course of the lode and placing a well-built mound at each end of the claim, in cases where the side lines or corners were unknown, (see page 6, circular of Mineral Instructions, January 14, 1867,) were decided to be incomplete, and subsequent instructions required the side lines to be in all cases actually run, surveyed, and marked, thus confining their surface or working-ground to the land surveyed, which, in many cases, (at points remote from the discovery or worked portions of the lode) would be hundreds of feet from the vein or lode, and absolutely valueless for working purposes. The local law of this Territory, *i. e.*, the act of the territorial legislature, allows 50 feet on each side of the lode for working purposes. It would, therefore, be impossible to locate the exact position of the side lines to a claim in accordance therewith until the lode had been traced and defined on the surface its entire length, which, in many cases, would be impossible, from the fact that lodes do not always crop out on the surface, and in other cases it would require the expenditure of thousands of dollars in useless surface tracings.

Another great cause of complaint is the requirement of the land office that applicants should prove that no other known veins or lodes exist on the ground surveyed. This requirement seems to be almost a complete estoppel to acquiring title to any valuable lode, for the reason that, as soon as any lode has been discovered and proved to be valuable, hundreds of prospectors and "wildcat lode-stakers" immediately repair to the vicinity and dig the whole surrounding country full of shafts, tunnels, prospect-holes, "coyote holes," &c., staking and recording every lode, spur, seam, and even boulder, as if running in every conceivable direction. Some of these may prove to be separate lodes, and may even cross the original lode. The owners of these separate lodes would of course be entitled to hold them, and it would be impossible for the owners of the original and valuable lode to prove that on any defined piece of land which they might have surveyed there were no other known lodes existing at the time of their application. This requirement seems unnecessary, and even unjust, considering the provision of the act limiting the location to one vein or lode, and the provision that the owners of a mine shall have the "right to follow their vein or lode with its dips, angles, and variations to any depth, (and I think it is the spirit and intention of the law to mean in any direction) although it may enter the land adjoining, which land adjoining shall be sold subject to this condition."

Lodes are generally narrow, crop out at one point, and it may be not again for a long distance; no survey can follow them. If they dip, as they almost always do, no straight line can follow them on the surface, in a hilly country, owing to the change made in the surface course of the lode by the dip coming into contact with the hills or depressions in the surface. How, then, can the law require a surface survey, when that surface survey almost invariably must fail to cover the lode sought to be secured? If it be the *lode* that is sold, then all metes and bounds, except the lines limiting the length of the claim, are unnecessary. Such end lines can be as easily run, surveyed, marked, located, witnessed, and perpetuated by monuments, and platted in the office as though side lines were surveyed therewith and a defined *tract* of land enclosed, and there could be no possible mistake or question in regard to the locus of such claim. If it be surface ground that is sold it cannot by any possibility be shown that no other lodes exist on the ground surveyed, neither can it be shown (when no surface indications exist, which is generally the case) that the lode sought is situated its entire length on the tract surveyed. In fact, I think the greatest difficulty that exists in the working of the law will be found in the incompatibility of the words "*lode*" and "*tract*."

When miners and mill owners apply for patents to defined tracts of land for mill sites, they do not seek nor desire to obtain title to any mines that may exist on such land; they merely apply for title to the surface land without including any mines or minerals; nor do they intend to debar miners from working such mines should they exist. This simple segregation of mining and surface rights has always worked satisfactorily and smoothly in the mining regions; and it seems to have been the intention of the framers of the mineral land act to legalize such segregation in accordance with the local customs and usages.

The only suggestion I can make in regard to an amendment of the present law, is to completely eradicate the words *acre* and *tract*, when applied to vein or lode mines, and place a price per foot linear measurement on the lodes, granting in conjunction therewith, a perpetual lease or privilege to the surface ground for a certain distance on each side of the vein, for working purposes. And that when any title is granted to tracts of surface ground in the mineral regions, for milling or other purposes, this mining privilege or right be reserved in the grant. Either this must be done, or a complete and absolute revolution in the mining rules, regulations, and customs of the western States and Territories must be made, and absolute titles to land granted in accordance with the maxim: "*Cujus est solum ejus est usque ad cœlum.*" Any such innovation upon long established customs and usages of miners, could only be accomplished with the greatest difficulty; and before any such radical change should be attempted, a commission of practical and scientific men should be appointed to fully investigate all of the local laws, usages, and customs of miners on the public domain.

Yours respectfully,

GEORGE B. FOOTE,

Deputy U. S. Mineral Surveyor, Mineral District No. 2, Montana Territory.

W. S. KEYES, *Mining Engineer.*

It will thus be seen, I think, that, without further emendation or addition, the law is both tedious and vexatious.

Second. It is excessively costly. In this particular I have the additional testimony of Captain W. W. De Lacy, United States deputy mineral land surveyor. His experience is that no patent can possibly be obtained at an expense less than $400, and if the distance be considerable it might cost $500. If, however, the claim be contested no estimate can be made of the possible or probable cost. Mr. Foote has made contracts to survey and perfect title for the sum of $400. Moreover, expensive as the survey is to the miner, the compensation allowed to the surveyor is entirely inadequate. He receives only $10, currency, per diem; out of this he must pay at least one assistant $5 per day; must further pay his own transportation and hence there is little or nothing left for his professional services. Under such circumstances it is extremely difficult to engage the services of competent men.

Another hardship is that two surveys must be made. The first may be entrusted to any surveyor; the second must be performed by one of the regularly appointed deputies of the surveyor general after compliance with certain prescribed formalities. No further proof is, I think, necessary to establish the second objection, viz: that the execution of the law is excessively costly and bears heavily on the mining interest.

Third. Even the issuance of the patent does not materially diminish the probability of litigation.

Instructions to the local surveyors would seem to imply that the surface as patented must contain the lode; and it is especially ordered that where the lead makes a turn, stakes must be set. The theory of the law would, therefore, make the patent a general notice to all men that the ground so included embraces the well-defined boundaries of the claim. Prior to full exploration this is an utter impossibility, and to demonstrate this point fully and satisfactorily would often require the expenditure of thousands of dollars. A gallery may be driven on the vein, under favorable conditions, as low as $10 currency per foot, and if it were required to follow the vein a distance of 2,200 feet it would cost no less than $10 \times 2200 =$ $22,000; *i. e.*, it is practically impossible, under the law, to give a surface within which the vein shall surely be found.

Again, if there be a throw or fault in the vein, no foresight can fix its position; and, as a consequence, no surface location can, *à priori*, be made. To avoid this difficulty the local laws and customs permit the claim-holder to follow his lode wherever it may run, and as this provision has been recognized in the law of 1866 the surface patent is practically valueless, and after, as before, costly excavations may be required to prove whether two contested locations be or be not one and the same vein.

It might further be a question as to what right a patentee had in the surface patented after his lead should have been proven to have passed out of such surface, and, per contra, whether he had a right to other 50 feet where his lead does actually run.

So that, all things considered, a patentee is no better off than if he had obtained no patent, and may be called upon to prove his vein in the same manner as now.

Fourth. The law has brought and can bring little or no revenue to the general government. Mr. McLean, the receiver of the United States Land Office, informs me that, under the law, 43.93 acres have been entered, and as fractions are chargeable at the same rate as full acres, there has been received in all the sum of $285, a paltry total for the length of time the law has been in force.

The small number of applications up to the present time, and the general apathy, still more conclusively prove that few if any further applications will be made. Indeed I do not myself believe that the general government should seek to draw from the mineral lands any revenue over the necessary expenses other than the incidental advantages to be derived from an increased production of the precious metals. It is unnecessary, I trust, to bring any argument to substantiate this proposition so generally recognized in all the legislation of every enlightened government.

Enough has, I think, been adduced to prove that the present law is vicious and inexpedient, that its provisions bear hardly upon the mining interests, and that it ought to be either repealed or essentially amended.

Objection, it may be argued, is easy, and fault-finding possible, to the lowest order of intellect. To offer a remedy is, therefore, rightfully to be demanded of all objectors.

In examining the question, then, on the broad ground of statesmanship and an enlightened political economy, we must consider not only what is absolutely best, but also how nearly such a standard can be approached in a manner feasible and acceptable to the people.

I am well aware that the mining communities look upon all legislation touching the mines with great jealousy, and will resist, as far as they can, any encroachments upon what they consider their vested rights—vested, because the government has for so long a time made no attempt to assert its paramount title. Hence a *laisser faire* policy is the only one likely to meet with any general approbation.

In view, however, of the ever-increasing importance of the mineral interests of the United States—interests embracing an area of country more extensive than the average kingdoms of Europe, and destined to build up towns and cities and to support a population far more numerous than our present grand total of all the States; in view of the magnitude and far-reaching scope of the industry, it behooves our legislators to do nothing hastily, and to make no laws whatever without first carefully searching the whole subject and comparing the mining laws of every other country. On such as bigotedly refuse to listen to the experience of other mining countries, and believe that no good is possible unless it be a home production, no impression can be made. That such men make up no small proportion of a mining community will be evident even to the most superficial observer.

With all diffidence I venture to suggest the following as the only feasible and statesmanlike solution of the difficulty: Let Congress appoint a commission, consisting of two or three representatives of the people and one or more prominent mine-owners from each of the mining regions. Let the commissioners secure all possible testimony directly bearing on the mining interests. Let them be empowered to call for persons and papers; to examine experts, mine-owners, and people from the mining States and Territories. Let them, further, investigate the general laws governing mines in foreign countries; and let them obtain the fullest exposition of the local laws and customs governing mining claims throughout the national domain.

For such a commission we have, as a precedent, the action of the English Parliament, prior to taking action in regard to purchasing the rights of the Hudson's Bay Company's territory in British America. That such a commission would entail a heavy expense upon the government is no valid objection, for the reason that the interests and communities to be affected by its action are as worthy of consideration as any others. In no other way, in my judgment, can any general legislation be inaugurated which shall not work wide-spread injustice and cripple, if not demoralize, the entire industry.

In my humble opinion, fortified by years of familiarity with the mining laws of Germany, of Mexico, and of the various mining districts of the United States, the "local rules and customs" are too uncertain for security, and are entirely inadequate to prevent that litigation which is and has been the curse of our mining system. I totally dissent from that portion of the local law which gives the mine-owner the right to follow all the dips, spurs, angles, and variations of his lode, even though it may enter the land adjoining, unless it be amended by forbidding parallel locations within a reasonable distance of the first point of discovery. I object to the law as it now is, for the reason that it is the fruitful source of litigation and violence.

No law should be tolerated which does not give a reasonable freedom from assault; and the vicious system at present in vogue, of allowing subsequent locations in close proximity to the first, has fostered and will foster the most vexatious litigation. As long as nothing of value is found, no attempts are made to interfere with exploration. As soon, however, as a valuable deposit of ore is reached, a multitude of claimants appear, under the specious plea that the development is upon a dip, spur, angle, or variation of some previously discovered lode; and all the technicalities of the law are at once brought to bear to obtain possession.

It is this uncertainty of title, fear of litigation and black-mail, which do more to retard mining than all other causes combined.

Hence I can see no usefulness in any law which does not render unassailable, or at least reasonably so, a title once obtained from the highest authority. To this end I can conceive of no enactment unless one which gives a surface beneath which, even to the centre of the earth, every precious or useful metal shall be the property of the patentee, or which forbids parallel locations within a certain distance of the point of discovery. Further, I would not admit the practical possibility of two true fissure veins running parallel within say 300 feet of one another.

Most of the vexatious lawsuits, once so prolific in Nevada, arose from parallel locations. The one-lode theory has there become pretty generally accepted, and it is due to the resulting freedom from litigation as much as anything else that the Comstock lode now yields an increased percentage of profit on the gross amount produced.

Even if a general mining law be unadvisable, it is palpable that the public sentiment of the older States will insist upon its passage; and the miners should therefore endeavor so to shape legislation that the mining interest shall receive no detriment. The burden of proof that such a law should not be passed remains with the objectors, for the simple reason that all mining countries, both ancient and modern, have approved of such a course. The *Ordenanzas de Mineria* of old Spain, which to this day are in force in all the Spanish American States, have stood the test of nearly three centuries.

All the kingdoms of Europe have general mining codes. England may, however, properly be excepted, for the reason that all, or nearly all, the mines are on land owned by individuals.

The Mexican *Ordenanzas*—in many respects the best mining code in the world—give a lode and a certain surface which is determined according to the dip of the lode. Moreover, they require that the mine be worked at least eight months in the year, unless a prorogue for cause be first obtained from the mineral inspector of the district. Litigation is unfrequent, and the mere fact that a mine is claimed is in general sufficient to prevent any attempt at "jumping." Such laws would not be efficient amongst a population as active and grasping as ours. It is necessary therefore that the mine-owners have full and undisputed title.

How this might best be obtained should, I think, be determined by a government commission.

Further, in revising the general mining law I would respectfully suggest that Congress make provision whereby title can be obtained to lands bearing the following described natural products, viz: borax and soda lagoons; saltpetre, either in caverns or as a surface efflorescence; alum-bearing clays; sulphur beds; coal deposits; asphaltum deposits; petroleum; ozocerite, or natural wax, (called by the Germans *Erd-wachs;*) and salt-beds or springs.

The above products are all of commercial importance; and lands carrying such are of more value than simple agricultural localities. As the law now reads no title to such deposits can be obtained prior to survey. Hence there is no encouragement to the prospector to seek for them; and, even if discovered by accident, no profit is possible, because it is impossible to acquire title. It is further unjust to a heavily burdened people that such lands should be sold by government for no more than $1 25 per acre. I would suggest that lands bearing such deposits be sold in bodies of say 40 acres, and at a price not to exceed $2 50 per acre.

At the last session of the Montana legislature a general placer mining law was passed; but little notice was taken of the fact at the time. One of our newspapers has repeatedly attacked it during the last summer. Two gulches, within my own knowledge, have been taken up in pursuance of its provisions; and my own observation is that a large number of miners approve of the measure. Its best feature is that ground once taken cannot be cut down by subsequent arrivals. Much injustice has, in times past, been inflicted upon the discoverers by new-comers, who, without the energy to prospect for themselves, are desirous of turning to their own advantage the labors of others. The text of the law is as follows:

AN ACT relating to the discovery and possessory right to all placer mines.

Be it enacted by the legislative assembly of the Territory of Montana: SECTION 1. That any person or persons who may hereafter discover any gulch, bank, bar, or hill claim or claims, shall be entitled to one claim by discovery-right, and one claim each by pre-emption.

SEC. 2. That all gulch claims shall be two hundred feet up and down said gulch and extending two hundred feet upon each side from the centre of said gulch.

SEC. 3. That all bank, bar, or hill claims shall be two hundred feet square.

SEC. 4. That a gulch with its banks, bars, and hill-sides shall constitute but one district.

SEC. 5. That all claims owned or claimed to be owned by any person or persons shall be represented by actual working of said claim or claims at least two days in each week, except at any time when such claim cannot be practically worked, which shall be determined by two-thirds of the claim-holders of the district.

SEC. 6. That there shall be, in each and every district, elected one recorder for such district, whose duty it shall be to record such claims in a book of record, to be at the inspection of all persons, and to give to any person or persons a certificate of such pre-emption; and for such record said recorder shall be entitled to a fee of one dollar.

SEC. 7. And that before any record shall be made under the provisions of this act there shall be placed at the extremity of each claim or discovery-claim one stake, said stake to be at least two inches in diameter, containing the name of the person or persons pre-empting such claim, and that said person or persons shall have at least fifteen days from staking of said claim to record such claims.

SEC. 8. That nothing contained in this act be so construed as to prohibit any person or persons from holding one or more claims by purchase.

SEC. 9. That any person or persons holding one or more claims by pre-emption or purchase, and working upon one or digging drain or other ditch for said claim, shall be considered an actual representation.

SEC. 10. That nothing in this act shall be so construed [as] to prohibit any body of miners to the number of thirty, from making any and all local laws which they may wish upon a call of the miners of any district, or upon the posting of a notice of such in three public places giving at least three days' notice, specifying the time and place of holding of such meeting: *Provided*, That said laws shall not conflict with vested rights under authority of this act acquired prior to said meeting.

SEC. 11. This act to take effect from and after its passage and approval.

Approved December 11, 1867.

SECTION IV.

NOTES ON IDAHO.

CHAPTER XVII.

REPORT OF MR. WILLIAM ASHBURNER, OF SAN FRANCISCO, ON CERTAIN MINES IN IDAHO.

The principal mining region of Idaho, in which most of the capital has been concentrated, is in the southwestern corner of the Territory, in what is known as the Owyhee district, the chief town of which is Silver or Ruby City, as it is sometimes called. Here there are many noted mines, which have already produced largely, paid well, and have mainly caused the great reputation of this Territory. The more productive of these mines, and, in fact, the only ones now being worked, are situated near the summit of a high mountain, situated back of the town of Silver and known as War Eagle mountain. Here within a limited space, are grouped together the Poorman or the New York and Owyhee mine, the Ida Elmore, the Golden Chariot, and the Oro Fino. All of these veins are encased in granite. The present supply of bullion is derived entirely from the Poorman and Ida Elmore, though both the Golden Chariot and Oro Fino are now merely awaiting the erection of hoisting works, and will soon be in operation again.

The ores in all these veins are simple and easily worked by the ordinary process of amalgamation. The ores of the Poorman consist principally of the chloride and sulphuret of silver, associated with but little copper and antimony; and the bullion resulting from their treatment contains about $\frac{150}{1000}$ of gold and $\frac{843}{1000}$ of silver, though from the lower workings of the mine the percentage of gold is less. This company is now engaged in extracting all the ore above the 358 feet level, and filling in the excavation; and the value of the bullion per ounce, which is now about $4 19, will be less when this is accomplished and work is again resumed in the lower levels.

This company has 1,650 feet of ground and owns an excellent 20-stamp mill with 16 pans and 8 settlers. They appear to work their ore very closely, and the metallurgist, Mr. Adams, states that the loss does not exceed 10 or 12 per cent. of the assay value.

The distance from the mine to the mill is four and one-quarter miles, and from $3 to $3 50 is paid per ton for hauling the ore. The total expenses of this concern are now about $9,500 per month, of which one-third is for mining and the other two-thirds for milling. The mining costs from $10 to $12 per ton, and the milling from $12 50 to $15. The present monthly production is not far from $60,000. In April and May last the total production was $124,300, which was obtained by working 850 tons, which would show an average yield of $146 24 per ton, and this may be regarded as the present value of the ores. In 1866, however, the ore which was taken from near the surface was very much richer, having averaged $229 41.

The results obtained by this company from July 19 to November 1, 1866, were as follows:

Tons, at different mills.	Yield.	Average per ton.	Value of bullion per ounce.
369¼	$25,200 48	$68 25	$3 44
362¼	62,220 81	171 88	1 87
771¼	203,586 71	264 05	1 74
880	255,683 59	301 91	1 73
2,382¾	546,691 59	Mean 229 41	

About 14 tons were selected from the above ore before it was worked and sent to Newark, New Jersey, where it was treated, and the yield was at the rate of $4,000 per ton.

It is not to be anticipated that these brilliant results will be realized again. The vein is narrower than it was formerly, being now only a few inches in width where the best ore is found, though widening in some places to five feet in the poorer portions of the mine; still there are no reasons for supposing that this will not prove a productive property for years to come.

Not far from the Poorman, and in close proximity to each other, lie the Ida Elmore, Golden Chariot, and Oro Fino mines.

The vein of the Ida Elmore is about three feet wide and has been sunk upon to a depth of 150 feet. The mine is worked for gold, which contains a large proportion of silver. The present yield of the rock is at the rate of $140 per ton, and the total monthly production about the same as the Poorman, or $60,000. It is impossible to say how much this mine has produced in the past, but it is known that, during a space of eight months, $400,000 were extracted by a mill of 10 stamps, and large sums in addition were expended for litigation, so that it is probable that at least $600,000 have already been taken out. The mine is yielding at the present time as well as ever.

The Golden Chariot adjoins the Ida Elmore and is upon and part of the same vein. It has been sunk upon to a depth of 150 feet, and some $200,000 extracted, most of which, however, went towards the expenses of the litigation and armed contest with the Ida Elmore. This company is not producing bullion at present, but will be in operation again during the coming autumn or as soon as the hoisting works are completed.

The Oro Fino is a claim of 580 feet in length, running parallel on the surface of the ground with the Ida Elmore and Golden Chariot. The vein varies in width from 3 to 14 feet, and dips east at a steep angle. It has been sunk upon to a depth of 220 feet, and drifts have been run the whole length of the claim. Moore & Fogus, the former owners, worked some 12,000 tons from this mine, which realized $392,000, or at the rate of nearly $33 per ton; and it is generally considered that, owing to the dishonesty of the miners and the abstraction of a large amount of rich specimens, at least $60,000 more should have been obtained. After the failure of these persons, two years since, the property went into the hands of their creditors, who, in eight months, extracted a further sum of $122,000. The average yield of the rock is from $40 to $45 per ton, and the expenses of mining and milling from $25 to $27. The bullion which was derived from the rock taken from near the surface was worth $10 or $11 per ounce; is now only worth $3 60.

As we proceed towards the north and south from War Eagle mountain the veins contain much more base metal, and the ores will require careful roasting before amalgamation, entailing a great additional expense for their metallurgical treatment.

In the Flint district, at the town of Owyhee, nine miles south of Silver City, is the Rising Star mine, which may be regarded as a representative and typical mine.

There are 1,200 feet in this claim. The vein is encased in granite, like all the other veins of the district; it bears north 10° 20′ west, and dips east at an angle of about 79°. The ore is an antimonial silver, containing a little copper, and is associated with white barren quartz, from which the richer portions are selected by hand. This property was formerly owned by Moore & Fogus, and passed into the hands of the present proprietors, who are mostly San Francisco gentlemen, in December, 1867. These parties have attacked the vein by means of an adit 110 feet long, which strikes it at a depth of 50 feet from the surface. From its intersection with the vein at this point the lode has been drifted upon towards the north 39 feet, and towards the south for a distance of 110 feet. At the extremity of the northern drift the vein is seven feet wide, and well defined. Towards the south, although the vein was somewhat more broken, its appearance was rapidly improving as the works progressed in that direction.

At the point where the adit intersects the vein this latter is divided into two branches by a seam of rock containing a large proportion of mineral, principally iron pyrites, but entirely destitute of silver. The eastern branch of the vein at this point is 3½ feet wide, while the western is 5 feet in width.

In addition to the above described works the company have sunk a vertical shaft to the depth of 118 feet, cutting the vein where it is eight feet wide, 65 feet from the surface. From near the bottom of this shaft a drift has has been run southerly, upon the course of the vein, 65 feet, developing very excellent ore, containing ruby silver in considerable quantity.

In July last about 160 tons of selected ore had been taken from this mine, which assayed at the rate of $280 per ton. The metallurgical treatment of this ore will be costly, and will require skill and care for its successful accomplishment.

The Rising Star company is now erecting a 30-stamp mill, with furnaces for the treatment of their ore. This mill will probably be completed in December. The old mills, which were built a few years ago, are all of them miserable concerns, containing a variety of new-fangled machinery, and entirely unfitted for treating the rebellious ores of this district.

The shipments of gold and silver from Ruby city between August, 1865, and July, 1868, or for a period of 35 months, have amounted to $2,969,647 97, or at the rate of $84,847 per month. During a portion of this time there was no production, owing to the entire suspension of the mills and mines in the neighborhood. During the last ten months the shipments have averaged $100,000 monthly from this district, which is the only silver producing region of Idaho. About three-fourths of the total production of the Territory is gold, almost entirely derived from the shallow placers, which are decreasing in value yearly.

At present the rates of wages are very high in the principal mining districts of the Territory; $5 a day in gold being paid almost universally to the most ordinary miners. The Chinese find limited employment, at a great reduction, but the prejudice existing against them is as strong in Idaho as elsewhere, and the Indian difficulties have prevented any large immigration.

The prices of the principle articles necessary to a mining enterprise in the Owyhee or Flint districts are as follows: Wood, $7 per cord; lumber, $60 per thousand; salt, 9 cents per pound; sulphate of copper, 21 cents per pound; iron, 14 cents per pound; flour, $6 50 per 100 pounds. Freight from San Francisco to Umatilla, on the Columbia river, is two cents a pound, and from Umatilla to Owyhee five cents.

By November the Central Pacific railroad will be completed to Gravelly Ford, on the Humboldt, from whence the distance to these mining regions is only about 150 miles.

The agricultural resources of a large portion of Idaho are good, and, in fact, excellent as compared with the Great Basin; there are extensive and fertile valleys, well adapted to grazing purposes, and to the cultivation of cereals. Moreover it is not likely that the cost of fuel will be excessive for many years to come, as there are well wooded mountains within a few miles of the principal mining centres.

CHAPTER XVIII.

THE WAR EAGLE TUNNEL.

The following paper, addressed to eastern capitalists, is interesting because it shows that the writers are alive to the importance of a deep tunnel under War Eagle mountain. I sincerely hope the enterprise may succeed:

We, the undersigned residents of Owyhee county, Idaho Territory, believing that the development of the mineral resources of said county is an object of great importance not only to those whose local interest will be affected thereby, but to the whole northern region of the Pacific slope, and will favorably effect the entire commercial and monetary system of our whole country, and if judiciously managed will afford abundant returns for all the capital necessarily employed for that purpose; to the end that the attention of eastern capitalists may be directed to this point as a proper field for their enterprise, we join in the following statement of facts:

The existence of precious metals in the Owyhee regions in quantities sufficient to repay the labor of extracting them was first discovered during the summer of 1863, and the stream known as Jordan's creek and its tributaries have ever since been worked for gold deposits found therein. During that season several quartz lodes of remarkable richness were discovered and located, among the first of which were the Oro Fino, Morning Star, Whiskey, War Eagle, Silver Legion, and Silver Chord; and during the year following the Home Ticket, Baltic, Boorman, and numerous other valuable lodes were discovered.

The first quartz mill was built in the summer of 1864, and since that time ten other mills have been erected in the county; and although many of them were built by parties who had little or greatly inadequate capital to meet the expenses of their enterprise, still it is believed that all who have persevered have received a remunerative return for the meoney invested.

The quartz mining district of Owyhee is situated in a peculiarly favorabl position for the advantageous development of its mineral wealth, the principal obstacle being its great distance from any commercial centre; but this objection is being fast overcome by the rapid construction of the Central Pacific railroad, which will in a few months time place us within forty-eight hours travel from San Francisco. The mineral belt appears to traverse the country in nearly a north and south direction, and the lodes found within it to preserve, with occasional deviation, the same general course. The Owyhee group of mountains is composed of four or five high peaks surrounded by many smaller ones, of which the one known as War Eagle mountain is the highest, and unconnected with any mountain range. They are surrounded by the valley of Snake river on the northern and eastern sides, and the valleys of smaller streams on the southern and western sides. The War Eagle rises to an elevation of about 3,000 feet above the valley of Snake river, is of granite formation, and is traversed by hundreds of gold and silver bearing quartz veins, varying in width, where they cut the surface, from a few inches to eight and ten feet. Many of these veins are the richest ever known; and it is believed that all, or nearly all, of them contain the precious metals in sufficient quantities to pay for working them when the proper facilities have been provided. It is a characteristic feature of nearly all these quartz lodes that they increase in width and richness as they have been followed downward from the surface of the earth. The deepest level yet reached is about 400 feet from the surface, where the ore surpasses in richness and quantity anything found above it. The constantly and rapidly increasing expense of raising the ore and water to the surface as the work progresses has been found in Owyhee, as elsewhere, the principal impediment to the profitable working of the mines. For this purpose a constant outlay of money for hoisting works, pumps, steam-engines, fuel, and labor is now indispensible; the aggregate expense of which, if it could be saved, would form no inconsiderable part of the profits of the best mines among us.

To avoid this the obvious and only expedient is to penetrate through War Eagle mountain with a tunnel of sufficient size to afford drainage and an outlet for all the ore that may be found within it; and fortunately the formation of the mountain is peculiarly inviting to such an enterprise. It is situated between the two streams known as Jordan creek, on the southwestern side, and Sinker creek on the northern and eastern sides; and those streams are about two miles apart.

A tunnel commenced on Jordan creek at a point opposite the highest elevation of, and continued through the mountain in an easterly direction to a point of equal elevation, on Sinker creek, would cut through at nearly a right angle all the lodes now worked, and all that appear upon the surface, and probably as many more "blind lodes," which are usually the richest. It would intersect the best and most productive of them now known, at a depth of from 300 to 1,600 feet below the surface. It would probably penetrate beds of ore surpassing in richness anything ever known before. It would certainly pay a good interest on the capital invested by way of tolls from the owner of mines, who would use it to transport their ore to the surface. To such an enterprise the laws of this Territory hold out very great inducements, giving to the owners of the tunnel all the blind, unlocated, and forfeited lodes reached by such tunnel for 500 feet on each side of the tunnel. In view of the great benefits and advantages which must *certainly*, and the still greater benefits that will *probably* accrue to the parties who will carry into execution the object above mentioned, we have no hesitation in recommending the prosecution of the enterprise to all who desire to make a profitable investment of capital.

In regard to the amount of capital necessary to be employed, it is impossible to give a very accurate estimate, depending as it must upon the plan and means adopted, the unforseen obstructions or facilities it may meet with, and the degree of economy exercised in its execution; but there is every reason to believe that the enterprise will become not only self-sustaing, but profitable before it is half completed. The undersigned are well acquainted with Mr. George Collin Robbins, the gentleman who has undertaken to organize a company to construct such a tunnel. He has been identified with the progress of the Owyhee mining region since its earliest development. He was the superintendent of the New York Gold and Silver Mining Company, (now Owyhee Mining Company,) and to his judgment, energy, tact and perseverance, that company is largely indebted in securing the "Poorman" and the other valuable mines it owns. He has perhaps a more thorough and correct knowledge of our mines in general and in detail than any other man; is well acquainted with the people of this section, and possesses their friendship and confidence in an eminent degree. He has good judgment, untiring energy and perseverance, great self-reliance, is a good manager and economist, and is well qualified to conduct an enterprise of this character to a successful issue.

D. H. Fogus.
J. M. Wilson.
L. W. Greenwell.
Gilmore Hayes.
O. Davis.
Hiram Gove.
A. J. Sands.
A. W. Clifton.
Thy, Ewinn & Co.
James H. Slater.
A. Goodman & Bro.
G. W. Grayson.
R. E. Hallock.
James A. Rupert.
J. F. Dye & Co
D. Prescott.
R. H. Leonard.
W. B. Crane.
Dudley Hoyt.
Martin Jones,

W. J. Davis,
L. J. Lewis,
Cosmos Silver Mining Company.
Charles S. Neck,
Ex-Superintendent Poorman.
George L. Story.
Webb & Myrick.
R. Fregaskis.
Thomas Cole & Co.
Blake & Co.
Hill & Millard.
Butcher & Lenoir.
T. D. Beckett.
C. G. Stafford.
Hill Beachy.
J. L. Martin.
J. C. Geer,
Collector of Internal Revenue.
L. F. Cartee,
Surgeon General Idaho.

I have some knowledge of the quartz lodes of War Eagle mountain, am personally acquainted with G. Collins Robbins, and nearly all the gentlemen whose names appear above. I believe the enterprise feasible, and to promise rich remuneration for invested capital. I endorse Mr. Robbins as an enterprising gentleman, of vigorous and comprehensive mind and practical mining experience, and gentlemen whose names appear above as men of capital, character, and experience.

D. W. BALLARD.

CHAPTER XIX.

BULLION PRODUCT.

The annexed is a statement of the amount of bullion assayed in Owyhee county, Idaho Territory, for the term of one year, ending June 1, 1868.

June, 1867, by Thomas McDonald	$1,703 54
July, 1867 do	831 20
Sept., 1867 do	3,168 29
Oct., 1867 do	11,179 85
Nov., 1867 do	30,826 73
Dec., 1867 do	78,008 54
Jan., 1868 do	88,702 62
Feb., 1868 do	67,793 00
Mar., 1868 do	72,881 96
Apr., 1868 do	69,854 66
Total	424,950 39
June, 1867, by Webb & Myrick	$17,765 73
July, 1867 do	37,097 39
Aug., 1867 do	40,428 77
Sept., 1867 do	40,010 59
Oct., 1867 do	25,162 83
Nov., 1867 do	43,886 79
Dec., 1867 do	27,669 71
Jan., 1868 do	37,040 72
Feb., 1868 do	68,819 12
Mar., 1868 do	27,140 50
Apr., 1868 do	4,030 59
May, 1808 do	1,915 90
Total	371,868 64
June, 1867, by Blake & Company	$13,331 29
July, 1867 do	45,283 53
Aug., 18 7 do	70,433 12
Sept., 1867 do	59,421 51
Oct., 1867 do	45,795 16
Nov., 1867 do	29,416 57
Dec., 1867 do	30,071 98
Jan., 1868 do	72,836 05
Feb., 1868 do	84,097 61
Mar., 1868 do	89,985 36
Apr., 1868 do	33,328 42
May, 1868 do	219,558 70
Total	793,559 30
Recapitulation by Thomas McDonald	$424,950 39
Recapitulation by Webb & Myrick	371,868 67
Recapitulation by Blake & Company	793,559 30
	1,590,378 33

CHARLES HILTON,
Assistant Assessor Internal Revenue, Third Division, District of Idaho.

SILVER CITY, IDAHO TERITORY, *June* 27, 1868.

The total bullion product of the year in Idaho is estimated by Mr. A. D. Richardson, in the American Year Book for 1869, at $7,000,000. Mr. Richardson's extensive acquaintance with the west makes him competent authority.

I had intended and expected to present as full an account of the mining districts of Idaho as of Montana, but found it impossible to make a personal examination last season, and was without the means to employ assistants. I hope in the coming season to obtain more complete information than has hitherto been published concerning Idaho, New Mexico, Washington, and Oregon.

SECTION V.

NOTES ON OTHER MINING FIELDS.

CHAPTER XX.

ARIZONA.

From the address of Governor McCormick to the fifth legislative assembly of Arizona, delivered at Tucson, November 16, 1868, I take the following summary of the mining operations of the year in that Territory:

> The Wickenburg gold mines are worked without interruption, and steadily yield a large revenue. The Vulture lode, the Comstock of Arizona, now has a wide and merited fame. It is one of the richest, most extensive, and remarkable deposits of gold quartz upon the continent; and its returns, up to this time, are believed to be but an earnest of what may be expected from it in the future. Unfortunately the mills erected in the vicinity of Prescott were put either upon worthless lodes or upon those in which ores predominate which cannot be made to pay by ordinary treatment. The chlorination process has lately been introduced there, and it is expected to prove as successful as in California and Colorado.* If such is the case, the hopeful people who have clung to that part of the Territory, under most annoying delays and disappointments, will speedily reap the reward due to their patience and pertinacity. Upon the Colorado river little is doing in mining; the low price of copper has not warranted the continuous working of the lodes at William s Fork and other points, although a renewal of operations at an early day is promised. From the Eureka district there is a steady and profitable shipment of lead ore to San Francisco; and work upon several silver lodes in that district is vigorously prosecuted, as it is upon several gold lodes near La Paz and Hardyville. Below the Gila the Cababi mines continue to yield a good return of silver. and a fine mill is in process of erection at Apache Pass, where the gold lodes are attracting much attention and give excellent promise. Confidence in the mineral resources of the Territory is unshaken, and those most familiar with them believe that, once secure from Indian depredations, and made accessible by the iron rail, Arizona will take front rank among the gold and silver producing districts of the world.

The only mine from which I have accurate returns is the Vulture, alluded to in the above-quoted address. This mine, described in the last report of Mr. Browne, (Mineral Resources, &c., 1868, page 478,) has been productive throughout the year. The 20-stamp mill of the company has been running steadily, and is now running. A new 10-stamp mill has been erected by another company upon an adjoining claim. The Vulture mine is being thoroughly opened; the buildings, machinery, &c., are receiving constant improvements, and everything promises splendid results. According to Mr. Browne's report the mill crushed, from November 1, 1866, to September 1, 1867, 4,834 tons of quartz, yielding $145,633, or an average of about $30 per ton, mostly as free gold. The continuation of working results from September 1, 1867, to August 31, 1868, 12 months, is as follows: During this period the mill crushed 10,640 tons of ore, producing $254,110 gold, an average of about $24 gold per ton.

The agricultural capacities of Arizona are beginning to attract attention, and when the Indian difficulties are settled will doubtless invite a considerable immigration. Most of the valley and river bottoms through out the Territory are succeptible of high cultivation. Wheat, maize, barley, and vegetables grow to perfection; the small attempts made to raise the fruits of the temperate zone have been successful; and excel-

* I think the governor is mistaken as to Colorado; chlorination is not established in that Territory, so far as I know.

lent pasturage for cattle is unlimited. Large tracts of table-land are well supplied with timber and water; and a great portion of what is now called desert has a rich soil, and only requires irrigation to render it productive.

Artesian wells and windmills would work miracles in this and many other portions of the Pacific Territories, now barren and desolate.

CHAPTER XXI.

UTAH.

Little can be said of the mining operations of the year in this Territory. The mines in the neighborhood of Salt Lake have remained idle, and the few discoveries of placer and quartz gold in the Wasatch range have not received development. In the southern part of Utah, in Piute county, some mines have been found, and prospecting has been carried on with considerable vigor. Beaver city is the nearest town, 40 miles away; Salt Lake city is 144 miles, and Pahranagat about 200 miles. The accounts of prospectors represent the country as very favorable to mining, and abounding in gulch and placer diggings, (paying $5 to $6 per day to the man,) and veins of gold and silver ores.

During my stay in Salt Lake city I had an interview with Mr. Brigham Young, president of the church of Latter Day Saints, and with several leading members of that church. They expressed a cordial desire for the completion of the railroad, and a willingness to have all the natural resources of Utah developed and utilized; disclaimed any hostility to mining, but admitted that they discouraged their own people from engaging in it because they thought agriculture would be far more profitable. Mr. Young expressed the opinion that the ores of Utah had never yet been skilfully treated. "What we used to call lead," said he, "and dig and melt up into bullets, these fellows call silver now! But if anybody is fool enough to come and mine for it, he may do so, and welcome!"

The private members of the church are not quite so indifferent to the subject as the leaders, but, on the whole, the Mormons have been satisfied to sell grain and vegetables to the mining districts, and let mining alone. I met their wagon-trains hundreds of miles away from Salt Lake, in White Pine and other districts, where their wares were in great demand.

The vast immigration arriving this year at Salt Lake is due, I believe, to the closing up of the Mormon missions in Europe, and the gathering of converts, as rapidly as possible, to the headquarters of the church. It is said that the policy for the future will be that of internal improvements and gradual occupancy of the Territory where they have planted themselves, and that the foreign missionary work will be abandoned. If this be true, we may expect their interests as settlers to overcome any prejudices which they may have cherished towards any particular industry, and the mineral resources of Utah, whatever they may be, will receive, no doubt, the attention of her citizens. This is already the case with the coal-beds of Weber cañon, which furnish an excellent quality of fuel, and supply the city of Salt Lake. The Pacific railroad will, doubtless, make use of it also.

CHAPTER XXII.

MINERAL RESOURCES OF THE ISTHMUS OF PANAMA—BY I. BLANCHARD MINING ENGINEER.

Of the many countries which American enterprise has traversed and explored there is perhaps none so little known, in proportion to the endless crowds of travellers passing yearly over it, as the Isthmus of Panama. Many wonderful tales have been told about it at one time or another; but for some reason, probably the bad reputation of its climate, it has not yet attracted on any extended scale the attention of the mining or scientific world. It may not be untimely, therefore, to present a few considerations concerning the mineral treasures, topographical and climatic conditions of this geographically so important country.

There have been many things to prevent a thorough exploration of the isthmus, such as difficulty of access and communications, scarcity of food, exposure to fevers, &c. Yet there are many attractions there for the naturalist, especially the botanist. But the chief features of the country are geological and mineralogical, as might be naturally expected, from the peculiar agencies to which this strip of mountain between two seas has been subjected in the swift alternation of plutonic and neptunic forces. Nowhere do we find geological phenomena more diversified and diametrically opposed than here. Close upon neptunic deposits, and overlying them, there are vast surfaces of congealed lava, trachytic, and phonolitic masses—strong indications of once active volcanic powers; and the metalliferous character of the country itself shows the results of this wild and apparently lawless succession of geological processes. Unlike the well formed and regularly defined veins of California and some parts of Europe, where the same mineral deposit sometimes maintains for thousands of feet along its course the same appearance and size, the veins of the isthmus are frequently faulted, thrown out of their true dip, pinched, or otherwise made to vary in character. The difference between the gold region of the isthmus and that of California it is interesting to notice. In the latter State, nature has done much to facilitate the exploitation of her treasures by men. The California gold deposits are described as belonging to three epochs. The quartz veins form the earliest; next to them follow the deep diggings, which are the first neptunic secondary deposits; and finally, out of these secondary deposits are formed the recent placers. In the isthmus, on the other hand, mineral wealth is not so widely diffused, but more confined to its original localities. The third class of California deposits, the rich gold-bearing alluvial beds, does not exist there; the other two classes are represented.

Of these the veins, as being the oldest, first claim attention. A great many laws have been suspected or invented to systematize the occurrence of auriferous veins in general. Some consider them as particularly belonging to the tropics; but this view is not in accordance with facts which show us that gold and gold veins abound in all quarters of the earth. Those who hold the theory of the essentially tropical character of gold-bearing veins ascribe them to the greater relative velocity of the earth's revolution at the equator than at the poles. Others, again, connect them with the supposed great tides in the interior of the earth, simultaneous with the ebb and flow of the ocean tides, which are known to be extreme in the tropics. Others believe in a regular tenor and value of ore down to sea-level, and an increase or decrease in definite ratio below that line. All these theories being set aside, the facts are simply that the veins of the isthmus combine with their great irregularity, above mentioned, an extreme narrowness, but good average richness of ore. Those of the north are generally richer than those of the Pacific slope. Their thickness varies from 6 to 12 inches, their dip is generally 75° to 85° southeast, and their course mostly northeast and southwest. The quartz is dense, compact, without selvages, abundantly intermixed with epidote, micaceous iron, copper pyrites, copper glance, peacock ore, galena, zinc blende, arsenical pyrites, &c. Gray copper and antimonial ores I never noticed either on the Atlantic or the Pacific side. Silver does not occur in independent ores, though it is found alloyed with the gold, which is very minutely divided in the ore, and often, even in the surface ore, not to be discovered by the usual test of washing in a horn spoon. Fire assay alone determines it. Free gold occurs near the surface; in depth the ore becomes richer, because impregnated with sulphurets, but at the same time unfit for amalgamation. It is yet to be ascertained whether this non-efficiency of quicksilver upon the sulphuret-bearing quartz is caused by a chemical association. On this point careful and suitable scientific investigations must decide.

The value of the gold quartz of the isthmus, as given by cupellation assay, averages from $40 to $120 gold per ton; the value of sulphurets from $120 to $600. In so-called "red-ores," containing a great deal of the peroxide of iron from the original sulphurets, there is of course an exceptional richness. Not everywhere does the quartz appear, as above described, in dense flinty masses. This is the case in the richest and narrowest veins; but in some others, and particularly in the wider ones, and those which break in porphyritic rocks, the whole vein seems to be intersected with threads and seams, themselves imbedded in a matrix of kaolinitic feldspar, in which the very crystals of quartz, though still retaining their hexagonal form, have been disintegrated by the action of earths and alkalies. The veins of the Pacific side of the isthmus are generally distinguished by their smaller contents of sulphurets. Their thickness and dip are about the same as those of the Atlantic lodes. The value of the ore seems to range from $30 to $60 gold per ton. The gangue is mostly porphyry.

The leading rocks of the isthmus gold formation are varieties of greenstone—diorite (amphibole, feldspar, a little quartz) and diabase. Gabbro never occurs; nor are granite and gneiss found as leading rocks; but common porphyry and the variety known as feldstein are frequent. These rocks are variable in appearance. The diorite, for instance, shows more or less extended segregations of a feldspathic character, often considerably decomposed. The violence of the geological revolutions which have affected this region is clearly shown in the veins. They are frequently faulted, and sometimes large zones of the vein are moved out of their true plane, leaving to the miner little or no indication whether he is to seek the lost lode above or below, to the right or to the left, since the connecting cross course has often become under pressure so thin as to be almost imperceptible, and the nature of the country rock gives no clue in what direction it would be most likely to yield or fracture.

Among the auriferous deposits we shall consider first the *cerros.* This name is generally applied in Spanish America to the slopes of mountains or hills, (as for instance the historic Cerro Gordo,) and, in reference to mining particularly, to plateaux formed of eruptive masses overlying auriferous deposits. Whether the gold is accumulated in these deposits by the action of water, or brought there by mere primary geological agencies, is not settled; for the first supposition speaks the rounded form of the particles, but the fact that these plutonic masses always cover it seems to indicate some relation of causality. It is probable that the primary neptunic deposits being formed, were afterwards covered by emissions of fiery fluid masses. The contact of these masses has metamorphosed to some extent the underlying strata, changing clay and gravel to a kind of cement; and the working of a cerro, even with more perfect tools than the natives have at their disposal, would be difficult, and not very remunerative.

From these facts it is easy to predict that the third variety of deposits—the secondary neptunic or proper placers cannot be very extensively represented on the isthmus. The Atlantic slope is short and steep, giving little opportunity for such formations; and even if the topography were favorable, the cerros are so shielded by the overlying rocks from denudation that such a collection of gold in recent river beds and bottom lands as California presents is out of the question. This is confirmed also by experience. The beds of creeks and rivers on the isthmus do not yield much gold—not more than five or six centigrams in 15 kilograms, or three or four cents to the panful.

It is evident, from what has already been said, that there is little chance of profit in working any of the isthmus gold deposits, unless the quartz veins. We shall now consider, in closing these remarks, what are the conditions afforded for the successful working of such veins in this locality.

The isthmus enjoys a wide and well-deserved reputation for insalubrity. Nowhere is this evil fame more justified than in the districts west of Aspinwall, in Cocle and Veraguas, on the Atlantic slope, where the most numerous and valuable veins are. The atmospheric currents, one from the south, saturated with moisture, and the other cold from the Atlantic, meeting incessantly on the water-shed of the Cordilleras, produce by their reciprocal condensations the torrents of rain which desolate the unhappy slopes, (hence Ver-aguas, country of floods;) and the vegetation, overstimulated to rank luxuriance by this excessive moisture and the heat of the climate, aids in attracting and precipitating the rains. Most of the Atlantic districts have no well-defined dry season, and several of them none at all. Of course, out of these perpetual floods, together with the gases evolved by the continual decomposition of vegetable matter, much poisonous miasma must arise, adding its injurious effects to those of the hot sun and the floods. Thus it comes to pass that a portion of the isthmus is shunned by men. From Aspinwall to Bocas del Toro, and from the mountains to the Atlantic, an area of about 1,200 square miles, there are but a few miserable settlements, supported in wretchedness by the catching of fish and turtle.

The exceptional climate renders the preservation of food and the construction of roads alike almost impossible; timber is very scarce, and spongy trees make the worst possible fuel. From Aspinwall to Bocas del Toro there is not one real harbor. The coast is dangerous, as the Gulf Stream is very violent and hurricanes are frequent. Roads on land do not exist, except the official highways, and they exist only on paper! In a country so situated, estimates of the cost of a mining enterprise are necessarily uncertain. Freight is a heavy but a variable item; labor is scarce, and fluctuates with political changes; the veins themselves are narrow, and cannot be relied upon for a large production of ore, nor for a *uniform* production on any scale. Then all supplies of food, &c., must be brought either on men's backs over the mountains from the Pacific, or by sea, on the Atlantic side. None can be obtained in the country. Finally, delays must frequently be suffered from swollen rivers or a stormy sea. Such are the economical conditions of mining in this region. In spite of their uncertainty we shall attempt to give an approximate idea of the expenses and profits of the business.

EXTRACTION.

	Metres.
Average width of the vein we will set down at	0.25
Width of drift, for two men	0.80
Height of drift, for two men	1.40
Monthly progress of men, (25 shifts of 10h)	2
	Cubic metres.
Total monthly excavation of two men as above	2.20
Of which nearly one-third is good ore, or	0.70

At a specific gravity of 3 this gives a weight of 2.10 kilograms, or two tons of ore. If the vein be worked simultaneously at 15 points (more are scarcely possible) the monthly yield will be 30 tons as the work of 30 men, besides outside laborers and assistants, carpenters, &c. The number of the latter being estimated at 20 and their wages at about 80 cents per day, while the miners get $1 50, (food included,) we have a monthly expense of $1,830, increased by medical attendance, clothing, and interest on the capital employed in bringing laborers to and from the mines, to at least $2,000. The ore thus obtained may be either worked at the mine or conveyed to metallurgical works.

Transportation of ore to Europe or the United States.—A brief calculation would show that the expense of freight will be far too heavy, unless the ore has previously been stamped and concentrated. Of course it is not easy to give an exact estimate of the stamping cost, but it would be rather high as compared with California. Hauling is cheap, but fuel dear. In the concentration there is a loss, of course. Then the expense of maintaining a road to the sea, procuring a vessel for transportation, shipping, storage, commissions, and final sales to some metallurgical establishment, finish the list of transactions. All these expenses must be defrayed out of the net value of the ore, after mining cost is subtracted, or about $133 per ton. Transportation from the mines to the sea is also difficult on account of the rivers, which present everywhere a series of rapids, and are liable to sudden floods and droughts.

Working ores at the mines.—The prospects under this system would not be much more favorable. The bad fuel, scarcity of material for construction, and lack of roads by which to obtain supplies, make stamping costly; and the treatment of the stamped ore presents an embarrassing question. Smelting is out of the question. Amalgamation is useless.

On the southern side of the isthmus labor and fuel are much cheaper; the country is accessible and cultivated; but these advantages are annulled, as we have seen, by the smaller value of the ore, narrowness and irregularity of veins, and scarcity of timber, fuel, and water power. Under these circumstances, therefore, there is scarcely a chance of working the gold deposits of the isthmus at a profit, and hence they cannot be objects of attention to American adventurers, even leaving out of view the far greater and more enticing advantages of the Pacific States and Territories of the Union.

PART II.

RELATIONS OF GOVERNMENTS TO MINING.

"The sovereign should afford the mine and those who work it all facilities, endue them with gracious privileges, without which mining cannot be maintained, protect the works, and show himself most benignant to them, in order to encourage them. Hence should he help poor and struggling miners by gifts of money and timber, by remission or reduction of taxes, and by other means, and strive in every way to stimulate the mining business. For this purpose, it is very beneficial if a sovereign makes a well-founded mining law, and after its publication takes pains to have it observed by his officials and mining establishments. He should, moreover, see to it that places of trust are filled with devout, faithful, intelligent people, experts in mining, and that these are so paid as to have no cause to seek profit in evil ways. He should also keep a watchful eye on the mines, and not permit the use of unlawful force against any of them in operation, nor the practice of any swindling, nor that the silver they produce shall be paid for at the mint with money inferior in quantity or quality, since it brings the miners to despair if they receive only copper for the silver they have obtained with sweat and blood. Finally, the sovereign should, from his own treasury or otherwise, provide the means of driving deep tunnels, which are the heart of mining, and for keeping the same in good repair, that the mountains may be conveniently laid open for mining."—*Johann Fried. Zedler, Gross. Univ. Lex. Halle,* 1733, *Art. Bergherr.*

INTRODUCTION.

Mining and agriculture are the two great forms of productive industry. Strictly speaking, agriculture is the most important, since without it men could not exist; yet mining is almost as essential, since without it men could only exist as savages. All human activities, in material things, are based upon the products of these two, their manufacture and exchange. But there are great differences between mining and agriculture, which indicate that while these arts stand on a par as fundamental sources of the wealth of nations, they do not occupy the same position in all respects, and cannot be treated by governments exactly alike. Of these differences I shall point out a few of the most important ones.

1. The products of mining are in general far less perishable than those of agriculture, and, in proportion to their first cost, of greater, because more prolonged, use to mankind. Who can estimate the blessings diffused by a ton of iron, mined, smelted, wrought into forms of beauty and usefulness, serving for generations the needs of men, and repeatedly reforged, and reappearing, as by a material metempsychosis, to enter upon new periods of beneficence? More difficult still is it to measure the importance of gold and silver, the production of which, aside from their application in the arts, is so subtly connected with the profoundest problems of political economy. The sophistry that gold and silver money is a conventional matter altogether is trivial. So is all society conventional; and the things upon which mankind have agreed are the things which God has ordained. Gold and silver are world's money, or means of exchange; and this accepted medium must bear a certain relation to the volume of the world's business. Experience, speaking louder than the philosophers, has shown that, in spite of all contrivances of barter, credit, and paper money, the supply of the precious metals is of vital importance to all commercial nations.

2. Gold and silver are especially valuable as articles of export. If a country produces more grain than it can consume, it must seek a market elsewhere for its surplus, and this market may not be readily found. Besides, there is danger of loss or deterioration by transport and storage. The precious metals, on the other hand, command the markets of the world. They can be shipped or hoarded without deterioration, and they form the best basis of international exchange.

3. But these advantages of mining are counterbalanced by the fact that its sources are not perpetual. Men till the same soil for generations, and, if it is properly cared for, it is as able at the end as it was at the beginning to sustain the desired crops. But every mineral deposit is certain, sooner or later, to be exhausted. Sometimes this exhaustion is absolute. The valuable mineral is all extracted, and the end of the deposit is reached. This was the case a few years ago with the silver mines of Andreasberg, in the Hartz mountains.* Sometimes the exhaustion is merely an economical one. The deposits continue, but it no longer pays to work them. This is the disaster looked forward to within the next century by English economists with regard to the coal mines of Eng-

* The Hanoverian government exerted every effort in vain to discover new veins or continuations of the old ones. The social problem presented by the cessation of the mines, depriving a considerable population of its hereditary profession and only subsistence, was a sad and difficult one Transplantation of the miners into other districts, at higher wages, was but partially successful, owing to their home-sickness. The Andreasberg mines are now abandoned.

land. In either case the source of wealth is closed, and great national changes are often the result. We may say, then, that mining yields a permanent form of wealth from a transient source, while agriculture presents a perennial source of perishable wealth.

4. The mistakes of mining are always to a greater or less extent irretrievable. Wasteful and ignorant farmers may exhaust the soil; but nature, time, and skill will restore it. Even the wanton destruction of timber entails upon a nation only a temporary evil, since trees will grow again. But the economical exhaustion of a mine, or a whole mineral region, can be brought about by reckless mining beyond the possibility of restoration. There are mines in Mexico, for instance, known to have been rich, and to carry in depth the continuation of the same deposits; but the improvidence of former owners, and the ignorance of engineers, have left the mines without adequate timbering or supports, full of water, (which, owing to the irregular nature of the excavations, cannot be drained nor pumped out, except at enormous expense,) and practically inaccessible. The loss of precious metals by ignorance or indifference in the treatment of the ores is another generally irreparable loss. It is the fashion to say that science will discover means by which the "tailings" of our gold and silver mines may be profitably worked, and many inventors claim to have found the long-sought secret. But the secret is in a more thorough treatment of the ores in the first place. Experience shows that the majority of the tailings in the Pacific States contain gold and silver which cannot now be extracted at a profit. Five dollars per ton, for instance, is not often enough to pay for handling and reducing gold or silver tailings.* And in the best circumstances the loss in the tailings is never recovered, since that which was a net loss becomes, in subsequent working, only a gross yield.

5. Finally, the resources of mining are not so equally distributed among nations as those of agriculture, and, as a consequence, the relative power of nations depends largely upon their mines. The iron and coal mines of England are well known to be the secret of her commercial strength; and in our own country the State of California owes her wonderful progress and increasing power to the mines. Even the enormous agricultural capacity of that State (however much her farmers may sneer at the idea) would never have been known nor developed but for the gold mines.

In view of these peculiar relations of mining, it is evident that governments are in a certain sense trustees of the wealth stored in the mineral deposits of their realms—trustees for succeeding generations of their own citizens and for the world at large. It is not a matter of indifference to the citizens of this country whether our mining fields be ravaged and exhausted in one or even five centuries, when they might last a score. Nor is this danger far-fetched. The condition of the Comstock lode, after less than eight years of extensive operations, bears witness at once to the unprecedented energy and the almost incredible rapidity with which that rich ground has been exploited. The Comstock lode, producing in 1867 one-fifth, at least, of the total value of bullion yielded by the mines of the country, bids fair to be economically exhausted in two or three years more; and can apparently only be saved from that fate

*I do not here allude to cases in which, from the very outset, arrangements are made for catching, concentrating, and beneficiating the ores that escape from the first processes in gold or silver mills. That is part of the regular and wise system of working. It is where that has not been done, and the tailings, accumulating in the bed of some stream or in heaps by the mill, have afterwards been made the basis of independent operations, that success has so often been wanting. In other words, the mistakes of bad management are not to be altogether remedied by subsequent economy.

by the timely aid of the Sutro tunnel. Certainly one such example should be sufficient to show us the necessity of economy and forethought in mining operations. If economy had saved and forethought had expended, within the past five years, the money necessary to construct a deep tunnel, these mines would not now be threatened with ruin.

The true relation of governments to mining arises out of the position they occupy as representatives of nations and trustees for their future welfare. As I shall hereafter show, by historical review, the notion of a divine right of the crown to the minerals in the soil is almost everywhere extinct; and certainly in this country it could find no foothold nor analogy. The questions for us to decide are two: what is the duty of the government towards the miners; and what is its duty towards the nation and the future?

In accordance with the spirit of democracy, it must be granted that the fewest possible restrictions should be laid upon individual enterprise and industry, and that the function of government in this respect is to "secure liberty." It is this securing liberty that makes legislation necessary, and hence legislation is demanded of us by way of, not interference, but protection. The miner (and I mean to include the capitalist, investing money in mines) needs protection by law, and this protection should be uniform and just to all. Experience has shown that in the important matter of ownership, leaving matters to take their own course has been productive of much confusion and loss. Capital has been wronged by the regulations established by labor; and the laboring miners themselves, now asking in vain for the assistance of capital, would gladly welcome the establishment of a uniform system by which the title to mining property could be acquired from the government. The law of 1866 was an important step in the right direction, but its recognition of local customs was too sweeping, and in many districts its provisions cannot be complied with. Only one patent has been issued under the law, and that for a quicksilver mine. There is imperative need of amendment, and then of prompt execution, of the law. I believe it is acknowledged that taxation of the mines for purposes of revenue to the government would be a disastrous policy. Mining can carry no extraordinary burdens of that kind. It needs every assistance and encouragement that can properly be given to it.

But when the government has discharged its duty towards the miners, there still remains the obligation to do something for the protection of the nation. There are not wanting thoughtful men who doubt the wisdom of surrendering entirely to the patentees of mines the mineral title.* Whether this step was wise or not, (and I think it was wise,) the government cannot now recede from it without trouble, and it remains to inquire what methods are still open to us to prevent wasteful and unscientific mining, and to secure the maintenance of a steady product of bullion, so important to the country. Detailed legislation, regulating the operations of mining, the rights of partners, the proper measures of safety, and the forms of litigation, must be left to the different States. The true and only course which the federal government can take in the discharge of its duty as trustee of our vast mineral resources is to establish some agency for the spread of knowledge among the mining communities, and

* "Considerations of public policy may yet demonstrate the evil of granting an absolute title by the United States, absolved from all conditions, by placing the subject-matter of the title beyond the reach of State legislation, leaving us, as a nation, beyond the reach of some wholesome mining system or code, which has always signalized nations rich in the precious and the useful metals." (Legal Titles to Mining Claims and Water Rights in California under the Mining Law of Congress, by Gregory Yale: San Francisco, 1867.)

to facilitate, in every possible way, the development of those communities into regular forms of society. Communication established among the thousands, all engaged in mining, and all wrestling with the same natural and economical difficulties, opportunity once given for every man to obtain the information he seeks in regard to his business, and the evils of the present state of things will vanish before the enlightened self-interest of those who, owning the mines, will be most desirous to work them with true economy and forethought.

Following the succession thus indicated, I shall discuss, first, the question of a national mining law, and second, the various ways in which the government may, while it assists rather than interferes with mining, protect the interests of the country by bringing about a better system of mining, and putting an end to the reckless and ignorant practices now so common.

The relations assumed by governments toward the industry of mining have differed widely in different ages, and the character and prosperity of that industry has been directly affected, in different countries, by the course pursued in this respect on the part of the state. In the United States the problem is now presented on a large scale for the first time, but it is a mistake to suppose that no light can be thrown upon it by the experience of other nations. On the contrary, history is full of instructive lessons upon this subject, and I think these lessons, rightly construed, confirm the decision to which the genius of our institutions and the nature of our present circumstances would naturally lead us. In adopting a wise and permanent policy toward the mining interests of this country, we cannot fail to be assisted by the study of the past, and the experience of those nations in which mining has been most successfully carried on for centuries may serve us as a general rule. Impressed by these considerations, I have compiled the following digest of the history of mining law, which is sufficiently complete to illustrate the views which I shall venture to present.

SECTION VI.

MINING LAW.

CHAPTER XXIII.

MINING AND MINING LAW AMONG THE ANCIENTS.

The main subject of the present discussion being the history of mining jurisprudence, and the consideration of that subject being limited as far as possible to its bearings on the immediate problems of legislation in the United States, I shall not attempt to collect, in this chapter, all that is known of the practice of ancient nations in regard to the arts of mining and metallurgy. The theme is an exceedingly attractive one, and on another occasion may be not inappropriate. I am aware that a more extended treatment of it would add greatly to the popular interest of this report, but I consider it more important to preserve the continuity of the argument which I am endeavoring to construct, and to introduce no threads which cannot be gathered into the conclusions which I hope to establish. Our knowledge of the legislation of earlier times has to be, however, in great part inferred from circumstantial evidence, or from the records which remain of ancient practice. A frequent reference to the history of mining, as distinguished from that of mining law, is unavoidable; yet this chapter must not be considered as even a complete outline, much less a comprehensive summary of all that is known to antiquarians on this interesting subject.

In comparison with the literature concerning the dress, language, mythology, and poetry of the ancients, we have very few books about the much more important questions connected with their proficiency in the mechanical arts, and especially the arts of mining and metallurgy.

Authorities.—Two books published during the last century are the only ones which have come to my knowledge in which the indications and fragmentary facts contained in ancient literature or existing ruins, observed by travellers, have been collected and systematically arranged. One is the work of Caryophilus, *De Auri et Argenti Fodinis Veterum*, of which I have not yet been able to find a copy in this country, though it is accessible in several libraries abroad; the other is a dissertation in the German language, by Dr. J. F. Reitemeier, published in Göttingen, 1785, and entitled *Geschichte des Bergbaues und Hüttenwesens bei den alten Völkern.* This admirable essay received the prize of the Royal Society of Sciences at Göttingen. There is a copy in the city library of Boston, to the superintendent of which I am indebted for the courtesy with which he placed the book at my disposal. Ancient authorities are more numerous, but not so satisfactory, since they give us mostly mere allusions or accidental revelations. Among them we may mention the Bible, Herodotus, Strabo, Pliny, Diodorus, Agatharcides, Clement of Alexandria, Aristotle, (*de mirabilibus, de cura rei familiaris, etc.*,) Dioscorides, Livy, and Polybius, not to mention a multitude of classic writers from whose works intimations of importance can be gleaned, such as Xenophon, Cæsar, Plutarch, and even the legendary poems of Homer and Hesiod. To these sources of information must be added the works of various mediæval and modern travellers, and the researches of antiquarian scholars in special fields of inquiry, too numerous to be catalogued here.

The origin of mining.—The art of mining is linked with so many others, which are the fruit of civilization only, and must be practiced under so many natural difficulties, which only advanced science has been able to overcome, that we may naturally believe it to have had neither a very early nor a very rapid development. No doubt the first races were led to the discovery of one metal after another by accident rather than systematic study of nature. Probably the first metals used by men were those occurring in a native state—such as gold, silver, and copper. The discovery of bronze, or the secret of hardening copper by rude metallurgical processes and mixture with other metals, was a step in the progress of the human race so important that it marks an epoch of pre-historic time, known as the age of bronze. The peculiar properties of gold and silver—their beauty, malleability, and above all their resistance to oxidation, which rendered their preservation possible through long periods, were undoubtedly the ground of that high esteem in which they have always been held, and which is at the present day enhanced by their relative scarcity, and the difficulty of obtaining them. The knowledge of these metals seems to have been indigenous in all countries where they occur, whether among the tribes of Asia, of Siberia, or of North America. Gold and silver are the A and B of the alphabet of metallurgy; and, although the mastery of the whole alphabet and its combinations in the literature of civilization has been the laborious work of ages, and is not yet complete, these first letters of it were beneficently made easy for man to discover. The rudiments of mining are first found in those countries where the human race itself probably had its origin. The Bible informs us that even before the Noachian deluge, some of the peoples of Asia understood the use of iron—but this knowledge does not appear to have been propagated among other nations. The Siberians and the Peruvians most certainly did not possess it, and other nations have made the discovery at a comparatively late period; but this only corroborates what we have already said, that the knowledge of metals was not, in the beginning, transmitted from one nation to another, but was the child of circumstances and accidental discovery in different parts of the world. At any given epoch of the first historic eras, before commerce and literature had produced an interchange of commodities and ideas, it is to be supposed that some nations would be more advanced than others in these respects. If the use of iron was confined to the race destroyed by the flood, then it perished with them.

At a much later period we learn that the Chaldeans and Assyrians possessed gold, silver, and "brass." The Phœnicians had also an abundance of metals; and it is more certain, in their case, that they obtained their supply from some sort of systematic mining. Their country itself was not rich in mineral wealth. Possibly they worked the copper mines at Sarepta, but these were their only mines at home. But their extended commerce brought them into connection with other countries abounding in the treasure they sought; and they went to islands of the Mediterranean for gold and other metals, including iron, of which they understood the use, ascribing its discovery to two of their mythical heroes. They are known also to have mined in Spain, (probably for "Tyrian lead" and silver,) and they even touched the distant shores of Britain in their bold explorations, and gathered the tin ore of Cornwall and Devon.

But at least an equal antiquity, and a much greater elaboration and system, must be recognized in the mining of the Egyptians. Under the reign of Osiris, the Egyptian mines of copper, silver, and gold were in productive operation. Both on the Ethiopian and the Arabian border, and near Saba, (which may or may not be Sheba of the Bible,) they worked the ores of their country. The Sinaitic desert, through which the Israelites travelled, contains to this day the ruins of mining works, the origin of which is shrouded in mystery, but may well be ascribed to that wonderful people the Egyptians, the extent of whose achievements in many directions the world is just beginning to estimate aright. They did not learn the use of iron so early as that of some other metals. Abraham found gold and silver used for instruments, ornaments, and currency among them, but no mention is made of iron. In the time of Moses, however, as is evident from two passages in Deuteronomy, the Egyptians smelted iron.

Mines of the Persians and Egyptians.—In the early times, as in all subsequent periods, conquest was one of the foes of mining. The Egyptians were twice conquered by the Ethiopians, and had several Assyrian wars, which must not only have produced such a disturbed condition of affairs as prevented the prosecution of mining, but also have drawn into the military service the classes of laborers employed in that business. The final establishment of the Persian dominion removed the disturbances from without, but the tyranny of the provincial governors produced numerous revolts, which doubtless had a disastrous effect upon mining. The Persians, however, amassed much treasure from their conquests, and obtained from the Egyptian mines, in particular, the finest silver. The strength which wealth imparted to this dynasty was painfully felt by the Greeks, in the vast armies which invaded their territory and the bribes with which their leaders were corrupted. The first period in the history of mining closes with the overthrow of the Persian empire by Alexander, and the transfer of the treasure and resources of the Orient into European hands. Meagre as are our data for this period, we are nevertheless led to a reasonably certain conclusion with regard to the tenure and authority under which mining was carried on. We hear of kings, like Crœsus, enriching themselves from the product of the mines; but there is no indication that these sources of wealth were open to private citizens. The immense quantities of gold and silver employed by governments, and their use in constant wars, also confirm our conjecture that the mines of Asia and Africa were the property of the rulers, and that they were worked by slaves. This was certainly the case in Egypt, in the following period. It is probable, therefore, that the doctrine of ownership by the crown of the metals in the earth was originally established by tyranny, and that before its establishment mining, like agriculture, was carried on by the citizens. The story of Joseph, in the Bible, shows by what means the despot of Egypt was able to destroy the individual industry of agriculture, and to turn the whole kingdom into his own farm. Doubtless the process of "consolidation" in mining followed a similar course.

In the second period there was apparently still greater activity and extent of mining operations; at least our information on the subject is more satisfactory. Gold, silver, copper, and iron were obtained in Ethiopia, and iron at least in Libya. Possibly the recent discoveries of gold in Africa, which are now attracting considerable attention from the English, are but rediscoveries of the fields worked centuries before Christ. India and Caramania produced gold, and the latter country also silver, copper, and cinnabar. The people, however, are said by Strabo to have been very ignorant of the art of working metals. The Derbæ did not know how to melt their gold dust into lumps, and the Indians sold crude specimens of rich ore to foreigners. The Chalybeans, on the other hand, became famous as workers in iron, and derived their principal revenue from this source. In Asia Minor the gold mines formerly owned by Crœsus were worked down to the times of Xenophon, but Strabo says that in his day they were exhausted, and only traces of them remained. There were iron mines and skilled workmen in Palestine. Arabia Felix is celebrated by many ancient writers as possessing very rich gold and silver mines, but no traces of them now remain, nor have modern travellers observed auriferous sands in any of the streams of that country. Historical testimony on the subject is, however, quite positive and unanimous, and the matter may be considered as still in doubt. It is not impossible that the ancient writers, who were not always exact in such statements, mistook the treasure obtained by the Arabians through their Indian commerce for a product of their own soil.

We may well believe that this wide-spread development of mining, accompanied as it was with a diffusion of government, brought about some change in the mining law. The loosely-strung empire of Alexander fell to pieces after his death, and no doubt the mines became the property of governors, generals, nobles, and wealthy citizens. We have, however, in Egypt a type of the general systems which obtained, on a greater or smaller scale, throughout the petty despotisms which divided the world. Diodorus gives us a picture of Egyptian mining, partly taken from the earlier work of Agatharchides. According to this account the mines of Egypt were the property of its kings, who obtained immense sums from them.

Those were in one sense the palmy days of mining; for the king got his mining ground gratis, worked only the richest deposits, captured or reduced to slavery the necessary laborers, and levied contributions on his kingdom for the necessary food and other mining supplies. Rich mines, worked at no expense, naturally paid handsome dividends. Machines were not employed to any extent, since human power was cheaper. The Egyptian monuments which remain to us represent the most stupendous works of engineering, as accomplished by the labor of countless multitudes of men. The labor of the mines was performed by prisoners of war, convicts, and purchased slaves. As the Egyptians were not a warlike people, and seldom returned from battle victorious, it is not likely that their prisoners were numerous. Neither could the convicts have supplied their extensive mines. It is probable that the greater portion of their miners were purchased slaves. We are, in fact, informed that the workmen in the Egyptian mines spoke different languages. To prevent conspiracies and escapes, the different gangs were placed under overseers who were not their countrymen, and all hope of flight was finally extinguished by fetters, by constant confinement in contracted caverns, and by the nature of the region itself, which offered no opportunity for successful escape. The lot of these unhappy creatures in the mines and furnaces was indeed a hard one. They were forced to labor day and night, without rest or hope, and under the most dreadful hardships and cruelties. They were entirely naked, and neither age nor sex, sickness nor wounds, excused them from the severity of discipline. The stronger ones hewed the rock in the mines, the half-grown youths carried the ore to the surface, persons over thirty years (so soon was their vigor destroyed) were set at the easier task of crushing it in mortars, and the women and old men ground it fine in hand-mills. The historian adds, with laconic pathos, that they continued to labor until they dropped dead beneath their burdens.

Ancient mining in Siberia and Europe.—The far northern country of the

Massagetes is said by ancient writers to have produced gold and copper, but no silver nor iron. This is the nearest approach to a mention of mining operations in Siberia which history presents. But the observations of travellers, especially those recorded by Pallas, Lepechin, Gmelin, and Rytchkow,* afford convincing evidence of the existence of extensive workings for gold and copper in Siberia. The tradition of the Russians, that these early miners were Scythians, is groundless. Tartars they were not, since they were unacquainted with iron, which the former knew how to use. A nomadic race they are believed to have been, since no traces of buildings or masonry remain in those regions. All that we can conclude with probability is that, before the irruption of the Tartars into Siberia, very extensive but rude mining operations were carried on in that country by tribes not far removed in culture from the aborigines of North America. The tools which they employed were either of stone or copper—never, so far as has yet been discovered, of iron.

The smelting of copper appears to have been successfully carried on, even with somewhat refractory ores. Traces of mining accidents, of the voluntary abandonment of very hard rocks, of great economy of labor in "dead work," &c., taken together with the indications above mentioned of the social condition of this unknown people, prove to us that they carried on their mining operations by individual enterprise, as freemen, and probably without reference to particular ownership of the soil. Although this system (if system it may be called) stands in favorable contrast, on grounds of humanity, with the cruel and tyrannical practices connected with mining in the southern Orient, and especially in Egypt, yet it is evident that its result was superficial exhaustion, abandonment, and finally burial in oblivion of the mines. From the very dawn of history, therefore, these two representative voices of Egypt and Siberia warn us that neither mining by the crown, nor nomadic, superficial mining by the individual, is the true method of utilizing with economy the mineral resources of any country. The first is inconsistent with liberty, and the second with stable industry.

Concerning the earliest beginnings of mining in Europe little can be said. The civilization of the East, as is well known, communicated itself first to the Mediterranean nations. As mining is an essential condition to the progress of civilization, so we may reasonably conjecture the progress of mining at any given period from the culture of the people. We are justified, therefore, in assuming that mining in Europe takes its rise with the emergence from barbarism of the Mediterranean tribes. Strabo, Pliny, and Herodotus declare that Cadmus, a Phœnician, opened the first gold and copper mines in Thrace—a statement which is philosophically, if not historically, true. The Phœnicians certainly carried on mining in the islands of the Mediterranean, and even along the coast of distant Spain. But it is not probable that their operations contributed much to the spread of the art among the barbarians; since they not only, with characteristic selfishness, carried away all the products of their industry to enrich their own land, but kept to themselves whatever knowledge they acquired. They cannot be regarded as the teachers of European nations in this art—a credit which belongs rather to fugitives and exiles from other parts of Asia, who opened mines, or communicated the knowledge of mining, in the regions where they took refuge. The nature of the laws or customs regulating mining differed, therefore, according to the source of the art. The labors of the Phœnicians seem to have derived extent and comparative permanence from the conservative influence of commerce rather than tyranny.

* The treatise of Pallas is found in *Actis Soc. Imp.* 1780, published at St. Petersburg, 1784; and that of Rytchkow in Busching's Magazine, part 8.

Mining in Greece.—The mining works of ancient Greece are remarkable for extent, antiquity, and improved arrangement. The Greeks mined in the mother country and in their eastern and western colonies, and maintained through many centuries this industry, improving it by their own experience, and even studying it by scientific methods. The works of Theophrastus and Philo on metals are unfortunately lost, as is that of Strabo on machines and methods of parting metals. The remains of Greek mines are too nearly obliterated to afford us any evidence. We must learn what we can from incidental passages in Greek literature, and these refer almost entirely to the mines of Attica.

The history of Greek mining may be divided into three periods. The first includes the activity of the mines upon the islands, the oldest of which belonged to the Phœnicians; the second period comprises the operations of the Greeks themselves, on the main land; and the third is characterized by the working of new and productive mines in the provinces of the Macedonian Philip, which finally, with the rest of the Greek mines, fell into the hands of the Romans. The operations of the first period must be mainly inferred from passages in the Iliad and Odyssey; and these are of course to be interpreted with due allowance for their poetic form. When it is said that Helios, or the sun, invented gold, and the mythical, not to say allegorical, Erycthonius discovered silver, while copper was brought to light by the investigations of workmen directed by the gods, we may infer that the order in which these metals became known to the Greeks was similar to that which, as we have already seen, obtains in the history of other peoples. Iron is said by an old Greek inscription to have been discovered at a period corresponding to 1431 B. C. of our calendar. These gleams of early history help us to understand how gold and silver, more than any other metals, have come to be considered the property of sovereigns. They were the earliest known, and that at a time when sovereigns took all they could get and could get almost anything they wanted. Homer's descriptions of the magnificence of Greek princes, if we may interpret them as historical, indicate no small surplus of gold and silver in Greece. It is to be remembered, however, that in the absence of that diffusive action which commerce maintains, and of that great demand for the precious metals to which their use as currency gives rise, the accumulation in a few hands of a comparatively small amount of gold and silver might well justify the glowing descriptions of Homer; and also that if the rich men of the present day were to spend their wealth, not on the means of comfort and enjoyment, not on books and works of art, not on public improvements, but only on plate, armor, jewelry, and chariots, they could far outshine the splendor of Homeric heroes.

The islands in which the Greeks carried on mining operations included Crete, (iron,) Thasos, (gold,) Eubœa, (iron and copper,) Cyprus, (gold, silver, copper, and iron,) Delos, (copper,) Rhodes, (copper, iron, and lead,) Milo, (alum and sulphur,) Seriphos, (iron,) and Siphnos, (now Siphanto, very rich gold and silver mines.) From the mines of the latter island one-tenth of the product was sent every year to the shrine of Delphi. In later times, this payment having been discontinued, the mines were drowned by the rising of the neighboring sea; and this disaster was ascribed to the wrath of Apollo at being deprived of his divine royalty!

In addition to these mines upon the eastern islands, there were others, probably of later origin, upon the islands near Italy. Pithecusa, opposite Cuma, was rich in gold; Sicily and the Liparian Islands were also famous for various ores.

The petty rulers of the islands were the only or principal owners of the mines, and the labor was doubtless performed by slaves, according to rude and simple methods.

The second period of Greek mining, comprising the operations on the mainland, in Greece proper, is better known and more important. The Spartans, under the influence of their political system, established no important industry of this, or, indeed, of any kind; but the Athenians became distinguished in the administration of the rich silver mines of Attica, and the productive colonial gold mines in Thrace and Thasos. Thessaly had also rich gold ores, Bœotia produced iron, and Epirus possessed mines of silver. These resources seem to have been developed about the time of the Persian war. The public revenue from the Attic mines at the beginning of that war was equivalent to about $30,000, and afterwards increased to much larger sums, which, together with the product of the colonial mines, had a great deal to do with the splendor and power of Athens. The unhappy Peloponnesian war put an end to Athenian mining. In vain Xenophon exhorted his countrymen to reopen the sources of their former prosperity, and prophesied the continuance in depth of the rich ores they had once so successfully worked. The poverty of the citizens, and the exhaustion (in spite of Xenophon) of the mines, were obstacles which could not be overcome. Neither, as we shall see, was the system of the Athenians favorable to the persistent working of mines under discouragement. We may take leave to doubt, at the present day, whether the mineral deposits of Attica are really exhausted; but at that time a temporary barrenness was equivalent to a complete failure. For nothing can carry forward such an industry over its periodical seasons of depression except despotic power on the one hand, or on the other hand that faith in the future which is the result of accumulated experience, called science; and the Athenians had neither of these. Their failure in mining was due to the same cause as their failure in political science; there was no education of the people to take the place of centralized power.

The administration of the Athenian and that of the Egyptian mines differed as widely as did the political systems of the two countries. The State indeed appears to have held a certain title to the minerals, but its rights did not extend to absolute possession, or at least were not strictly insisted upon. Before the Persian war the income of the mines was annually distributed among the citizens, from which we may conclude that the republic either mined for itself or leased its mineral lands. After that war, however, this distribution of profits was discontinued on the advice of Themistocles, although the State still received payments from the mines. It is not improbable that certain mines, especially ancient ones, were rented on special terms, as the property of the republic; but the general practice was adopted of encouraging the development of mineral resources by a liberal and universal code. Taxes on gross production were remitted; citizens and friendly aliens alike were encouraged to mine under the light royalty of one twenty-fourth part of the net profits. The number of private adventurers thus encouraged to mining enterprise must have been very great. Even Demosthenes, in whose day Athenian mining was already on the wane, speaks of them as a class, like farmers and merchants.* The labor was performed by slaves, hired from their owners. The overseers were also slaves skilled in mining. It is probable that in many cases the lessees themselves were slaves, as it was not uncommon in Athens for masters to lease to their slaves factories, workshops, and farms. In such leases the slave-superintendent usually paid a daily net sum *per capita* for the number of

*Demosth. adv. Aristocratem.

laborers employed. The owner of slaves employed in mining received daily one obolus for each. The lessee was responsible for the food and clothing, and, in case of flight, for the value of the slaves—possibly also for their lives. No doubt this was a much milder slavery than that of the Egyptians, yet, as the slaves were strictly watched and always kept in fetters, it was oppressive enough. Slave-labor must always be lacking in individual skill and zeal, and make up for this deficiency by increased numbers. Accordingly we find that the slave-miners of Athens amounted to many thousands, or, as Athenœus says, to myriads. History speaks of a miners' revolt, in which the insurgent slaves took possession of Mount Sunium, and from that point made many destructive raids upon the Attic realm. The extent to which the republic attempted to prevent such perils by laws, regulating the number of laborers in each mine, or to control in general the operations of lessees, is unknown. That a certain governmental supervision was exercised appears from the fact that a director of mines was appointed, who indicated to adventurers, upon application, where they might prospect for ore, and that there were laws to determine the methods of mining, and the location, direction, and extent of veins, as well as the proper distance between different claims upon this same field.

Ancient mining in western Europe.—Before the time of the Roman dominion, mining was carried on in many parts of western Europe; and although there are little or no traces left of the laws which regulated the industry of the barbarians, I shall briefly mention the localities referred to, partly to complete this historical outline, and partly because the mining jurisprudence of the Romans, like their mining science, was affected by their conquest of those countries where the natives already practiced this art.

The Etruscans and the Sabines, in Italy, were acquainted with the use of copper, and the former made early discovery of iron on the neighboring island of Elba, the specular ores of which are famous to this day. The Salassians, in Lombardy, turned the Po into canals, and established extensive washings for gold. The region of the Taurisci and Norici was rich in gold, and at one time the natives invited laborers from the south to assist them in its production; but the result was an overstocked market, and a fall of one-third in the value of gold, which caused them to send home their laborers and reduce production to maintain the price. The tribes of Gaul obtained gold, silver, copper, and iron. But Spain exceeded in its treasures of gold, silver, copper, tin, lead, and iron all the countries of the ancient world. The barbarian natives obtained these metals from superficial deposits or outcrops, and the Phœnicians and Carthagenians, and afterwards the Romans, extracted them by deep mining. In fact, the art itself was planted in Spain by these foreign nations. The mere use of surface deposits can no more be called mining than the gathering of bunch-grass and pine nuts by our Nevada Indians can be called agriculture. Probably the Phœnicians themselves, in their distant operations in Spain and Britain, engaged rather in commerce than mining, buying the metals of the barbarians. But the Carthagenians, we know, established in Spain and Sardinia most extensive and productive mines, the revenue of which enabled them to support a numerous army of mercenaries and to wage long and costly wars with Rome. No doubt these mines were in some form the property of the state. The British islands were the scene of a considerable native industry, comprising gold, silver, iron, copper, lead, and tin. Strange to say, the Britons seem to have lacked or despised the art of manufacturing copper, though they practiced the more difficult metallurgy of iron. The Phœnicians traded with them secretly for tin, and the Romans, by following the Phœnician ships, finally discovered the mystery of the Cassiterides. But the Britons continued, until their conquest by Cæsar, to work their own mines of lead and tin. The tin of Cornwall was shipped first to the Isle of Wight, and thence to the coast of Gaul, where it was loaded upon horses and transported to Marseilles—a journey of 30 days.

Mining of the Romans.—Almost all the nations celebrated for their mines in ancient times became at last the prey of the Romans; and Roman mining was therefore a very wide-spread industry. Our knowledge concerning it is, however, mainly confined to Europe; since neither the hints of classical writers nor the observations of modern travellers have thrown much light on the Roman mines in Asia and Africa.

The poverty of the early Romans indicates that they did not work the mines of their native land. They struck the first silver coins shortly before the first Punic war, when, by rapid conquests in middle and lower Italy, they acquired mines which furnished them the means to greater undertakings. The wars against Carthage made Rome mighty among nations, and eminent in the history of mining. The first two Punic wars delivered into her power the important mines of Sardinia, Sicily, and Spain. Oriental conquests added mines in Asia Minor, Greece, and Macedonia, and at a subsequent period the remaining mines of the east, in Asia and in Egypt, were acquired by the victorious arms of Pompey and Augustus, and those of northern Spain and Gaul yielded to the legions of the Cæsars. The tin mines of Britain were their latest conquest of this sort; and after these had been gained Rome was mistress of all the important mines of the ancient world, and gathered into her coffers the wealth which had before been the strength and glory of many different nations.

As the mines had been acquired by conquest, they became the property, not of private citizens, but of the republic, and afterwards of the empire. In the period after the first Punic war the revenues of the republic were collected, indirectly, through contractors; and the censor, to whom belonged the duty of farming out the finances, awarded at certain times the leases of the mines. Ordinarily, as for instance in upper Italy and Spain, the lessees worked their ground with purchased slaves. In a few districts, however, the native inhabitants were held to a certain amount of labor in mines and furnaces, as a sort of vassalage, like that of the crown-serfs of Russia a few years ago, and this crown-right over their services was granted to the lessees of the mines. The treatment of the slaves was not less inhuman than that practiced by the Egyptians. Diodorus describes both in nearly the same language. The increased money value of a slave among the Romans might indeed have caused some amelioration of his condition for the sake of prolonging his life; but probably this was lost sight of in view of the immediate profit derived from the rapid and reckless robbery of the mines. It was the swift exhaustion and waste of their mineral resources, and not any considerations of humanity towards barbarians, which led the Romans to change their policy of leasing the mines. From an economical point of view no system of mining could have been more injurious to the state. The lessees cared nothing for the future; they took no pains to utilize all the treasure in the earth; they were absorbed in the endeavor to realize as much profit as possible during their limited term of possession, and to this end they employed vast armies of slaves and ruthlessly laid waste the mining lands. Polybius says that the lessees of a single district in Spain employed in their mines no less than 40,000 purchased slaves; and this evil grew to such a size in the gold mines of upper Italy that the censor, in order to delay the exhaustion of the mines and prevent the sudden depreciation of the precious metals, made it a condition of lease that the number of laborers in those mines should not exceed a certain limit. Of course under these circumstances the art of mining made no progress. The Romans took it as they found it among the conquered nations, and rather fell behind their teachers than surpassed them. The system of Egypt, bad as it was, was better than this. The selfishness of despotism was at least more provident than the indifference of democracy. The period from the first Punic war to the empire was characterized by an immense production of metals, and ended with the exhaustion of many of the mines. The despotic emperors took the matter in hand, and, though the past could not be repaired, they reformed the causes of the evil. They began to work the mines through regularly appointed officials, instead of leasing them to unscrupulous speculators; and as it was not feasible for the government to obtain so many slaves as had previously been employed by private parties, the system of feudal service from the inhabitants was gradually extended, and the oppression of the former irresponsible administrations was lightened. The crown-serfs, so to speak, were allowed to own and to sell land, but the purchaser acquired, together with the property, the obligations of service resting upon the former owner. Slaves were also employed, but these were rather condemned convicts than purchased barbarians or captives of war. The emperors seem to have preferred to apply this system to the maintenance of mines already open, and to have willingly allowed private adventurers to discover and explore new ones. Thus Trajan allowed the Dacian gold mines to be worked by a sort of stock company, (*collegium aurariorum,*) and Valentinian I. gave free permission to prospect for metals on payment of a portion of the subsequent products. Instances are mentioned of private persons owning large and profitable mines, probably by special grant. A new impulse was thus given to mining, and gold mines were opened during the first hundred years of the empire in Dalmatia, Illyria, and Dacia. The supervision of this vast industry required numerous officials, of whom the names only are left to us, such as *Comes metallorum*, the *Comes sacrarum largitionum*, the *Comes Orientis*, the *Vicarii*, and *Rationales*. Probably their duties were chiefly of a financial or magisterial nature, although the *Comes metallorum* may have been a sort of mining engineer.

But agencies came into play which overpowered the good influence of the new system. The errors of the past were, to a great extent, irremediable; the impoverished mines could not compete with others more favorably situated; and finally the irruptions of the barbarians on the borders disturbed or destroyed the industry of many districts. The serf-laborers were quite as likely to join the invaders as to defend the mines against them. From the silence of the later historians we may infer that mining in the Roman empire declined rapidly after the third century; and after the fifth century, when the barbarian hordes overwhelmed with successive invasions the tottering empire of the west, it ceased entirely. The Byzantines maintained it a little longer, but after the seventh century they gradually surrendered their mines to the conquering Arabs. The mines of Asia Minor, Thrace, and Greece were the last which the empire retained. The victorious barbarians no doubt gleaned what they could from the abandoned works of their predecessors. This was done, we know, by the Arabs in Spain, the Franks in Gaul, and the Goths under Theodoric in Italy. But we have no record of their manner of operation, nor can we say in what way the mining of mediæval times grew out of this ruin of ancient mining. There is a chasm of centuries not bridged by historic records.

It is scarcely necessary for me to trace the evident parallel between the histories of Roman and American mining. The Romans, by an injudicious system of administration, plundered and wasted the then available resources of the known world; and when they awoke to the extent of the mischief it was too late to repair it. The system of indiscriminate free mining, permitted in this country for the last few years, though outwardly unlike the farming out of the Roman mines, possesses the same fatal evil. The mines are worked by those who have but a temporary interest in them, and do not hesitate to rob them for present gain, thus wasting the resources of the State. In ancient times, only despotism could cure such evils; but I am one of those who believe that freedom has means not less effective for reform, and I hope to establish on a firm historical, as well as philosophical basis, the propositions which I shall, in the present report, recommend as the true foundation for a democratic jurisprudence of mines.

CHAPTER XXIV.

MINING LAW IN THE MIDDLE AGES.

Mining is the only industry which extends its activity into the earth's interior.* The accidental boundaries which topography or commerce may give to landed estates can scarcely be the limits for the extent of underground work, which is rather controlled by the dimensions of subterranean mineral deposits. Mining was therefore even in pre-historic times already separated, as an independent industry, from other exploitations of the soil. It is carried on neither within the same boundaries nor by the same persons as agriculture. Under the influence of this distinction peculiar legal relations were established in Germany at a very early day, probably at the commencement of systematic mining, which have for their subject the subterranean deposits, and are not dependent upon the ordinary laws of property. In the form of a local custom, obtaining with remarkable uniformity in all the original centres of German mining, the principle of mining freedom (*Bergbaufreiheit*) established itself, permitting all persons to search for useful minerals, and granting to the discoverer of such a deposit the rights of property within certain limits. This principle of free mining emigrated with the German miners to all places whither their enterprise extended itself, and the original local custom became the general law. In this existence of an estate in minerals, entirely independent of the estate in soil, lies the distinctive character of German mining law. It is eminently a special law, not subordinate to the civil law, but co-ordinate with it. Its rules and maxims are self-created, and based upon its own peculiar experience. Where the mining freedom of which we have spoken does not exist, where the owner of the soil possesses, as in England, the exclusive right to the minerals contained in it, there can be no such thing as a distinct mining law.

The Roman law gave, as a rule, the mineral right to the land owner; but the opposite principle seems to have sprung up spontaneously in

* For a more elaborate discussion, see, among other works, the admirable commentary on the new mining law of Prussia, by Councillor R. Klostermann, from whose introduction the first paragraphs of this section are substantially borrowed.

Germany. The earliest record of the German custom is the mining treaty between Bishop Albrecht, of Trent, and the miners immigrating from Germany to that locality, bearing date March 24, 1185. In 1208 the mining customs were officially announced in Trent. The formation of the Iglau code in Moravia took place about 1250, and this system was rapidly extended through Bohemia also. The Schemnitz law in Hungary was formed somewhat later, but coincides exactly with that of Iglau. The code of Freiberg, in Saxony, was probably brought from the Harz, since Freiberg was first settled by Goslar miners. Its publication took place in the 14th century. The mining regulations of Massa, in Tuscany, date from the middle of the 13th century. The uniformity of these laws is striking, and extends not only to the common principle of free mining, but to special provisions thereunder, and even to certain formulated maxims, which lead us irresistibly to the conclusion that they have in the transmitted habits and traditions of wandering miners their common origin.

This origin was much earlier than the records above cited. Mining is known to have been carried on by the Germans at Andreasberg, in the Harz, since anno Domini 968. The famous Rammelsberg mines at Goslar were discovered anno Domini 972 by the pawing of a steed, named Rammel, tied to a tree in the forest. Before the return of the master the horse had "developed" a promising vein of ore, and the mountain was baptized in his honor. The Freiberg district was discovered about 1165, by a teamster of Goslar, who picked up a rich specimen of ore while passing through the then unpopulated region. A stampede of miners from Goslar, and the opening of many valuable mines, was the result. Since 1547 the mines of Freiberg have been steadily producing. The mines of St. Annaberg were discovered by one Daniel, said to have been guided by a celestial flame. The mines of Schneeberg were found about 1470 by a spice pedlar from Zwickau, who, travelling by this mountain, noticed a discoloration of the soil, and set some laborers at work. In 1477 the great mass of native silver was found at Schneeberg, and honored by the elector Ernest, who used it on a memorable occasion as a dining table. It was a slab nearly a foot thick, and about 12 feet long by 6 broad. When it was melted, it yielded some 20 tons of silver. The mines of Marienberg date from 1521, and those of Mansfeld, which are still prosperous, from 1199. But older than any of these is Hungarian mining, which can be traced as far back as A. D. 750. Reitemaier* says the German mines were undeniably opened by miners from Gaul; but I think it fair to conjecture from the great antiquity of Hungarian mining, that there was also a direct current of progress from the east, perhaps not unconnected with those operations of the tribes of the Danube to which allusion was made in a previous chapter. Whatever mining the Gauls did was done under Roman law, and certainly there is no trace of that law in the history of German mining. In this case, as in many others, the tide of Latin ideas broke in vain upon the rocky Saxon character, and retreating left no marks but such as time speedily erased.

The earliest records of mining law in the middle ages do not create, they only recognize and establish, the customs which were even then already old. If the source of these customs is lost in obscurity, so also is their gradual development; for, as I have said, the earliest publication of them was made in Trent—in other words, in a foreign land, where they came into collision with existing systems. Of their peaceful growth at home we have no trace. They suddenly appear in history, adult and strong. But they soon met with opposition and modification at home,

* *Geschichte des Bergbaues, etc. bei den Alten Völkern*, p. 150.

where the emperor and the territorial sovereigns laid claim, at the end of the 12th century, to the mining royalty. The German mining law is a product of this antagonism—a compound of mining freedom with mining royalty—(*Bergfreiheit und Bergregal.*) The contest between the two principles occupied part of the 13th and 14th centuries. It was the south against the north, Egypt against Siberia.* The proud dynasty of Hohenstaufen began the war. Frederick I claimed the mines of Trent as imperial royalties, (*regalia,*) and forced the bishop to accept a lease of them. The mines themselves were not interfered with. All that the emperor desired was a recognition of his prerogative, as a support to future claims; and, in general, the struggle of the German emperors for the royalty of mines was prompted, not by their desire to appropriate and work them, but by their claim of the right to levy on mining imperial taxes, independently of the different legislatures and sovereigns of the empire. Meanwhile, the territorial rulers saw their advantage in promptly adopting and employing for their own interest the theory of royalty, and finally the owners of the soil made themselves heard, and obtained a certain recognition of their claims to some non-precious metals.

During this conflict of ideas contradictory principles were proclaimed by different parties; and the thirteenth century presents a scene of confusion and uncertainty as to the relations of emperor, prince, landlord, and miner. The famous "Golden Bull" of Emperor Charles IV, dated January 9, 1356, simplified the contest by excluding from it two of the conflicting parties. That emperor was more inclined to augment his hereditary power as a Bohemian prince than to increase the prerogatives of his imperial authority, which would pass to some other German sovereign after his death. He therefore, in the imperial law referred to, surrendered the claims of the emperor in favor of the electors; and in fact the result of this partial surrender was the actual exercise of mining royalty by all the other sovereigns, as well as the electors. But the Golden Bull excluded also the land owner, putting all metals, precious and base, together with salines, under one rule, namely, the right of the territorial sovereign. Two forces were now left face to face, the royalty of the princes, recognized by the emperor, and the principle of free mining, already repeatedly recognized to a greater or less extent by the princes themselves. The relations of these two forces were not determined by the Golden Bull, which left the princes free to enforce their claims as far as they had already done so, or might be able to do so in future. The issue of the conflict, thus left to time, was different in different states; but the essential victory remained with the miners. The princes recognized the right of free prospecting and the right of the discoverer to the mineral deposit discovered, reserving to themselves only the usual tribute (finally the tithe) and the rights of police and magisterial jurisdiction. But although mining freedom thus obtained practical recognition, the rights of the sovereigns were exercised in exceptional cases in opposition to this principle. Mines and whole mining districts were granted without reference to the discovery; and the occasional feature of special grants was accepted as a part of the jurisprudence of mines. The procedure necessary to obtain property in minerals also suffered a change. Mere occupation by the discoverer was no longer sufficient; he must "denounce" his claim, and obtain his lease from the prince or his delegate—generally a regularly constituted office or court of mines, (*Bergamt, Bergbehörde.*) The maxim was still preserved, "The first finder is

* See remarks on Egyptian and Siberian mining in a previous chapter.

the first claimant;" but the greater weight was laid upon the "denunciation," *(Muthung,)* and the right of the discoverer was forfeited if he failed within a brief period to make his discovery known in the appointed manner. The princes of different states made use of their power to extend and modify existing regulations, so that mining codes proper took the place of the mass of traditional usages which had accumulated through four centuries, and which might have been called by partial analogy the common law of mines.

German mining codes of the sixteenth and seventeenth centuries.—One of the first steps taken by sovereigns to confirm by exercise their rights of royalty, was the endowment of certain cities and districts with peculiar privileges, on account of their mines. Turin and Vallensasco, in Italy; Mont Saut, in Languedoc; Truro and Pensance, in Cornwall; the Isle of Wight; Grünberg, Engelberg, and Melchthal, in the canton of Unterwalden; several iron mines in the canton of Berne; the Black Erzberg, in the valley of Filisur; Mount Guntzen, in the Alps; Goldberg, Reichstein, Zuckmantel, Kupferberg, and Gieren, in Silesia; Cremnitz, Schemnitz, Altsol, Neusol, Königsberg, Puggany, Tyller, and Eperies, in Hungary; Smaland in Sweden; and Casan in Tartary, are examples of this practice outside of Germany. The mining cities of Germany were very numerous. The Harz alone contained seven, which exist to this day, St. Andreasberg, Altenau, Clausthal, Zellerfeld, Grund, Lautenthal, and Goslar. In Saxony, and particularly in the realm of the Counts of Meissen, was the "ancient and honorable free mining city" of Freiberg, originally called Freistein, the origin of which is interesting as an illustration of the history of the period. The Freiberg district, as I have said, was discovered about 1165 by a teamster of Goslar, (the locality of the famous Rammelsberg mines in the Brunswickian Harz,) and first settled by miners from that place. A few years after, Duke Otto of Brunswick quarrelled with his director of mines, *(Bergvogt,)* and the latter, to revenge himself, marched to Saxony with all his workmen. They were joyfully welcomed by the Margrave, who not only granted them extraordinary privileges, but also, for the protection of the Freiberg mines in those uncertain times, surrounded them in 1176 with walls, and built the castle of Freistein in the midst of them. Saxony has many other mining cities, among which may be named St. Annaberg, Schneeberg, St. Georgenstadt, Schwarzenberg, Marienberg, localities of silver mining, and Altenberg, Eibenstock, Scheibenberg, Wolkenstein, and Ehrenfriedersdorf, localities of iron and tin mining. Arensberg at Cologne, and the copper mines of Riegelsdorf in Hesse, are also mentioned among the privileged mining districts. Watering-places were generally favored also, as appears from the following passage in an old essay on mining royalty:

> Regarding mineral springs, hot and metallic baths, it is not considered that a great prince should make a royalty of them, or demand of the guests at such places any payment for their use. For Almighty God did not cause these springs to flow for the sake of princes and rich people only, but also, and perhaps chiefly, for the healing of the poor. And it is to be feared that they may dry up, if this gift is abused, as indeed was the case with the Griesbach, not far from Strasburg, the water of which disappeared when a certain duty was imposed upon the spring, but reappeared again as soon as the duty was removed. For this reason the Emperor, Charles IV, granted a privilege to the Wildbad of the Canton Berne. If a prince, however, should tax lightly the guests at any spa and use the money for their benefit, as, for instance, in the erection of a church in that place, he may not be reproved.

The principal German mining codes *(Bergordnungen)* of this period are those of Electoral Saxony, Cremnitz and Schemnitz in Hungary, Treves, Joachimsthal, Brunswick-Lüneberg, Zohnstein, &c. There is also a Danish mining code, and a good statement of general principles in the celebrated work of Agricola, *De Re Metallica.* It would be scarcely profitable at this time to review these different systems in detail, or to burden the general description which I propose to give with constant references to particular sources of information. It will be quite sufficient for my purpose to present a picture of those features in which the codes of this period substantially agree, in order to show the general nature of the system which obtained throughout middle Europe during the period of "paternal government"—a period when political economy was imperfectly understood, and the doctrine that sovereigns might interfere for their own private ends with individual industry was replaced by the notion that governments ought to regulate for the general good all the affairs of the people.

It was principally the flow of precious metals, and afterwards of other products, from America to Europe which brought the industrial problem of the sixteenth and seventeenth century, and placed commerce in antagonism with the hitherto accepted maxims of government. At the end of the fifteenth century the value of the precious metals in Europe reached its maximum. The price of grain in 1494 was only half as much as in 1399; but it rose in the sixteenth century (or in other words gold fell) to three times, and in the seventeenth century to five times, the price of 1494. The effect of this change on mining was disastrous; and the arbitrary measures taken, in accordance with the spirit of the age, to abate the evil, of course failed of their intended effect. It must be remembered that at this time the laws regulating the guilds prescribed precisely how many masters, journeymen and apprentices there should be in every trade and what wares they might or might not produce; workmen were not allowed to labor outside of their proper city; heavy penalties attended the importation of any article which, in the opinion of the guilds, could as well be manufactured at home. It is not surprising that mining also was administered by the state under a bureaucratic system, and on false notions of political economy. It is amusing to read that in one instance the increase of the number of coal mines was forbidden, *lest the expense of so many deep workings should raise the price of coal*, while at the same time the owners of mines nearest the market were prevented from working, because it would not be fair to those whose mines lay further away! In spite of such follies as these, however, there grew up an elaborate and in many respects very wise system of administration, much of which has remained to the present day, and is well worthy to be studied.

A scheme of the organization of this industry would be something like the following:

1. The sovereign.
2. The director of mines, (*Berghauptmann.*) This officer represents the government, and is the highest authority. There may be more than one in the same state if it is a large one. Prussia recently had five, besides one chief director of mines, who was at the same time a sort of minister without a vote (*Vortragender Rath*) in the royal cabinet.
3. Mining councillor (*Bergrath.*) These are inspecting and consulting officers, who make periodical tours through the districts under their charge, and report to their superior. The director of mines and the councillors include within their duties also the administration of smelting works; but all ranks below them are restricted to one or the other department.
4. Master of mines, master of furnaces, (*Bergmeister, Hüttenmeister.*) This officer has charge of a single district, and inspects weekly.
5. Sworn inspectors of mines or of furnaces, (*Berggeschworene, Pochgeschworene.*) These officers inspect daily.
6. Surveyor, (*Markscheider.*)

These six grades must be filled by men of thorough education as well as experience.

7. Captains and foremen, (*Bergsteiger*, *Pochsteiger*, *Untersteiger.*) These officers may or may not be graduates of schools. They are chosen for their faithfulness and practical ability, and are constantly under the supervision of the various inspecting engineers.

8. At the smelting works there are assayers, counter-assayers, &c., and there is a paymaster (*Schichtmeister*) elected by the miners and confirmed by the mining court, who takes charge of the accounts of several mines at once.

This is an outline of the system which still prevails substantially in Germany. I am far from recommending, as the sequel will show, the adoption of such a plan by the American government; but mining companies in different districts would be greatly benefited if by free and voluntary association they could effect a similar cheap and effective administration. Under such a system the whole mining enterprise of the Comstock lode could have been superintended by the ablest men in the country at one-quarter the expense which has been incurred under the multiplied administrations of different companies.*

As I have said, great weight is laid, in the ancient codes, upon the denunciation of claims. Prospecting seems to have been in most cases unhindered. Says a German writer:

> Here occurs the question whether a private person has any right to dig for and mine metals on the ground of another. A doubtful question *a priori*, since "no one may go a-hunting on another's land." It is also forbidden for any one to seek treasure on the land of another, and we might naturally suppose gold and silver mines to be meant; nevertheless the contrary is declared, in view of the general benefit from the production of metals, and the particular advantage of the royalty to the coffers of the state.

This freedom of prospecting was, however, limited so far that the foundations of buildings must not be injured, and all damages done to the surface or to agriculture must be paid. The discovery of a vein must be immediately made known to the master of mines by a denunciation, either written, or, if oral, then followed within three hours with a written one. The master of mines must see that the first discoverer is not cheated of his rights. He also exercises a general authority over all the prospecting work, and when the vein is actually exposed, he issues upon the denunciation aforesaid a permit to work it, (*Muthzettel*, *Muthschein.*) No such permit can be issued unless the denunciation contains an accurate description of the locality of the vein; until such a definite statement is possible the work proceeds merely as prospecting. After the permit is issued, the miner may go on until he has developed the true dip and course of the vein and opened it to a sufficient depth to require "bucket and rope" for his operations. At this point the master of mines orders a survey and location of the field, which is then regularly leased to the holder of the preliminary permit. Denunciations of placers (*seifen*) may also be received, but the master must then visit the place in company with the royal gamekeeper and forester, and satisfy himself that the proposed operations will not be hurtful to timber, game, irrigating or draining canals, etc., when he may give a license for placer mining. This license, however, he may revoke at any time; and if wilful damage is done in these respects by the placer miners, he may not only eject them, but hold them for the repair of the said damage, and even proceed, if required, to punish them for the wrong committed. The erection of stamp-mills, etc., he may authorize, if not to the injury of others already erected. All mining leases require the work to be continuously prosecuted. Parties engaged in making preparatory shafts and tunnels are

* See chapter on Comstock mines, in this report.

allowed no interval, unless they are miners at work part of the time elsewhere. This provision was evidently intended to encourage prospecting by the workmen in their leisure hours, and to give them a chance to become mine owners on their own account; but at the same time to prevent capitalists from commencing work and then dropping it, while continuing to claim such rights as would exclude other adventurers. After the mines are open and ore is struck, the making of the survey and application for a lease is peremptory, and when the lease is once issued, certain delays, caused by natural necessity, are to be permitted; foul air or much water are good excuses. The longest interval of idleness, however, must not exceed one quarter for silver and two quarters for base metals. Other claimants offering at any time during such an interval, "time is called" upon the idle lessees, and they must presently resume operations or lose the lease, which may then be issued, upon new denunciation, to others. Parties receiving permits to reopen abandoned mines are not obliged to specify the vein or veins they will work, but must report them and take leases upon them as soon as they are discovered.

Leases were generally subject to the royalty, usually 1-10 or 1-20 of gross product, paid to the sovereign. Where the mines were upon private lands, the landlord received a second tithe in lieu of damages. It was common also to give the Elector, "by ancient usage," one-eighth of the stock in every leased mine. This he retained, liable to the same assessments as any other stockholder, and if he at any time declined to pay his share of assessments his stock was forfeit. Poor mines, and in many cases iron mines, were freed from the oppressive tithe. Yet the coal mines were frequently held subject to the metallic royalty. The Counts of Schaumburg are said to have derived as much revenue from coal as other princes from silver. In Holland and Lower Saxony, even peat was laid under royalty, and it was not uncommon to include the manufacture of saltpetre in the same category.

Mining leases covered a certain area of the surface and a space below the surface, either bounded by vertical planes or by surfaces parallel with the dip of the vein. The first was called a square location, (*gevierdtfeld*,) and the second an inclined location, (*gestrecktfeld*.) The practice of following to any distance outside of the vein leased the "dips, spurs, and angles," was unknown; and I am unable to discover any traces of it in ancient or modern times except in the mining customs of this country. The possessor of an inclined location was generally allowed to work about 30 feet in the hanging wall, and the same distance below the foot wall, (*Vierung, viertehalb Lachter ins Hangende, und viertehalb Lachter ins Liegende.*) Within these limits all the ore discovered might be extracted by the lessee. In case of veins crossing the elder location took precedence, but could only maintain the right to a zone of 30 feet on each side of its vein. In cases of doubtful controversy the matter was compromised by a union of the two mines. The simple square location was applied to beds, masses, and even to true veins, when they possessed a dip of not more than 15° below the horizontal plane. The size of this kind of location varied with the locality and the circumstances, such as the number of associates or stockholders, etc. A frequent size seems to have been about 200 feet square, with the discovery shaft in the centre. The length of a claim upon a vein was also variable. In Freiberg, I believe, 400 feet were allowed; in Hungary 200, and elsewhere, ordinarily, 300. According to the general rule, the discovery shaft stood in the middle of the claim. A mine was generally divided into 128 shares, (*Kuxe*,) which might be held by one man, if he could afford it; but such was scarcely ever the case. An old authority says "a silver mine needs 32 stockholders, a copper mine 16, and a tin mine 8."

Wood for timbering was furnished, when possible, by the royal forester. Where there were no crown lands and forests, the companies must agree with the owners of timber, and it was the duty of the master to preserve harmony and fair play between the two interests. The mines were mostly worked under contracts with the laborers, and the price per foot or fathom (*Lachter*) was fixed by the master and sworn inspector, according to the varying hardness of rock and difficulty and danger of the work.

The driving of adits or deep tunnels was the privilege of the prince, but it was almost universally permitted, under certain regulations, to private parties. There were peculiar rights connected with such a work. One was the tunnel-right, (*Stollenhieb*,) entitling the lessee to all ores found within about eight feet (5 *Viertellachter*) above the water level of the tunnel, and for a distance of two feet on either side. The second right was the tunnel-royalty, (*Stollengerechtigkeit*,) entitling the tunneller to one-ninth of the profits of any mine drained and ventilated by his tunnel. To gain this, however, the tunnel must really and effectively drain and ventilate; and this royalty might be taken away by the opening of a deeper tunnel, which thus acquired the right to one-ninth the mining profits. In order to gain either of these privileges a tunnel must be a certain distance "under grass"—in Saxony 70 feet, and in some states as much as 120. A new tunnel, in order to be entitled to the royalty already enjoyed by an older one, must strike the mine at least 30 feet deeper. Special contracts were frequently made between tunnels and mines, by virtue of which, when the ninth was too onerous and the mine was in danger of failure, a lower royalty was accepted.

CHAPTER XXV.

THE SPANISH MINING LAW.

The essential features of this law were given in the first report of Hon. J. Ross Browne, (page 257,) and I shall only recapitulate a few important facts in regard to it, referring to that report and to the full compilation of Mr. Rockwell.* The royal ordinance of the King of Spain, published in 1783, has been ever since substantially in force in Mexico It asserts the right of sovereignty over all species of metal, and authorizes the concession of mineral rights only while the mine is worked. It is also very full in its directions as to the manner of mining, experience having shown that a mere temporary ownership of mines tends to a reckless and insecure method of exploitation. This law is remarkable for an attempt to reconcile the two systems of square and inclined locations by an elaborate graduation of the size and shape of the surface claim according to the dip of the vein. Chapter VIII of the ordinance, containing this plan, deserves to be quoted. It runs as follows:

SECTION 1. Experience having shown that the equality of the mine measures established on the surface cannot be maintained under ground, where, in fact, the mines are chiefly valuable, it being certain that the greater or less inclination of the vein upon the plane of the horizon must render the respective properties in the mine greater or smaller, so that the true and effective impartiality which it has been desired to show towards all subjects of equal

* A Compilation of Spanish and Mexican Law in Relation to Mines, &c., by J. A. Rockwell, New York, 1851.

merit has not been preserved ; but, on the contrary, it has often happened that when a miner, after much expense and labor, begins at last to reach an abundant and rich ore he is obliged to turn back, as having entered on the property of another, which latter may have denounced the neighboring mine, and thus stationed himself with more art than industry—this being one of the greatest and most frequent causes of litigation and dissension among the miners—and considering that the limits established in the mines of these kingdoms, and by which those of New Spain have been hitherto regulated, are very confined in proportion to the abundance, multitude, and richness of the metallic veins which it has pleased the Creator of his great bounty to bestow on these regions, I order and command that in the mines where new veins, or veins unconnected with each other, shall be discovered, the following measures shall in future be observed:

SEC. 2. On the course and direction of the vein, whether gold, silver, or other metal, I grant to every miner, without any distinction in favor of the discoverer, whose reward has been specified,* 200 yards, taken on a level, as hitherto understood.

SEC. 3. To make it what they call a square, that is, making a right angle with the preceding measure, supposing the descent or inclination of the vein to be sufficiently shown by the opening or shaft of 10 yards, the portion shall be measured by the following rule:

SEC. 4. Where the vein is perpendicular to the horizon, (a case which seldom occurs,) 100 level yards shall be measured on either side of the vein, or divided on both sides, as the miner may prefer.

SEC. 5. But when the vein is inclined, (which is the most usual case,) its greater or less degree of inclination shall be attended to in the following manner:

SEC. 6. If to one yard perpendicular the inclination be from three fingers to two palms,† the same hundred yards shall be allowed for the square, as in the case of a vertical vein.

SEC. 7. If to the said vertical yard there shall be a departure of—

Amount of departure.	Side of square allowed.	Dip, in degrees.	Depth.
Two palms, three fingers	112½ yards	60° 39′	200 yards.
Two palms, six fingers	125 yards	58°	do.
Two palms, nine fingers	137½ yards	55° 30′	do.
Three palms	150 yards	53° 08′	do.
Three palms, three fingers	162½ yards	50° 55′	do.
Three palms, six fingers	175 yards	48° 50′	do.
Three palms, nine fingers	187½ yards	46° 50′	do.
Four palms	200 yards	45°	do.

So that if to one vertical yard there correspond a departure of four palms, which are equal to a yard, the miner shall be allowed 200 yards on the square of the declivity of the vein, and so on with the rest.

SEC. 8. And supposing that in the prescribed manner any miner should reach the perpendicular depth of 200 yards, by which he may commonly have much exhausted the vein, and that those veins which have greater inclination‡ than yard for yard, that is to say of 45 degrees, are either barren or of little extent, it is my sovereign will that although the declivity may be greater§ than the above-mentioned measures, no one shall exceed the square of 200 level yards, so that the same shall always be the breadth of [claim upon] the said veins by the length of 200 yards, as declared above.

SEC. 9. However, if any mine-owner, suspecting a vein to be run in a contrary direction to his own, (which rarely happens,) should choose to have some part of his square [laid off] in a direction opposite to that of his principal vein, it may be granted to him provided there shall be no injury or prejudice to a third person thereby.

SEC. 10. [Provides that banks, beds, or other accidental depositories of gold or silver shall be apportioned into claims by the miners themselves, attention being paid to the richness of the place and to the number of applicants, and preference given only to the discoverer. The government reserves the right to revise such local mining regulations so as to prevent unfair dealing.]

* The reward of the discoverer (chap. iv, secs. 1 and 2) consists in three "portions" of the vein when in a mountain where no shaft nor mine has ever been opened before, and two portions when in a mountain known and worked in other parts. This grant is conditioned upon denunciation within 10 days, and, like all others, becomes void by four months' neglect to work the mines.

† This corresponds to a "dip," as now estimated by mining engineers, measured by the angle between the plane of the lode and that of the horizon, of 85° 25′ to 63° 20′. In the following section I have added to each specification the dip in degrees, and also the depth in yards at which, according to this law, the vein, *if it held a regular dip*, would pass out of the mining field into the neighboring one.

‡ The word "inclination" is the same as I have previously translated "departure," and a greater inclination than 45 degrees would be, in modern phrase, a smaller one, that is, the vein would dip less than 45 degrees below the horizon. See remarks on this section, below.

§ Less.

SEC. 11. The portions being regulated in the manner described above, the denouncer [that is, each claimant] shall have his share measured at the time of taking possession of the mine, and he shall erect around his boundaries stakes or landmarks, such as shall be secure and easy to be distinguished, and enter into an obligation to keep and observe them forever, without being able to change them; though he may allege that his vein varied in course or direction, (which is an unlikely circumstance;) but he must content himself with the lot which Providence decreed him, and enjoy it without disturbing his neighbors. If, however, he should have no neighbors, or if he can, without injury to his neighbors, make an improvement by altering the stakes and boundaries, it may be permitted him in such case, with previous intervention, cognizance, and authority of the deputy of the district, who shall cite and hear the parties, and determine whether the causes for such encroachment are legitimate.

It is frequently said that the Spanish mining law is the best that was ever devised. It certainly is one of the most elaborate, and perhaps was well fitted to the knowledge and social conditions of the era when it was formed. But a careful study of it is sufficient to show that it is now antiquated. The chapter above quoted, for instance, is evidently based on two assumptions: first, that mineral veins very seldom change their course and dip, and that an opening ten yards deep is enough to show what these characters are; and second, that no mine can be profitably worked to a greater depth than 200 yards. The first of these assumptions is not justified by experience; and the second has long since been rendered obsolete by the steam-engine, deep tunnels, and other appliances of modern engineering. The Spanish system in Mexico has certainly stimulated mining, after a fashion, in that country. The mines of Mexico have produced vast quantities of bullion, but a closer examination reveals that the art of mining itself has made little progress; the lack of permanent proprietorship has led to reckless robbery of mineral deposits; very valuable veins have been so unskilfully opened as to render deep workings impossible; the profits of mining have not been expended in permanent improvements, but either carried out of the country or wasted in civil wars; in short, Mexico has been plundered, not developed. She is just so much poorer to-day by the millions she has yielded to man; and those millions are proof only of the magnificent endowment which nature bestowed upon the land, not of any extraordinary wisdom in its administration. At the present time the policy of the Mexican government is to tax mining just as much as it will bear. A recent reduction in the exorbitant charges upon the extraction and exportation of bullion was the result merely of the determination of the mining companies to stop work if these tyrannical exactions were continued; and I do not yet see the signs of an intelligent and liberal policy towards this industry. The spirit of old Spain, which regarded the treasures of the earth as a prize to be avariciously grasped and selfishly appropriated, is still dominant in republican Mexico. An indolent people desires mining to prosper, not that agriculture, manufactures, and all other forms of industry may also prosper, but that all these industries may be unnecessary. The cure for this evil is to alienate the mines from the government, make them private property, put them on a level with other property, relieve them from unjust taxation, and make them a part of a wise general system of internal administration. Whether such a change could be effected as would extend the miner's title along the dip of the vein in depth, I do not pretend to decide. In Prussia the inclined location has been abolished; but that country has been so long the scene of mining operations that almost every group of mineral veins has been sufficiently explored to determine its peculiarities. Hence, by a proper selection of ground on the surface, a mining lessee may secure all the advantages of an inclined location. Whatever be the case in Mexico in this respect, it is, I think, quite necessary at present in our comparatively unexplored mining regions to give the miner what in early days the German law gave him, the right to follow his vein.

CHAPTER XXVI.

MODERN GERMAN CODES.

The elaborate administration of the mining interest on the part of the state which characterized Germany in the middle ages is giving way to a more democratic policy. Even so late as a century ago, the mining code of Frederick the Great made it the duty of the authorities to superintend all mining operations, to inaugurate them in one district, regulate them according to scientific principles in another, or sustain and protect them where they were already properly established. This policy is no longer necessary. The spread of knowledge and the activity of commerce renders it safe to leave to the mining communities in the main the management of their own affairs. The new Prussian mining law, which took effect October 1, 1866, replacing the former systems of Prussia, Nassau, Hanover, Electoral Hesse, Frankfort, and other provinces, presents the best example of the modern idea, in which education takes the place of government; and I shall content myself with a brief review of its characteristic features, omitting any detailed description of the present codes of Austria, Saxony, and other German states, as prolonging too far this already extended historical sketch.

1. According to the general mining law of Prussia,* the following minerals are excluded from the proprietary rights of the land-owner: Gold, silver, quicksilver, iron, (with the exception of bog-iron ores,) lead, copper, tin, zinc, cobalt, nickel, arsenic, manganese, antimony, sulphur, ores of alum and vitriol, pit coal, brown coal, graphite, rock salt and other salts occurring with it, and salt springs. These minerals are objects of mining, and the law prescribes the manner in which a title to them can be obtained. The state surrenders entirely its claim to mineral rights, and stands henceforward on the same footing as private citizens, retaining only the rights of police, justice, and finance, which it exercises over every other form of property and labor. Special grants, made under the ancient system, are not interfered with. To be properly objects of mining, the minerals enumerated must be (1) in their natural deposits, and (2) in such forms as can be utilized. Alluvial deposits, such as gold or tin placers, are included; the rare metals, precious stones, amber, petroleum, &c., are either left to the land-owner or made subject to special regulations. Marble and building stone generally are not held as objects of mining. In provinces once Saxon, as in the present kingdom of Saxony, coal belongs to the owner of the surface.

2. Prospecting, (*Schürfen*,) whether by open cuts, pits, shafts, tunnels, or bore-holes, is allowed to all under the following limitations: It must not be carried on upon any public square, street, or railway, nor in grave-yards, nor in places where the authorities forbid it on grounds of public interest, nor, without express consent of the owner, within 200 feet of any building on grounds belonging to the same, nor in gardens or yards. Whoever wishes to prospect on the grounds of another must seek his permission, but every land-owner must give such permission to all applicants, unless some one of the objections above enumerated can be shown to exist. Probable injury to wells, mineral springs, ponds, or neighboring mines is sufficient ground for prevention of prospecting by the mining authorities. The prospector is bound to pay the land-owner annually

* Perhaps the best manuals on this subject are those of Mining Councillor R. Klostermann, Berlin, and Director A. Huyssen, of Halle, both of which I have freely used, in various portions of this report.

in advance for the use of his land, if it be necessarily withdrawn by the prospecting operations from other uses, and to return it to him at the close of such occupancy, with damages for any depreciation of its value. All disputes arising are settled by the proper court. The prospector must make formal application in every case to the authorities, and receive the necessary license, before commencing to work. The proprietor of mines in operation cannot forbid prospecting in his field for metals to which he has not acquired the right; but, like the land-owner, he may demand security in advance for possible damages to his own property; and, when the new prospecting work actually threatens the safety or the undisturbed operation of the older mines, the authorities may refuse to allow it. But the owner of a mine has the preferred right to apply for permission to work for other metals than those already granted to him if the authorities decide that the former had better be mined in common with the latter. If the prospector, therefore, discovers them, the previous miner in the same field may claim them.

3. The discovery of a vein must be followed by its regular denunciation, *(Muthung.)* This act, like the recording of a claim in American mining districts, gives the miner at once the right of property in the mineral. The denunciation, which is also an application for license to mine, is made in writing, and in duplicate. Each copy is endorsed with the day and hour of presentation to the authorities, and one is then returned to the applicant. It must contain the name and residence of the applicant, the name of the metal or metals to be mined, a description of the locality in which the vein or deposit has been discovered, and the title by which the mine is to be known. A title already applied to a mine in the same district is not allowable. As I have said, the mere presentation of this document gives the applicant a *prima facie* ownership; but this right is still conditioned upon the investigation of the mining authorities, as to the validity of the alleged discovery. The metal or metals mentioned must be found, by official examination, to exist at the point described, in natural deposit, *i. e.*, not brought there by human agency, and in such quantity as to justify mining. The latter question is a delicate one, and the facts are generally construed with great liberality towards the applicant, who, after all, assumes the greatest risk of loss, if the deposit be poor. But certainly the rights of a land-owner are not to be disturbed to favor some crack-brained adventurer who has found a seam of coal an inch thick, or a lump of galena as large as a walnut. Under this rule the mining authorities of Bonn refused to grant a license on the strength of a few particles of pyrites in the rock. It should be also borne in mind that such a refusal is no real hardship to the prospecter, unless he desires to deceive some one, or the public, as to the value of his claim. He is still free to continue prospecting as before. Finally, the authorities have to be satisfied that the proposed concession of a mining field does not conflict with the rights of other parties, whether earlier discoverers or neighboring mine-owners. For this purpose due notice must be given, and a certain time allowed. Meanwhile, the applicant must have the field surveyed by the official surveyor, and file duplicate maps, upon which the discovery-point and boundaries are laid down. This must be done within six weeks after the denunciation, otherwise the latter fails of validity—a very important provision, calculated to secure the *bona-fide* prosecution of a claim by the discoverer. The actual discoverer of a vein has, for one week after his discovery, the prior claim, even though another make earlier denunciation; but after the lapse of that period the date of denunciation determines priority of right.

4. Mining rights are granted, as far as possible, in fields bounded on the surface by straight lines, and in depth by vertical planes. The ancient custom of granting "inclined locations" on the dip of the vein is thus entirely abolished, and modern authorities in Europe do not hesitate to condemn it as productive of great uncertainty and litigation.* The size of the field on the surface may be a little over five acres in most parts of Prussia, but is restricted to quarter of an acre in a few districts, for special reasons. These areas give only the maximum; of course smaller fields may be granted. The shape of the field may vary, straight lines being the boundaries, and the greatest length not exceeding for a five-acre field about 13,600 feet (2,000 Prussian *Lachter* or fathoms,) and for a quarter-acre field one-fourth that distance. The discovery-point must lie within the field, though not necessarily in the centre.

5. All preliminaries being complete, the deed (*Verleihungsurkunde*) is made out in the name of the king, and published in the official newspaper of the district. It contains the name, business, and residence of the grantee, the name of the mine, the area and boundaries of the field, with a description of its location as to parish, county, civil and mining districts, the names of the metals to be mined, the date, and the seal and signature of the authorities. Three months are allowed for the assertion of conflicting claims, after which the rights of such claimants, in ordinary cases, expire.

Under certain conditions, which I will not pause to enumerate, the consolidation of adjacent mines is permitted. The division of one field into several, or the exchange between neighboring mines of portions of their respective fields, is generally permitted by the authorities; but such divisions or exchanges are not permitted as would leave segregated mining fields too small to be worked independently.

6. The nature of the property thus conveyed to the grantee is defined as "the right to obtain and utilize the minerals excluded for reasons of political economy from the title of the land-owner, and to construct, above and under ground, all necessary buildings and apparatus for this purpose." This right may be sold, mortgaged, and levied upon, like real estate. It must be exercised, however, under certain regulations, justified by the general good, and fixed by the state, and, when these conditions are not complied with, the right itself may be impaired or forfeited. A few of the more important conditions will be enumerated. The mine-owner is bound to keep the mine in operation, if so required by the authorities. It is no longer, as formerly, forbidden to let a mine lie idle for more than a certain period. On the contrary, work may be suspended at any time, without the formal permission of the authorities; and they can only demand its resumption when clearly required by public interests. A great lack of the metals produced, and an impossibility of obtaining a supply from other quarters, would be a satisfactory reason for such a demand. The owner has six months' time in which to comply with this demand, and, even before it is issued, is entitled to a hearing of his protest. He may also appeal to the minister of commerce. If he intends to resume work, he gives the authorities four weeks' notice of the fact. But if he fails to comply with their demand, they may proceed to deprive him of his grant, unless the circumstances which made the demand proper have in the mean time changed. Every mine must be worked according to a plan, which must previously be submitted to the government officials, and approved by them. If no objection is made, the mine-owner may proceed with his plan. If the plan is

* This question will be found elsewhere discussed, with reference to the particular condition of this country.

objected to, which can only be on grounds of safety to the mine, the miners, and the public, the mine-owner must either convince the authorities that their objections are unfounded, or change his plan to obviate them. Violation of this rule is punished with fine, and if necessary the authorities may suspend operations at the mine. Every mine must have an exact map of the underground workings, and this must be periodically perfected as the work advances. The responsible managers and superintendents of mines must be reported to the authorities, and if necessary examined as to their capacity for their several positions. If a person not recognized as competent by the mining authorities is put in charge of a mine, they may demand his removal, or suspend the operations of the mine until a competent person is appointed. Superintendents are responsible for the proper working of the mines according to the plans agreed upon, and bound to afford the proper officials free opportunity for inspecting the works, and all desired information. The mine-owner is bound to furnish, at stated periods, the statistical information called for by the minister of commerce. He must also permit persons bearing the permission of the authorities to enter his works. (This provision is most beneficial to students at a German school of mines, since they enjoy by virtue of it an opportunity of studying practical operations, such as they could not otherwise obtain.)

7. The mining authorities are: 1. The district officials *(Revierbeamten;)* 2. The supreme mining bureaux *(Oberbergämter;)* and 3. The minister of commerce. The district officials are inspecting and reporting officers or surveyors. The names given in a previous chapter, on the codes of the middle ages, are mostly retained, but the superintendents and mining captains are no longer government officials. The mining bureaux are presided over by the directors, as formerly. They issue licenses and grants, and have the general administration of the law in their hands. The minister is appealed to in the last instance.

8. In addition to these authorities there are the courts, the jurisdiction of which is determined by statutes, and is not at present important for us to consider. It is, however, a fact not without significance that all the German states have various courts, in which cases arising in mining operations may be adjudicated, often without the tedious forms attendant upon ordinary suits. The English court of the stannaries is an institution of this kind, and the English "cost-book" system of stock companies is also the counterpart of the immemorial *Gewerkschaften* of Germany. Our American mining districts contain many examples of mining partnerships or associations of a similar character; and no doubt it will be found advisable in the course of time to establish courts and rules of procedure adapted especially to this state of things, as has been done in all older states. Further remarks on this subject will be found in the chapter on English mining law.

9. The Prussian law in respect to the taxation of mines has been greatly simplified, but there still remain many complicated provisions which must be regarded as legacies of the past. In view of the history of that kingdom under the most remarkable dynasty of modern times, its gradual increase from the original limits of the little duchy of Brandenburg, by constant territorial acquisitions, to its present imperial proportions, and the respect which it has always shown towards existing laws and privileges, and towards its own past contracts and grants, it is not wonderful that those differences in legislation which I have mentioned in a previous chapter as growing up in the petty states of Germany should still be to some extent perpetuated in the provinces of Prussia. The present Prussian mining law is based upon nearly a score of ancient codes, and

recognizes many local exceptions to its general provisions. There has been, however, a steady progress towards unity and simplicity, and the general outline of this progress is instructive.

According to former laws all mines were bound to pay the sovereign a royalty of one-tenth of their gross product free of mining cost to him. This was reduced by the law of 1851 to one-twentieth; by the law of 1861 a gradual decrease was established amounting to one-fifth of the royalty per annum, until the royalty should be reduced to two per cent.; by the law of 1862 iron mines were declared entirely free of royalty, and a new decree established with regard to all mines, by virtue of which, after January 1, 1865, the royalty was to be but one per cent.; and this is the present amount paid to the state under that head. The state pays its share of the expenses of reducing ores, but receives its percentage of gross product free of mining cost.

But in addition to the royalty there were formerly innumerable taxes and commissions paid by the mines to cover the expenses of the scientific and financial administration carried on by the state. In some provinces (as I have said in a previous chapter) the sovereign had a certain share of the stock of every company as a complimentary gift; and on this he could draw his dividends like any other stockholder, being bound at the same time to pay assessments or forfeit his interest. There were quarterly dues, additional quarterly dues, dues for measurements, for specimens, for inspections, for auditing accounts, for supervision and direction, for affidavits, for weighing, for assaying, for surveying, in short for every act which the government officials performed; and these were not fees but fixed sums assessed upon the mines, as a hotel-keeper on the Rhine charges for candles, attendance, etc., the same amount in every guest's account. All these petty payments are now abolished, and in place of them a regular "tax of supervision," amounting to one per cent. of the value of the product, is levied on mines in actual operation. When surveys or other special services are performed for any mine, the official is merely paid a proper fee for his labor. Many of the services formerly performed by the officials may now be done by others, the authorities reserving only the right to insist upon the employment of competent persons. The tax of supervision of one per cent. is therefore nothing more than a contribution from the mines to secure thorough scientific inspection and direction of their works at a far cheaper rate than would be possible under any other arrangement. What American mining company, even among the wealthiest, could obtain the service of a whole board of able engineers and metallurgists, such as the directors and inspectors of every German mining district, by the payment of one per cent. of its product? Certainly in that vast number of our mines which are just beginning to produce, and need more than any others wise counsel and direction, much time, labor, and money are wasted, because competent direction is too expensive. I think it possible to devise a plan, not inconsistent with American ideas of individual liberty, by which the opportunity to acquire such assistance may be afforded to our mining districts. But a national school must first give us the material in the shape of thoroughly trained engineers, before we can expect either legislation or association to secure so great a reform.

To recapitulate: the Prussian law, apart from local exceptions, imposes a royalty of one per cent., which is net revenue to the state, and a tax of one per cent., which the state expends for the good of the mines themselves. I shall urge, in the sequel, that the United States ought to repudiate the whole doctrine of a royalty, as such, and leave the mines free from taxation under that head. The late bullion tax was something of that nature, and has properly been abolished. But that the mines, thus relieved of all burdens, may rightfully be required to contribute something toward the expense of such necessary provisions for their own benefit as they cannot make, in their isolated condition, for themselves, is a far more reasonable proposition, and one which deserves serious consideration. A tax far lighter than the late bullion tax might be so expended as to save to the mines themselves millions of dollars every year. Prussia received from her mines, in 1865, a little over $9,000,000 gold (American.) This was partly the product of mines actually worked by the state, and partly the royalty from others. The expense incurred by Prussia on account of the mines in the same year was more than $7,000,000, leaving a net profit of only $2,000,000. The steady reduction of taxes under such circumstances shows that the government has adopted the wise and liberal policy of administering the mining law so as to secure, not an immediate revenue to itself, but an energetic and skilful development of the resources of the country, rightly deeming the increased production and use of the metals to be worth more to the nation than a few thousands of dollars, obtained by stifling this most beneficent industry.

CHAPTER XXVII.

THE CODE OF FRANCE.

It was the law of April 21, 1810, in the formation of which the Emperor Napoleon I took so large a part, which gave its present constitution to the mining industry of France. Under the ancient monarchy the mines were regarded as a dependency of the royal domain, and only the sovereign could grant permission for their exploitation. Such grants had only a temporary character, and were most frequently encumbered with onerous conditions of payments into the royal treasury, besides those which in the majority of cases must be made to the owner of the soil.

After the abolition of feudal rights, the mines and mineral deposits of France were placed, by the law of July 28, 1791, at the disposal of the nation, and the government was authorized to make "concession" of them; but this concession was at the same time forbidden to be otherwise than temporary; and, moreover, all that part of every mineral deposit lying within a hundred feet of the surface was expressly reserved to the landed proprietor, who also had a right of preference in obtaining the concession. These provisions nearly amounted to a prohibition of general mining. It was made easy to mine in the case of those persons only who, being farmers, would probably not care, or know how to mine; and it is no wonder that, under these restrictions, little progress was made in the exploitation of mineral deposits.

The law of 1810 declared, in accordance with the Code Napoleon, that the property in minerals goes with the property in land; but stipulated that the government might separate the two, granting the mineral right, even in perpetuity, to another than the land-owner, on the single condition of a tribute paid to the latter. It made this property in minerals negotiable and taxable like any other, putting it on a basis as secure as that of real estate. In this way protection was given to capitalists desiring to engage in mining, and an era of prosperity, previously im-

* This summary of the subject will be found, subtantially, in the splendid official publication, *Resumé des Travaux des Statistique de l'Administration des Mines*, 1853–9, page 6.

possible, was inaugurated for the mines of France. The law, in making this distinction between surface and subterranean proprietorship, has included in the class of mines only those substances which by reason of their nature or the manner of their occurrence must be exploited in a certain way, according to special rules. All other minerals are left to the proprietor of the soil, and may be worked under a simple permission, or without such permission, subject to the police regulations established by goverment. *Minières*, or surface works, such as beds of iron-ore, workable by open excavation, pyritous earths, suitable for the manufacture of copperas, or deposits of peat, require the permission referred to; quarries (*carrières*) of building-stone, marble, granite, sandstone, &c., require only observance of the police regulations. Mines, in the sense of the law, capable of becoming the objects of a concession, include therefore mineral fuels, bitumens, sulphur, alum, and metalliferous deposits of every kind except the beds of iron specially classed as *minières*. Among the substances thus legally subject to segregation from the surface proprietorship, only two, mineral fuel and iron, are worked to any large extent in France. Aside from these, there were in that country in 1860, only 247 mines of all kinds, classified as follows:

Graphite and bitumen	50
Pyritic and aluminiferous ores	15
Rock salt and salt springs	29
Antimony	24
Manganese	20
Lead and galena	18
Lead and silver	27
Copper	9
Copper, lead and silver	17
Lead, silver, zinc, copper, and other metals	30
Gold and silver, separate or together	3
Arsenic, separate or with gold and siver	2
Tin	2
Sulphur	1
Total	247

At the time when the law of 1810 was passed, however, the mines of France were not so limited in number. The productive provinces west of the Rhine, which now belong to Prussia, were then included in the empire of Napoleon; and the principles of mining law, as well as the rates of taxation established by the French law of 1810 and the imperial decree of 1811, remained in force under the Prussian supremacy until the end of 1864. The only change made by the Prussian law in regard to royalty is the subjection of salt mines and springs in those provinces to the state. This was necessary on account of the monopoly of salt maintained by the Prussian government. In all other respects the law of Napoleon virtually continued in west Prussia.

The provisions with regard to taxes were these: Each mine paid a certain fixed sum per annum, according to the size of its field, and also a tax of 5 per cent. on its *net* profits. To this amount one-tenth was added to cover incidentals. The net profit was ascertained by subtracting the current expenses only, not the cost of permanent improvements, from the total production. These taxes amounted in the aggregate to about 2 per cent. of the gross product; and since the 1st of January, 1865, they have been replaced by a single tax of that amount. It is, of course, much easier to collect a tax on gross receipts than on net profits, and the result is the same to the mines. Prussia has also declared the iron mines free of tax. Thanks to the law of Napoleon, which swept away with vigorous hand the accumulated privileges and forms of the past, or, perhaps, we might rather say, thanks to the revolution which burned off the forest-growths of centuries and left him an open field, and finally, thanks to the judicious legislation of Prussia, less hampered here than in her eastern provinces, the districts west of the Rhine enjoy one of the simplest and most efficient mining codes in the world.

CHAPTER XXVIII.

MINING LAWS OF SWITZERLAND.

On this subject Hon. John Hitz, consul general of Switzerland, writes as follows:

I can only state that, after a careful perusal of the federal laws of Switzerland, I find nothing having reference to mining privileges. As you are aware, the federal government of Switzerland owns no territory in the cantons, and therefore exercises no authority whatever over the mineral or other deposits contained in such cantons. If any laws exist relative to mining, they must be cantonal regulations; and among these which now lie before me I find no other mention than in the laws of Glarus, which provide (Art. 42) that "within the jurisdiction of the *Landesgemeinde* (cantonal government) fall * * * * * * * the regulation of salines and forests, water rights, game, and fisheries, wine tax, market, and *mines*, as well as the purchase and sale of real estate;" and in the laws of Valais a passage which declares, (Art. 29,) "The following are the powers of the Grand Council: * * *. 9. It shall issue concessions of mines, and may authorize their transfer to third parties." As you are aware, even cantonal authorities do not own territory as public domain. Every inch of ground belongs either to private individuals, corporations, or communes; and the two cantons above named are the only ones known to me who claim to be the dispensers of mining privileges, unless the extraction of salt is considered such a privilege, in which case the canton of Aargau owns, and either operates itself or leases, certain salt wells on its territory along the Rhine, near Rheinfelden.

It is evident from the foregoing statement of the consul general that the mining industry of Switzerland is not sufficiently important to call for general federal legislation, while the democratic policy of the Swiss has entirely destroyed the doctrine of any inherent right of royalty to minerals residing in the government.

CHAPTER XXIX.

MINING LAW OF ENGLAND.

The English law of mines is, like all English law, the growth of centuries, and complicated with many local regulations and "immemorial customs." The oft-quoted "case of mines," in the reign of Elizabeth, referred the crown right to the common law, and the decision of the judges was that all gold or silver ores belonged to the crown, whether in private or public lands; that any ores containing neither gold nor silver belonged to the proprietor of the soil; that the king* could grant

*Plowden, 31, 310, quoted in Hon. J. Ross Browne's first report, p. 217. The quaint reason given by Onslow in this case was that, "because gold and silver are the most excellent things which the soil contains, the law has appointed them, as in reason it ought, to the person most excellent, and that is the king." (See Pettus, Fodinae Regales.)

away mines of gold or silver, but not without express words in his patent, demonstrating his intention to sever the mines from his royal patrimony. It is indeed not improbable that the crown once laid claim to all mines, and it is well known that at a comparatively recent period it was attempted to comprise within the royal prerogative all those of copper and tin, on the ground that these ores necessarily contain some portion of gold or silver. In the reign of William and Mary, however, two enactments* secured to the subject the enjoyment of all mines in which tin, copper, iron, or lead are found, notwithstanding any quantity of the precious metals mixed. The property in minerals unsevered from the land, whether held together with the property in the land or separate from it, is what the law terms a corporeal hereditament, as distinguished from the mere right to work for them, which is an incorporeal hereditament. Apart from the claims of the crown, the property in minerals is *prima facie* in the owner of the fee of the land, whether in possession, remainder, or reversion, or subject to the tenancy of other persons. But the property in minerals is not necessarily accompanied by the right to work for them.† Indeed, when the owner of the fee is not in possession, nobody can work for the minerals; not the tenant, lest he commit waste;‡ not the lord of the manor, because he has not possession of the surface, nor even of the subsoil. The minerals are part of the demesnes of the manor, and naturally follow the fee in every case. Thus, for instance, minerals found on the sea-shore below ordinary high-water mark belong *prima facie* to the crown; between the ordinary and extreme high water mark, to the owner of the adjoining freehold; in land suddenly left by the retirement of the sea, to the crown; in land formed by the casting up of alluvial matter, to the lord of the manor.

The property in minerals, and the right to search for them, may be vested in other persons than the owner of the fee, by alienation, prescription, or custom.

In the case of alienation there is an important distinction between such a conveyance as confers an estate and such as merely confers a right to dig, without property in the minerals until severed from the soil. A conveyance of the former class is binding forever, whether the owner of the minerals continues to work for them or not. This distinction of law between an estate in minerals and the right to mine is an important one; it describes exactly the step which the United States government takes, in the mining law of 1866, by which a perpetual estate is granted to those who had up to that time only been able to enjoy a possessory title, conferring the right to mine. According to the English statute of frauds no legal interest in minerals beyond that of a tenancy at will can be created or transferred otherwise than by writing. The effect of this and other statutes is to make an instrument under seal necessary for the conveyance of any interest beyond that of a tenant at will, or for less than three years, as also for the conveyance of a right to dig for minerals. The most general forms of conveyance for particular interests are either leases of the minerals or licenses to dig them for a term of years. A license is not exclusive in its nature unless expressly so drawn; the grantor may work himself for the minerals, or he may license other persons to do so. Conflicting claims, arising out of different licenses, would probably be decided in equity in favor of the party in possession and actually working.

* 1 Wm. and M., c. 30; 5 Wm. and M., c. 6.

† For these and other points, see authorities quoted in Collier's Law of Mines, p. 14, *et. seq.*, from which much of this sketch of the English law is taken.

‡ Tenants may dig *open* mines to get for their own use gravel, clay, marl, or manure, and, it has been held, coal and iron also.

A lease is necessarily exclusive of the rights of all other persons, vesting in the grantee the absolute possession of the whole of the subject-matter demised.* The legal estate in mines can only be alienated in the modes thus noticed; but an equitable interest, with a title to a share of produce, may be acquired by agreement, either written or spoken, express or implied, attended with equitable rights against coadventurers, and with legal liabilities to the public. A mining company, for instance, can only acquire title to mines by deed (*i. e.*, by an instrument under seal) or by prescription or custom, of which I shall speak presently; but each stockholder may acquire effective title to his share of profits by virtue of a mere certificate, or, rather, by a mere agreement, of which the certificate is the convenient expression or result. This kind of title in mines is subject to the statutes affecting partnerships, joint-stock companies, and cost-book mines.†

Prescription and custom, as has already been said, may also vest in other persons than the owner of the fee the property in minerals, or the right to search for them. According to Coke,‡ prescription is a personal

* The granting clauses in the form of a lease of metals, with license to dig, use of water, &c., are as follows:

"In consideration of * * * he, the said A B, hath given, granted, and demised, and by these presents doth give, grant, and demise unto the said C D, his executors, administrators, and assigns, all copper, and all other ores, metals, or minerals (except coals) to be found in, under, and throughout the lands and premises comprised within the limits hereinafter described, * * * together with full and free liberty, license, and authority to dig, mine, work, and search for the same, and to raise and bring to grass all such copper and other metals and minerals, * * * to carry away and convert the same to his and their own use and uses, and at his and their wills and pleasure to pass and repass, carry and recarry, and to drive, dig, work, and make any new or other adit or adits, shaft or shafts, pits, drifts, leats, and watercourses in, over, upon, and through any part of the said premises, and to use those already made and driven, and to erect thereon any shed or sheds, mill or mills, engine or engines, or other buildings as he * * * shall from time to time think necessary and convenient for the more effectually working the premises aforesaid, and for working, washing, dressing, cleaning, manufacturing, bringing about, and making merchantable such copper and other ores, metals, and minerals, * * * to have and to hold, use, exercise, and enjoy all and singular the several powers, liberties, and authorities hereby granted and intended so to be, (excepting and reserving and subject as aforesaid,) * * * from the day of the date of these presents for and during the term and time of —— years now next ensuing, and fully to be complete and ended." * * * *

The grant is qualified by various agreements between the parties The use of water may be granted for the purpose of mining, subject to the rights and privileges of others already acquired, and to such other reservations as the circumstances require. The time, manner, and amount of payment of rent or royalty is specified, (*tribute* is not strictly rent,) and the lessee is bound to keep proper accounts, accessible to the landlord, to work the mine with all reasonable expedition "regularly and effectually, and in every respect according to the most approved modern practice of good miners," &c., &c., with greater or less fulness of detail, according to the whim of the parties. My experience in this country rather favors the drawing of a mining lease in general terms, leaving it for the courts to decide, in case of disagreement, what is fair dealing on either part. Detailed specifications in the lease do not obviate, but complicate, litigation.

† The cost-book system in use in Cornwall and Devonshire differs from ordinary partnerships on the one hand, and joint-stock companies on the other. The principal distinction from ordinary trading partnerships appears to be the absence of the *delectus personæ*, and consequently a limited liability; while the organization differs from that of a stock-company in the fact that its powers are not delegated to an aristocracy of directors, but directly exercised by the whole body of shareholders

The following is the form of transfer of share in a cost-book mine:

"I, —— ——, do hereby, for valuable consideration, sell, assign, and transfer unto —— —— —— parts or shares of and in a certain mine or adventure, called ——, situate in the parish of ——, county of ——, together with the like share or proportion of and in all engines, tools, tackle, materials, ores, halvans, moneys, and all other appurtenances thereto belonging, together with all dividends and profits in respect of the said part —— or share, and all interest, privileges, and advantages to be derived therefrom. As witness, &c.

"I —— - —— do hereby accept the said —— shares, subject to the same terms and conditions, rules and regulations, as the said —— —— held the same."

‡ 1 Inst., 113.

usage, as that such an one and his ancestors or those whose estate he hath, have used, time out of mind, to have such an advantage or privilege. Prescription can be claimed only by the owner for the time being of the freehold; an incorporeal hereditament only can be subject of it, and it must be of origin beyond the time of legal memory; in other words, the right to work for minerals, but not the legal estate in them, may be subject of prescription.

Custom is defined to be a usage of the inhabitants of a certain district, and requires three things for its validity: It must have its origin beyond legal memory, ("from time whereof the memory of man runneth not to the contrary;") it must have been uninterrupted; and it must be reasonable. The law is very careful to guard against the abuse of this right. In fact, the whole institution of "immemorial custom" is based only upon the principle that it is better to allow certain deviations from the rules of abstract justice laid down for general practice, than to commit the greater injustice of invading the established usages of society, and disappointing the well-grounded confidence of honest citizens therein. The notion that a custom may be arbitrarily created or modified at any given time, "by popular sovereignty," so as to affect the vested rights of property, is foreign to English and to every other law worthy of the name. It really overthrows the whole foundation on which this humane maxim has been built.

A good illustration of an immemorial custom, affecting the right to mining property, is the "tin bounding" which formerly prevailed in Cornwall and Devonshire, and is still valid, though comparatively disused in those districts. A charter granted in the third year of King John to the tinners of Cornwall and Devon speaks of it as already ancient.* In the recent case of Rogers *vs.* Brenton, 10 Q. B., 26, the custom was stated and confirmed by the jury as follows: "That any person may enter on the waste land of another in Cornwall, and mark out by four corner boundaries a certain area; a written description of the land so marked with metes and bounds, and the name of the person for whose use the proceeding is taken, is recorded in an immemorial local court, called the stannary court, and proclaimed at three successive courts held at stated intervals; if no objection is succesfully made by any other person the court awards a writ to the bailiff of the court to deliver possession of the said 'bounds or tin-work' to the bounder, who thereupon has the exclusive right to search for, dig, and take to his own use all tin and tin ore within the described limits, paying to the land-owner a certain customary proportion of the ore raised under the name of toll-tin. The right descends to executors, and may be preserved for an indefinite time, either by actually working and paying toll, or by annually renewing the four boundary marks on a certain day." Similar customs exist in Derbyshire, in the forest of Dean, and in various parts of Europe. In the case above alluded to, Rogers, the plaintiff, claimed his exclusive rights as a bounder, though he had neglected the mine for many years, pleading that the bounds had been regularly renewed. The defendant was agent of a company which had begun to work the mine and refused to recognize the alleged rights of the plaintiff. Much evidence was given concerning the nature and prevalence of the custom. The witnesses agreed that the bounds could be preserved by mere annual renewal without working, and some of them doubted whether even the ceremony of

* Quod possint (stammatores nostri) omni tempore libere et quiete absque alicujus hominis vexatione fodere stammum, et turbas ad stammum fundendum * * * *sicut solebant et consueverunt.* et emere buscam * * * et divertere aquas ad operationem eorum in stammariis *sicut de antiquá consuetudine* consueverunt.

renewal was necessary, except as evidence of the right. They also differed as to the consequence of neglecting to renew on the exact day. None could assign any limit to the surface of land that might be included within the four corners, but it was said to be generally very small. One of the most experienced witnesses remembered a pair of tin-bounds "a quarter of a mile each way," but this was the largest he knew of. Only one instance was recollected by any witness of bounds recently proclaimed; all the wastes of tin-mining districts were supposed to be already under ancient bounds. The jury found, as to the question of fact, a verdict for the plaintiff, on the ground that working was not essential to the custom. The court, however, decided that the custom as found to exist by the jury was unreasonable in as far as it conferred a right to bounds on a person not actually working. The opinion pronounced on this occasion by Lord Denman is a most thorough and elaborate explanation of the principles underlying the case, and deserves to be studied by American legislators. I quote a few passages:*

Upon the ownership of the land, giving a *prima facie* title to minerals, the custom of bounding has been engrafted. * * * In substance it is this: the mine is parcel of the soil; the ownership is in the owner of the soil, but it is a parcel which, to discover and bring to the surface, may ordinarily require capital, skill, enterprise, and combination; which, while in the bowels of the earth, is wholly useless to the owner as well as to the public; and the bringing of which into the market is eminently for the benefit of the public. If, therefore, the owner of the soil cannot, or will not, do this for himself, he shall not be allowed to lock it up from the public; and, therefore, in such case (unless, by enclosure, he may seem to have devoted the land to other important purposes inconsistent with mining operations, such as agriculture or building) any tinner, *i. e.*, any man employing himself in tin mining, may secure to himself the right to dig the mines under the lands, rendering a certain portion of the produce to the owner of the soil.

It is right to observe, in passing, how every step, even in this strong invasion of the rights of ownership, still is made with reference to them. In the first place, the land to be bounded must be wastrel; if it be several and enclosed, it must have been anciently bounded while wastrel, and so, in the language of the country, assured for wastrel; the liability must have first attached on it, therefore, before enclosure and devotion to other useful purposes. Then after the tinner or bounder has commenced by cutting the turves, and so making out the limits within which he will work, proceedings are to be taken in the stannary courts, of which the owner has notice, and sufficient time is allowed before the bounder's title becomes complete, during which the owner may still intervene and preserve his rights entire, so as he will exercise them for the benefit of the public. If he abstain from any interference it may well be considered that he has consented to the bounder's proceedings: and the customary render of the portion called toll-tin† may be a very sufficient consideration to him for what he gives up of his original exclusive rights. * * * This then brings us to the point which was more especially contested on the argument, whether this customary right can exist without continuing *bona fide* to search for tin, and to work the land for mining purposes with the enclosed limits; whether it is sufficient to renew the bounds annually by a new cutting of the turves as at the commencement. Assuming for the present the validity of the custom, if the *bona fide* working within the bounds be made a part of it, and assuming that it is a custom which is to be tried by the tests‡ established by the common law for ascertaining whether a custom be good or not, it appears to us that without this qualification it cannot be sustained. Customs. especially where they derogate from the general rights of property, must be construed strictly; and above all things, they must be reasonable. Bounding is a direct interference with the common law rights of property; it takes from the owner of the land, who is unable or unwilling at a particular moment to dig for tin under his waste land, the right to do so, it may be forever, and vests it in a stranger, making only the customary render in return;

* The opinion may be found in 10 Q. B., 26, and the passages here quoted, with others, in Collier's Law of Mines, p. 33 *et seq.*

† "The custom in Devonshire, as declared in the convocation rolls of the stannary parliaments for that county differs from that in Cornwall, principally in being a freehold interest descending to the heir, and being unaccompanied by the obligation to pay any toll or compensation to the land-owner. The Cornish custom having been mainly supported on the ground of its being accompanied by this obligation, there seems little reason to doubt that the custom in Devonshire, if found by a jury to exist in fact, would be deemed void in law."—*Collier's Law of Mines, American edition, page* 41.

‡ According to Cudden *vs.* Estwick, 6 Mod., 124, and other cases, the conditions are, that the party bound should have a benefit, the party claiming be at some charge, and that it should have a reasonable commencement.

it empowers the stranger not only to extract the mineral from beneath the surface, but to enter on the surface, and cumber it with machinery, buildings, and refuse stuff which the operations below occasion,* and all this without the least regard to the convenience or interests of the owner. The only things which make this reasonable are the render of the toll-tin to the owner, and the benefit to the public secured thereby in the extraction of the mineral from the bowels of the earth. Both these are not only lost, but the latter, it may be, positively prevented, if the bounder may decline to work and yet retain the right to exclude the owner. Instead of insuring that the minerals should be brought to the surface, the custom so construed may be made the means of keeping them locked up within it, and at the same time preventing any improvement in the surface. Many bounds may become the property of the same owners, who may think their interests best served by limiting the supply and diminishing competition, while the owner will decline to spend his capital in building or agricultural improvements, because at any moment the bounder may renew his operations, and entirely and without compensation defeat the purposes of his expenditure. If it be said that the public good is best served by that regulated supply which best serves the private interests of the bounder, that wherever it is for the interest of the public that the mine should be worked, the interest of the bounder will be to meet the demand by an adequate supply, and that when the mine is not worked, it is only because it is for the interest equally of both that it should not be; without admitting or denying the truth of these assertions, one answer is that, where such a state of things has existed so long and so decidedly as to amount to reasonable proof that the original purpose with which the bounds were enclosed has been abandoned, it is unreasonable to maintain the bounds themselves. It may have been that the owner did not enclose the land or work for the mineral himself, only on account of a temporary inability, or the temporary existence of the same causes which the bounder now alleges as the ground for his ceasing to work. Why then is he to lose his earlier and better right forever, and under the same circumstances the bounder to preserve his? Another answer is drawn from regarding the original purpose of the custom, which was not founded on the doctrine of demand and supply, but on the expediency simply of bringing the mineral to the surface for the use of men.

In view of these and other considerations, the court held that the provision in question was void, because unreasonable; and there are good grounds for supposing that the unqualified right claimed was also historically to be refuted, as but an abuse of the original limits of the custom.†

I have quoted this exposition of the law at some length, because the principles laid down are universally applicable and just. They apply with equal force to the case of mines in public lands; and the frequency with which they are violated by the whimsical "regulations" of mining districts in the United States is an evil which requires immediate attention, now that those regulations have been formally recognized as valid to some extent in law, and as furnishing a proper basis for the acquisition of the estate in minerals from the general government. I shall discuss this subject more fully in the sequel.

I do not find any traces in the law of England of a recognition of the right to follow mineral deposits in depth outside of the boundaries marked upon the surface.

Statutes regulating the manner of working mines, the employment of children, &c., have from time to time been made by Parliament. So, for instance, a bill passed February 14, 1860, provides for the regulation and inspection of mines, and prescribes general rules as to safety-lamps, ventilation, guide-rods, &c.‡

The laws and equities relating to mining in England are administered generally by the courts of chancery and common law. There is, however,

*According to the legal maxim, "Cuicunque ali quid conceditur, conceditur etiam id sine quo res ipsa non esse potuit." The right to obtain minerals comprises the right to do all that is necessary thereto.

†The ancient charters were granted to tinners "operantes in stannariis," and "dum operantur." In Carew's *Survey of Cornwall*, fol. 136, ed. 1769, it is said, "These bounds he is bound to renew once everie yeere, as also in most places to bestow some time in working the myne, otherwise he loseth his privilege." Collier, quoting from Smirke, gives these and other instances.

‡Levi's Annals of British Legislation, ix. 1861.

a court of very ancient origin,* called the stannaries court (formerly several courts, called stannary courts, held before the stewards of the four stannaries) and now presided over by the vice-warden of the stannaries. This court has both common law and equitable jurisdiction, concurrent with that of the superior courts and the county court, and affords an easy and expeditious method of settling such disputes as arise out of mining transactions. The proceedings in equity concern chiefly the mines operated on the cost-book system, and contrast favorably with the prolonged, complicated, and expensive operations of the courts of chancery. The late Prince Albert was lord-warden of the stannaries.

CHAPTER XXX.

MINING REGULATIONS IN AUSTRALIA.†

Gold was discovered in Australia in 1851, by Hargraves, a miner from California. A considerable immigration of miners ensued, and laws were enacted in 1852 and 1853 by the legislative council of New South Wales, "for regulating the management of the gold fields, raising a revenue therefrom, and for the preservation of order thereon." The first of these laws authorized the governor general to grant to British subjects only leases and licenses for mining purposes, for terms not exceeding 20 years, and by the eighth section, aliens were to pay twice the license-fees and royalties payable by British subjects. The ordinary license-fee to mine and dig for gold in any waste lands of the Crown was 30 shillings per month. For a grant of permission to work a quartz vein, the fee was £25; and for each renewal, the same sum was paid. The act of 1853 removed the distinction between British citizens and aliens, admitting the latter to "the like privileges of working the gold mines and gold fields of the colony. and of employing themselves thereon, as now are or hereafter may be enjoyed by British subjects. The fees are reduced to 10 shillings for a license to dig or mine for gold upon Crown lands, and one-half of that rate for license to mine upon private lands, already leased from the Crown for pastoral purposes.

CHAPTER XXXI.

MINING LAWS OF CANADA.

The different provinces of the Dominion have, I believe, different local codes. The most instructive for my purpose are those of Nova Scotia and Ontario. The letter of Hon. P. S. Hamilton, commissioner of mines at Halifax, published in the last report of Mr. J. W. Taylor, United States commissioner, on the resources of States and Territories east of the Rocky mountains, contains an outline of the law of Nova Scotia, from which the following paragraphs are taken:‡

*Confirmed rather than created by charters, 3 John and 33 Edw. 1, often subsequently recognized and defined, and finally established in its present form during the reign of William IV.

†This account is taken substantially from Mr. Gregory Yale's Book on Mining Claims and Water Rights, San Francisco, 1867.

‡ A still more full and complete account of the law of Nova Scotia may be found in the Guide to Nova Scotia, by Alexander Heatherington, editor of the Halifax Mining Gazette.

Whoever may be the owner of the land, gold mines in Nova Scotia belong in the first instance to the Crown. At least this is practically the case as yet. There are portions of land in the province which have been granted without reserving to the Crown any minerals, but upon such unlimited grants no gold has yet been discovered. As a rule, out of all land granted in Nova Scotia there are reserved to the crown all mines and deposits of gold, silver, lead, tin, iron, copper, and coal. All other mineral substances are conveyed with the soil. The regulations improvised by the governor and council on the first discovery of gold in Nova Scotia, as also the first "gold field act" passed by the provincial legislature, were framed, as might naturally enough be supposed, with but a very imperfect knowledge of what was requisite to a gold-mining community anywhere, still more of all that was peculiar in the Nova Scotian gold fields, and would most conduce to their development. Consequently they were hampered with many provisions which experience soon proved to be useless, but which bore heavily and vexatiously upon those who engaged in mining enterprises. There is little room to doubt that the check thus given to such enterprises at their very conception is, in its results, felt to some extent even yet. The law now in force, which with its subsequent amendments was framed by the writer of this paper, (Mr. Hamilton,) has been found to work satisfactorily to all parties concerned, although of course every year's additional experience suggests some further amendation.

According to the existing law, the intending miner having determined upon the site of his future operations, it not being preoccupied by another, may in the first instance apply at the department of mines for either a prospecting license or a lease. There is no limit to the extent of ground that he may apply for. To obtain a prospecting license he must pay at the rate of fifty cents per acre; and where the ground applied for is not Crown land, must enter into a bond to reimburse the proprietor thereof for any damage that may be done to his land. This license holds good for three months, but is renewable for a further term of three months upon the prepayment of 25 cents per acre. This gives him the exclusive right to explore on the whole tract applied for, and select any part, or the whole of it, upon which to carry on mining operations.

Before entering upon any such mining operations, he must, whether he has previously held a prospecting license or not, apply for a lease of such unoccupied ground as he may have selected for his purpose. On making such application he is required to pay at the rate of $2 for each area of 250 feet in length by 150 feet in breadth, and also, when the ground applied for is private property, to make an arrangement with the owner of the soil for any damages the latter is likely to sustain. Thereupon he receives a lease for 21 years, reserving a royalty of 2½ per cent. upon all the gold mined. The law further requires him to have labor performed annually at the rate of 100 days' work for every 250 by 150 feet leased by him, and to furnish quarterly and swear to a return showing, among other things, the amount of work and when performed, the quantity of quartz mined, the mill to which it was sent, and the quantity of gold obtained from it. Any person is liable to a heavy fine who runs a quartz-mill without a license. Before obtaining this license, for which there is no charge, he must give bonds with ample sureties for the performance of his duties as required by law. The licensed mill-owner must every month make and swear to a return showing the quantity of quartz crushed, the mine whence it came, and the quantity of gold taken from it; and out of this gold he himself pays to the mines department the royalty reserved by law, receiving three per cent. out of that royalty as commission for his trouble.

Under the law thus described by its author, about $3,000,000 have been extracted from the gold mines of Nova Scotia within the past six years. He says the law works satisfactorily; but the slow development of the mines under it leaves room for the suspicion that its burdens are too heavy for this industry to support.

Certainly the province of Ontario has found the taxation of mines a source of no revenue, but a cause of much ruin to mining. In February or March, 1868, the legislative assembly passed an act of extraordinary character, which, besides fixing in a very arbitrary manner the size and shape of mining claims, and providing that both alluvial and quartz mines should be bounded by vertical planes in depth, limited the period of lease to one year, made the lease liable to forfeiture by one week's intermission in the working, and imposed a royalty upon all gold and silver mines, whether on crown lands or private property, of not less than two nor more than 10 per cent. of the gross amount of gold and silver mined. Fortunately the lieutenant governor was empowered to fix the tax between these limits, and even to grant mineral lands by order in council, on any terms he might see fit to prescribe.

I presume the experience of a single summer has been sufficient to show the unwisdom of this law. At all events, it has been repealed, almost or quite unanimously, at the session of the assembly which closed a few days ago, (December, 1868;) and an act* has been passed abolishing all royalties, taxes, and duties imposed by any previous patents, and rescinding all reservations of gold and silver mines contained in previous grants. The fee simple of the minerals is made over to the owner of the soil, and no reservation or exception of gold, silver, iron, copper, or other mines or minerals may hereafter be inserted in any patent from the crown granting lands sold as mining lands. Exploration for minerals on crown lands is declared free to all persons, and actual mining may be carried on upon crown lands, either by the purchase of the ground as mining land or by the procurement of a miner's license. The license must be renewed annually, is not transferable, and authorizes the licensee personally, and not through another or others, to mine during one year from the date of said license on any unsold crown lands within the mining division therein mentioned, and not for the time being marked or staked out and occupied by any other licensee. Each mining claim on a vein shall be 200 feet along the vein, by 100 feet on each side thereof, measuring from the centre of the vein or lode. Companies of two or more persons, who each hold a miner's license, may stake out and work additional feet along a lode by the above width, in the proportion of 100 additional feet in length for every additional miner, not to exceed 1,000 feet in length altogether, and work the claim jointly. Mining claims shall be laid out as far as possible uniformly, and in quadrilateral and rectangular shapes; measurements of all mining claims shall be horizontal, and the ground included in every such claim shall be deemed to be bounded under the surface by lines vertical to the horizon.

These provisions indicate that deep mining is as yet unknown in the province. If mining claims are to be bounded beneath the surface by vertical planes, then 100 feet on each side of the vein is too little for the security of the miner. However, all this arrangement of mining under license is evidently intended for individuals without capital, and such

* This account is based upon a copy of the act as introduced by the ministry. I presume it is the same as that which passed the assembly. The newspapers have not to my knowledge mentioned any important amendments, and the introduction of the bill was received by all parties with cheers.

persons cannot be expected to carry on operations to a great depth. The tendency of the law will be to encourage the purchase of mineral lands from the crown, since that releases the owner from all necessity for license, or limitation of claim by a fixed standard of surface measurement. This is a beneficial tendency, unless it goes so far as to lock up the entire territory in the hands of surface-owners and prevent all independent mining. The laws of Canada, as will be seen from these examples, are fundamentally the same as those of England, modified by old grants of the crown, and by the legislation of the different provinces. The general character of that legislation hitherto has not been very favorable to a rapid development of mining, but the new and more liberal policy is gaining ground, and doubtless the example of Ontario will be followed by other provinces. The principal reform—a release of the miners from onerous taxation—once effected, other necessary or advisable improvements will follow as they are dictated by experience.

CHAPTER XXXII.

CONCLUSIONS.

History gives us a partial explanation of the causes which have made Germany, ever since the middle ages, the school of the world in the art of mining. In that country, and we might almost say in that country alone, has mining been pursued for centuries, comparatively undisturbed by wars and conquests, and continually fostered by the state, and assisted by the progressive science of each succeeding age. In laws, in histories, in her miners' dialect, and, above all, in the not yet obliterated traces of ancient operations, Germany presents to us a complete and instructive picture of the mining industry of the past, whilst her numerous and well-appointed schools, with their armies of accomplished graduates, her local populations of (so to speak) hereditary miners, her wise and elaborate system of legislation for mines, and her multifarious manufactures, based upon mining, keep her still the foremost nation of Christendom, if not in every branch of this industry, or in all the steps of invention and progress which attend it, yet at least in its general stability and settled economy, and in its harmonious relations to other forms of organized labor as a recognized element in the prosperity of the state.

Spain had once an excellent mining code; but it was based upon an incomplete science, and upon institutions of labor which have passed or are passing away; and the Spanish code (familiar to us as the present system of Mexico) has stood still while the world advanced. England has a vast and productive mining industry; and English statesmen are not slow to recognize its importance as the foundation of the commercial power of that country. But the intricacies and local complications of English law are proverbial, and the mining codes are no exception to the rule. We can probably copy little from England, save those principles of common law which we have already. France has the most modern system, (if we except our own, which is as yet scarcely worthy of the name,) for the clean sweep of the Code Napoleon did not spare the ancient regulations which fettered the mining industry of that nation. But France has unfortunately few metal mines, and her experience can afford us, therefore, but little light. It is to Germany that we must look for our best models of legislation, as of applied science. No popular notion is more erroneous than that which ascribes to the Germans, as a people, learning without practical skill and tact; and nothing can more strikingly illustrate the error of this impression than the manner in which the Germans have brought to bear upon the art of mining the sciences of chemistry, mechanics, mathematics, law, and political economy.

It is not, however, by closely imitating the course of any nation that we can successfully establish an American system. The one thing to be studied in all nations is the degree of wisdom with which they have adapted their legislation to their circumstances; and it should always be borne in mind that we occupy a position widely different from that of a state bound by precedents and privileges, and, at the same time, possessed of greater central power than democratic governments can or should ever acquire. Our American system cannot be a delicately balanced and nicely administered one: the hoofs of each new party riding into power would trample such workmanship to pieces. It must be broad, simple, and, as far as possible, automatic. Our institutions are not like philosophical apparatus, closely watched and often adjusted; they are rather like the ocean, lashed by storms and swayed by mighty tides, yet keeping its own level after all, and asking no man to supply its deficiency or drain its surplus.

It is no small task to apply the teachings of history and the examples of successful states to these new conditions; yet it were folly to forget those teachings, and, blindly disdaining all examples, to blunder forward in a path where every false step wastes the energies and delays the progress of a great people.

I think the foregoing analysis and historical summary proves the truth of certain principles, which harmonize also with the democratic policy of this country. Among these I would name the following:

1. The assertion of any right of royalty in the precious metals is unfounded in nature, and unwise in practice. The most enlightened nations have abandoned the idea of anything more than a general supremacy of the state over mining in the interest of the people.

2. The benefits derived by government from the mines must be indirect. No tax for revenue should be laid on mining any more than on agriculture. Taxes sufficient to cover the cost of the necessary supervision of the mining interest are, properly enough, levied in all nations except the United States. We had a bullion tax, and spent none of it for the miners; now we have no tax, which is better, at least, than the former system.

3. The question, whether the government should sell the mines or only license their working, is to be answered, in this country, in favor of the first alternative, unless we are prepared to establish and administer a vast mining system over our scattered districts. I think the true course is to alienate the mines from the United States as soon as possible, and to do this upon a general and uniform policy, preventing the necessity of special legislation.

4. The manner of conveying titles to the mines should be so regulated as to avoid as far as possible all litigation in future, and at the same time encourage mining. For, it must be remembered, in surrendering the title to the mines wholly to the patentee, we remove that stimulus to their development which the conditions of the possessory title formerly maintained; and we can only rely on the natural laws of supply and demand to secure the continued working of the mines. According to those laws, profit limits production, and mining must be profitable to the individual, if it is to be continued for any length of time. Now, passing a title to the miner which is indefinite or ambiguous, and brings him into conflict with his neighbor, is laying a heavy burden on mining, and so, without gain to any one, diminishing the product of bullion.

5. The nature of the property conveyed is such that ordinary measurements cannot always define it. The Spanish and English laws, as I have shown, invariably bound mining claims by vertical planes, just as the property of land-owners is bounded. The modern Prussian law does the same thing. But according to the present codes of other German states, and the ancient codes of all, inclined locations may be granted, with the right to follow the vein in depth, without reference to the surface ownership. The American miners' law is unlike either, and, so far as I know, has no parallel in history. It comprehends the vein, its dips, spurs,* and angles, to any depth; and under this provision, when two veins are found to meet in depth, the oldest location is held to be the main lode, and the other is confiscated as a "spur." There is no justice in such a provision. On the other hand, there is no limit in American local regulations as to the distance between parallel locations, which, no matter how closely they lie together, are presumed to be on different veins until proved to be on the same. This state of things both invites and protracts a litigation which is seldom settled except by exhaustion and compromise.

There are not wanting those who urge the adoption of "square locations" exclusively, as the cure for these evils. But with such, after mature reflection, I cannot agree. The great aim of the government in disposing of its mines should be to secure their permanent and systematic working. To define the boundaries of mining ground by vertical planes does indeed lessen the danger of litigation, but it also lessens the value of the claim; and, in most cases, the value thus subtracted from one property is not added to any other. Thus a miner under the Spanish law loses the right to work his vein, because at the depth of 600 feet it passes out of his surface boundaries into the neighboring claim; but the neighbor is not much better off for knowing that 600 feet below the surface he may find a vein of ore. To the miner who has already reached that depth, it is valuable; to the miner who must dig and blast 600 feet to find it, it may be worth nothing. Meanwhile, it is undoubtedly for the interest of the country that the work should be continued in depth; and the proper person to carry it on is evidently the one who has commenced it and prosecuted it thus far. The Spanish precedent I have already discussed elsewhere, and shown that its effect has not been favorable to permanent mining. England and Prussia present more modern and plausible systems. Prussia is most deserving of attention, since in that country the inclined location has been abolished, and it is natural to suppose that experience has proved its inferiority. This cannot be accepted, however, without due consideration of the circumstances of the case. Mining has been carried on in Germany for centuries. We may safely assume that every mining district is thoroughly studied and known. The local peculiarities of the veins are understood; and it is not difficult to locate a surface claim so that it will cover the ground upon a vein to the greatest depth to which mining can be carried. Besides, most of the mines are already opened; many of them are worked under inclined locations of the old sort; and these are not interfered with.

In the United States, on the other hand, we are comparatively ignorant of the peculiarities of our mining districts, and our mineral veins have shown themselves in many, I might almost say in most, cases, to vary in dip to an extraordinary degree. The veins of Lander Hill may be cited as an example. Some of them dip at the outcrop 60° below the

* The word *spur* is omitted from the United States law of 1866, but the sweeping recognition in that law of "mining customs" virtually restores it.

horizon, and, at a depth of 300 feet, are found to run for a considerable distance almost horizontally. Only very large square locations, tracts of 40 acres at least, could cover such mining ground; and I consider it impracticable to grant the mineral lands containing gold and silver in such parcels, though, no doubt, capitalists would prefer such large areas.* For the present stage of mining in this country, as for the earlier stages of mining in Germany, the inclined location must be accepted as the best for lodes.

But it does not follow that the boundaries of an inclined location cannot be defined at all. They used to be so in Europe, and they may be so in this country. The location should give the right to a certain distance each side of the vein, so many feet in the hanging wall, and so many in the foot-wall. When two claims cross in depth, the elder location simply holds its course through the other, taking only so many feet away, and leaving to the second party the right of way to follow and find his vein again. If one claim joins another in depth, the two being branches of the same vein, the elder location takes the whole in depth, but does not take the "spur" above the junction, except so far as its right extends in the two walls. At the same time, the surface location of veins should be regulated by law, and the making of new parallel locations close to older ones should not be allowed. Of this I shall speak presently.

6. Although history abundantly shows that mining flourishes best when the property in minerals is distinguished from the ownership of the soil, it seems to me good policy for the United States, in selling the mines, to sell also the surface. In most cases the land will never be taken up for agricultural purposes, and if the miner does not buy it no one will. I do not mean that the ownership of minerals shall go invariably with the soil, but that, where the United States has both for sale, both should be sold to the same party, who may afterwards dispose of either as he likes. The present law partially recognizes this policy by selling inclined locations at so much per acre. Under one interpretation of this rule, the same acre may be sold over and over again, and, strictly speaking, not belong to any of the purchasers, since all they receive is the right to use it for mining purposes.

The foregoing conclusions will be better understood in their application to American mining after a brief analysis of the United States law. For an able commentary upon the law, and the earlier instructions under it, issued from the General Land Office, I would refer to the interesting work of Mr. Gregory Yale, of San Francisco, on mining titles and water rights in California. I shall not go minutely into the analysis on the present occasion, since it is rather my purpose to suggest amendments to the law than to discuss constructions of it.

The first and second sections of the law of 1866 provide for two classes of miners in this country. The first section *licenses* all miners upon the public domain. They are not trespassers, neither are they owners; they are simply licensed to mine, under such regulations as may be prescribed by law or agreed upon among themselves. The second section makes it possible for certain persons or associations to step out of the class of licensed miners into that of actual proprietors. This section *distinctly applies to veins or lodes only*,† and leaves all placer, gulch,

* Let any one attempt to calculate the value of a square location of 40 acres on the Comstock, or Lander Hill, or Treasure Hill, at White Pine!

† A recent decision of the Commissioner of the General Land Office includes placer, gravel, and cement mines under the operation of section 2. The words of the chairman of the Committee on Mines and Mining, in reporting the bill to the Senate, May 28, 1866, were: "*By this bill it is only proposed to dispose of the vein mines.* * * * * It is not proposed to

hydraulic, and cement miners, together with all those who do not acquire patents to veins, on the broad ground established by the first section. Nor does the second section make it obligatory upon any person to acquire a title to the vein of gold, silver, cinnabar, or copper he may be working under the general license of the first section.

The second section declares that a diagram may be filed, conforming to the local laws, customs, and rules of miners, and a *tract* entered and patented, *together with* the right to follow the vein, &c. This, it seems to me, distinctly conveys the surface ownership to the patentee, together with the right of inclined location. But the mining customs do not recognize a surface ownership, vested in the miner, and hence much confusion has arisen, since the law leaves the size of the "tract" to be determined by local customs. Nor is confusion the worst result that may be expected. Miners will begin to make regulations expressly to influence the subsequent operation of the patent law. It is said that the only patent thus far issued is one conveying several hundred acres of land, the "custom" having been, no doubt, conveniently established for the occasion.

Section third provides, among other things, that no plat, survey, or description filed for patent shall cover more than one vein or lode. Under this provision what is the status of a vein existing, but not discovered until after the patent has issued, within the borders of a certain tract? If the vein was previously known, then the patent could not issue for the tract covering it, and the boundaries of each tract must be so drawn as to exclude all veins except the one on which the patent is applied for; but if the second vein is discovered within the tract patented, I think the legal position is this: the patentee owns a piece of land, and the mineral right to one vein, cropping out on the surface within his property. The United States, which formerly owned both surface and mineral, still owns all other veins within the tract, except the one patented, *and under the spirit of the first section* any one may mine upon the other veins, simply paying damages, not royalty, to the patentee.

Recommendations.—I have the honor to recommend, as necessary amendments of the present law, the following provisions:

The size of the *tract* decided by patent and the number of feet upon the lode should be fixed by law, in spite of all conflicting miners' customs. Vested rights must be adjusted by agreement among owners; but it should be at once announced that the United States will hereafter regard the locator of a vein as entitled to claim, say, 200 feet on each side of the vein; that no other locations subsequently made within that distance will be recognized as patentable; that subsequent locations made within less than 200 feet of the boundary of the first location will be shorn of so much of their width on that side, being limited by the elder locations; that the patentee shall pay to the United States, say, $5 per acre for his land, and a fee of, say, $10 for each separate vein discovered and worked within the tract, after the first vein, upon which the

---

interfere with, or impose any tax upon, *the miners engaged in working placer mines.*" The words of the law are, "*vein or lode of quartz, or other rock in place, bearing gold, silver, cinnabar, or copper.*" There is no possible construction of these words which will include placer mines, or alluvial deposits, or beds. The Commissioner argues that there are different kinds of veins, and that it is difficult to decide how a vein was ormed—all of which does not touch the case. Amid all the discussions of geologists about vein-formation, the distinction between all veins and alluvial deposits has never been disturbed. It is found in the earliest laws, and is perfectly comprehended by the ordinary miner. The United States law of 1866 cannot be applied to mines of the latter class; it was an experiment, applied only to "quartz mining," and the attempt of the Land Office to extend it over placers, before a single quartz mine has received a patent under it, only tends to bring the whole law into contempt.

issuance of the patent is based. The right to follow the vein, its dips, variations and angles should remain unaltered, and all ores found within 30 feet of the vein in the hanging or foot wall should be considered as belonging to it. In a case where two veins cross in depth the elder location should keep its right to 30 feet in either wall; if the veins unite and become one the elder location would take the whole vein below the junction, but not the whole spur above, being restricted on that side to its right of 30 feet.

It is true that this system would not prevent all collision of interests. A and B might, for instance, locate side by side on parallel veins 400 feet apart, and each might subsequently discover a vein within his tract near the boundary line between them. In working these they might find themselves close together and liable to interfere. But in such a case it would at least be only a question between A and B, not between them and a score of piratical locators, only intent on mischief; and disputes arising between owners in this way would be much easier to settle by compromise than the present class of suits, where one party has nothing to lose and everything to gain. Besides, no patent should be granted until the vein first located is sufficiently developed to show its course and width. Until that has been done the miner should be content to work under the free license granted by the United States; and when that has been done the chances of subsequent discoveries of valuable and separate veins within 200 feet are in most districts not very great. In fact, the majority of the "float locations" made under present customs in the immediate neighborhood of developed veins are worthless, except for purposes of black-mail, robbery, and litigation; and if the privilege of working such subsidiary out-crops belonged only to the patentee of the vein in the centre of the tract they would never be worked.

Again, the conditions on which the possessory title depends should be made uniform in all the mining districts; and I am of opinion that in no case should claims be held without being worked a reasonable period every year. The present chaotic state of the practice in this respect is described by a committee of the Nevada legislature as follows:

> In one district the work required to be done to hold a claim is nominal; in another, exorbitant; in another, abolished; in another, adjourned from year to year. A stranger, seeking to ascertain the law, is surprised to learn that there is no satisfactory public record to which he can refer; no public officer to whom he may apply who is under any bond or obligation to furnish him information or guarantee its authenticity. Often in the newer districts he finds there is not the semblance of a code, but a simple resolution, adopting the code of some other district, which may be a hundred miles distant.*

My predecessor repeatedly urged this point; and in the absence of the necessary federal legislation the evil has certainly not diminished. I think the provisions of the "quartz laws" of Nevada county, California, might be adopted in this regard, with advantage, as the universal rule. They require work to the extent of $100 in value, or twenty days' faithful labor, each year, and make the regularly elected and sworn county clerk or recorder the mining recorder also. The spirit of the law should be to prevent all parties from holding claims who do not mean to work them. This is a legitimate sequence of the position in which the United States law places such parties. They have free permission *to mine*, not to "squat," and prevent other people from mining. They should not treat the mines as their *property* until they have bought them from the United States. It is said, "sometimes the miner, having found a vein, is obliged to wait for capital or for better times to work it." But if he has a *bona fide* intention to work he can do as much as will hold his

* For a full statement of these evils see the report of the committee, quoted in J. Ross Browne's report for 1867, page 227.

claim. The secret of much opposition to such a wholesome provision is that those to whom the United States generously gives the free license *to mine* do not wish to mine, but to speculate. A few men organize a district, locate hundreds of thousands of feet, pass laws to protect their "rights," and then, by working one or two rich veins, try to attract a population and sell out their claims. The law is not intended to protect speculators of any class.

Nor should patents be granted on veins not opened and traced. When a man has chosen a vein, worked it to the extent of $1,000 expenditure, and determined to buy it, he is entitled to the special protection of the second section of the law.

There need be no difficulty in executing these provisions. If miners do not desire to enter the class of owners, they can remain licensed to prospect and mine on the public domain; but the protection afforded by such provisions as I have recommended against piratical locations would make applications for patents very numerous, especially in new districts. Nor is there any hardship in excluding later locations within 200 feet of the original one. We grant a man the right to own and work a vein which he has discovered, because we assume that he expended skill and labor in the discovery, and that his working will benefit the public. But these considerations do not apply to the individual who makes haste to follow the discoverer, and "locates" the nearest piece of quartz, hoping either to find by chance the main lode, (the discoverer having found by skill and labor only a spur or branch of it,) or else to get down to the vein located by the discoverer, and extract a quantity of rich ore before, by the slow process of drifting along the vein into his stopes, it can be proved that he is a trespasser. I could adduce many instances in which men have sunk vertical shafts to cut a rich deposit which did not belong to them, and, while they were taking out large quantities of valuable ore and turning it into money, coolly said to the real claimant, "You tell us this is your vein: *prove it*, and we will give it up at once." The courts invariably demand that kind of proof which requires a connection to be made between the works of the claimants, either by surface cuts or by drifts under ground, and, so far as I know, never award any damages on account of the ore which the intruder, finally ejected, may have extracted and sold "in good faith." The present law gives no greater security to capitalists than the mining customs, for under the latter a company could at least locate all the outcrops in its neighborhood, and so prevent piratical locations; and that is the most that can be done under the law. The patent must cover but one vein, but the patent is kept from being made worthless by interference and litigation only through innumerable surrounding locations made by the patentee! Is this what we call securing the title of the miner?

What are these mining customs to which the law pays such sweeping respect? They are edicts passed at 24 hours' notice by mass meetings of from five to 500 men; it requires no more formalities to abolish or amend them than it did to make them—a notice pasted on a door, a "mass meeting" next day, and the thing is done. The records of titles are kept by an officer called the recorder, not known to the law nor answerable for malfeasance in office, except that if he were known to tamper with the books in his charge his life might be taken by the party wronged. The records are kept in a few districts in fire-proof offices and in suitable form, but more frequently in small blank-books, pocket-books, or scraps of paper, stowed away under the counter or behind the flour-barrel or the stove of a store or bar-room. These are not exaggerations. The title to millions of dollars' worth of property depends on records no better cared for than this. The whole record book for the Philadelphia district, Nevada, was burnt up, and the district "jumped;" and the game would have succeeded but for the unusual circumstance that a second copy of the records was in existence. If I am correctly informed, this second copy was only a partial one, and there was a good deal of litigation and trouble, involving some bloodshed, as the result of attempts to enforce old claims on oral testimony. The Sheba mine, in Humboldt county, is another instance (see account of that mine) of the shifting and *unrecorded* nature of these mining laws. In regard to the size of claims and the tenure by which they are to be held, it is best to make one uniform federal law, overriding these regulations.

I have the honor to recommend also, as an advisable addition to the law, that the United States deputy surveyor under the act shall be required to examine whether a mineral deposit proposed to be patented is a vein or not. If not, the same area shall be deeded as before, but without the right to follow the vein out of the limits of vertical planes from the surface boundaries. And I recommend in general an extension of the law to cover placer claims, by providing that such claims may be sold by surface area, in "square locations." The question of size is not vital, since it regulates itself. After the United States has once sold two adjacent properties, it cannot prevent their being united. Hence, by combination and by different purchases, companies will be able to acquire as much land as they desire.

In carrying out any such measures, no conflict with the miners is to be feared. The law is not compulsory. It simply opens the door to admit members of the licensed class (which includes all citizens and those who have declared their intention to become such) to enter the class of patentees by purchase, (which may include also aliens.) The motive applied is an improvement of the title. The miners' or possessory title, in spite of its frequently vaunted validity, is not one upon which money can be safely lent. It is a curious fact that miners can hardly ever borrow money to develop their claims, while they frequently sell the claims, undeveloped, for much more than they failed to borrow. The insecurity of the mining title lies in this: that an absentee owner or mortgagor is at the mercy, 1st, of the laws which the miners may at any time enact; and, 2d, of the agent on whose compliance with those laws his whole title depends. A capitalist in San Francisco lent to a miner from the interior $10,000 in gold, to help him develop a very promising gold mine, and took a mortgage on the mine as security. The miner returned to the district where the property was located, stopped work for a certain number of days, and allowed the mine to be "jumped" or re-located as abandoned by a friend of his own. The friend became, by miners' law, the owner; the two rascals divided $10,000 between them; and the capitalist was left to muse upon the instability of the "possessory title."

The substitution of a perfect title for this shifting one is a benefit to every poor miner. It will enable him to borrow money on his mine, a much better course than to hurry a sale of it to some speculative company before its value is half determined. The miners will hasten to avail themselves of the provisions of the law if it is made easy for them to do so. But the expense, delay, perplexity, and contradictory decisions which have hitherto marked the administration of it have produced discouragement and indifference.

The present law is not operating at all; therefore the question of its benefits can hardly be answered. But I think that such amendments as I have suggested, together with one more practically important, would remove most of the present difficulties in its way. The latter touches the question of expense. The compensation of deputy surveyors under the law is notoriously inadequate, especially in the new and sparsely settled districts. (See letters included in the chapter on Montana.) The result is that the miners are subjected to extra legal expense, or the work is not properly done. In view of the fact that new mines should be encouraged, and that producing mines should bear the expense (as they do everywhere else in the world) of the system devised for their own good, I recommend a bullion tax of one-quarter of one per cent. to be applied, one-half to the necessary expenses of mineral surveys over and above the present legal fees, and one-half to the maintenance of a national school of mines, on the plan set forth in another chapter.

SECTION VII.

MINING EDUCATION.

CHAPTER XXXIII.

MEANS OF DISSEMINATING INFORMATION WITH REGARD TO MINING METALLURGY.

The object of the government in taking measures for the spread of information concerning the mineral resources of the country and the proper methods for their exploitation is three-fold. The first end served is to increase the confidence of its own citizens in the natural wealth of the country, and to augment the credit of the country throughout the world. One reason why the credit of the United States is so much lower than that of other nations far less able to pay their debts, is the fact that this nation makes no such thorough periodical exhibits of its sources of strength as do European states. In other words, they advertise more than we do; and their immense statistical official publications have a fine effect upon their financial standing with the world. A second good result from the spread of the kind of information alluded to above, is the communication of valuable advice and knowledge to the mining populations, rendering the business of mining more profitable, and thereby encouraging an increased production of bullion. The third object to be attained is the protection of the country against reckless and wasteful mining, by the inculcation of sound principles, and the enlightenment of the miners as to their own best interests. This is not in the nature of a lesson, forced upon them, but of a boon which they desire and would gratefully welcome.

The means by which the government can act in this important matter are three: a commissioner, a bureau, and a national school. I shall briefly discuss the first two, and pass to a more detailed consideration of the third.

The provision of Congress, under which Mr. J. Ross Browne and myself have served, was certainly a measure of great benefit, so far as it went. No one can deny that the two reports of 1867 and 1868 throw a great deal of light upon the previously obscure and almost fabulous subject of the mineral resources of the country. The eagerness with which they have been sought for by the citizens of all the States, exhausting the official editions, and justifying the publication of editions by private houses besides, is a proof of the estimation in which they are held by the people. Both those reports, and the present one, were too much occupied with a presentation of the resources of the country west of the Rocky mountains, and of the general condition and prospects of the mining industry, to leave space for the discussion of topics more directly instructive to the miners themselves; but if the work is continued, future reports may deal with such topics, and no doubt considerable good would arise from the discussion. But while many things which the commissioner attempts to do are necessary to be done, I do not think that he can cover the whole ground. He cannot receive and reply to letters from miners who desire advice; he cannot serve as a medium for exchanging information. To do that, he must have clerks and a bureau. Now there are many reasons which make a national bureau of mines desirable, and, in default of any better means, necessary; but I am decidedly of opinion that the duties of both commissioner and bureau, and a great many more beside, could be best and most economically performed by a national school.

To this subject I have given much attention, and I deem it one of the most important that can be brought before Congress for consideration. All attempts to enlighten our miners, and preserve from waste and ruin our mines, will be but partially successful, unless we can establish a living and progressive agency of intelligence in their midst. The advantages to be gained by the creation of such a school as the bill of Senator Stewart, introduced last year, proposes, may be enumerated as follows:

1. It would give us the right kind of scientific engineers and metallurgists. The excellence of many foreign schools is acknowledged, and numerous American students attend them to obtain that education in the arts of mining and metallurgy which they need to practice at home.

But, while the principles of theoretical science remain everywhere the same, all questions of the best modes of applying those principles vary with circumstances. The economy of different methods and processes is so intimately connected with the price of labor and fuel that the process which is the best in one country is cast aside in another. It is a severe requisition that we make upon a young graduate of a foreign school of mines, when we ask him to adapt his acquired science at once to our widely different circumstances. Every such graduate has to reconstruct, alone and for himself, the whole art which he has learned—a work requiring genius as well as intelligent perseverance, and one in which many men fail, who, *if they had been educated in the region where they were to practice*, would have been respectably and deservedly successful all their lives. A school of mines would speedily give us a settled and digested American science of mining and metallurgy, and the reproach that has been cast upon science would pass away.

It is undeniable that many of those now engaged in mining sneer at educated engineers, the graduates of foreign schools. This contempt is partly justified by the failure of foreign engineers and metallurgists to adapt their ideas to our conditions; but it is mainly unjustifiable. Many charlatans have imposed upon the credulity of the public by parading the names of foreign schools—like that Isenbeck, who professed to practice upon black rock ores the "Freiberg flux process;" but that is no reason for despising really well educated men. Another great cause of this feeling is the fault of the public. When American (or foreign) young men come here from the schools of Europe to take part in mining, the true wisdom is to give them subordinate positions at the mines, where they may gradually learn the new conditions of the problem, and fit themselves for higher positions. They are generally good surveyors, assayers, and draughtsmen. But the general rule has been to take such young and inexperienced men as superintendents, or, worse yet, send them as experts, to inspect totally undeveloped mining lands, and say whether they will "pay dividends on judicious investment of capital." Now, of all the branches of knowledge in the world, this one of prophesying the future of a newly discovered mineral deposit in a newly opened territory is not and cannot be taught in a school. It requires the basis of a thorough education, coupled with years of field experience, and a familiar acquaintance with the locality examined. Besides, men fresh from countries where ores are worked much more cheaply than here, would naturally be tempted to consider veins "highly promising," or "very rich," which were only so according to foreign standards. Their flattering reports once made, their services were no longer needed; and unskilled overseers proceeded to waste what little chance of profit there might be in the case. No wonder that when the mistakes of scientific, but not practical, and practical, but not scientific men are heaped together upon the head of science, they seem to cover her with shame. But all this arises from the notion that there is something recondite and approaching sorcery in the sciences of geology, mineralogy, and metallurgy. In fact, science is merely knowledge, and knowledge is power. Let every miner have a chance to hear lectures and witness experiments in the sciences which interest his calling, and he would conceive for science a true respect, equally removed from the vulgar superstition on the one hand, and the boorish contempt on the other, with which she is too often regarded. Then our thoroughly trained American engineers would be received with confidence by the people, and they would justify that confidence by inaugurating and maintaining reforms in mining and metallurgy, increasing both the gross product and the net profit of our mines, and securing the future by wise forethought. None of the objections urged against foreign schools hold good against a national school among our own mines.

2. It would serve all the purposes for which a commissioner is now appointed. The work of compiling statistics and other information for the use of Congress and the people is expressly turned over to the faculty of the school by the terms of the bill; and their annual reports would no doubt be more valuable than the opinions and statements of any single man. The professors are also enjoined to travel through the mining districts, and address popular and instructive lectures to the miners—both parties gaining by this acquaintanceship.

3. It would serve all the purposes of a bureau or department of mines. The delays and difficulties which have arisen in the administration of the mining law by the General Land Office show how hard it is to manage such matters at such a distance. For an industry so constantly progressive as that of mining, the best kind of bureau is a school; because that remains always in vital connection with the people, hears of the latest improvements, tries experiments, publishes results—is, in short, in sympathy with the work for which its pupils are trained.

4. It would tend to unite different sections of the country, the mining interests of which are now separate and isolated. The interests of miners are alike. The miners in Oregon and in New Mexico are wrestling with essentially the same problems as those of Colorado and Carolina. What they need is one central point to which all experience shall gather, and from which light may radiate to all. The scientific collections, apparatus and library of such an institution would be worth more to the country than a score of inferior ones, costing in the aggregate ten times as much. This is one reason why the work cannot be left to private enterprise, or State liberality. No one private or State school can command the support and collect the experience of all the mining communities. For that, a national school is required. It has been shown by experience in other countries that such a school, devoted to the mining sciences only, and maintained by the state, has a powerful influence on the productiveness and permanence of the mining industry, while a mere department in some institution of learning, or a school smothered in a capital, away from the mining regions, has never been found to affect so widely the actual work of mining, although, no doubt, such endowments do much good. Let us have as many private schools, State schools and college schools as can

be supported; they will all succeed the better for the existence of that of which none of them can take the place—a national school among the mining regions. I no not underrate the advantages of private schools. On the contrary, I highly esteem them and rejoice in their prosperity. The school of Columbia College, New York, the Sheffield School of New Haven, the Rensselaer Institute at Troy, the Massachusetts Institute of Technology, the Pardee scientific department of Lafayette College, Pennsylvania, have all given considerable space to mining and metallurgy; and the first is devoted entirely to the branches of theoretical and applied science which relate to the extraction and beneficiation of useful minerals. Now there is work enough in the United States for twenty local mining schools, one in every State or Territory where mining is carried on; but there is neither room nor need at present for more than one national school, to stand in the midst of all local institutions, to concentrate and utilize the efforts of all. Such a school would simply take the place of the foreign academies to which our young men are now obliged to go, after they have learned what can be taught them here; and *as soon as it shall thus become possible to complete a thorough course without the expense of a foreign residence, our mining schools, great and small, would have twenty students where they now have one.*

5. Such an institution is more and more urgently needed every year, because the difficulties of mining in the Pacific States and Territories are constantly increasing. The steady annual decline of bullion product is partly due, as I have elsewhere remarked, to this cause. An average uniform product is only to be attained by a system of mining which does more than merely extract the richest ores and then abandon the mines. It is a significant fact, that the largest part of the bullion from lode-mining this year comes from the same mines that furnished it last year, and the year before, and the year before that. Mines like the Eureka of Amador, and the Eureka, North Star, Empire, and others of Grass Valley, would be much more common if skill and wisdom were more common among miners. Individual enterprise might in time correct this evil; but it has not yet done so, and we cannot afford to wait for so slow a reform nor to pay its frightful cost. The very extent of our mining territory is a fatal inducement to avoid rather than to overcome the growing difficulties of the work. It is so much easier for ignorant men to try their luck on virgin ground than to continue the exploration of ground already open, that in the absence of an organized effort to enlighten the people on this subject, we may expect to see our vast mining fields overrun and pillaged before an earnest and systematic development is undertaken. The praiseworthy efforts of single men to stem the tide are almost insignificant in comparison with the general tendency. One might as well expect the Indian to commence stock-raising while the prairie swarms with buffalo. He cuts out the hump and the tongue, throws away carcass and hide, and laughs at all notions of economy and industry. A despotic government would stop this waste by arbitrary measures; but the democratic policy of moral suasion by education is at once more feasible and more effectual.

6. An objection has been advanced which is plausible enough to merit a brief reply. It is said that the government is not called upon to interfere, simply because individuals are not successful in mining, any more than in case of depression in any other business. This objection confounds the distinction between individual and national loss. In point of fact, I think that individuals or companies have lost less money in mining this year than last, and less last than the year before. Mining is regulating itself according to the laws of self-interest. Those who are

not making money for the time being stop; only the best mines will be worked, and those only in such parts and for such periods as will secure the quickest and largest dividends. It is safe to say that not more than one-quarter of this year's bullion product has been obtained at a profit over and above costs; while, balancing the whole yield against the whole outlay, there is no profit left. The tendency of individual enterprise is naturally to abandon all the unprofitable mines, thus reducing the yield to one-quarter of its present amount—a reduction which could not be wholly compensated by robbing newly explored districts of their surface ores. It is the country, not individuals, that loses by such a course; and any measure which promises to encourage individuals to persevere, and offers them the means of obtaining that exchange of experience and impartation of knowledge which will render their work (so important to the country) profitable to themselves, is worthy of serious attention. It is a measure of national policy, not a "governmental interference."

The value of a national school of mines being acknowledged, it becomes a question of importance where it shall be located. That it ought to be, as the bill of Senator Stewart provides, west of the Rocky mountains, is evident from the following, among other reasons: It is the gold and silver mining industry which needs support, is most closely connected with the national credit and welfare, and gets, at present, the least aid from any quarter. The government does not own the iron and copper lands in the east, and is not directly interested in their product. Yet they are protected while gold and silver are not, nor can be, except by such a measure as this. Besides, the older States are better provided already with educational facilities.

Again, the Pacific States and Territories have, and will continue to have, a large and growing population interested in mining; they will furnish numerous students to such a school, and the school in return will gain in efficiency by its location in the midst of the mining districts. This is indispensable, if the provision requiring the professors to travel every year among the mines is to be made effective. A miners' meeting, held at Nevada City, near Grass Valley, last summer, passed the following resolutions, which, I think, express very clearly the substance of this matter:

Resolved, That we cordially recognize the importance to our mining industry of a national school of mines on the Pacific slope, substantially upon the plan advocated by the Secretary of the Treasury and J. Ross Browne, late United States commissioner of mining statistics, and embodied in the bill now before the United States Senate.

Resolved, That such a school, to exert its full measure of influence and achieve complete success, must be situated in the immediate vicinity of mining and metallurgical operations, so as to combine the benefits of actual practice with those of scientific instruction; and that we will not, so long as this fundamental condition is fulfilled, embarrass this important measure by the assertion of particular local interests; and we call upon the miners of the Pacific States and Territories to support the plan in a similar spirit of liberality.

The choice of location is wisely left to the directors of the institution. I venture to suggest that for the first year or two no permanent selection need be made. The erection of buildings would entail a considerable expense, which might better be avoided at the outset. Regarding the enterprise as an experiment, (however our hopes for its success are fortified by reason, analogy, and history,) I think that place should be chosen for a commencement which offers the best advantages *for the time being*, such as accessibility to students, neighborhood of well-managed mines and reduction-works, and cheapness of living.

The abolition of the bullion tax raises the question, how the school is to be supported. Before considering this, I would say a word or two concerning the probable expenses of the enterprise. The bill in its present form (see report of J. Ross Browne, 1868,) contemplates a large expenditure at the outset. This might, no doubt, insure an earlier maturity, but it is not absolutely necessary. As I have already suggested, the cost of permanent buildings may be avoided for the present, by a temporary location and employment of cheap or hired buildings. It is not necessary to make instruction absolutely free. The national mining school of Saxony is managed upon a compromise system. The students do not pay all the expense, but they do bear a part of it, and the government supplies the deficit. In the present instance, an equitable and acceptable arrangement is not difficult. There are certain expenses, such as the salaries of the principal instructors, procurement of collections, library, &c., which are necessary and constant, whatever be the number of students. There are other expenses, which vary with the number of students, such as the cost of laboratory accommodations, the salaries of assistants, etc. It seems fair that moderate fees should be received from the students, to cover expenses of the latter class; and as the number of students increased, these fees might amount to such a sum as materially to reduce the proportion paid by the government. The directors should fix these charges with care, low enough to offer no hindrance to any who desired the benefits of instruction, and high enough to cover the variable expenses alluded to, and to insure appreciation of the privileges offered. Even aside from the saving to the government, I think this plan would increase the efficiency of the school. The sum of $100,000 currency, judiciously expended, would be sufficient, in my opinion, to put the school in operation with the most necessary collections, apparatus, &c.; and the annual cost of maintaining it (apart from the erection of buildings) need not exceed that amount, the expenses incident to the increase of students being covered by fees. I recommend that $100,000 be appropriated for this purpose for the first year. Subsequently, perhaps some acceptable plan could be adopted, by means of which the mining industry itself might bear a portion of the expense. A bullion tax of one-eighth of one per cent. would cover the whole, and be an insignificant burden, besides affording, what is now lacking, a ready indication of the prosperity and productiveness of the mines every year. If the Sutro tunnel is constructed by government aid, a portion of its revenues might be annually set aside by law for this purpose; but for the present an appropriation is the most direct means. I believe the nature of the object would justify this in any event; but it is especially reasonable in view of the fact that considerably more than a million dollars has been paid by the miners within the last four years, in the shape of a special tax on bullion. In view of the whole relation of government to mining, discussed in a former chapter, I claim that such a tax is only justified when its proceeds are applied for the benefit of the mining industry; and hence the appropriation asked, for the establishment of a national school of mines, is but a slight return for the extra burden which has been imposed upon mining.

In conclusion, I would urge the importance of immediate action upon this subject. It will be at least a year before the school, on the most moderate scale, can be put in operation, and the necessity for it grows stronger every day. If we delay until threatened evils are actually upon us, if we allow our country to recede from her foremost position among mining nations, we cannot excuse ourselves. On the other hand, a timely support to this industry will strengthen the hands of others, stimulate the settlement of our vast territory and the organization of stable communities upon it, and secure the future material progress of the country.

The history of the world proves that all nations eminent for profitable and permanent mining have employed two agencies for success—a national mining code and a national mining school. These the United States must have.

I append accounts of several European schools, which will serve to show the nature and compass of their activity. The schools of London, Schemnitz, Leoben, Fahlun, and other places also deserve attention; and, in fact, a thorough study of the organizations of foreign schools should precede the adoption in detail of a plan for our own. Such an examination is provided for by the bill of Senator Stewart, establishing a national school of mines.

CHAPTER XXXIV.

THE FREIBERG SCHOOL OF MINES.

By Benjamin Smith Lyman, of Philadelphia.

In view of the probable establishment before long of a national school of mines in America, it is worth while to look at similar schools in other countries. The following account of the Freiberg mining school was published five years ago, in a newspaper not specially devoted to mining interests, and has long been out of print. Few important changes there have taken place since then. The younger Weissbach has become professor of mineralogy in place of Breithaupt, and has from illness been compelled for some months past to interrupt his teaching. The number of Americans at the school has greatly increased, and was 35 a year ago, and is perhaps even greater now.

It would be well if former students of the Berlin and London mining schools, or of those at Clausthal, Liege, St. Etienne, Prizibram, Schemnitz, Leoben, and elsewhere, would likewise give the American public some account of these institutions.

The Royal Saxon Mining School, or academy (Bergakademie.) now 97 years old, is situated at Freiberg, 25 miles southwest of Dresden. It is surrounded for miles by mines, chiefly of lead and silver, that have been worked for 600 years, and is within two or three miles of two large smelting works. Freiberg is a town of 17,000 inhabitants, and has recently been connected with Dresden by railroad. The smelting works near Freiberg and some of the mines belong, as well as the school, to the government, and the rest of the mines and furnaces throughout Saxony are thoroughly under government control, so that not only are very good opportunities given the students of visiting the mines and furnaces and of working practically at them for their instruction, but the oversight of all these works, in the interest of their proprietors or of the government, gives permanent employment of many grades and kinds to Saxon graduates of the school.

There are about 140 students at the academy; less than half of them are native Saxons.

State students.—About five-sixths of the native students receive aid from the government; that is, they pay only $37 (American money) yearly for tuition. In return, they are required to pass examinations and are carefully watched over in their studies; and they bind themselves not to settle outside of Saxony after graduation without paying all that has been remitted to them by the government on the score of instruction or otherwise.

Admission to the school.—Free State students, as they may be called, must apply for admission to the school as early as the end of February; they must show by their birth certificate that they are between the ages of 16 and 23; they must bring a physician's testimonial of health, strength, and soundness, and a certificate of vaccination; they must bring written testimonials of their good character up to the date of their application; if under age, they must bring a certificate from parents or guardian of approval of the application; their previous education must fit them for the profitable pursuit of the studies they desire to pursue, and in the absence of satisfactory certificates to that effect from certain public institutions they must pass an examination. This examination is about equivalent to that required for admission to Harvard College, and includes algebra and geometry, equations of the first and second degree, stereometry, plane trigonometry, and the use of logarithms. Some facility in drawing, and a good, neat, legible handwriting, are also required; and some knowledge of French and English is considered an advantage. If the applicant comes from a school where Latin is not taught, the examination in this is omitted, but that in the mathematical and practical branches is made the more strict.

Preparatory mining course.—After a satisfactory examination of this kind, the student has to spend four months in following a preparatory practical course at the mines. For the first four weeks he must spend at the mines four six-hour shifts each week, and for the rest of the course five a week. The first eight weeks are spent on the mechanical preparation of the ores; the next six in practical work of different kinds in the mine, such as drilling and hammering stone; one week in seeing how the ore is raised from the mine; and from one to two weeks in observation of the various timbering and masonry work in the mines. During the course the student is helped to information in every detail by the overseer of the mine or his subordinates, and a report is made out monthly to an appointed academical instructor of the student's regularity, industry, zeal, and behavior. The student must also hand in, every month, to the same instructor, a complete journal of his daily work, its object, and what he has been taught about it, as well as his own observations. At the same time he has to pursue at the school certain preparatory studies in mathematics and drawing. Neglect of the duties during this course, or a betrayal of physical unfitness for the fatigues of a miner's life, may yet prevent the student from entering the school. But if the course is satisfactorily finished, he has to spend the remaining time until the beginning of the academical lectures in getting generally oriented in regard to the mines by visiting them under the special direction of the aforementioned instructor, and from time to time in his company. Those students who have already worked a year practically in mines are excused from the practical preparatory course, but not from at least two months of this general orientation.

Preparatory metallurgical course.—There is also a preparatory metallurgical course that must be attended in the long vacation by those students who wish to hear the lectures on metallurgy the following year. This preparatory metallurgical course begins about the first of August and lasts four weeks. The students meet every morning at six or seven o'clock at one of the smelting works, and have to write down, at the dictation of an instructor, a detailed description of the different metallurgical processes and operations. The rest of the morning is spent in visiting in company with the instructor the different parts of the works.

Each student must hand in, weekly, to this instructor a journal, containing not only the dictations but original observations and explanatory drawings; and this journal is handed in at the end of the course to the professor of metallurgy.

Academical instruction.—The students are encouraged to continue their visits to the mines and furnaces near Freiberg throughout the year, especially on Mondays, when there are for that very purpose as few academical exercises as possible; and in the vacations they can make excursions to more distant works. The most deserving of the students receive state aid for the longer excursions, and so travel into distant countries in the long vacation. In the spring and summer the professors themselves occasionally conduct excursions of a half day or a whole one, or of two or three days, to furnaces and mines, and to points of geological interest, and they sometimes make a long vacation journey with a few students.

The academical lectures are given in yearly courses that begin on the first Tuesday of October and end with the last week of the following July, with vacations of about two weeks at Christmas, Easter, and Whitsuntide, and with pretty frequent single holidays. The number of years to be spent at the academy by a student is not prescribed, but is commonly three or four. The student is also free to choose the courses of lectures that he will attend; but he must make known in writing at the beginning of June his choice for the following year, and that choice must be in accordance with the final examination that he intends to pass, and with the progressive nature of the studies themselves.

The students are obliged to take notes of the lectures and their accompanying practical exercises, and to exhibit a journal of the same from time to time to the several professors. During each course of lectures there is now and then a recitation in order that the professor may know the success of his lessons and the diligence of his pupils. At the end of July a public yearly examination of the students all together is made, and at this their journals, exercises, drawings, and the like are all exhibited as proof of their industry. This is, however, a parade or exhibition rather than an examination. If a student wishes to leave the academy, he must announce his intention, and he may have a testimonial. At the end of the whole course of study the student who wishes to enter the service of the state must pass the state examination, as it is called.

State examination.—The state examination takes place in October, but notice of intending to pass it must be given before the end of June. Not more than three candidates are examined at once, and the examination is open only to the students and certain officials, and to the relatives of the candidates. The examination is of four kinds: for those who wish to become miners, surveyors, constructors, and metallurgists.

The miners are examined in mineralogy, geology (with ore deposits,) mining, elementary mechanics, bookkeeping, mining law, general surveying, physics, drawing. They must show, too, that they have diligently followed the courses on practical surveying, general chemistry, metallurgy, and civil architecture. In default of such showing they must be examined in these branches.

The surveyors are examined in general and special surveying, mineralogy, but only in the most important characters, geology, ore deposits, mining law, drawing, physics. They must bring, too, good testimonials of their attendance on the courses on mining.

The constructors are examined in mining, physics, civil architecture, bookkeeping, general surveying, drawing, higher mathematics, elementary mechanics, construction of machines. They must have heard, also, the courses on general chemistry, metallurgy, mineralogy, and geology.

The metallurgists are examined in theoretical and analytical chemistry, dry and wet assaying and blow-piping, metallurgy, physics, mineralogy, elementary mechanics, mechanical preparation of ores, bookkeeping, drawing. They must have heard the courses on geology, civil architecture, mining law, and mining.

The candidates of all kinds must bring to the examination large drawings already made. One day is spent in making the oral examination in the different branches. On the second day is made an examination in drawing, principally in sketching after the models or after oral descriptions; also in writing short original papers on given subjects, to be finished in a short time, in connection with the performances in drawing. The third day is given to an examination of the metallurgist in practical assaying. Moreover, the candidates of all kinds must have handed in before the end of September a paper on a subject that has been given them at the time of their announcing their intention to stand the examination. The examination in each branch is declared "excellent," "good," or "satisfactory;" and if "satisfactory" is not obtained in a single branch, the candidate cannot be admitted to the practical course, but may try the examination again the next year.

Practical courses.—After the State examination, those who wish to practice their profession in Saxony must spend a whole year in practical work at the mines, or, if they are metallurgists, at the Royal Smelting Works. During the year at the mines they must practice all the different kinds of work, from the lowest to the highest, including that of overseers, two, four, eight, or twelve weeks at a time. They must go daily to the work, and remain at it during a full shift; and are paid for their labor $1 12½ a week. They are required to hand in monthly a brief journal of their daily work. They must not turn their attention to other branches of study or work than that they have selected; but they may be allowed, from time to time, to visit other mines when something special is to be learned of importance. Those who wish to enter the service of the Royal Smelting Works must work there half a year at the practical metallurgical operations, and another half year at the work of the different officials of the establishment. They must remain daily at the furnaces from six in the morning until four; they are paid at the rate of $1 12½ a week. If their work does not prove satisfactory, they are dropped from the employment of the government, and sent away from the furnaces. Those metallurgists who do not wish to join the service of the Royal Smelting Works are not allowed to spend more than eight weeks in practical work at the furnaces, and receive no pay for their work.

Subsequent employment.—Three of the best metallurgists are selected at the end of the year's course, in case their services are required, to assist the officials, and to continue at the furnaces as before. The others may receive permanent employment elsewhere, and, while waiting, are paid $1 12½ a week; or, if they must wait long, or are especially deserving, $1 50 a week.

Those who wish to practice the profession of surveying must, after the state examination and the year's practical work in the mines, perform a given trial piece of surveying, lasting several months and testing thoroughly their professional capacity. The rest at the end of the year's practice are employed in various mining or geological matters, according to each one's special fitness, until some permanent position is found for them. Those who intend to study law at the university after their mining studies must announce this intention before entering the mining academy, and must pass, either before that, or after leaving the academy, the ordinary examination for admission to the university. They are not obliged to go through with the year's practical work after the state examination.

Independent students.—The students who receive no aid from the government have to pay from $7 50 to $22 50 for each course of lectures, besides an annual fee of $11 to the academy; so that an industrious student of this class has to pay commonly $75 or $100 a year for his instruction. In order to be admitted to the academy, these students must be more than 16 years old; they must bring testimonials of good character up to the time of their coming there, as well as testimonials of fitness to pursue the intended academical studies; and if they are Saxons, they must bring their birth certificate. They are allowed to take part, if they choose, in the practical preparatory mining and metallurgical courses, and in the recitations and other exercises of the course, as well as in the yearly and state examinations; but those preparatory courses and the state examination must be specially paid for. These students are also allowed—two at a time—to have a practical course of eight weeks at the smelting works. Before leaving the academy they must announce their intention to do so, and they may have a testimonial to take away with them.

The professors.—There are 13 academical instructors, and they give in all 33 courses. They receive themselves the money that is paid for their courses by the students. Most of the instructors hold also other positions under the government connected with the mining or metallurgical interests of the state.

Breithaupt gives the courses on mineralogy, on crystallography, and on the paragenesis of minerals.

Weissbach gives two courses on elementary mechanics, (one general, the other with reference to mining;) a theoretical course, and a practical one on the construction of machines, and a course on general surveying.

Gaetzschmann gives two courses on mining.

Von Cotta gives a course on geology, one on paleontology, and one on ore deposits.

Scheerer gives a course on theoretical chemistry; one on practical chemistry,(qualitative analysis, and preparations;) one on analytical chemistry, and one on the metallurgy of iron. The last two chemical courses are accompanied by practical exercises in the laboratory.

Junge gives two courses on mathematics, (one on cubic and undetermined equations with alligation, progressions with interest, plane and spherical trigonometry, analytical geometry; the other on the elements of the differential and integral calculuses with their applications, and the principles of higher mechanics; one on descriptive geometry, and one on practical surveying. The last is accompanied by practical exercises in the mines and above ground, and in the plotting room.

Fritzsche gives a course on metallurgy, one on assaying by the dry way, and one on assaying by the wet way. The courses on assaying are accompanied by practical exercises in the metallurgical laboratory.

Heuchler gives a course on civil architecture, and the instruction in drawing.

Kressner gives a course on mining law, and one on mining business style of writing.

Richter gives a course on the blow-pipe, accompanied by practical exercises.

Proelss gives instruction in French.

Albin Weissbach (the son) gives a course on physics, and one of practical exercises in mineralogy.

Gottschalk gives instructions in bookkeeping.

The buildings and collections.—There are three buildings occupied by the academy; the principal one, the metallurgical laboratory, close by, and the chemical laboratory, at a distance from the other two. The principal building contains three lecture-rooms, a large mineralogical collection, a geological collection, a collection of machine models and a shop for making them, a large library, a shop for the sale of minerals, the dwelling of the superintendent of the academy, that of the janitor, and a few other rooms, including the academical prison. The metallurgical laboratory building contains laboratories for dry and wet assays, and for the blow-pipe practical exercises, a large room for the office work of the surveying exercises, and a lecture-room. The chemical laboratory building contains, besides the laboratory, a lecture-room and the dwelling of the professor.

The mineralogical collection is open to the students two or three days in the week; and, as the minerals are mostly in drawers, these drawers are opened for the students by one of the mineralogical professors. A separate small collection of, say, a thousand specimens of minerals is usde for the course of practical mineralogical exercises, and the students are allowed to handle them freely.

Admission to the geological collection can be obtained at almost any time, and also to that of machine models.

The library is open twice a week, and books can either be consulted there or taken out and kept several weeks.

The discipline.—The academy, under the finance department of the state, has now its own police and its own criminal court, and punishes violations of its own laws; and its discipline extends over all the students without exception.

Its laws forbid to the students immoral behavior in general; noise in the academical buildings during the lectures; gaming and drinking bouts; disturbance of the public quiet; large meetings, for pleasure, or fencing, or anything else, without special leave; extravagant living and accumulating debts; fighting; challenging; duelling; defamation; negligence of studies; encouraging others to negligence; neglect of the regulations about visiting the mines or furnaces; neglect of the special directions of mining or furnace officials; walking alone in the mines; firing off the holes drilled for blasting; selling minerals; injuring anything in the library, collections, or laboratories.

The punishments are reprimanding, either by an instructor in the name of the rest, or in the presence of the teachers' meeting, or in presence of the academical court; reporting to parents or guardian; setting tasks for whole or part of the vacations; imprisonment from one day to a week, or from one week to four, either during the daytime only, or day and night; withdrawal of state aid in whole or in part, temporarily or permanently; threatening of advice to leave the academy; advising to leave the academy, either for a time or forever; expulsion from the academy and town—either simple expulsion, or expulsion together with a public announcement of it. Moreover, a combination of several of these punishments may be inflicted. Behavior at the academy may also affect the future position of a student who enters the service of the state.

The students are allowed to have societies among themselves, provided they are not for political purposes; and the chief officer of each society must report to the academical authorities a list of its officers and members, and state its place and time of meeting. There are three such societies.

*American and English students at Freiberg.**—The following list, compiled from official records, includes all Americans and Englishmen who studied at the Freiberg academy from its foundation in 1766 to its centenial, 1866. It will serve not only to show to what extent these countries are indebted to Saxony for the education of their sons, but also to expose the swindlers who pretend to come from Freiberg. The absence from this list of the name of any American or Englishman who claims to have studied at the academy before the year 1866 will be conclusive proof of the falsity of his claim:

Name.	Country, as given at entrance.	Year of entrance.
J. Hawkins	England	1786
A. Champernowne	England	1789
Thomas Barcker	England	1790
Thomas Weaver	England	1790
John Hailstone	England	1792
John Coke	England	1793
George Mitchel	Ireland	1798
George Tuthill	England	1798
Thomas Holland	England	1798
Robert Jameson	Scotland	1800
John Henry Vivian	England	1803
Wm. H. Keating	United States, (Philadelphia)	1819
Stephen de Mornay	England	1829
Richard G. Killaly	Ireland	1830
Aristides de Mornay	England	1832
Alex. de Mornay	England	1832
Edward Steut	England	1833
Lewis Gorden	Scotland	1838
Theodore F. Moss	United States, (Philadelphia)	1838
Christian E. Cheeswright	England	1839
Frederick Bridgeman	England	1846
William L. Faber	United States	1846
Ricardo de Bayo	England	1846
Robert Pigott	England	1848
John W. Osborne	Ireland	1848
Henry Rohdewald	United States, (Baltimore)	1849
Franz Lennig	United States, (Philadelphia)	1849
Walter McClelland	Scotland	1850
John Betts	England	1850
Eugene Hilgard	United States, (Illinois)	1850
John G. Ellery	United States, (New York State)	1851
Arthur P. Vivian	England	1851
William Bradley	United States	1852
William Ketchell	United States, (New Jersey)	1852
Hillary M. Bauermann	England	1853
John Blandy	United States, (New York)	1853
John D. Eastor	United States, (Baltimore)	1853
Henry F. Blanford	England	1853
Samuel Minton	England	1853
Stewart D. Birch	England	1854
George Brush	United States, (Brooklyn)	1854
Herbert Reynolds	England	1854
John Sturz	England	1855
George P. Wall	England	1855
James Hague	United States, (Albany)	1856

* The preceding account of the Freiburg school of mines, and the following chapter on the Paris school, both the work of Mr. Lyman, are extracted from the columns of the American Journal of Mining, published in New York city. The chapter on the Berlin academy, by Mr. Ward, is taken from the same source. This list of American and English students, however, and the regulations of the Berlin academy in a subsequent page, were not originally a part of the chapters in which they are placed, but have been added by myself.

R. W. R.

List of names of Americans and Englishmen, &c.—Continued.

Name.	Country, as given at entrance.	Year of entrance.
John F. Powles	England	1856
William Powles	England	1856
Raphael Pumpelly	United States, (New York)	1856
Leopold Bierwirth	United States, (New York)	1857
Carl Froebel	United States, (New York)	1857
Louis Janin	United States, (New Orleans)	1857
Henry Janin	United States, (New Orleans)	1857
William A. Kobbe	United States, (New York)	1857
William Hustler	England	1857
James Latham	England	1857
Edwin Parkyn	England	1857
William V. Russel	England	1857
John Taylor	England	1857
Rudolph E. Werthemann	United States, (San Francisco)	1857
Frank T. Williams	England	1857
Lewis Falkenau	United States, (New York)	1858
Alfred P. Rockwell	United States	1858
William B. Richardson	Scotland	1858
John H. Boalt	United States, (Ohio)	1859
S. M. Crafts	United States, (Boston)	1859
Robert H. Lamborn	United States, (Philadelphia)	1859
Ernest Moss	United States, (New Orleans)	1859
Francis Washburn	United States, (Boston)	1859
Clement Foster	England	1859
William Galloway	Scotland	1859
Edmund B. Preston	Calcutta	1859
John F. Lewis	United States, (South Carolina)	1860
Rossiter W. Raymond	United States, (Cincinnati)	1860
Augustus Steitz	United States, (St. Louis)	1860
Louis Vogel	United States, (St. Louis)	1860
Harry Bowman	England	1861
Hugh Bowman	England	1861
Walter Crafts	United States	1861
Edward H. Jackson	United States	1861
Winfield S. Keyes	United States, (New York)	1861
Benjamin S. Lyman	United States, (Massachusetts)	1861
Eugene N. Riotte	United States	1861
James B. Smith	United States	1861
Eckley B. Coxe	United States, (Philadelphia)	1862
William S. Lee	United States, (New Jersey)	1862
William N. Symington	United States	1862
Charles J. Duval	United States, (New Orleans)	1863
Fritz Gillmann	England	1863
Philip H. Lawrence	England	1863
Charles Madge	England	1863
Louis F. Reichert	United States, (California)	1863
Augustus J. Bowie	United States, (California)	1864
George L. Bradley	United States	1864
Howard Crittenden	United States, (California)	1864
Walter L. Kane	United States	1864
Samuel F. Emmons	United States, (Boston)	1864
Marshall Hastings	United States, (California)	1864
Maximilian Koester	United States, (California)	1864
Ethebert Watts	United States, (Philadelphia)	1864
John H. Caswell	United States, (New York)	1864
J. W. Cortlan	United States	1864
William M. Curtis	United States, (New York)	1864
Thomas M. Drown	United States, (Philadelphia)	1864
William B. Foster	United States, (Pennsylvania)	1865
Robert Hazen	United States, (San Francisco)	1865
Arnold Hague	United States, (Boston)	1865
Almon D. Hodges	United States	1865

List of names of Americans and Englishmen, &c.—Continued.

Name.	Country, as given at entrance.	Year of entrance.
Edward R. Howe	United States	1865
Alexis Janin	United States, (New Orleans)	1865
Richard J. Inge	United States, (California)	1865
George J. Johnson	United States	1865
Lebeus H. Mitchell	United States, (Massachusetts)	1865
O. A. Moses	United States	1865
Lyman Nichols	United States, (Boston)	1865
Philip Oettinger	United States, (New York)	1865
John B. Pearse	United States, (Philadelphia)	1865
Edward D. Peters	United States, (Boston)	1865
William H. Pettee	United States	1865
Frederick Prime	United States, (New York)	1865
Thomas C. Raymond	United States	1865
Charles C. Rueger	United States, (California)	1865
Duncan D. Templeton	United States, (New Orleans)	1865
Sydney W. Tyler	United States, (Connecticut)	1865
Gardner F. Williams	United States	1865

Total, 124. Britons, 48; Americans, 76, of whom 33 entered in the years 1864 and 1865. The number in 1866 is said to have been still larger. Nearly or quite all the Americans in the above lists have graduated and returned to this country.

CHAPTER XXXV.

THE PARIS SCHOOL OF MINES.

The French imperial mining school (*École Impériale des Mines*) at Paris was first founded in 1783. The special object of its instruction is the mining and working of minerals; also, the study of steam machinery, the discovery and care of mineral springs, drainage and irrigation, building and running of railroads, and in general the arts and occupations connected with mineral manufactures. The instruction includes the branches of machinery, metallurgy, mineral chemistry, mineralogy, paleontology, geology, (both pure and applied to agriculture,) administrative law, mining and manufacturing laws, as well as the principles of construction needed in the practice of government mining engineers and of managers of mines and furnaces.

The students of the school, the instruction, the management and discipline, and the building and collections will be spoken of in turn.

The whole number of students is little more than a hundred, and is made up of government students, outside students, foreign students, and free students.

Government students, (elèves ingénieurs.)—The government students are taken only from the graduating class of the polytechnic school. These graduates are allowed, in the order of their school rank, to choose which branch of the government service they will go into; and it almost always happens that the full number of places in the mining school is filled by the very highest scholars. The number taken each year depends upon the demands of the service; half a dozen years ago the yearly number for several years was six, but of late it has been only three. Their age on entering the mining school averages more than twenty-one years.

After graduating at the mining school they become ordinary mining

ERRATUM.

THE following names were omitted by clerical error from the list of enrolled students at the Freiberg Academy, commencing on page 236:

James Watt,	England,	1787
Stephen D. Buchan,	England,	1836
Adolph Steinhäuser,	England,	1836
Alfred Betts,	England,	1852
Wm. T. Blanford,	England.	1854
Henry Bleidorn,	New-York.	1854
R. J. Kernick,	Cornwall,	1856
Thomas Macfarlane,	Scotland,	1856
Wadsworth Bush,	England,	1861

It should be added that the list does not include students under private tuition, nor those who may have visited Freiberg in the course of their professional education, without enrolling themselves among the members of the Academy, and regular attendants upon the lectures.—R. W. R.

engineers of the third class, and are assigned to duty in some part of France. The higher grades, to which they may rise in course of time, are: ordinary mining engineers of the second and first class, mining engineers-in-chief of the second and first class, and general mining inspectors of the second and first class. The ordinary engineers have charge of the mining and railroad interests of the government, and the inspection of steam boilers, in larger or smaller districts, according to their rank; the engineers-in-chief have, in like manner, the oversight of several such districts; and five of the general inspectors, who are in all only about a dozen in number, have charge of the five great divisions of the whole of France. Moreover, the care of the Paris mining school, and of the two other lower mining schools of France, and other special duties, give occupation to a few of the mining engineers of almost every grade. The whole number of mining engineers in the service of the government is about 130, and there are about 20 more on unlimited leave of absence, or in the service of companies, making about 150 in all.

The government students have a salary of 100 francs a month, and, during journeys, 150 francs a month, besides an outfit of 100 francs, and eight francs for every day of travelling.

Outside students, (elèves externes.)—The outside students are intended to become managers of mines and furnaces in the owners' interest. They are admitted to the school on a competitive examination, and have the same instruction and practical exercises as the government students. A preparatory year of instruction is also provided for those who wish to become outside students, but are not fitted for admission to the studies of the first year.

A candidate for admission to the preparatory year, with the view of becoming an outside student, must be French by birth or by naturalization, and at least 16 years old, and at most 22 on the foregoing 1st of January. His application must be sent to the minister of agriculture, commerce, and public works by the 1st of September, and be accompanied by a birth certificate, and, if need be, his naturalization papers; by a certificate of good character from the authorities of his dwelling-place; by a physician's certificate of having been vaccinated, or having had the small-pox, and, if need be, by an official certificate that the preliminary examination is unnecessary. This preliminary examination is made before the middle of October by government mining engineers designated for the purpose, and must be passed by all candidates, except those who have passed the examination at the end of the first year of the polytechnic school. The final examination is made at Paris, in the first half of November, by the council of the mining school. The candidate must write and spell well, and must know arithmetic, algebra, geometry, plane trigonometry, analytical geometry, descriptive geometry, and physics, and must be able to draw from copies. There are commonly perhaps 15 French students following the studies of the preparatory year.

Candidates for admission as outside students to the studies of the first year must be French, in like manner, and a year older than the candidates for the preparatory year—that is, about 18 at least on the opening of the school term in November. They must also hand in their application in the same way together with similar certificates; and all must likewise pass a preliminary examination, except those who are graduates of the polytechnic school, or are licentiates of the mathematical sciences, or have passed the examination at the end of the preparatory year. The final examination is made by the council of the school in the first half of November. The requirements are good handwriting and good spelling, a knowledge of the differential and integral calculus, of mechanics, of descriptive geometry and its applications, of those parts of physics that treat more especially of gases and of optical instruments, of general chemistry, and geometrical drawing, and water-color washing. Before the examination each candidate must hand in at the school a page of French written from dictation, five drawings of descriptive geometry, (exercises on the straight line and the plane, solution of three principal cases of trihedral angles, tangent plane to a surface of revolution, section of an oblique cone by a plane, development of a truncated cone, intersection of two cylinders,) three drawings of stone cutting, (an oblique door in a battering wall, a straight descending vault, an unclosed winding staircase,) a drawing of carpentry, (a roof of truss with all the pieces in detail,) a washed drawing of a screw and nut shaded.

About 20 outside students are admitted every year to the studies of the first year, and about 12 every year receive diplomas at the end of their studies.

Foreign students, (elèves étrangers.)—Foreigners are permitted to share in the instruction of the school in all its branches, including the preparatory year; and are admitted, without examination, on the simple recommendation of the ambassador at Paris of each applicant's government. Of course it is desirable for all students to have the same fitting and age as the French students have, in order to profit by the studies of the school. Foreign students can have places in the labratory and in the drawing-room, only in case places happen to be vacant there. They may pass the same examinations as the government students, and are expected to pass one of them each year; and at the end of their studies they may have a certificate of the manner in which they have studied, and of their examination marks; but no diploma is given them, and they have no right to practice the profession in France, except as assistants of French engineers. The foreign students are subject to the same discipline as the French, but are less cared about and less closely watched over, so that they do pretty much as they like. Half a dozen years ago, the number of foreign students in the preparatory year was perhaps a dozen; in the first and second year of the regular course, about half a dozen, and in the third year, three or four. There are commonly two or three Americans among the foreign students of the school.

Free students, (elèves libres.)—Besides the above-mentioned students, others, called free students, are allowed to take such portions of the school instructions as they may choose, but are required to pass at least one examination each year. They have much the same privilges as the foreign students, and, like them, receive no diploma at the end of their studies. The free students are few, perhaps a dozen in the whole school.

The instruction.—The instruction is three years long, (besides the preparatory year,) and is given in lectures, (without recitations,) practical exercises in chemistry, drawing, mineralogy and paleontology, and in occasional excursions. With French generosity, it is made quite free of cost to all the students, French and foreign alike; and the lectures on mineralogy, geology and paleontology are open to the public. The students of the second and third years have to travel in mining regions in their long summer vacations.

The students are not left to grope in their ignorance for a fitting arrangement of their studies, but a well-planned regular course of study is prescribed, and things are learned in their proper connection, a matter of great importance.

Preparatory year.—The instruction of the prepatory year begins at the middle of November and lasts until the end of summer.

Professor Haton de la Goupilliere (ordinary engineer of the first class) lectures on the differential and integral culculus and in mathematics.

Professor Fuchs (ordinary engineer, second class) lectures on descriptive geometry and the parts of physics that treat specifically of dynamical electricity and optics.

Professor Moissenet (ordinary engineer, first class) lectures on general chemistry.

The students of the preparatory year also practice geometrical drawing and water-color washing under Mr. Amoroux, the drawing-master of the school.

First and second years.—The lecture courses of the first and second years are given together; that is, some of them are two years long, and the students who enter the school one year begin with the second part of the course of those who entered the previous year; but the lecture courses are so arranged that some begin one year and some the next. The courses that are only one year long alternate with each other, so as to be equal in number each year. It is necessary, therefore, to be at the school at least two years in order to get the most important part of the instruction. Ten lectures of about 16 hours in all are given each week, and the courses last from the middle of November until the middle of April.

Gruner, (general inspector, second class,) professor of metallurgy, gives a two-year lecture course, that begins the even years, (1860, for example,) with general metallurgy, furnaces, fuels, and the like, and iron; and the next year takes up copper, lead, silver, gold, quicksilver, tin, antimony, bismuth, and zinc.

Rivot, (engineer-in-chief, second class,) professor of mineral chemistry, gives a two-year lecture course, that begins in the odd years, with the metalloids, alcalis, and earths, together with cements, mortars, mineral waters, soils, and manures; and the next year treats of the metals. He has also charge of the laboratory, where each student works in periods of three weeks at a time, alternating with the drawing exercises. In the laboratory the students begin with making preparations of different bodies, and then make analyses and dry assays. A written account of the laboratory work is required from the student.

Daubrée (engineer-in-chief, first class) is professor of mineralogy, in the place held half a dozen years ago by the much lamented De Sénarmont. The lecture course is only one year long, but it is repeated every year, and it is expected that the students generally will follow it two years running before getting the needful practical familiarity with the minerals. A few, however, are able to pass the examination satisfactorily at the end of the first year. Besides the lectures, there are, for some weeks before the examination, practical exercises in the presence of the professor.

Callon (engineer-in-chief, first class) is professor of mining and machinery, and gives a one-year course on each of these subjects in alternate years, beginning the one in mining on the odd years, and the one on machinery the even years.

Elie de Beaumont (general inspector, first class) is professor of geology, but he gives only four or five of the lectures himself, and the rest are given by his colleague, Mr. De Chancourtois (engineer-in-chief, first class.) The lecture course is but one year long, but it is repeated every year, and the examination comes at the end of the second year, and hearing the lectures is only required that year. Besides these lectures, there are, in the spring, weekly excursions of a whole day in the neighborhood with both these professors. After the spring examinations are over, there is every year, in the beginning of June, a geological excursion of a whole week to some distant part of France, as, for example, to the Ardennes, or to the Jura. On this yearly excursion, Elie de Beaumont himself takes the lead, and does it most admirably; long may he be spared the strength for such fatiguing labors! The party numbers some forty, counting the professors and two or three of their assistants and friends and the students, to all of whom transportation is furnished free.

Bayle (engineer-in-chief, second class) is professor of paleontology. He began with paleozoic fossils in 1859; and in 1860 took up secondary fossils; and in 1861, probably, went on with tertiary fossils, making really a three-year course of it. The student, however, is required to follow this course only through the first year; but as the examination does not come until the end of the second year, together with the geological examination, he finds it to his interest, if only for that reason, to hear the lectures of both years.

Professor Fuchs (ordinary engineer, second class) teaches surveying, with practical exercises above ground and in the catacombs underground, in the summer between the first and second years lectures.

The drawing exercises of the first and second year under Mr. Amouroux, consist of machine drawing from copies and from real machines, plotting, mapping; and later, in the second year, in making original drawings in solution of given problems in mining, machinery or metallurgy.

Third year.—The lectures of the third year are comparatively few in number, and mostly on subjects of less interest and importance to foreign mining engineers than the lectures of the other two years.

Couche (engineer-in-chief, first class) is professor of construction, and lectures on railroads and machine construction.

Professor Lamé-Fleurs (engineer-in-chief, second class) lectures on mining laws.

Professor Delesse (engineer-in-chief, second class) lectures on agriculture, drainage and irrigation. Excursions are sometimes made to large farms in the country.

The drawing exercises of the third year are original designs connected with the solution of problems in mining, machinery or metallurgy.

Mr. Schlessinger teaches German to the students of every year; but the study of it is optional, and few study it after the first few days.

Mr. Elwell teaches English, in like manner, to those of any year who choose to study it.

Examinations.—The examinations at the ends of the lecture courses are both written and oral, and a week is given to the examination in each course. The written examination takes place in the library, and two or three questions are given to all the students together for each to answer. Each student may make use of his lecture notes or of any books he may bring with him or find in the library; and, if he wishes, he may work upon the answers all through the day until four o'clock; but the time required for his work is noted. The questions in metallurgy, one year, to give an example, were how to adjust the charges of two iron furnaces in order to produce good foundry iron in one and forge iron in the other, at less than certain given prices, with three ores, and forge cinders of certain given composition and cost, and with labor of a certain given cost. The geological questions, one year, required a description of the coal measures proper, their characteristic structure, composition and fossils, and their difference from other coal formations; also an account of the principal conditions in which limestone occurs on the globe, and the origin of different limerocks; also an account of the different tin ore deposits in the world, and the conjectures as to their probable mode of formation. The written examination in mineralogy consisted, under De Sénarmont, of crystallographic computation. In the oral examinations the students are examined one at a time by the professor of each branch and a couple of other gentlemen, and the questioning lasts from ten minutes to half an hour. In mineralogy the student is asked the names of six or eight materials placed before him. In geology and paleontology, he is tried in the same way with a few fossils as well as questioned on geological points, and required to explain a specimen or two of ore veins. The examinations of the second year include, also, the subject of the first year's lectures.

Journeys.—Besides the geological and agricultural excursions already mentioned, the students of the second and third years have to travel for at least 100 days in the second half, that is, the summer of those years; commonly two or three students together. They have to make known their plans beforehand, and have them approved of; and after their return, have to hand in a journal of what they have seen. Both French and foreign students are furnished with circular letters of introduction to the government mining engineers, and to all managers of mines and furnaces in France, who take pains to show all needful attentions to the students. In this way there is really as good a chance to see mines and furnaces to advantage as if the school were placed in a mining region, and a long period of time were specially set apart for this purpose. At the end of their studies those government students who have sepcially distinguished themselves at the school are allowed to travel for a time in foreign countries.

Management.—The mining school is under the control of the ministry of agriculture, commerce, and public works, and is managed by a general inspector of the first class, [now Mr. Combes,] who has the title of director of the school. Under him, a general inspector of the second class, [now Mr. Gruner,] or an engineer-in-cheif, is charged with the direction of the studies and the details of the management, and has the title of inspector of the school. The council of the school, which meets at least once in two months, consists of the director and the inspector of the school, of two general inspectors, and of the professors; and it deliberates on the standing of the students, and the cases of extreme punishment, and arranges the lecture courses. Another council, called the improvement council, consists of the director of the school, a general inspector of the first class, two general inspectors of the second class, the inspector of the school, and two of the professors. It meets at least once a year, and its business is to consider the merits of the work of the students taken as a whole, and to propose improvements in the instruction of the school.

Punishments.—The penalties that can be inflicted on the students are: a reprimand given either privately or in presence of their comrades, by the professors, by the inspector, or by the director of the school; temporary exclusion, for a week or fortnight, from the rooms for study, and from the laboratory or from the school; public mention; censure by the council, with or without public mention; delay of promotion from one class to the next; final expulsion from the school.

Hours.—The lectures are given at half-past nine in the morning and at noon, and there are in the first and second year, commonly, two each day. The students are required to sign their name in a register before each lecture, and at half-past three in the afternoon. They may leave the school between the two lectures, or from half-past eleven to twelve, for their breakfast; but they must stay there from noon until signing at half-past three. They can stay later if they like, and some work at their drawings by lamplight.

Rank.—The rank of the students is determined by their merit, taking account of their industry, their examinations, and their capacity shown in the practical exercises, and the journals of their journeys.

Dress.—There is a uniform prescribed for the government students, but none for the others. The undress uniform is simply three narrow bands of gold lace around the cap.

The building and collections.—The school with all its appurtenances is contained within one building, which contains also the dwellings of the director and inspector of the school; but none of the students lodge at the school. Certain portions of the school have been built within the last half dozen years, and it is now handsomely furnished with laboratories, drawing-rooms, and rooms for the library and the mineralogical, geological, metallurgical and machine model collections. The collections of fossils and minerals are very large and fine; and they are open to the students and to the public on certain days in the week. The specimens, except the duplicates, are in glass cases on the tables, so that they can be easily seen but not handled. There is a small collection of fossils and minerals that is always accessible to the students, and can be freely handled. The large library is open daily and all day.

The collections of the museum of natural history at the plant garden are also open to the public on certain days of the week, and are therefore available, especially the fine collection of minerals, for the study of mining students. There are other mineralogical collections likewise accessible, in the city, as well as libraries, machine models, laboratories, for private instruction under excellent chemists, and other valuable facilities for study; to say nothing of the great benefit, both directly to the student and indirectly through its effect on the professors, of the presence in the city of a very large number of scientific men.

Further details of the organization of the school may be found in the laws and decrees of the *annales des mines* for 1856; and details of the examinations for admission, in the same for 1861 and 1867.

CHAPTER XXXVI.

THE PRUSSIAN ROYAL SCHOOL OF MINES AT BERLIN—BY WILLARD P. WARD, M. E.

Of this excellent institution but little is known in this country in comparison with the wide reputation of the Freiberg, Clausthal, and Paris schools. The main reasons for this are the comparative recentness of its foundation and the fact that it is not situated in a mining region. The practical part of a mining engineer's education is probably best gained by studying at a school situated in some great mining region, where he will see nothing but mines and hear nothing but mining matters discussed.

On the other hand, there are many things which it is necessary for an educated miner to know which he can learn just as well in one place as another, so far as the advantages of location are concerned. These are the kindred sciences of chemistry, geology, mineralogy, the theory of the treatment of ores, assaying, &c., which are necessary to a rational system of mining.

The large attendance of the excellent mining schools connected with Columbia College, the Troy Polytechnic, and others, shows that the American people appreciate the value of these sciences to the mining engineer.

As every young man who is about to enter upon the study of mining, for one reason or another, cannot go to Europe to spend three or four years there in prosecuting his studies, it is a fine thing for the country to have these schools, which I believe to be excellent; and far be it from me to say anything to injure them in any way. Still some—partly because they appreciate the advantages of a European residence, and partly because they consider the advantages to be enjoyed there greater than those offered by the schools of this country—will go to Europe to study; and to each a knowledge of the merits of the Berlin school may be of value.

The advantage of being a member of this school consists not only in being able to hear the lectures and have the valuable advice and friendship of the professors, but it gives one free entrance to all the mines and smelting works of Prussia. So great is the courtesy of the Germans that almost anybody, on making proper application, can see nearly all their works; but a letter of introduction from the director of the Berlin school will secure a degree of civility which under other circumstances would be wanting, and admission to certain works which would otherwise not be shown at all, or shown in such a way that one would be but very little the wiser after seeing them.

With regard to the lectures it may be said that they are all of the best. The Prussian government has spared no pains or money to give the students all the opportunities possible for obtaining a thorough theoretical and, so far as models and collections can be of assistance, practical knowledge of his profession. The student has the advantage in Berlin of being able to attend the lectures of Gustav Rose on mineralogy, whose name is almost as familliar to mineralogists as that of his lamented brother, Henry Rose, is to chemists; of Beyrich on geology, who is regarded by many in Germany as a second Cuvier in the realms of paleontology; and to make use of the large mineralogical and paleontological collections of the largest university of Germany.

The director of the school and professor of mining, Hauchecorne, is a man of very extended practical knowledge in his branch. He has been for many years a mining superintendent in Westphalia and Upper Silesia.

Professor Kerl, on general smelting and assaying, is sufficiently well known, even in America, to render anything I could say of him superfluous. Professor Wedding, on iron smelting, has a large experience in his subject, but is probably better known in England than in this country. Professor Rammelsberg, on mineral chemistry, and Professor Hoffman, on general chemistry, are professionally, and through their books, well known in this country. Professor Werner, on machinery, is regarded as authority in Germany. The large and well-appointed laboratory is under the charge of Dr. Finkler, one of the most promising of the former pupils of Henry Rose. There are but few, if any, other schools which possess such corps of instructors.

In the summer vacation trips are made to various mining regions by the professors of metallurgy and mining accompanied by the students, the travelling expenses of the party being paid by the government.

To the above general account I add the following, translated from official publications, for which I am indebted to Professor Bruno Kerl, of Berlin:

REGULATIONS OF THE ROYAL ACADEMY OF MINES.

§ 1. *Object.*—The Royal Academy of Mines, at Berlin, is established for the purpose of affording to those who would educate themselves in the management of mining, metallurgical, or saline works, opportunity to obtain the necessary professional knowledge.

§ 2. *Control and administration.*—The academy is under the general control of a director, appointed by the King, and responsible to the minister of commerce, trade, and public works. The financial and statistical departments (bureau work) are conducted by officials of the ministerial department of mines, furnaces, and salines.

§ 3. *The curatorium.*—This consists of five members or curators, appointed by the King, and assists in the arrangement of the organization, the determination of the various courses, and the nomination of instructors.

§ 4. *Duties of the director.*—Besides the general management of the institution, the director has the following special functions:

1. The issuance of permissions to enjoy the benefits of the academy, according to the conditions in §§ 10–12.

2. The superintendence of the systematic progress of lectures and instruction.

3. The control of collections and apparatus, (for which the instructors in each branch are primarily responsible,) and the preservation of buildings and personal property.

4. The preparation and transmission of estimates.

6. The procurement of apparatus, furniture, &c., and the receipt of moneys within the limits of the estimates.

6. The transmission of annual accounts, and the reception and editing of notes and reports.

7. The rendition of annual reports.

8. The convocation of regular instructors, to consult upon the plan of instruction, and other matters relating thereto, as often as may be required, and at least semi-annually.

§ 5. *Regular instruction.*—Regular instructors (professors) are appointed by the minister of commerce, trade, and public works, on the nomination of the director and approval of the curatorium, for the principal subjects included in the courses, and are bound to deliver certain lectures and give certain instruction in their respective branches.

§ 6. *Extraordinary instruction.*—The director may also, with the consent of the curatorium, grant permission to any regular instructor of the academy, to any professor or teacher of other institutions of learning, and to other duly qualified persons, to lecture upon special subjects.

§ 7. *General plan of instruction.*—The lectures at the academy continue from the 15th of October to the 15th of the following August, with an Easter vacation of three weeks.

§ 8. *Subjects.*—The following subjects are included in the plan of regular instruction: mines, salines, general metallurgy, metallurgy of iron, mechanics, machines, surveying, drawing, construction, projections and shadows, recitations and colloquies upon mineralogy, geognosy, and paleontology, and on mathematical processes, mining law, mineral chemistry, iron founding, mechanical technology of the metals, applied chemistry in the arts, blow-pipe assaying, general chemical analysis, with practical instruction in the laboratory, assaying in the dry and humid ways, theoretically and practically, &c., &c. A catalogue of the lectures and lecture fees is published semi-annually.

§ 9. *Reception of students.*—Permission to attend the academy is granted by the director, according to the conditions of §§ 10–12, upon application made during the first 14 days of the semester, and accompanied by the necessary attestations. This permission is endorsed upon the application and given to the student by the registrar of the academy.

§ 10. *Qualifications of students.*—The following have a right to be admitted to the academy:

1. Those students of mines, furnaces, and salines, who desire to devote themselves to the Prussian government service.

2. The matriculated students of the Royal Frederick William University of Berlin.

3. The matriculated students of the Royal Academy of Practical Arts, (*Gewerbe Akademie.*)

§ 11. *Admission of other students.*—The director may also grant to other persons the permission to attend such lectures as they may name in their applications.

§ 12. *Applications.*—The students admitted according to §§ 10 and 11, note, in the proper column of the application blank, the lectures which they desire to attend during the semester, and deliver it to the registrar for signature.

§ 13. *Fees.*—Within four weeks after the beginning of the semester, (half year,) the applications (§ 12) are to be handed in, the fees paid into the academical treasury, and the students are to report themselves to the instructors.

§ 14. No instructor is allowed to accept the application of a student, or admit him to lectures and recitations, before the fee has been paid and receipt endorsed upon the application-blank, except where fees are remitted. (§§ 19, 20.)

§ 15. *Fees.*—Lectures and recitations are partly for fees (privation) and partly gratuitous, (public.)

§ 16. In the case of private lectures included in the regular courses, the fee shall not exceed one thaler (73 cents gold) for each weekly hour per semester. The fee for a course of lectures occupying five hours of each week through the half-year, for instance, would be five thalers. Fees for instruction in drawing and practice in the laboratory are subject to special arrangements.

§ 17. The fees for extraordinary lectures are fixed by the instructors in accordance with the curatorium. The rule adopted for ordinary lectures is in general, however, not to be exceeded.

§ 18. The fees paid in for extraordinary instruction are received by the respective instructors from the treasury at the end of the semester.

§ 19. *Remissions.*—In cases of personal indigence, attested by the proper authorities, the minister of commerce, trade, and public works may, on the application of the director, remit to native students half the fees for ordinary instruction. There is no remission of the fees for special courses of lectures.

§ 20. The remission is endorsed by the director on the application-blank; and the student binds himself thereupon, in writing, to refund to the treasury of the academy the amount so remitted within six years after leaving the institution.

§ 21. *Refunding of fees.*—Fees are refunded to students when the lectures do not take place, or are broken off during the first half of the semester, or are held at different times from those first announced. The amount so refunded must be drawn from the treasury during the first four months of the current semester, otherwise the claim is void.

§ 22. *Certificates.*—Remarks as to the degree of industry and proficiency manifested by the student are entered at the close of each semester in the proper columns of the application-blank. At the request of the students the director will issue, upon surrender of the application-blank, a certificate as to his conduct and progress while in attendance at the academy.

Students who have attended the academy for at least two semesters may be subjected to an examination and receive certificates of their attainments. With reference to this point the following rules are established:

REGULATIONS FOR THE EXAMINATIONS OF THE ROYAL ACADEMY OF MINES AT BERLIN.

§ 1. The students of the Royal Academy of Mines may, upon leaving the same, for the purpose of obtaining proofs of their acquirements, undergo an examination, the result of which will be embodied in an official certificate, made out for them.

§ 2. Only those students can apply for such an examination who have attended the lectures or taken part in the practical exercises of the academy for at least two semesters. Nothing more is necessary for admission to examination than proof of such attendance.

§ 3. The examination may cover all the sciences and accomplishments taught at the academy. The candidates have to name those branches in which they desire to be examined.

§ 4. The commission conducting the examination consists of at least three members, including the director of the academy as president, an the instructors in those branches covered by the examination.

§ 5. The examination is both written and oral. The candidate must present, upon a subject named by the commission, a written thesis, for the preparation of which a period of six weeks is allowed him. If he is to be examined in several branches, he may choose the one to which the subject of the thesis shall belong. The candidate is also at liberty, however, to present, besides this one obligatory work, other written productions or drawings. All work so presented is to be accompanied with the written assurance that it has been performed without assistance; and the thesis must be in the candidate's own handwriting.

§ 6. Applications for examination must be addressed in writing to the director of the academy at least six weeks before the close of the semester, and accompanied with the necessary proof of two semesters' attendance. The examining commission then determines the subject for the thesis, so that this may be prepared during the vacation. The completed work is to be handed in to the commission within the six weeks before mentioned, a discretionary prolongation of which period is only to be made by the commission in cases of extraordinary hindrance. The oral examination takes place at the beginning of the following semester.

§ 7. The examining commission prepares a diploma or certificate concerning the result of the oral examination and the examination of the written thesis. These degrees of proficiency are recognized and entered on diplomas with the words, "*mit Auszeichnung*," (with distinction,) "*gut*," (well,) and "*genügend*," (pretty well, or sufficiently.) Each examiner proposes the verdict in his own department, and the question is determined which grade of proficiency shall be certified by the vote of a majority of the commission. For those branches in which the candidate has not borne examination even "sufficiently" well, no entry whatever is made.

§ 8. The candidate is free to apply after the lapse of half a year, to be re-examined in those branches in which he failed on the first trial; but after a second failure no further application will be granted.

§ 9. The examination fee, payable to the academical treasury when the application is made, is 10 thalers for an examination covering not more than four branches. For every additional branch an additional fee of three thalers is required; but the whole fee can in no case exceed 20 thalers.

The following are the regular courses of lectures for the winter semester of 1868–'69:

	Lectures and instructors.	Half-yearly fee.
1.	Mining Technology—five lectures weekly by Bergrath Hauchecorne	5 thalers.
2.	Technology of Saltworks—one lecture weekly by Bergrath Hauchecorne	1 "
3.	General Metallurgy—four lectures weekly by Professor Kerl	4 "
4.	Metallurgy of Iron—four lectures weekly by Bergrath Wedding	4 "
5.	Founding and Moulding—three lectures weekly by Dr. Dürre	4 "
6.	Chemical Technology—two lectures weekly by Professor Kerl	2 "
7.	General Assaying—six lectures weekly by Professor Kerl	9 "
8.	Blowpipe Assaying—two lectures weekly by Professor Kerl	3 "
9.	Assaying of Iron—three lectures weekly by Bergrath Wedding	4½ "
10.	Petrography—four lectures weekly by Professor Beyrich	4 "
11.	Geology, with special attention to the stratified formations—four lectures weekly by Professor Beyrich	4 "
12.	The Geological Formation of the Globe—one lecture weeky by Dr. Lossen.	Gratis.
13.	On Volcanoes—one lecture weekly by Professor Roth	Gratis.
14.	Mineralogical Repetitions—four lectures weekly by Professor G. Rose	Gratis.
15.	Mineralogical Exercises—four lectures weekly by Dr. Eck	4 thalers.
16.	Chemistry of Minerals—three lectures weekly by Professor Rammelsberg	Gratis.
17.	Repetitions of Analysis of Minerals—four lectures weekly by Dr. Finkener.	Gratis.
18.	Practical Instruction in the Analysis of Minerals—(*a*,) quantitative; five hours daily by Dr. Finkener	20 thalers.
	(*b*,) qualitative; four hours weekly by Dr. Finkener	8 "
19	Analytical Geometry—five lectures weekly by Professor Bertram	5 "
20.	Mechanical Science—six lectures weekly by M. Hormann	6 "
21.	Applied Mechanics—six lectures weekly by M. Hormann	6 "
22.	Surveying of Mines—four lectures weekly by Berg-Assessor Kauth	4 "
23.	Instructions in Drawing—eight lessons weekly by Berg-Assessor Kauth	Gratis.
24.	Laws of Mines—two lectures weekly by Geh. Oberbergrath Ackenbach	Gratis.

Bergrath (mining councillor) Hauchecorne is the present director of the academy.

CHAPTER XXXVII.

THE SCHOOL OF MINES AT CLAUSTHAL, PRUSSIA.

Since the annexation of the kingdom of Hanover to Prussia, the old and famous academy at Clausthal, in the Hartz mountains, has been, so to speak, dismantled. Some of the best professors have been called to Berlin; the former director (the celebrated mineralogist, Roemer) is dead; and little that is important remains of the school except its excellent courses of practice in mining and metallurgy. These are retained, because the location of Clausthal, in the midst of an ancient and still actively worked mining region, renders it peculiarly suitable for such practical instruction as cannot be imparted at the Berlin school. Prussia maintains, therefore, at Berlin a school of theory, and at Clausthal a school of practice. The method pursued at the latter place will appear from the following description:

The object of the practical course is to impart to the student a complete insight into all particulars and details of every branch of mining and smelting. This is effected—

1. By examination of all interesting mines, dressing and smelting works of the Upper Hartz.
2. By inspection of all the apparatus and machinery used.
3. By study of different processes in actual operation and of their proper manipulations.
4. By actual experience in every department as a workman.

The course begins in the first week after Easter, and lasts six months, of which two are devoted to mining, two to metallurgy, and two to the study of dressing-works and processes, including hydraulic engineering.

In all these departments, complete theoretical instruction is given at the academy in Clausthal. The practical course in each department is placed under the supervision of a mining official of high degree, as teacher, who assigns the pupils, in squads of two or three, to subordinate officials, connected with the administration of mines and furnaces in operation. Under the guidance of his special instructor the student enters the mines every morning, (Saturday and Sunday excepted,) and is made to take note of everything in their operations. Beginning with the simplest manipulations and proceeding to the most intricate and difficult, all is explained to him. The peculiarities of special cases before him, difficulties and the means by which they are overcome, the improvements which progress in the art of mining has effected, are all illustrated by actual examples, such as can only be furnished in mines of great antiquity, and among a population to whom this profession has been for centuries hereditary. In this manner about six weeks are spent in one or two mines, each of which is a labyrinth of shafts, drifts, and stopes, and an epitome itself of the history as well as the science of mining. The student having during this period obtained a general knowledge of the subject, and, by manual labor, acquired a certain necessary familiarity with details, he spends the next fortnight under the same guidance in excursions to the important copper, lead, iron and zinc mines of the Upper Hartz.

The courses in dressing ores, hydraulic engineering, and metallurgy, are similarly conducted. In the latter the student takes part, with the assistance of the friendly workmen, in the whole course of the metallurgical processes, and finally produces, with his own hands, the pure silver bar from the ore. Copper, iron, zinc, and lead furnaces, sulphuric acid, alum and copperas works, and the art of the assayer, are all made subjects of attention, and that familiarity with their practical operations is acquired which doubles the value of subsequent theoretical study.

Saturdays are given to the sketching of machinery, and to explanations by the instructor of those points not fully made clear during the week.

The Clausthal administration has earned the gratitude of all by its liberality in this arrangement. We say gratitude, for the sacrifice of time and valuable labor involved in such a system has been incurred only for the good of science. Of this no one will entertain a doubt when we state that the fees paid by the student for this six months' practical course amount to $13 in American gold.

APPENDIX.

Statistics of bullion, ores, &c., at San Francisco, for the year ending December 31, 1868.

IMPORTS OF TREASURE.

The imports of treasure (exclusive of those from Victoria, which are included in the receipts from coastwise ports,) for the past five years have been as follows:

Year	Amount	Year	Amount
1864	$1,845,909	1867	$2,252,851
1865	1,872,697	1868	2,815,961
1866	1,298,311		

RECEIPTS OF TREASURE FROM THE INTERIOR.

The receipts of treasure from the northern and southern mines of our State during the past five years have been as follows:

	Uncoined.	Coined.	Total.
1864	$40,130,090	$5,330,325	$45,460,415
1865	41,903,649	4,361,951	46,265,600
1866	39,299,850	4,565,359	43,865,209
1867	43,807,656	4,812,788	48,620,444
1868	39,318,042	6,614,694	45,932,734

RECEIPTS OF BULLION.

The receipts of bullion from Washoe, Esmeralda, and Reese river (Nevada State) for the past five years have been as follows:

1864	$15,797,585	1867	$18,000,000
1865	15,181,877	1868	15,250,000
1866	15,215,218		

RECAPITULATION.

The imports, coastwise receipts, (including Victoria, V. I.,) and receipts from northern and southern mines, (including Nevada State,) during the year 1868, were as follows:

Imports	$2,815,961
Receipts coastwise (including Victoria)	3,757,137
From northern and southern mines	45,932,736
Total for 1868	52,505,834
Total for 1867	56,726,856
Decrease 1868	4,221,022

TREASURE EXPORTS.

The exports of treasure during the years 1867 and 1868, respectively, were as follows:

To—	1867.	1868.
China	$9,039,530 07	$6,192,995 40
Chile	723,450 97	....
Central American ports	654,498 85	728,474 00
England	5,905,799 49	6,226,097 68
France	1,659,951 00	1,091,343 26
Japan	648,049 52	777,459 46
Mexico	34,000 00	13,000 00
New York	29,356,424 67	21,104,611 17
Sandwich Islands	47,032 32	89,110 00
Society Islands	500 00	....
Vancouver's Island	155,000 00	135,000 00
Total	48,224,236 89	36,358,090 97
Add net duties	7,622,827 00	7,760,411 16
	55,847,063 89	44,118,502 13
Decrease 1868	....	11,728,561 76

The recapitulation for 1868 is as follows:

	Steamers east.	China, &c.	Total.
Gold bars	$16,302,848 98	$1,262,375 92	$17,565,224 90
Silver bars	10,966,672 75	2,935,421 79	13,902,094 54
Gold coin	1,894,004 38	748,868 05	2,642,872 43
Gold dust	....	30,606 60	30,606 60
Mexican dollars	....	2,217,292 50	2,217,292 50
Total	29,163,526 11	7,194,564 86	36,358,090 97

MINT STATISTICS.

The coinage of the United States branch mint for the month of December has been $2,340,000 gold and $82,000 silver; together, $2,422,000. The coinage for the year, monthly, as compared with the year 1867, has been as follows:

Months.	Silver.	Gold.	Total coin.	Total.
			1868.	1867.
January	$17,000	$80,000	$97,000	$124,000
February	120,000	520,000	640,000	1,022,000
March	60,000	515,000	575,000	978,535
April	15,000	695,000	710,000	1,895,000
May	54,000	660,000	714,000	2,505,000
June	57,000	865,000	922,000	1,420,000
July	50,000	2,305,000	2,355,000	1,152,000
August	70,000	1,395,000	1,465,000	2,380,000
September	10,000	2,445,000	2,455,000	1,989,000
October	25,000	2,390,000	2,415,000	2,361,000
November	47,000	2,550,000	2,597,000	2,369,000
December	82,000	2,340,000	2,422,000	1,900,000
Total	607,000	16,760,000	17,367,000	20,095,535

In the first months of the year, when freights were low to the eastward, and the supply of coin abundant, the disposition was to ship bullion. In the latter months of the year coin became scarce and eastern credits full. The mint, therefore, absorbed the larger proportion of the supply, and the operations have been immense. Every 60 days an amount has been turned out equal to the whole projected capacity of the mint for a year when it was built. In the last two months there has been silver coinage from deposits of White Pine bullion. The total supply of bullion reported has been, for the last three years:

Bullion.	1866.	1867.	1868.
Sent to mint	$17,617,096	$19,265,376	$17,367,000
Export gold bars per steamer	23,707,064	18,222,246	16,302,849
Export gold bars per sail	1,268,460	1,404,927	1,262,376
Export gold dust per sail	20,000	62,770	30,606
Export silver per steamer	9,039,036	9,759,890	10,966,671
Export silver per sail	3,946,114	5,468,370	2,935,422
Total	55,597,770	54,183,593	48,864,924

The decline in the supply of bullion is due to the falling off in the product of the Washoe mines. In the last quarter of the year, however, the White Pine region has become very productive. The leading mine there, the Eberhardt, has sent down over $500,000, of which a considerable portion has passed through the Refining Company.

The exports of bullion have been less than last year, the falling off having been greatest in the last six months of the year. The silver bars have been rather less abundant, and the gold has gone rather to the mint than abroad. In the first part of the year the low freights caused the shipments to be considerable, leading, with other operating causes, to a scarcity of coin in the autumn. The opposition steamers being then withdrawn, freights advanced and the bullion was turned into the mint. This movement is seen in the following table, showing the monthly deposits of gold at the mint, the monthly exports, and the range for bars:

Months.	Gold.		Prices of bars.
	Minted.	Exported.	
January	$80,000	$2,715,692 12	900 to 910
February	520,000	1,215,400 61	910 to 920
March	515,000	2,039,925 22	910 to 920
April	695,000	1,604,651 11	890 to 900
May	660,000	2,267,520 95	880 to 900
June	865,000	1,578,139 94	880 to 900
July	2,305,000	1,851,846 70	880 to 890
August	1,395,000	1,442,501 31	880 to 890
September	2,445,000	750,906 31	860 to 890
October	2,390,000	699,152 21	830 to 870
November	2,550,000	585,458 51	840 to 860
December	2,340,000	813,827 21	850 to 860
Total	16,760,000	17,565,022 20	860 to 865

Thus, for the whole year, about half the gold bullion was sent to the mint, a good deal of it extracted from the silver refined for the China market by the San Francisco Refinery Company, and the other half exported. Of the deposits at the mint the San Francisco Assaying and Refining Company made $9,400,000 of gold, and $225,000 of silver; together, $9,625,000—or more than half the whole. In the first six months only $3,928,000 was sent to the mint, and $11,431,676 was exported; in the last six months, $12,632,000 went to the mint, and $6,133,356 only was exported—reversing the operation. The coin thus turned out by the mint was greatly needed in the autumn months. The disposition of it for the year was, monthly, as follows:

	Exported.	Duties paid.	Total drain.	Coined.
January	$454,894	$592,279	$1,047,173	$80,000
February	239,190	668,691	907,881	520,000
March	160,140	759,753	919,893	515,000
April	389,345	683,094	1,072,439	695,000
May	152,263	672,554	824,797	660,000
June	154,787	652,202	806,989	865,000
July	89,471	910,082	999,553	2,305,000
August	149,270	740,361	889,631	1,395,000
September	202,042	881,779	1,083,821	2,455,000
October	225,564	654,873	880,237	2,390,000
November	147,533	713,782	861,315	2,550,000
December	211,393	631,022	842,415	2,340,000
For 1868	2,642,872	8,560,411	10,403,283	16,760,000
For 1867	4,001,825	7,541,247	11,543,217	18,331,287

The actual drain diminished monthly as the year drew to a close; at the same time the mint supply was larger, giving a greater surplus for general use:

		1867.		1868.
Coined		$18,331,287		$16,760,000
Shipped	$4,001,825		$2,642,872	
Duties	7,541,247		7,760,411	
		11,543,072		10,403,283
Excess coinage		6,788,216		6,356,717

Thus the result for the 12 months shows nearly as great a supply of coin; but if we divide the year into periods of six months the result will correspond with the above table of coinage:

	1867.		1868.
First six months, excess coinage	$2,197,119.	Deficit,	$1,666,521
Second six months, excess coinage	4,591,098.	Excess,	8,023,238
Year, excess coinage	6,788,217.	Excess,	6,356,717

COAL STATISTICS.

The receipts of coal from the Monte Diablo, California, mines for the past five years have been as follows:

	Tons.		Tons.
1864	37,458	1867	83,174
1865	60,530	1868	109,095
1866	84,024		

The aggregate imports and receipts from all sources have been:

	Tons.		Tons.
1864	143,492	1867	230,884
1865	154,251	1868	262,889
1866	188,519		

EXPORT OF COPPER ORES.

To—	Tons.	Value.
Great Britain	1,503	$51,750
United States—Boston	130	9,800
United States—New York	3,444	166,375
Total for 1868	5,077	227,925
Total for 1867	7,833	421,546
Decrease, 1868	2,756	193,621

EXPORT OF QUICKSILVER.

To—	Flasks.	Value.
Australia and New South Wales	1,550	$47,828
Central America	1	45
China	16,785	505,081
France	500	15,000
Great Britain	3,500	105,000
Mexico	14,121	440,518
New Zealand	30	1,238
Peru	2,500	79,425
Vancouver's Island and British Columbia	20	919
New York	4,500	135,000
Total for 1868	43,507	1,330,054
Total for 1867	28,824	929,726
Increase, 1868	14,683	400,328

EXPPORTS OF FLOUR AND WHEAT.

Total to all ports for the years 1867 *and* 1868.

	Flour, bbls.	Value.	Wheat, sacks.	Value.	Total value,
1867	519,428	$3,178,598	4,604,080	$9,340,497	$12,519,095
1868	465,273½	2,973,538	4,071,837	8,635,854	11,609,392
Decrease, 1868	54,154½	205,060	532,243	704,643	909,703

Total value of domestic exports other than treasure during 1867 *and* 1868.

1867	$16,654,638
1868	17,821,809
Increase, 1868	1,166,971

This increase is mainly in the items of barley, lumber, salmon, leather, mustard seed, skins and furs, and wool. The exports of ores have been as follows:

Ores.	1867.		1868.	
	Tons.	Value.	Tons.	Value.
Gold	93	$16,475	1	$500
Silver	106	24,763	68½	15,310
Copper	7,883	421,546	5,077	227,925
Lead	184	8,665	....	....
Manganese	....	....	1,657	26,830
Various	458	17,629	69½	1,860
Totals	8,724	489,078	6,873	273,225
Decrease in 1868	....	....	1,851	$215,853

The cessation of the export of lead ores is due to the establishment of metallurgical works at San Francisco, which manufacture at home the lead ores formerly exported.

IMPORTATIONS OF METALS, ETC., DURING 1868.

Castings, barrels	33	Iron:	
packages	56, 150	Railroad bars, number	178, 186
bundles	28, 054	Safes, number	303
pieces	82, 068	Old, tons	10
Fire-clay, barrels	188	Steel bars, number	2, 753
casks	182	bundles	5, 321
Coal:		cases	1, 016
Eastern, tons	31, 413	Lead:	
hogsheads	935	Bar, cases	13
casks	2, 706	kegs	266
Chili, tons	8, 511	Pigs, number	5, 672
English, tons	29, 868	Sheet, casks	5
Sydney, tons	32, 390	rolls	25
Russian Asia, tons	204	Pipe, reels	235
Vancouver, tons	23, 397	Marble, tons	400
Coos bay, tons	10, 425	packages	5, 000
Bellingham bay, tons	14, 000	boxes	406
Copper, packages	768	Yellow metal, cases	715
Steam engines	40	old, packages	50
Iron:		Mineral water, packages	989
Bars, number	271, 151	Coal oil, cases	127, 186
bundles	134, 371	Ore:	
Sheet, bundles	18, 609	Copper, sacks	70
number	17, 393	Silver, sacks	233
cases	550	Plumbago, packages	40
Plates, number	23, 001	Tin:	
Hoop, bundles	10, 902	Plate, boxes	38, 496
cases	1, 743	Pigs, number	1, 820
Pipes, number	16, 512	Foil, cases	20
Tubes, number	15, 435	Ware, packages	409
bundles	14, 734	Zinc, rolls	30
Pig, American, tons	2, 642	casks	775
Scotch, tons	15, 371		

O

Henry R. Worthington,

HYDRAULIC WORKS,

Office, 61 Beekman St., New-York.

STEAM PUMPING ENGINES

FOR ALL PURPOSES, SUCH AS

WATER-WORKS ENGINES,

Condensing or Non-Condensing; Stationary and Portable Steam Fire Engines; Boiler Feed Pumps; Wrecking Pumps; Mining Pumps;

PUMPS FOR HYDRAULIC PRESSURE;

Water Meters, Oil Meters, Water Pressure Engines; Stamp Mills, for Gold, Silver, and Copper Ore; Steam and Gas Pipe, Valves, Fittings, etc.; Hydraulic Cranes and Hoisting Machinery,

IRON AND BRASS CASTINGS.

Manufactory: Van Brunt Street, near Hamilton Ave.,

BROOKLYN, N. Y.

VALUABLE WORKS

ON

MINING AND METALLURGY

FOR SALE BY

D. VAN NOSTRAND, 192 Broadway, N. Y.

MINERAL RESOURCES OF THE PACIFIC STATES AND TERRITORIES. By J. Ross Browne. 1 vol. 8vo, cloth.

REPORT UPON THE PRECIOUS METALS. Being statistical notices of the principal Gold and Silver producing Regions of the World, represented at the Paris Universal Exposition. By William P. Blake. 1 vol. 8vo, cloth, $2.50.

PRACTICAL HAND-BOOK FOR MINERS, METALLURGISTS, AND ASSAYERS. Comprising the most recent improvements in the disintegration, amalgamation, smelting, and parting of the precious ores, with a comprehensive digest of the Mining Laws, greatly augmented, revised, and corrected by Julius Silversmith. Fourth edition. *Profusely Illustrated.* 1 vol. 12mo, cloth, $3.

TREATISE ON ORE DEPOSITS. By Bernhard Von Cotta, Professor of Geology in the Royal School of Mines, Freiberg, Saxony. Translated from the second German edition by Frederick Prime, Jr., Mining Engineer, and revised by the author. With numerous illustrations. *In Press.*

A TREATISE ON THE METALLURGY OF IRON. Containing outlines of the History of Iron Manufacture, Method of Assay, and Analysis of Iron Ores, Process of Manufacture of Iron and Steel, etc. etc. By H. Bauerman. First American edition, revised· enlarged, and illustrated by numerous engravings. 12mo, cloth, $2.50.

THE MINING AND METALLURGY OF GOLD AND SILVER. By J. Arthur Phillips, Mining Engineer. 8vo, *illustrated,* cloth, $15.75.

A PRACTICAL TREATISE ON METALLURGY. Adapted from the last German edition of Prof. Kerl's Metallurgy. By William Crookes, F.R.S., and Ernest Röhrig, P.H.D. 2 vols. 8vo, illustrated with 207 wood engravings, cloth, $9.

A MANUAL OF PRACTICAL ASSAYING. By John Mitchell. Third edition. Edited by William Crookes, F.R.S. 1 vol. 8vo, cloth, $14.

VAN NOSTRAND'S ECLECTIC ENGINEERING MAGAZINE. Selected from Home and Foreign Serials. Conducted by A. L. Holley, Engineer Bessemer Steel Works, etc. Issued monthly at $5 per annum.

*** Copies of our new Catalogue of American and Foreign Scientific Books, 56 pp. 8vo, sent to any address on receipt of six cents in postage stamps.

OFFICE OF

The Bishop Gutta Percha Co.,

113 Liberty St., N. Y.

BISHOP'S IMPROVED ELECTRIC FUSE.

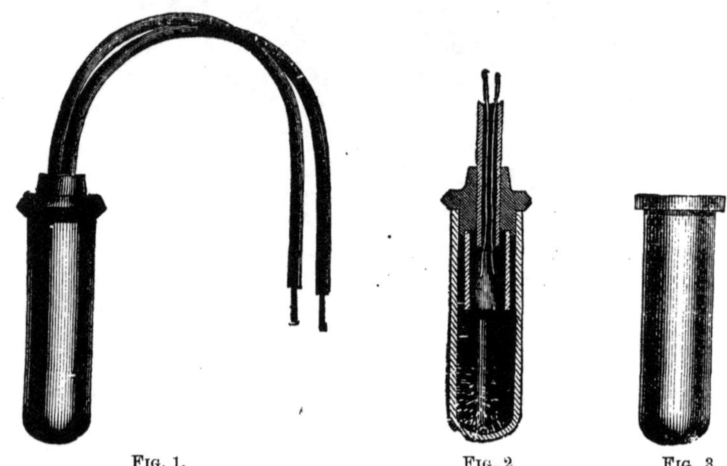

FIG. 1. FIG. 2. FIG. 3.

The accompanying cut represents the Fuse, which can be used for the explosion of

Powder or Nitro-Glycerine.

The two Conducting Wires (3½ feet long) are each separately insulated and tested before using. This mode has been adopted as the best and surest one, and most reliable, as the insulation

Can be thoroughly Tested in Single Wire,

and *can not be* where two wires are insulated in one covering.

Fig. 1 is a perspective view, and Fig. 2 a vertical section, showing the internal construction. Fig. 3, shown in the accompanying cut, is to be used with match fuse, for blasting with Nitro-Glycerine; the Fulminate is the same as used in No. 1, and is sure fire.

We offer to the public this IMPROVED FUSE for Blasting Powder or Nitro-Glycerine. The Primer and Fulminate is prepared by Dr. J. G. POHLE, of New-York, whose reputation is a sufficient guarantee for the quality of this portion of the Fuse.

The manufacture of the Fuse is under the charge of CHARLES A. BROWNE, formerly Electrician at the Hoosac Tunnel. The Insulated Wires are of our own manufacture, and of pure copper and pure gutta percha.

We feel confident, therefore, that we can offer the best article in the market. We are making an

ELECTRIC MACHINE,

to use with this Fuse, of an entirely new and much improved pattern, from a design by Mr. BROWNE, which we feel sure will please, and be sold at very much less than the present Machine in use.

The Fuse will be packed in boxes of 100 and 1,000 each, and in this manner will be sold, ready for shipment. Prices will be graded by quantities wanted, and will be as low as the same quality of Fuse can be had in market.

For any further information, and Pamphlet with full instructions, apply to

SAMUEL C. BISHOP, General Agent,
113 LIBERTY STREET, N. Y.

HOISTING.

BOILER.

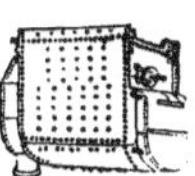

ANDREWS'

PATENTS.

Friction Grooved Noiseless Hoisting Machines

Run without noise or jar. Speed changed or reversed instantaneously.

Smoke-Burning and Super-Heating Boilers

Are Economical and Safe.

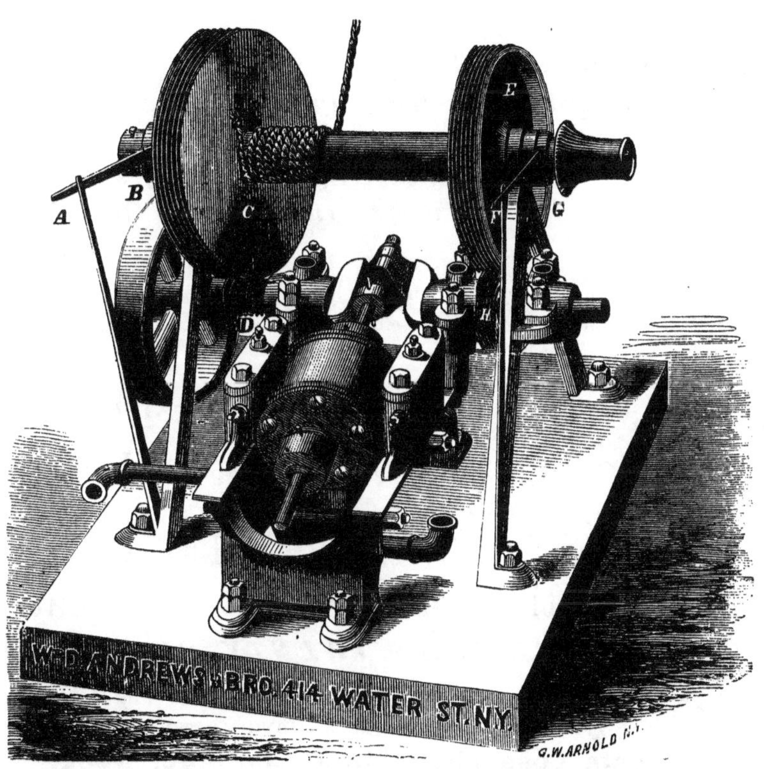

OSCILLATING ENGINES

Sizes, one half to 250 Horse-Power. Require no Foundation, leave the shop ready for use

CENTRIFUGAL PUMPS

Pass Sand, Gravel, etc., etc., without injury. Capacity, 90 to 40,000 gallons per minute.

ALL COMPACT, LIGHT, AND DURABLE,

For Descriptive Circulars, address Patentees and Manufacturers,

WM. D. ANDREWS & BRO.,

412 to 416 Water Street, New-York.

ENGINE.

PUMP.

www.ingramcontent.com/pod-product-compliance
Lightning Source LLC
LaVergne TN
LVHW010236110826
845151LV00004B/1310

* 9 7 8 1 4 2 5 5 2 4 8 8 3 *